OVER AND OVER AND OVER AGAIN

Cultural Inquiry

EDITED BY CHRISTOPH F. E. HOLZHEY
AND MANUELE GRAGNOLATI

The series 'Cultural Inquiry' is dedicated to exploring how diverse cultures can be brought into fruitful rather than pernicious confrontation. Taking culture in a deliberately broad sense that also includes different discourses and disciplines, it aims to open up spaces of inquiry, experimentation, and intervention. Its emphasis lies in critical reflection and in identifying and highlighting contemporary issues and concerns, even in publications with a historical orientation. Following a decidedly cross-disciplinary approach, it seeks to enact and provoke transfers among the humanities, the natural and social sciences, and the arts. The series includes a plurality of methodologies and approaches, binding them through the tension of mutual confrontation and negotiation rather than through homogenization or exclusion.

Christoph F. E. Holzhey is the Founding Director of the ICI Berlin Institute for Cultural Inquiry. Manuele Gragnolati is Professor of Italian Literature at the Sorbonne Université in Paris and Associate Director of the ICI Berlin.

OVER AND OVER AND OVER AGAIN
Reenactment Strategies in Contemporary Arts and Theory

EDITED BY
CRISTINA BALDACCI
CLIO NICASTRO
ARIANNA SFORZINI

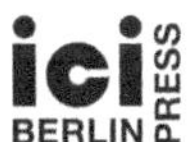

ISBN (Hardcover): 978-3-96558-027-5
ISBN (Paperback): 978-3-96558-028-2
ISBN (PDF): 978-3-96558-029-9
ISBN (EPUB): 978-3-96558-030-5

Cultural Inquiry, 21
ISSN (Print): 2627-728X
ISSN (Online): 2627-731X

Bibliographical Information of the German National Library
The German National Library lists this publication in the Deutsche Nationalbibliografie
(German National Bibliography); detailed bibliographic information is available online at
http://dnb.d-nb.de.

Cover design: Studio Bens

In Europe, the paperback edition is printed by Lightning Source UK Ltd., Milton Keynes,
UK. See the final page for further details.

The digital edition can be downloaded freely at: https://doi.org/10.37050/ci-21.

ICI Berlin Press is an imprint of
ICI gemeinnütziges Institut für Cultural Inquiry Berlin GmbH
Christinenstr. 18/19, Haus 8
D-10119 Berlin
publishing@ici-berlin.org
press.ici-berlin.org

Contents

The Reactivation of Time ix

From Re- to Pre- and Back Again
SVEN LÜTTICKEN 1

I. UNCOVERING THE HISTORICAL PAST,
PERFORMING THE POLITICAL PRESENT

The Reenacted Double: Repetition as a Creative Paradox
ARIANNA SFORZINI 19

'The Reconstruction of the Past is the Task of Historians and
not Agents': Operative Reenactment in State Security Archives
KATA KRASZNAHORKAI 29

The Collection of Jane Ryan & William Saunders:
Reconstruction as 'Democratic Gesture'
PIO ABAD 37

Insistence: The Temporality of the Death Fast and the Political
ÖZGE SERIN 47

'Interrupting the Present': Political and Artistic Forms of
Reenactments in South Africa
KATJA GENTRIC 57

Resounding Difficult Histories
JULIANA HODKINSON 69

Archival Diffractions: A Response to Le Nemesiache's Call
GIULIA DAMIANI 81

Archival Reenactement and the Role of Fiction:
Walid Raad and the *Atlas Group Archive*
ROBERTA AGNESE 91

II. AESTHETIC FORMS OF REHABILITATION

Unintentional Reenactments: *Yella* by Christian Petzold
CLIO NICASTRO 101

Everyday Aesthetics and the Practice of Historical
Reenactment: Revisiting Cavell's Emerson
ULRIKE WAGNER 113

Speculative Writing: Unfilmed Scripts and Premediation
Events
PABLO GONÇALO 121

Reenactment in Theatre: Some Reflections on the
Philosophical Status of Restaging
DANIELA SACCO 131

Re-search, Re-enactment, Re-design, Re-programmed Art
SERENA CANGIANO, DAVIDE FORNARI, AND AZALEA SERATONI . . 141

In the Beginning There Is an End: Approaching Gina Pane,
Approaching *Discours mou et mat*
MALIN ARNELL 151

Performance Art in the 1990s and the Generation Gap
PIERRE SAURISSE 161

III. RESISTANCE AND RECONCILIATION IN THE MUSEUM

Re-Presenting Art History: An Unfinished Process
CRISTINA BALDACCI 173

Reconciling Authenticity and Reenactment:
An Art Conservation Perspective
AMY BROST 183

UNFOLD: The Strategic Importance of Reinterpretation for
Media Art Mediation and Conservation
GABY WIJERS 193

Unfold Nan Hoover: On the Importance of Actively
Encouraging a Variable Understanding of Artworks
for the Sake of their Preservation and Mediation
VERA SOFIA MOTA AND FRANSIEN VAN DER PUTT 205

Living Simulacrum: The Neoplastic Room in Łódź:
1948 / 1960 / 1966 / 1983 / 2006 / 2008 / 2010 / 2011 /
2013 / 2017 / ∞
JOANNA KILISZEK 219

'Repetition: Summer Display 1983' at Van Abbemuseum:
Or, What Institutional Curatorial Archives Can Tell Us about
the Museum
MICHELA ALESSANDRINI 231

'Political-Timing-Specific' Performance Art in the Realm of
the Museum: The Potential of Reenactment as Practice of
Memorialization
HÉLIA MARÇAL AND DANIELA SALAZAR 239

'We Are Gathering Experience': Restaging the History of
Art Education
ALETHEA ROCKWELL 255

References 263
Notes on the Contributors 285
Index 293

The Reactivation of Time

Reappropriating, restaging, revisioning, remediating: at the crossroad of the new millennium, reenactment has undoubtedly emerged as a key issue in the field of artistic production, in theoretical discourse, and in the socio-political sphere. Taking an ever larger distance from notions of historical revival and 'Living History', current reenactments call into question whether the present can unpack, embody, or disentangle the past. Accordingly, to reenact is to experience the past by reactivating either a particular cultural heritage or unexplored utopias. If to reenact means not to restore but to challenge the past, history is thus turned into a possible and perpetual becoming, a site for invention and renewal.

Reenactment radically questions the idea of representation itself, together with the traditional notions of the subject and the object of knowledge. The idea of the uniqueness of truth, as well as the presumed connaturality between the human subject and a world accessible to epistemic procedures, came into question in the course of the twentieth century. Any representation of reality revealed itself to be de facto a remaking. Similarly, artistic creation is no longer thought of as a mimesis of reality, but the mimesis transforms itself into forms of critical re-presentations. Michel Foucault, Gilles Deleuze, Jacques Derrida are — among others — the main philosophical references to rethink the relationship between history, subjectivity, and reality, where 'repetition' and its 'difference' are at stake.

The horizon in which reenactment has to be considered is no longer that of an original act and its successive representations, its copies, but the virtually infinite possibility of reactivating an event through its *simulacra* and *Doppelgängers* — or even better — its translations and interpretations. Reenactment does not retrieve an essential and original truth of the past. It permits an explosion of sorts of the notion of truth in a multiple temporal scattering of events, not in order to invest into the supposed authenticity of history, but to create new forms of thinking and staging the relation to history itself.

The critical dimension is therefore essential to the notion of reenactment. Its conceptual and practical power does not reside in reproposing the past, in repeating it, but in questioning and reactualizing this same past and its memorial value through the act of its restaging. There is no such thing as 'neutrality' in the reactivation of a past event. In every act of repetition, there is a critical potential conveyed by the gesture of repetition itself. This critical force can then arise from different aspects of the act of reenactment, such as the choice of specific archives and historical materials; the place in which reenactment takes place; the subjective experience of the event; the positions of both the interpreter and (active) spectator.

When artists decide to reenact past performances, for example, every concrete aspect of reenactment virtually opens a critical dialogue with the past that is meant to be reactivated. One could argue that this critical dimension of reenactment resides above all in a distortion of historical time. But the temporal orientation does not proceed from the present to a presumed past with the objective of unveiling its secret original truth or meaning. It goes instead from a present that demands a transformation to a future where openness and contingency become visible because of the reactivation of the past. Therefore, to establish a critical relationship with the past does not mean to make a historical judgment, but to have the possibility of showing — through its repetition — that history is open to multi-layered approaches, that it is a constant requestioning of its assumptions, hierarchical positions, and values.

Through reenactment practices, authenticity, authorship, and originality lose their meaning as cornerstones of Western thought and arts. A whole 'regime of truth', to use a Foucauldian notion, is questioned and actively replaced by another, which is itself constantly shifting. As a consequence, the artistic gesture or work reveals itself to be a reenactment of a given cultural heritage, and every act is already contingent on an experience of the act itself, as well as on the various modes through which it is being remembered and historicized.

How do the arts rethink and reposition their role and value in this new 'regime of truth'? The process of creative repetition branches out into at least three directions: a manifold and asynchronous temporal dimension that entails the return/survival of the past understood as generating meaning and values for both the present and potential future/s, in terms of what one could call a symbolic archaeology; an epistemological-axiological challenge to the traditional dichotomy between true and false, original and copy; a performative bodily practice that physically restages events.

At the same time, methodologically the notion of reenactment can also be approached from three main directions: the archive, the arts, museum and curatorial practices. The present volume, which stemmed from the international symposium organized at the ICI Berlin in November 2017 as part of the Institute's 2016–18 research project *ERRANS, in Time*, is organized following these different investigative paths in an attempt to consider both the conceptual foundations and practical aspects of reenactment.[1] Starting from a genealogy of the concept and a comparison with related terms and their meanings (revocation, reconstruction, replica, repair, rehabilitation, revision, revelation, reinvention, among others), the volume focuses on the close relationship between repetition and seriality on the one hand and the emergence of neo- and post- movements of the twentieth and twenty-first centuries on the other: from neo-realism to the neo-avant-garde, from the post-modern to 'retro-futurism'. But also, as Sven Lütticken brilliantly points out in his introduction, that special temporal shift 'from re- to pre- and back again', to quote the title of his contribution.[2]

The first part of the book, *Uncovering the Historical Past, Performing the Political Present*, examines how, from a physical space for documentation and conservation, through reenactment practices, the archive can turn into an apparatus of cultural repair and political activism. The 'archaeological' experience, inspired by Foucault's mobilization of archives, is here crucial inasmuch as it reveals how historical subjectivity and a more inclusive transmission of collective memory are produced.

The second part, *Aesthetic Forms of Rehabilitation*, more closely examines reenactment as an artistic and also literary and theatre practice. Using different media (film, photography, sculpture, perform-

---

1   'Over and Over and Over Again: Re-Enactment Strategies in Contemporary Arts and Theory', symposium held at the ICI Berlin on 16–17 November, 2017 <https://doi.org/10.25620/e171116>.
2   See Sven Lütticken, 'From Re- to Pre- and Back Again', in this volume.

ance, writing …), artists play with the idea of authorship, originality, and authenticity, and, as a result, blur the borders between reality and fiction and multiply the strategies of *re*-presentation. The focus is on the critical effects of these practices, and especially their potential to bring to light oppressive narratives of history and therefore to be an effective tool for feminist, post-colonial, queer, and gender politics.

The third part, *Resistance and Reconciliation in the Museum*, elaborates on the way in which reenactment has influenced curatorial practices and changed the modality in which exhibitions are organized and studied. The reconstruction and restaging of a pivotal or previously underestimated exhibition or artwork is proposed as a new approach to the making and rewriting of the history/histories of art, presenting an entire set of challenging issues, such as: the relationship with institutional contexts and socio-political frames; the selection of artworks to be reconstructed, which is related to the promises of survival and conservation but also to the risks of recommodification; the differences that arise in the adaption/revision process; the crucial role of the participant audience.

As organizers of the symposium and editors of the volume, we would like once again to thank very much all the speakers who joined the conference at the ICI Berlin in 2017 and contributed to the stimulating discussion – including those whose papers do not appear in the volume: Natasha Adamou, Laura Almeida, Diana Baker Smith, Rosa Barba, Cory Browning, Filipa César, Kirill Chepurin, Leora Farber, Oleg Gelikman, Lieke Hettinga, Livia Monnet, Stefan Solomon, Edward A. Vazquez. Thanks also to the artists, museums, and image rights holders for their collaboration and availability. Our thanks go above all to the staff of the ICI Berlin, who supported us in all the different phases of this plurennial project. Thank you in particular to Christoph Holzhey, Manuele Gragnolati, and Claudia Peppel, without whom all this would not have been possible; and to Arnd Wedemeyer, for his great, never-ending advice and meticulous editing during the making of the volume.

CRISTINA BALDACCI
CLIO NICASTRO
ARIANNA SFORZINI

From Re- to Pre- and Back Again

SVEN LÜTTICKEN

While the term 'reenactment' has a complex history, both in the philosophy of history and in the popular domain of historical (usually: war) reenactment, it migrated to the sphere of contemporary artistic production around 2000. The aesthetic strategies of pieces such as Jeremy Deller's *The Battle of Orgreave* (2001) and Rod Dickinson's *The Milgram Re-enactment* (2002), as well as works by Omer Fast such as *Godville* (2005), clearly referenced popular forms of historical reenactment in the context of war reenactment societies and living history museums. This development indicated a new interest in the performative engagement with history in contemporary art. On the other hand, by 2000, performance art itself had accrued a significant history, which raised the question of how to preserve or actualize it. From happenings and Fluxus to later forms of performance and body art by practitioners ranging from Abramović and Ulay to Chris Burden, the performance art of the 1960s and 1970s had been canonized, or was just undergoing canonization; however, it was far from self-evident how these historical works could be presented for contemporary audiences.

HISTORICAL REENACTMENT

Some of the first exhibitions and publications that attempted to chart, historicize, and theorize the newfound relevance of reenactment

around 2005 consequently made various montages of artistic reenactments and other forms of historical reenactment, following cues
in artworks that already made such connections.[1] Rod Dickinson's
Milgram Re-enactment (2002), a careful restaging of Stanley Milgram's
infamous psychological experiment on obedience based on original
transcripts, referenced popular reenactment culture mostly in its title,
as the lab setting and repetitive succession of experiments with different test subjects was a far cry from popular war reenactment. By
contrast, Jeremy Deller's *The Battle of Orgreave* (2001; filmed by Mike
Figgis) actually took on the form of such a war reenactment, swapping
World War II and other armed conflicts for the political and social up-
heavals of Thatcher's Britain in revisiting the eponymous fight between
striking miners and police in 1984.[2] Deller frequently appropriates
popular forms; in this case, one can wonder if his attempt to politicize
the applied historicism of the reenactment culture was not undercut
by the wholesale adoption of its trappings.[3]

Such works are based on a popular type of reenactment immediately rooted in the American Civil War reenactments that took place
during the war's centennial in the 1960s, such as the 1961 Bull Run
(or First Manassas) reenactment on the battle's original site. These
events can be seen as historicist happenings for a wide audience. In its
most general sense, the term 'historicism' designates those tendencies
in modern philosophy, historical writing, and culture that attempt
to reconstruct various periods in their alterity, while also trying to
provide some kind of access to the inner workings of this culture and
its denizens.[4] With the advent of historicism in the decades around

---

1   Cf. *Experience, Memory, Re-enactment*, ed. by Anke Bangma, Steve Rushton, and
     Florian Wüst (Frankfurt a.M.: Revolver, 2005); an exhibition I curated, *Life, Once
     More: Forms of Reenactment in Contemporary Art*, ed. by Sven Lütticken (Rotterdam:
     Witte de With, 2005); *History Will Repeat Itself: Strategies of Reenactment in Contem-
     porary (Media) Art and Performance*, ed. by Inke Arns and Gabrielle Horn (Frankfurt
     a.M.: Revolver, 2007).

2   *The Battle of Orgreave*, dir. by Mike Figgis (Artangel Media, 2001).

3   See also Hito Steyerl, *Die Farbe der Wahrheit. Dokumentarismen im Kunstfeld* (Vienna:
     Turia + Kant, 2008), pp. 50–53.

4   On the history and the different interpretations of the concept, see Georg G. Iggers,
     'Historicism: The History and Meaning of the Term', *Journal of the History of Ideas*,
     56.1 (January 1995), pp. 129–52. On historicism in the arts, Hannelore and Heinz
     Schlaffer's *Studien zum ästhetischen Historismus* (Frankfurt a.M.: Suhrkamp, 1975) is
     still unsurpassed in many respects.

1800, past cultures were no longer regarded as just relatively different, perhaps falling short of some timeless cultural ideal, but as essentially and fundamentally different.[5] This was a project riven by internal tensions; Hegel's attempt to reintegrate the alterity of past epochs into a single metahistorical narrative was countered by the work of historians who attempted to reconstruct the past 'the way it really was' ('wie es eigentlich gewesen'), to use Ranke's phrase.[6]

The latter form of historicism in turn had its aesthetic counterpart and was itself in part dependent on aesthetic strategies; Stephen Bann has analysed the work of Ranke and Prosper de Barante in conjunction with the novels of Walter Scott.[7] To pinpoint similarities in strategies of description and narration is not, of course, to suggest identical intentions. Nor does it mean that historical writing does not have evaluative criteria that are specific to it. Rather, it examines the ways in which various disciplines (scholarly as well as artistic) engage in the fundamental problem of historicism: that of *presenting*, of making present, a past that has become problematic. For two centuries, theatrical and performative strategies have played a crucial role in this regard. As Walter Benjamin noted, the archetypal nineteenth-century interior aimed to give the bourgeois the impression that a historical event such as the crowning or the murder of an emperor could have taken place in the next room.[8] Follies like Walter Scott's quasi-medieval residence of Abbotsford, or the fantastic series of 'historical' rooms constructed by the writer Pierre Loti in his house in Rochefort-sur-Mer, provided their owners with such phantasmagoric interior, while parades and pageants provided more public forms of historicist theatricality.

A last hurrah for parades in which citizens dressed up in the garb of past centuries was the Kaiser-Huldigungs-Festzug in Vienna in 1908, which celebrated the continuity of Habsburg rule a mere six years be-

---

5   See Sven Lütticken, 'An Arena in Which to Reenact', in *Life, Once More*, pp. 17–60; it contains many additional references.

6   Leopold von Ranke, *Geschichten der romanischen und germanischen Völker von 1494 bis 1535. Erster Band* (Leipzig: Reimer, 1824), p. vi.

7   Stephen Bann, *Romanticism and the Rise of History* (New York: Twayne, 1995), especially pp. 17–29.

8   Walter Benjamin, *Gesammelte Schriften*, ed. by Rolf Tiedemann and Hermann Schweppenhäuser, 7 vols (Frankfurt a.M.: Suhrkamp, 1972–91), v: *Das Passagen-Werk* (1982), p. 286.

fore the outbreak of World War I. Meanwhile, the US was swept by a veritable craze for historical pageants — performed before a grandstand by a large troupe recruited from the town itself against a picturesque background, such as a castle.[9] Both in parades and in pageants, with their sequencing of successive groups or tableaux, the overarching historical narrative often trumped the experience of *Jetztzeit* or 'now-time' evoked by Benjamin. The forging of such a now-time was clearly intended with the 1920 mass spectacle of *The Storming of the Winter Palace* in Leningrad, which influenced the similar sequence in Sergei Eisenstein's *October*. Having little similarity to the actual events of 1917, *The Storming of the Winter Palace* was a mass spectacle that did have roots in late nineteenth and early twentieth-century pageant culture, and which yielded images that would be presented as documentary evidence of the 'real' event.[10] Only a few years had elapsed, but the act of monumentalizing that took place in 1920 showed that the October Revolution was already seen as an event similar in importance to the French Revolution — which, in turn, was brought close to the present in a revolutionary *Jetztzeit*.

One 1918 commemoration of 'October' took the form of a festival titled *The Burning of the Hydra of Counterrevolution*, inspired by a French revolutionary holiday.[11] With the action largely being confined to several stages erected in front of the palace, and with elements of allegorical abridgement in the script, the 1920 spectacle was still rather 'stagey' in comparison with reenactments and living history museums since the mid-twentieth century, which tend to emphasize immersion in a particular historical moment or era. The *Storming of the Winter Palace* oscillated between representation of the past and its *re*-presentation (the making present again in a flash of now-time). Today, the desire for *re*-presentation and immediacy prevails, but the growing

---

9   On historicist parades in Europe, see for instance Werner Telesko, 'Der Triumph- und Festzug des Historismus in Europa', in *Der Traum vom Glück. Die Kunst des Historismus in Europa*, ed. by Hermann Fillitz, 2 vols (Vienna: Künstlerhaus Wien, 1991), I, pp. 290–96; on US pageants, see David Glassberg, *American Historical Pageantry: The Uses of Tradition in the Early Twentieth Century* (Chapel Hill: University of North Carolina Press, 1990).

10   See *Nikolai Evreinov & andere: 'Sturm auf den Winterpalast'*, ed. by Inke Arns, Igor Chubarov, and Sylvia Sasse (Berlin: Diaphanes, 2017), pp. 251–71.

11   James von Geldern, *Bolshevik Festivals, 1917–1920* (Berkeley: University of California Press, 1993), p. 41.

emphasis on interactivity and experience — which has only become more pronounced with the emergence of video games, many of which revisit historical wars and battles — glosses over the sense that the present seems gridlocked and the historical horizon clouded.

Perhaps the most important prefiguration of this new popular reenactment culture is to be found in the distinctly highbrow form of R.G. Collingwood's early twentieth-century philosophy of history, which uses the notion of reenactment to denote a central intellectual tool, or faculty, of the historian. For Collingwood, when the historian tries to understand Caesar's actions at a given moment, this means that he (I'm following Collingwood's gendered language here) has to '[envisage] for himself the situation in which Caesar stood, and thinking for himself what Caesar thought about the situation and the possible ways of dealing with it'.[12] Collingwood thus posits a form of armchair reenactment: a mental exercise aimed at understanding historical processes. By contrast, much popular and artistic reenactment is open to the accusation of providing nothing but an escapist simulation of historicity. And yet, in attempting to overcome the alterity and non-identity of past actions and periods through subjective identication, Collingwood effectively arrives at a more considered and analytical version of what some of the more fanatical and dedicated contemporary war reenactors call the 'period rush' — the momentary illusion of being inside the original stream of events, not in a restaging.[13]

This focus on experience and immersion in contemporary reenactments complicates a familiar trope from 1980s theories of postmodernism: the waning of historicity, as symptomatically manifested in the replacement of a 'proper' engagement with history and its antinomies by superficial pastiches and retro fashions.[14] The 'hardcore' reenactors' penchant for authentic details and immersive experience can be seen as

---

12   R. G. Collingwood, *Human Nature and Human History*, Proceedings of the British Academy, 22 (London: British Academy, 1937), p. 13. See also William H. Dray, *History as Re-enactment: R. G. Collingwood's Idea of History* (Oxford: Oxford University Press, 2005).

13   See a popular account of Civil War reenacting: Tony Horwitz, Confederates in the Attic: Dispatches from the Unfinished Civil War (New York: Vintage, 1998); in addition, see Jenny Thompson, War Games: Inside the World of Twentieth-Century War Reenactors (Washington: Smithsonian, 2004).

14   The locus classicus is of course Fredric Jameson's *Postmodernism, or, The Cultural Logic of Late Capitalism* (Durham, NC: Duke University Press, 1991).

a critique of precisely this kind of postmodern negation of history, but in the process they come to identify and reify history with a concrete and delineated set of artefacts and events, and to espouse an ideology of concrete (co-)presence in the (restaged) event. Here, dramatic time annuls historical time, rather than establishing a productive dialectic with that time scale; historicist play absorbs and annuls history. As a result, this history is highly susceptible to endless instrumentalization: witness the problematic allure of Confederate soldiers and Nazi troops in war reenactment.

This is not to say, however, that the form cannot also be used in other ways — not by those claiming the ownership of history, but precisely by those who contest these masters of history and their own genealogies. Under the Duterte regime in the Philippines, the annual activist reenactment of the 1985 Escalante massacre gains in urgency, as a dismal now-time has emerged between the Marcos and Duterte eras.[15] Here, folk reenactment loses the 'national heritage' aspect it has in Deller's work (in spite of Deller's determination to infuse the demotic form with critical content). Joshua Oppenheimer's film *The Act of Killing* has former death squad leaders triumphantly reenacting their own crimes during the 1965 to 1966 mass killings in Indonesia; they have never been held to account and are glorified by a powerful right-wing militia. In this 'perennial 1965', so to speak, Oppenheimer and his associates use reenactment in an almost therapeutic manner — it is the role change from perpetrator to victim that finally causes their protagonist to break down. Both the Escalante reenactments and *The Act of Killing* are interventions in situations in which the past is all too present; they make the ongoing effects of these massacres perpetrated by US-backed regimes painfully sensible,, rather than offering an escape from the present to a more heroic past.

In a less directly interventionist mode, Eran Schaerf's *Scenario Data* presents a series of artworks focusing on the staging of history,

---

15   See, for instance, on the blog of the progressive union of agricultural workers UMA Pilipinas: '"Cultural Revolution" Pursued in Escalante Massacre Memorial', 20 September 2016 <https://umapilipinas.wordpress.com/2016/09/20/cultural-revolution-pursued-in-escalante-massacre-memorial/> [accessed 10 March 2019]; Barbara Mijares, 'Militants Reenact Escalante Massacre', *ABS-CBN News*, 20 September 2017 <https://news.abs-cbn.com/news/09/20/17/militants-reenact-escalante-massacre> [accessed 10 March 2019].

from seemingly innocuous war reenactments to more sinister forms of stagecraft. If the masters of history perpetuate the historical crimes that created their position of power and privilege in the first place, thus effecting a colonization of the now by a past that refuses to die, the perpetuation of this power in turn facilitates the remaking of history. *Scenario Data* is based on an elliptical scenario that Schaerf has realized in various media: in printed text/photo spreads, for instance, but also in large installations in which revolving slide projectors cast images related to the scenario on the walls. These images include Napoleonic reenactors, old chairs scattered around a campfire during the Yom Kippur War, and an astronaut in an eighteenth-century period room. This still, from the end of Stanley Kubrick's *2001: A Space Odyssey*, is reframed in an accompanying text by Schaerf:

> The American space agency Odyssey suspects the Kubrick Company's lost futurologist may be in an eighteenth century French salon. The agency has requested the support of the Israeli secret service. Meanwhile, the French Baron Edmund de Rothschild declared his intention to donate an eighteenth century French salon to the Israeli Museum of Period Rooms to ensure that in the case of the lost futurologist's return, it will be in Israel.[16]

At one point in Schaerf's allusive fiction, 'Israeli soldiers disguised as Palestinian women' come to blows with 'European war-gamers disguised as Napoleonic Guards'. This occurs, of course, in the 'Museum of Period Rooms', which has been advising the army on disguises.[17] The past is actualized and instrumentalized in perplexing ways; the fantasy of time travel reveals itself as temporal colonialism, as history is reenacted in order to perpetuate the present order that sprang from it.

NOTATION AND MEDIATION

If pieces such as *The Milgram Reenactment* or *The Battle of Orgreave* could be accepted as contemporary visual art, this was ultimately due

---

16 Eran Schaerf, 'Scenario Data #39', in *Life, Once More*, ed. by Sven Lütticken, pp. 9–16 (p. 9).

17 Ibid., p. 10.

to the performative turn in the art of the 1960s and early 1970s; after all, such pieces reintroduce some of the tropes of historicism into performance art. By the early twenty-first century, the work of the first and second generation of performance artists had itself become historical. How to deal with these works, which were, by their nature, ephemeral? Many of them had been documented in some ways (in the form of photos, films, videos, and written accounts); could and should they also be reenacted? In 2001, the project 'A Little Bit of History Repeated' at KW Institute for Contemporary Art in Berlin, curated by Jens Hofmann, put the issue of the reenactment of historical performance pieces on the map.

What is the status of the 'original' performance or performances of a given piece? Is the piece considered to be score-based and therefore repeatable, re-performable, in the manner of many musical compositions? In the wake of John Cage, during the early 1960s, Fluxus artists developed a type of event score that allowed for a wide range of interpretations. George Brecht's 1961 *Word Event (Exit)* was a case in point: the score, which is reduced to the word 'exit', can be performed by exiting a room, but Brecht also selected a readymade 'exit' sign as a realization of the piece. However, in spite of this openness of the post-Cagean score, specific 'historical' executions of such a score can still be auratized. Written accounts and especially auratic black-and-white photographs created a mystique around such iterations. This is especially true with charismatic performers such as Beuys, or with the more complex happenings staged by Allan Kaprow or Wolf Vostell.

Kaprow, for one, tried to counteract such mystification by increasingly refusing the mediation of his happenings, even doing away with live audiences and restricting them to active participants, while producing scores that would allow for a myriad of different realizations, not necessarily controlled by him. The 2006 to 2008 travelling Kaprow retrospective contained a number of 're-imaginings' of old Kaprow environments and happenings. What was problematic about these re-imaginings was that they seemed to have been executed with very little imagination; they were normalized, bureaucratic versions using an IKEA aesthetic. One space was dubbed an 'Agency for Action'. This was an office space in which one could find, for instance, photocopies with instructions for happenings. With its generic office look and its aura of administrative aesthetics, this space seemed singularly inappropriate and jarring. But perhaps this quasi-corporate version of Kaprow's piece is in fact an apt actualization, as it foregrounds the effects of institutionalization and the need to come to terms with the work under vastly different circumstances — situating it in the gap between then and now, rather than enshrining it in 'wie es eigentlich gewesen'.[18]

In the context of the neo-avant-garde, and indeed of the Fluxus network, Beuys is representative of a performative practice predicated on a single performer and his ritualistic act. While Beuys's pieces from *Filz TV* (1970) to *I Like America and America Likes Me* (1974) could be reduced to fairly simple instructions, any new version risks appearing as an impoverished knock-off, lacking its star performer. Furthermore, could a new performer — or even, in some cases, the same performer some thirty years later — not fall into the trap of going through the external motions, without arriving at a Collingwoodesque recreation of the impulses behind the actions? Marina Abramović has staged a number of versions of her own works, and those co-created with Ulay, as well of pieces by other 'historical' artists. Increasingly, younger performers take her place in new iterations of her pieces, though Abramović has only become more iconic as part of today's media-celebrity complex.

The use of other/younger performers in such restagings can be seen as a specific form of *delegated performance*; as such, it is part of a wider reconceptualization of performance art beyond the paradigms of the 1960s and 1970s.[19] This delegation of the performance of a historical piece to others, however, coexists (at times uneasily) with an increasing valorization of documentation engaging with a piece's past iterations. A contemporary version of Yvonne Rainer's *Trio A* (1966) in a museum, danced by a number of young performers simultaneously, does not take away the need for other forms of engagement with historical versions that were performed by Rainer herself.[20] The

---

18 'Allan Kaprow: Art as Life' ran at the Van Abbemuseum in Eindhoven from 10 February to 22 April 2007.

19 On delegated performance, see Claire Bishop, 'Delegated Performance: Outsourcing Authenticity', *October*, 140 (Spring 2012), pp. 91–112.

20 Such performances took place, for instance, during 'Yvonne Rainer: Space, Body, Language' at the Museum Ludwig in Cologne from 28 April to 29 July 2012.

last fifteen years have seen a marked increase in scholarly and theoretical interest in the afterlife of ephemeral performances and dance pieces. How are performances remembered and reconstructed after the fact? If critics and scholars once treated the 'actual' performance as a privileged event and relegated all mediations to secondary status, the process of mediation has now come to be seen as an integral element of performative practice. Oral and written accounts, film, and video are no longer seen as derivatives of the 'real' artwork but provide access to it even while (re)shaping it. In her study of Rainer, Carrie Lambert-Beatty foregrounds the fact that her object of study is 'a series of traces, shaped and serially reshaped by the interests, desires, and ways of seeing of everyone from the artist to the photographer who documented the events to the historian herself'.[21]

At first sight, the rise of performance reenactments would seem to indicate that, after all, we still long to experience the original event or some approximation of it. If most sophisticated performance scholarship has decisively abandoned the ontological privileging of the live performance over media representations that marked both historical performance art and performance studies, does this vogue for restaging performances indicate a relapse of sorts? There is no denying that many such reenactments hold the promise of getting a close approximation of the original event. The most successful reiterations of historical performances counteract this by acknowledging their mediated nature. Here one could think, for instance, of Babette Mangolte's 1993 film *Four Pieces by Morris*, which restages four significant dance/performance pieces from the period of Robert Morris's involvement with the Judson Dance Theater. Mangolte's version of the piece *21.3* (1964), which saw Morris lip-synching (not quite in synch) to his taped reading of an Erwin Panofsky text on iconology, is a black-and-white film that refuses to imitate the filmic documents of the period in any literal manner. Mangolte obviously based her restaging in part on the famous black-and-white photo of this piece, but she did not attempt to recreate Morris's look in detail. The voice on the tape is Morris's, and the performer, Michael Stella, is dressed and

---

21   Carrie Lambert-Beatty, *Being Watched: Yvonne Rainer and the 1960s* (Cambridge, MA: MIT Press, 2008), p. 16.

bespectacled in a way that seems to evoke the early 1960s, as well as the late 1980s and early 1990s; in this way, memories of Morris in the original performance may become mixed with more recent stage images. The film seems suspended between periods, fracturing Morris's already multiple temporalities as if in a colourless kaleidoscope.

Film was a crucial medium for the survival of aesthetic historicism in the twentieth century and beyond, from early films after Scott's novels such as *The Bride of Lammermoor* (1909) and *Ivanhoe* (1913) to Spielberg. *Saving Private Ryan* coexists and competes with live war reenactments, with many reenactors serving as extras during battle scenes, even as some may resent having the action cut up into film takes. Both forms, however, try to create a suggestive and immersive experience of the actual happening. Mangolte's take on film as a medium of historical reconstruction could hardly be further removed from this. Morris's original version already was a remediation of print in oral form, turning the performing subject into a neurotic puppet; in this sense, the performance was not 'original' in the first place. The mediacy rather than the immediacy of film is stressed.

A different piece by Morris, which took the form of a minimalist column standing erect on a stage and suddenly falling over (pulled by a wire), has more recently been recreated in Gerard Byrne's large video installation *A Thing Is a Hole in a Thing It Is Not* (2010). This work consists of a series of videos dealing with Minimal Art and its controversies. They include a restaging of Tony Smith's legendary New Jersey Turnpike ride and of the 1964 Public Radio broadcast *New Nihilism or New Art?* (1964) with Donald Judd, Dan Flavin, and Frank Stella. Here and elsewhere, Byrne's work often involves actors reading out historical texts — usually transcripts of interviews. In other words, the actors reenact conversations on the basis of their translation into print. Such forms of aesthetic practice double as potential aesthetic theory, providing crucial incentives for theoretical and historical writing. The best scholarship and theory on reenactment is just beginning to catch up with the ways in which art unpacks the complexities and contradictions of reenactment.

RE- AND PRE-

While performance scholars have increasingly focused on performance documentation as more than just a pale and passive reflection of the 'real thing', as archival materials with an intrinsic value and performative qualities in their own right, artists have increasingly taken to performing various archives within the context of exhibitions.[22] Examples include: Hans Ulrich Obrist's Swiss Pavilion at the 2014 Venice Architecture Biennale — in which documents of the work of Lucius Burckhardt and Cedric Price were activated through a choreography devised in collaboration with Tino Sehgal and other artists — and the 2015 Black Mountain College exhibition at the Hamburger Bahnhof in Berlin.

Analysing Jean-François Lyotard's take on the postmodern condition, Tom Holert argues that a specifically 'postindustrial and postmodern relationship between competence and performativity [...] opens up a new area of activity for the artist which, though performativity, is distinguished by a potential freedom of choice and interests and omni-accessibility to databases and archives'.[23] In the process, history has increasingly been transformed into a deposit of potentially valuable materials to be mined by artists and other post-Fordist workers (i.e., creative and cognitive workers). In other words, we are dealing with a productivist mobilization of the historical record.[24]

We can see this mobilization, in more or less critical forms, in projects such as the various iterations and divisions of Boris Charmatz's *Musée de la danse,* or pieces by Alexandra Pirici and Manuel Pelmuş

---

22   On the more productive role now accorded to documentation, see, for instance, Philip Auslander, 'The Performativity of Performance Documentation', in *Perform, Repeat, Record: Live Art in History,* ed. by Amelia Jones and Adrian Heathfield (London: Intellect, 2012), pp. 47–58, and Lambert-Beatty, *Being Watched.*

23   Tom Holert, 'Exhibiting Investigation: The Place of Knowledge Production in the Visual Arts *Dialogue/Discourse/Research,* 1979', in *Troubling Research: Performing Knowledge in the Arts,* ed. by Carola Dertnig, et al. (Berlin: Sternberg Press, 2014), pp. 28–81 (p. 50).

24   In this context the phrase 'performing the archive' and variations thereof become buzzwords. See for instance *Performing the Archive/Archives of Performance,* ed. by Gunhild Borggreen and Rune Gade (Copenhagen: Museum Tusculanum Press, 2013), or the programme of the 2015 NUI Galway conference *Performing the Archive* <https://performingthearchive2015.files.wordpress.com/2015/07/conference-programme-final.pdf> [accessed 10 March 2019].

such as *Public Collection of Modern Art* (2014). In such projects, performers enact various historical performances, or even (in the case of Pirici and Pelmuş) artworks in any medium, as well as political manifestos. The activation of the archive here becomes a matter of living labour; it is not just re-performed by someone pushing a button on a DVD player but through physical enactment by professionals or unskilled labourers, as well as by the visitors who are confronted with and challenged by the 'official' performers. Many of the pieces and texts reenacted on behalf of Pirici and Pelmuş in the Van Abbemuseum in 2014, during the first iteration of *Public Collection of Modern Art* speak of the utopianism of modernist and avant-garde movements. Vladimir Tatlin's Tower, Dada slogans, and a Piet Mondrian painting meet the Communist Manifesto and the Cyborg Manifesto, as well as the Accelerationist Manifesto.[25] That this genealogy ends with the cod vanguardism of Nick Srnicek and Alex Williams suggests Karl Marx's dictum about tragedy being repeated as farce; in the age of Twitter theory, utopian vistas have been become memeified fodder for the attention economy.

Some of Pirici's solo pieces play with a variety of projected futures. Her 2016 piece *Signals*, which was put on in a dark space by performers wearing motion capture suits, contained some elements that were also part of Pelmuş and Pirici's *Public Collection of Modern Art*, such as Tatlin's Tower, but it combined (art) historical and contemporary references with futurist entries such as 'EU flag with five stars collected by Tate Modern in 2032' and 'Abramović holograms for her 2030 MoMA retrospective'.[26] In the latter case, the performers *preenacted* a future sci-fi techno-reenactment. A notion that has come to the fore in recent years, preenactment is a rehearsal for a future that may or may not be actualized. One work reenacted by Pirici and Pelmuş's young performers at the Van Abbemuseum was the single-channel version

---

25   On the piece's conception, see Paul Dunca's interview with the artists, 'Public Collection: An Interview with Alexandra Pirici and Manuel Pelmuş', *Rivista Arte*, 14 December 2014 <https://revistaarta.ro/en/public-collection/> [accessed 23 March 2021].

26   For a list of the meme-like elements that make up *Signals*, see the artist website <http://alexandrapirici.com/> [accessed 23 March 2021]. However, this list is not the (entire) score: the components were performed in ever-changing sequences on the basis of a selection made by online users and a content-ranking algorithm.

of Harun Farocki's *Workers Leaving the Factory* (1995), which itself reuses historical films, starting with the 'first film' of workers leaving the Lumière factory, and continuing with subsequent scenes that could be regarded as (usually unintentional) remakes of that first film. At the Van Abbemuseum, the performers reenacted Farocki's work by leaving the exhibition space, only to return and continue with their gruelling schedule. The repetition suggests that you cannot leave the 'social factory'; it is a preenactment of a future that at present appears forestalled.

Milo Rau's *Congo Tribunal* (2015–17) presents itself much more assertively as 'the illusion of a future in which this symbolic would be to some extent normal' ('das Vorleuchten einer Zukunft, in der dieses Symbolische gewissermassen normal wäre').[27] An artist-led tribunal without any official status, the Congo Tribunal is part of a larger constellation of historical and contemporary activist and artistic tribunals, such as the various 'people's tribunals' from the 1960s and 1970s Russell Tribunals to the present. Rau is well aware of such precedents, with which the Congo Tribunal shares its absolute powerlessness in juridical terms. One could term this 'paralegal performance': its efficacy lies in publicity, not in the legally binding speech act of a judge or jury. Rau's *Moscow Trials* (2013) constituted a free replay of actual trials against artists and curators in Putin's Russia; they were a reenactment in which a jury had to arrive at verdicts that could (and did) differ from the actual verdicts. Rau conceives of such pieces as preenactments of a justice to come.[28] This is particularly pronounced in the case of the *Congo Tribunal*, which did not restage any prior event, in the absence of any actual political and/or juridical process that would stop the violence.

---

27   Milo Rau, *Das Kongo Tribunal*, ed. by Eva Bertschy, Rolf Bossart, and Mirjam Knapp (Berlin: Verbrecher Verlag, 2017), p. 24.

28   Drawing on psychotherapy, Céline Kaiser uses the term 'preenactment' in 'Auftritt der Toten. Formen des Re-, Pre- und Enactment in der Geschichte der Theatrotherapie', in *Szenotest. Pre-, Re- & Enactment zwischen Theater und Therapie*, ed. by Céline Kaiser (Bielefeld: transcript, 2014), pp. 44–58. Milo Rau, who participated in the *SzenoTest* project (see Kaiser, 'Vorwort', p. 7), has adopted and adapted the term for his practice: see, for instance, Avi Feldman>, 'An Interview with Milo Rau', *OnCurating*, 28 (January 2016), pp. 50–53 <http://www.on-curating.org/issue-28-reader/an-interview-with-milo-rau.html> [accessed 10 March 2019].

In contrast to the *NSU-Komplex auflösen* tribunal (2017), a grass-roots initiative for which Forensic Architecture produced a video reconstruction of the murder of Halit Yozgat by the NSU Neo-Nazi group, Rau's Tribunal is an authored project: a show with a clearly identified director who exploits his position of privilege. While certainly not beyond critique, the *Congo Tribunal* provides many productive points of departure for further elaboration, precisely through critical examination. Rau has used dramatic time not to represent, but to intervene in and (potentially) transform historical time. Recalling Harold Rosenberg's frequent play on the different registers of 'acting', from theatrical performance to political action, Rau stages an only partially scripted tribunal in which actors play themselves in a future courtroom.[29] This is history as preenactment, which is something different than visionary anticipation. In J. L. Austin's terms, one could conceive of the tribunal as an *illocutionary* speech act that, while not having the power of *perlocutionary* speech acts — 'I sentence you to ten years in prison' — can nonetheless have an effect through rhetoric and affect.[30] But what, precisely, is being preenacted? Would a 'real' Congo Tribunal be a proper historical event — such as, say, the storming of the Winter Palace, or even the Battle of Orgreave — that ruptures the status quo or would it prevent the further strengthening of the status quo though a UN-approved model of conflict resolution and population and conflict management?[31] It may not be a flaw, but rather, a quality — a feature rather than a bug — that the project raises such questions and provokes a chain reaction it cannot control. Semi-scripted though it may be, it opens onto an unwritten future.

In an essay on the concept of performativity that is highly critical of art-world uses and abuses of Austin's speech act theory, Andrea Fraser discusses the term enactment (without any prefix) in a framework informed by psychoanalysis. As an extension of the notion of trans-

---

29   On Rosenberg, 'action painting', and the slippage between different modes of acting in his writings, see Sven Lütticken, *History in Motion: Time in the Age of the Moving Image* (Berlin: Sternberg Press, 2013), pp. 223–27.

30   J. L. Austin, *How To Do Things with Words* (Oxford: Clarendon Press, 1962).

31   Oliver Marchart defines the theatrical preenactment as 'preforming' such a future event; see Marchart, *SoDA Lecture 09.07.2014 'The Art of Preenactments'*, Hochschulübergreifendes Zentrum Tanz Berlin (HZT Berlin), 9 July 2014, online video recording, Vimeo <https://vimeo.com/114242197> [accessed 10 March 2019].

ference to include nonverbal, physical elements, 'enactment' indicates that structures of relationships 'are produced and reproduced in all kinds of activity'. For Fraser, enactment implies 'that in the production and reproduction of these relationships there is *always* an investment, and that the meaning of the enactment, its significance, function, and effect, is intimately and inseparably tied up with that investment.'[32] What kinds of (psychological, social, economic) investments inform our re-, pre-, and other enactments? What do we perpetuate and what do we modify in each iteration? What is (re)produced in the process? These are some of the questions in the ongoing tribunal that accompanies any practice worthy of the name.

32   Andrea Fraser, 'Performance or Enactment', in *Performing the Sentence*, ed. by Carola Derning and Felicitas Thun-Hohenstein (Berlin: Sternberg Press, 2014), pp. 122–27 (p. 127).

I. UNCOVERING THE HISTORICAL PAST, PERFORMING THE POLITICAL PRESENT

The Reenacted Double
Repetition as a Creative Paradox
ARIANNA SFORZINI

As a starting point for my paper, I would like to take into question a short text by Michel Foucault that is at the same time an unfinished project: the screenplay of a film that does not exist (or better, has not existed for a long time). This Foucauldian screenplay is actually a *reenactment* of a *reenactment*, the repetition of an artistic repetition. It was written for a film never made (during Foucault's lifetime) about Pablo Picasso's *Las Meninas*, a series of 58 paintings that the artist created in the space of six months in 1957, taking up, updating, re-interpreting Diego Velázquez's famous 1656 painting of the same title. This artistic repetition will then allow us to reflect, theoretically as well as historically, on the value of the practice of reenactment as a critical and philosophical operation. The question that I would like to raise through this example (a question that is at the centre of both Foucauldian thought and theories of reenactment) is that of the critical dislocation of the place of thought. For Foucault, what is at stake is the notion of repetition as a practice that allows a current and creative reformulation of the question concerning the place from which one thinks, today, and the actual forms of historical subjectivity.

Velázquez's masterpiece *Las Meninas* has been astonishing its public for centuries in its ambiguous richness: who is really the subject of the representation? The infanta Margherita? Her retinue? The king and queen in the mirror? The painter depicting a portrait session? The space opened by the figure of the servant passing through the door in the back of the painting? Picasso repeats this *mise en abîme* of representation 58 times: in turn, the infanta and the details of her dress, the servants, the mirror, the space beyond the open door, become the subject of the work, in a mobile dance that makes any fixed role and any precise interpretation impossible.

At the end of the 1960s, Guy de Chambure imagined, for the Adrien Maeght Gallery in Paris, a film documentary that would stage Picasso's *Las Meninas*. To write the screenplay, he immediately thought of Michel Foucault, and not by chance: the publication of *The Order of Things* in 1966 had established Foucault as the philosophical thinker of *Las Meninas*, but of those of Velázquez, which Picasso reenacted, so to speak. Foucault accepted this proposal (there is a signed contract) and in the summer of 1970 wrote a script of about twenty pages, whose first part is entitled 'The Disappearance of the Painter' (La Disparition du peintre), a typescript kept in the Foucault Archives at the Bibliothèque Nationale de France (boîte 53, in three slightly different versions) and published in 2011 in an issue of the *Cahiers de l'Herne* dedicated to Foucault.[1] However, the film project was not realized under Foucault's supervision, for reasons that are both technical or legal and historical-political. Shooting was in fact impossible in the Spain of Franco's fascist regime. The original director Alain de Chambure was denied permission to shoot at the Prado and the material already filmed in Barcelona, where the complete series of Picasso's *Meninas* is located, was confiscated by Spanish authorities. In any case, this idea of a Foucauldian film about *Las Meninas* has not ceased to fascinate those who knew about it, and the project to finally shoot a documentary with the original screenplay of Foucault was finally realized in 2020 by director Alain Jaubert.[2] This film is therefore the reenactment of

---

1   Michel Foucault, 'Les Ménines de Picasso', in *Michel Foucault*, ed. by Philippe Artières, Jean-François Bert, Frédéric Gros, and Judith Revel, Cahiers de l'Herne, 95 (Paris: L'Herne, 2011), pp. 14–32.

2   *Le Subtil Oiseleur, Foucault de Velázquez à Picasso*, dir. by Alain Jaubert (Éditions Montparnasse, 2020). Michel Foucault's family asked the director Alain Jaubert to follow the same screenplay the philosopher had written fifty years before. The film was finally shot and edited in 2019 and 2020, and presented to the public in 2021 during the fourteenth *Journées internationales du Film sur l'art* at the Musée du Louvre. Foucault's

a reenactment, between artistic practice and philosophical thought, linking in a counter-linear historical temporality the Spanish court of the seventeenth century, Francoist Spain of the 1950s and 1970s, 1970s France, and France and Europe today, in the 'COVID-19 era' of film production.

As the title of the first part suggests, Foucault's screenplay plays with the painter's position, or rather the painter's non-position, in Picasso's repetitions. It thus transforms these paintings into an opportunity to rethink the role of the subject of thought, which was already central to Foucault's famous reading of Velázquez's painting *Las Meninas* at the beginning of his 1966 *The Order of Things*. The images are supposed to follow the movement of an extremely theoretical text, thus describing the passage from the subject of classical representation, which vanishes to let only the representation itself speak in its representative power of reality (Velázquez), to the subject of modern painting (Picasso): a divided, disparate, plural subject that gives itself in an image only to be able to disperse again from there in its infinite repetitions, in its 'doubles'.

Las Meninas by Velázquez is for Foucault in *The Order of Things* the emblem of a category of thought so fundamental to modernity that it defines for him its 'episteme', that is, the set of conditions of production and circulation of true discourse: representation. Velázquez's painting is the 'representation of Classical representation' and the 'definition of the space it opens up to us'. The representation is the modern, Cartesian dream of an order of thought in which each element finds its place, in a precise, methodical, measurable concatenation. The order of the world, of language and thought become superimposable, without remainder. *Las Meninas* by Velázquez would then be the representation that undertakes to represent itself in all its elements, with its images,

---

text runs through a subtle montage of the images of Picasso's paintings and is read by the voice of Fanny Ardant. The choice of Alain Jaubert is not a coincidence: he was a very committed journalist in the 1970s, participating in movements such as Le secours rouge and Le groupe d'information sur les prisons (GIP), he taught philosophy at the University of Vincennes (1970–1974) on the same chair held by Foucault in 1969, and then became a director for television and cinema. In 1971 (on 29 May), working as a journalist for *Le Nouvel Observateur*, Alain Jaubert was beaten up in a police bus while accompanying a detained person to the police station, and charged with resisting arrest. The case provoked strong reactions and Foucault, among other intellectuals, campaigned for his acquittal.

the eyes to which it is offered, the faces it makes visible, the gestures
that call it into being. But there, in the midst of this dispersion which
it is simultaneously grouping together and spreading out before us,
indicated compellingly from every side, is an essential void: the necessary disappearance of that which is its foundation — of the person it
resembles and the person in whose eyes it is only a resemblance. This
very subject — which is the same — has been elided. And representation, freed finally from the relation that was impeding it, can offer
itself as representation in its pure form.[3]

Representation as a historical 'episteme' of thought implies for
Foucault the impossibility of representing the subject of such representation: the subject of thought in its concreteness and empirical depth.
In Velázquez's *Las Meninas*, the place of the painter as well as that of the
spectator is empty, according to Foucault. Three groups of characters
allude to it: the painter in the picture, the servant leaving the door, the
sovereigns in the mirror. But the subject of the representation itself, in
its concreteness, is elided. This subject instead overwhelmingly invades
the scene with Picasso and his *Las Meninas*. As an insistent presence in
and through the canvases, the subject returns as the protagonist in all
its declinations: as eye, character, light, or 'demiurge' of the pictorial
world – world unfolded by the materiality of the painting. But this
presence is never embodied in a unique and stable point, in a 'true'
vision of the world. It is rather the continuously reactivated opening
of a multiple and evolving perspective. The classical representation for
Foucault is not only a mode of visibility, but a form of thought that
has shaped Western philosophy since Descartes. Representation is the
name of an emblematic experience for Western philosophical culture:
(1) the myth of an ordered scientific space transparent to the activity
of the subject; (2) the correlation between an object-world and an
a-historical subject, capable to dominate the world in its truth; (3)
the necessary expulsion from discourse of what is essentially unrepresentable: the disorder of non-sense, of madness, of unreason. The
impossible repetition of such representation by Picasso is, according
to Foucault, the sign of a new world of thought, which no longer offers

---

3   Michel Foucault, *The Order of Things: An Archaeology of the Human Sciences*, trans. by
     Matthew Chrulew and Jeffrey Bussolini (London: Routledge, 2002), p. 17–18.

itself in its transparent truth but emerges in a non-linear sum of perspectives that the subject must not only unfold but create in its activity. And it is precisely in the game of repetition (the 58 reenactments of Velázquez's canvas) that this creative position of the subject is staged.

It should not be forgotten that, immediately after the publication of *The Order of Things* and shortly before the project on Picasso, in 1967, Foucault himself experienced a subjective 'dislocation of thought'. He left for Tunis as an invited professor and remained there until 1969. In Tunisia he lived some fundamental political experiences (his 'May 1968') and held a series of important courses: (1) on fifteenth-century painting and geometric perspective as an archaeology of representation; (2) on philosophical discourse and Descartes, sketching a genealogy of classical philosophical thought; (3) on Manet, considered to be the first painter of modernity, who made the same gesture in painting as Nietzsche in philosophy or Mallarmé in literary language: the questioning of the traditional subject of thought and its representative relationship with reality. The representation and its form of visibility are therefore, for Foucault at the end of the 1960s, at the centre of a broad reflection on the Western history of thought. Foucault's aim in assembling a series of plastic, pictorial, and architectural references in various works of the 1960s and 1970s is to construct a counter-history of classical thought as a representative practice built on a dialectic of complementarity between the subject and the object of knowledge, and to offer new ways of doing philosophy. He tries to find forms of anti- or counter-representative thought in which artistic practices themselves remain an important element of criticism and historical concretization of the concepts at issue.[4]

---

4   'Penser l'intensité [...] c'est se rendre libre pour penser et aimer ce qui, dans notre univers, gronde depuis Nietzsche; différences insoumises et répétitions sans origine qui secouent notre vieux volcan éteint; qui ont fait éclater depuis Mallarmé la littérature; qui ont fissuré et multiplié l'espace de la peinture (partages de Rothko, sillons de Noland, répétitions modifiées de Warhol); qui ont définitivement brisé depuis Webern la ligne solide de la musique; qui annoncent toutes les ruptures historiques de notre monde. Possibilité enfin donnée de penser les différences d'aujourd'hui, de penser aujourd'hui comme différence des différences. [...] Théâtre de maintenant.' Foucault, 'Ariane s'est pendue' [1969], in Foucault, *Dits et écrits*, ed. by Daniel Defert, François Ewald, and Jacques Lagrange, 2 vols (Paris: Gallimard, 2001), I: *1954–1975*, text no. 64, pp. 798–99.

The notion of the 'double' is fundamental for the construction of such counter-representative thinking. Thanks to a deep dialogue with philosophers and artists such as Friedrich Nietzsche, Antonin Artaud, Gilles Deleuze, but also Pierre Boulez, Georges Bataille, Maurice Blanchot (to name but a few), Foucault elaborates an extremely important conception of the creative force of repetition, particularly through literary language. Repetition is the possibility of deforming and disturbing the traditional space of thought through a grotesque *mimesis*: an impossible imitation of the objective representation of reality by a unique and sovereign subject, the subject of the dialectics and teleologies of history. Andy Warhol comes to mind and his Marylin in series, or the repetition of Campbell's cans:[5] the position of the 'simulacra' of an image (or a concept or discourse) is a way of immediately contesting its unique and truthful meaning. A truth that is repeated can no longer be the only One. It is inevitably a truth that is said 'in the interstice', in the space between one repetition and another, and that thanks to this difference in repetition (Deleuze *docet*) can be criticized, transformed, made 'other' than itself.[6] Repetition, as artists who practice *reenactment* well know, has a creative power intrinsic to its constitutive monotony. The double is the same all over again and yet always different from itself. As an operation that is not only artistic but also aesthetic, philosophical, and political, it is then a force of agitation and restlessness, which allows us to put into question our ways of thinking and being. In the same way, the Foucauldian analysis, repeating Picasso repeating Velázquez 58 times, aims at questioning the consolidated forms of discourse and their relationship with the conceptions and positions of subjects and objects of knowledge. Repetition in philosophical discourse and artistic practice is a critical staging: a movement of transformation through plays of refraction, duplication, and multiplication of the realities and subjectivities at stake. To take up and

---

5   See Foucault, 'Theatrum philosophicum' [1970], trans. by Donald F. Brouchard and
     Sherry Simon, in *Essential Works of Foucault, 1954–1984*, ed. by Paul Rabinow, 3 vols
     (New York: New Press, 1998–2001), II: *Aesthetics, Method, and Epistemology*, ed. by
     James D. Faubion (1998), pp. 343–68. See also an unpublished text about Andy Warhol
     kept in Boîte 53, Foucault Archives, Bibliothèque nationale de France (NAF 28730).
6   Gilles Deleuze, *Difference and Repetition* [1968], trans. by Paul R. Patton (New York:
     Columbia University Press, 1994), and Deleuze, *The Logic of Sense* [1969], trans. by
     Mark Lester and Charles Stivale (New York: Columbia University Press, 1990).

paraphrase an expression used by Foucault in a famous 1984 essay on Kant's 'Beantwortung der Frage: Was ist Aufklärung', reenactment practices would then be a new way of thinking about the 'ironic heroization of the present, [the] transfiguring play of freedom with reality'.[7] They question the forms and limits of a historical configuration of thought, blurring its set of relations and opening up new possibilities for existence.

To return in conclusion to the starting point of this discussion: the screenplay of Foucault on Picasso on Velázquez. Its posthumous actualization and realization today is a reenactment of archival material through an artistic repetition, between the seventeenth and twentieth century, fifty years after its creation by Foucault. Yet what sense does it make to update this project today, situated as it is at the hybrid intersection between philosophical reflection, exploration of museum painting collections, audiovisual techniques, and archival fragments? Is it possible to recover, after so many years, the philosophical force that the screenplay imagined by Foucault should have embodied in the filmed reproduction of Velázquez's and Picasso's paintings? This project develops at a fertile crossroads between philosophical and political dimensions, aesthetic experience, the materiality of the archives, and the possibilities of reactivation, circulation, and creation made available by new technologies. The actual documentary on Foucault's screenplay exploits an entire series of digital potentialities unimaginable in 1970. It is moreover, inevitably, not only a film about *Las Meninas*, but also and above all a film about Foucault as an interpreter of the painters of the past, in a creative short-circuit between the (visual, this time) archives used by Foucault and the works of Foucault that have become his archive. Whether the documentary does indeed manage to convey this interweaving of creative and critical thinking is up to the audience to decide. It is, however, important to reflect — through Foucault's screenplay — on the power of repetition as an aesthetic and philosophical practice. Foucault's text is an archival material on works of art (*Las Meninas*), in which these works are not analyzed as simple aesthetic entertainments but as forms of visibility essential

---

7   Michel Foucault, 'What is Enlightenment' [1984], in *The Foucault Reader*, ed. by Paul
     Rabinow (New York: Pantheon Books, 1984), pp. 32–50 (p. 42).

to a historical configuration of thought (a way of thinking about the paradigms of discourse and the positions of the subject in history).

Repeating and reenacting Foucault's archives has therefore undoubtedly an immediate appeal from a marketing point of view. A Foucauldian documentary is probably first and foremost a 'good investment', as were its archives, acquired in 2013 by the Bibliothèque nationale de France for the exceptional amount of 3.8 million euros. The philosopher's archives are a 'treasure' not only in a cultural sense (the French Ministry of Culture did designate them a 'national treasure' to legally prevent their sale abroad, for example to American universities). But archives can also become the place of a repetition in a strong artistic and philosophical sense: they might be the material of a creative practice using the power of reenactment as a critical operation and a philosophical problematization. Foucauldian (and more generally philosophical) archives might in turn transform themselves, like the thought that unfolds there, also through forms of artistic *reenactment*, into an exercise of updating the critical effort.

Repetition, doubles, reenactments as historical-artistic and conceptual events have therefore a powerful philosophical and intrinsically political value. They allow us to reformulate the fundamental question concerning the place of thought today and for the future. Maurice Blanchot, at the beginning of a powerful critical text on Foucault, asked him this question directly, underlining the paradox of the archivist who, by digging to find the conditions of possibility for discourse in our history, risks undermining the very ground from which he takes his word: '*Monsieur* Foucault, from where do you speak — *D'où parlez-vous?*'[8] It is precisely the creative practice of repetition, the double as an aesthetic-philosophical instrument, that allows perhaps not for a solution to this paradox, which remains all too real, but to deploy it as a critical force. It is as if reality, intrinsically plural, were always 'excessive'. The forms of knowledge, the relationships of power, the techniques of existence always take place with a surplus of meaning and strength, which can be used in turn and which consequently makes history an open system. The possibility of resistance would be

---

8   Maurice Blanchot, *Michel Foucault as I Imagine Him* [1988], transl. by Brian Massumi and Jeffrey Mehlman (New York: Zone Books, 1990).

hidden in the power of repetition inherent in the relationships that make up the concrete fabric of our language and our world. According to Foucault, repetition games are political tools to reactivate this creative power immanent to reality. Taking advantage of the power of the double means being able to imagine another world and render it possible. Repetition is an exercise in freedom, a gesture of insubordination that Foucault himself never ceases to affirm through his practice of thought: a power of scandal, the force of *fiction*.

Foucault therefore dreams of a philosophical practice that takes up this power of repetition and short-circuits any search for univocal sense and any strategy that invokes 'meaning' and 'truth' in order to call to order. To use another of Foucault's key concepts, an 'ontology' of discourse and images understood through their power of duplication would consecrate them as 'heterotopias': the 'other spaces' that question and transform every given and ritualized place in a society. The language of fiction is the disturbing double of reality: a subtle yet radical fracture that marks the position of a real difference, the opening of a possibility of transformation. Like the performance of a court jester, the mocking imitation exposes its presumed model. 'The wound of the double [...] The present infinity of the mirage that constitutes, in its vanity, the thickness of the work, that absence within the work from which it paradoxically arises.'[9] Beyond any principle of economy of speech, the repetitive act of the double becomes a 'dépense' of sorts, in the sense that Bataille gives to this concept: a force always excessive to itself, and precisely for this reason capable of establishing new forms of meaning, reality, and existence.[10] Through repetition, a new practice of thought forges its path.

---

9   'La blessure du double [...] Infini actuel du mirage qui constitue, en sa vanité, l'épaisseur de l'œuvre — cette absence à l'intérieur de l'œuvre d'où celle-ci, paradoxalement, s'élève.' Foucault, 'Le Langage à l'infini' [1963], in *Dits et écrits*, I, text no. 14, pp. 287–88 (my translation).

10 See in particular Georges Bataille, *La Notion de dépense* [1933] (Paris: Lignes, 2011) and *La Part maudite* (Paris: Minuit, 1949).

'The Reconstruction of the Past is the Task of Historians and not Agents'
Operative Reenactment in State Security Archives

KATA KRASZNAHORKAI

Approximately two decades have passed since reenactment in performance art[1] started to influence contemporary cultural theory in exhibitions,[2] and later in game-changing books, such as Rebecca Schneider's *Performing Remains*.[3] It has also been more than twenty years since the first national secret service archives in former socialist

---

1   The term 'performance art' is used here to describe all performative artistic strategies by visual artists, i.e. happenings and actions. Although the term 'performance' was rarely used in Eastern Europe in the analysed period, it is an umbrella term that covers all tendencies in live-art actions that did not originate in theatre or musical performance. The term 'reenactment' has become increasingly ubiquitous in recent years, used lavishly to simply describe a 're-doing' of any cultural activity. In this essay, it refers to Rebecca Schneider's definition, relating to a certain type of historiographic analysis that takes place in a 'syncopated time', with the involvement of the bodily experience in memory, in: Rebecca Schneider, *Performing Remains: Art and War in Times of Theatrical Reenactment* (London: Routledge, 2011), partly published in an earlier version: 'Performance Remains', *Performance Research*, 6.2 (2001), pp. 100–08.

2   See, for example: 'A Little Bit of History Repeated', curated by Jens Hoffmann, at the KW Berlin from 16 to 18 November 2001; 'Life, Once More: Forms of Reenactment in Contemporary Art', curated by Sven Lütticken, at the Witte De With, Rotterdam, from 27 January to 27 March 2005; and 'History Will Repeat Itself: Strategies of Reenactment in Contemporary (Media) Art and Performance', curated by Inke Arns, at the HMKV Dortmund from 6 to 23 September 2007.

3   Rebecca Schneider, *Performing Remains*.

European countries started to (partly) open their doors for scientific research: first the Stasi Records Archive (BStU) in Germany in 1990, followed by archives in Budapest (1996), Warsaw (1998), Bucharest (1999), Sofia and Prague (2007), and finally Tirana (2017). However, although the accessibility of these archives has since led to research in history, sociology, and literature, until recently, no systematic, comparative, and analytical research was undertaken on performance art in relation to secret service operations.[4] Nor was the interrelation between the state security archives and performance art reconsidered from the perspective of reenactment strategies.

The scope of this paper does not allow me to give a hint of explanations for these issues. This paper aims to provide a preliminary, rough outline highlighting only the potentials of analysing the relation between reenactment strategies in state security methods and in performance art. This analysis hopefully contributes not only to the understanding of the relationship between secret services and the performance art scene but also, in a broader context, to the interrelation between reenactment strategies in art and 'operative reenactment' by the state security. Furthermore, this paper attempts to shift focus to the possibilities that lie in the intertwined relationship between reenactment theory in performance art and operative theory in secret service practices.

Analysis of secret services' records and documents on performance art shed new light, not only on the systematic oppression of subversive art forms that opposed state-socialist cultural directives but also on the reenactment strategies of secret service informers who performed in order to effectively disrupt performance artists and prevent performance art from becoming public.

But why were performances, happenings, and actions — mostly carried out by almost unknown artists in marginal places in front of

---

4   *Artists & Agents. Performancekunst und Geheimdienste*, ed. by Kata Krasznahorkai and Sylvia Sasse (Leipzig: Spector Books, 2019) (forthcoming in English) and the exhibition 'Artists & Agents' curated by Sylvia Sasse, Kata Krasznahorkai, and Inke Arns at the HMKV Dortmund from 26 October 2019 to 19 April 2020. The exhibition magazine is free for download here: HMKV Exhibition Magazine 2/2019, ed. by Inke Arns, Kata Krasznahorkai, and Sylvia Sasse (Dortmund: Hartware MedienKunstVerein, 2019) <https://www.hmkv.de/files/hmkv/ausstellungen/2019/AGENTS/05_Publikation/HMKV_AGENTS_Magazin_DE-EN.pdf> [accessed 20 February 2020].

small audiences — so alarmingly dangerous in the eyes of the state security? The potential of being reenacted was one of the decisive reasons that performance art became one of the most surveilled spheres of art in certain countries, such as in Hungary or the German Democratic Republic. From the perspective of the secret service, this artistic genre was a nightmare for several reasons: (1) it was a (in some cases spontaneous) live event, so real-time-control during an action was almost impossible; (2) it had no prior screenplay and was thus not eligible for prior control and censorship; (3) it was in some cases an improvised action, so officials only knew about the performances either shortly before or after the event, and sometimes only realized during the performance what was happening; (4) the majority of the performances took place in public spaces, such clubs, the basements of museums, or outdoors, but also in private flats that were also under surveillance, but where it was harder to 'get in';[5] and (5) the genre was supposed to have originated in the West and therefore had the potential to infiltrate the youth with 'nihilistic' and 'anarchic' ideas. Most importantly, performance art as a live event could be reenacted anywhere and anytime without providing a tangible object of surveillance. It had no manifest output — unlike sculpture or painting, which were easily recognized as art. One of the major difficulties for the state security was to detect *what* and *how* to put under operative control, and how to *re-act* what was seen or reported.

Before proceeding with an overview of reenacting and re-acting between the state security and performing artists, the difference between reenacting and re-acting must be clarified. 'Reenacting' refers to the acting out of a fixed role constructed by state security officials, with which the informant had to identify. As a result of a successful reenactment, the bodily (in style and manners) and mental (in ideology, cultural definitions, etc.) identification with the person under operative control would ideally be reached. In the state security terminology of the GDR and Hungary, this was called the 'legend'

---

5   On the relationship between public and private spheres of the surveilled places of performances, see Kata Krasznahorkai, 'Surveilling the Public Sphere: The First Hungarian Happening in Secret Agents Reports', in *Performance Art in the Second Public Sphere: Event-based Art in Late Socialist Europe*, ed. by Katalin Cseh-Varga and Adam Czirak, Routledge Advances in Theatre & Performance Studies (London: Routledge, 2018), pp. 127–38.

— the role that an actor played and with which they later became identified. It was these 'legends', or life stories, that were tailored to the operative scenario (the task the agent or informant had to fulfil), which was agreed upon in writing at the time that the informant was 'taken on'.[6] As in the special case of surveilling performance artists, it was difficult to obtain relevant information from these artists' closed circles, and thus informants of central importance had to come from their innermost circles, usually close friends of the surveilled person. These informants had to perform their 'legends' and re-enact these roles in similar, repetitive manners also in the most intimate situations. That led in some cases to the formation of multiple personalities within one person. The permanent reenacting of these different personae often resulted in broken identities and serious disturbances in the personalities of those artists, who had to be informants and artists in one. Reenacting roles and identities prescribed by officers and integrating these roles into one's personal life produces a crucial idea regarding the theoretical implications of reenactment formulated by Sven Lütticken in 2005: 'If one is always re-enacting roles partially scripted by others, one might just well use re-enactment against itself by recreating historical events.'[7]

'Re-acting' was the state security officers' methodology for using information in the reports that were delivered via the effective operation of agents using and reenacting 'legends'. Re-acting was at the core of the officers' tasks once a report was delivered to them. The key instrument for operative staff to counter performance art was the systematic writing and archiving of reports; both surveillance and report writing were carried out following guidelines created by the secret service itself. These guidelines were meticulously orchestrated, highly repetitive and monotonous. Once a report had been handwritten and delivered, the process repeated itself: first the document went to the secretary to be typed (if it was classified as important enough), then

---

6   'MfS-Dictionary: Werbung', *Stasi-Unterlagen-Archiv*, ed. by Der Bundesbeauftragte für die Unterlagen des Staatssicherheitsdienstes der ehemaligen Deutschen Demokratischen Republik <https://www.bstu.de/mfs-lexikon/detail/werbung/> [accessed 17 November 2020].

7   Sven Lütticken, 'An Arena in Which to Reenact', in *Life, Once More: Forms of Reenactment in Contemporary Art*, ed. by Sven Lütticken (Rotterdam: Witte de With, 2005), pp. 17–60.

sorted in many different operative files and forwarded to higher levels if necessary. There were certain artists who were surveilled and 'operatively treated' for more than a decade by at least three (but often more than ten) long-term informants. One can imagine that in the flood of reports, in some cases written every other week, there was a continuous flow of surveillance, handwriting, typing, and forwarding, a cycle that repeated itself again and again and again. Actual 'actions', like tapping phones or house searches, were rather rare in this monotonous flow of mostly repetitive information gathering about the surveilled persons and stand in stark contrast to the obsessive repetition and emphasis of the supposed 'danger' emanating from this new artistic form. These paranoid fears were triggered by the rhetoric of the documents themselves, particularly by the ongoing, almost mantra-like repetition of the dangers that socialist society was facing from performance artists, with some sentences repeated verbatim in many reports over a number of years. This was the permanent reenactment of fake facts produced in order to create internal enemies, based on the repetitive evocation of prefabricated fictions. Repeating how dangerous these 'negative-nihilistic' artists were for society also gave legitimization to the massive personal and financial efforts that kept the machinery of state surveillance alive for more than twenty years.

It is thus unsurprising that artists were not only monitored by the state: the secret services also attempted to discuss, define, and, in any case, intervene in this new development in art. It was thus crucial for the secret service to develop theoretical tools to detect whether an action or artist was a threat to socialist society or not. The Hungarian secret service repeated the definition of 'the happening' over and over again in countless reports and operational plans to emphasize and enhance the assumed danger. As a consequence, the fake facts led, in the case of some artists, to attempts to criminalize and pathologize them;[8] in other cases, the artistic activities of the underground were actively hindered by the closing of locations, the disruption of performances

---

8   Kata Krasznahorkai, 'Heightened Alert: The Underground Art Scene in the Sights of the Secret Police — Surveillance Files as a Resource for Research into Artists' Activities in the Underground of the 1960s and 1970s', in *Art Beyond Borders: Artistic Exchange in Communist Europe (1945-1989)*, ed. by Jérôme Bazin, Pascal Dubourg Glatigny, and Piotr Piotrowski (Budapest: Central European University Press, 2015), pp. 125–39.

in public spaces, and public undermining of an artist group's work.[9] In other cases, the secret service acted against performance art with performative methods resulting in 'counter-performances' as acts of subversive affirmation.[10]

One report compiled by an unofficial informant with the former GDR state security reads: 'The principal content of "action art" is the production and subsequent destruction of decadent artistic forms, and the documentation of the sequence of motions involved.'[11] It is this 'sequence of motions', the continuous serialization of movements and situations, which led to a certain 'Stasi aesthetic' in documenting artistic actions, with the aesthetic of the archive itself creating a kind of involuntary 'archive art'. For example, this absurd aesthetic is manifested in a photo series made by a secret service agent photo-documenting people visiting the illegal gallery of Gabriele Stötzer in Erfurt. This photo series gains a certain 'artistic' value due to the minimalist and serial aesthetic depicting people opening the door to a banned gallery: fifty different persons, always from behind, documented in the very same moment.

Reenactment strategies were also a form of the artistic reclaiming of the archives after the system change. After 1990, artists turned to their own state security records as a new source of artistic material. The absurdity of the fabrication of danger with the repetitive mantra of irrelevant, seemingly unimportant, and banal details is the focus of the German artist Cornelia Schleime, who left the GDR in 1984.

---

9   Such was the case with the GDR group of artists gathered around Galerie Clara Mosch, which was systematically deconstructed by the Stasi with the help of the group's photographer, Rolf-Rainer Wasse (Codename 'Frank Körner') as a central informant.

10   This interference is described by Sylvia Sasse as 'subversive affirmation' of the state security. For more detail, see: Sylvia Sasse, 'KGB: The Art of Performance. Action Art or Actions against Art?', *Artmargins*, 30 December 1999 <http://www.artmargins.com/index.php/2-articles/449-kgb-or-the-art-of-performance-action-art-or-actions-against-art> [accessed 28 February 2019], and in the forthcoming publication Sylvia Sasse, *Subversive Affirmation* (Berlin: Diaphanes, 2022).

11   BStU, MFS, BV Karl-Marx-Stadt, Auswertungs- und Kontrollgruppe, AKG — 10088, 18.10.1977, 'Information über ein Treffen der Kunstschaffenden des Verbands bildender Künstler der DDR in Leussow', Comrade Siegfried Lorenz, 00094, cited in Sylvia Sasse, 'Stasi-Dada. Was KünstlerInnen aus ihren Geheimdienstakten machen', *Geschichte der Gegenwart*, 16 February 2016 <http://geschichtedergegenwart.ch/stasi-dada-gabriele-stoetzer-las-im-cabaret-voltaire-aus-ihren-akten/> [accessed 20 February 2018].

She used exactly this repetition of sentences and recurring phrases from her photographic records and reenacted her own files by re-staging repetitive phrases and descriptions of her personal and artistic life written by unofficial informants and officers in her series *Looking Forward to Further Collaboration Nr. 7284/85.*

What does the research on reenactment strategies of the state security concerning performance artists contribute to performance theory? Above all, the archives document the actions of the secret services themselves and their operative practices, not the artistic actions. The secret service archives can thus be treated as a reservoir of state performative practices. Repetitive actions and strategies to reenact long contradicted what was thought about performance art, an art form considered to be one that could not be saved, documented, and repeated.[12] The state security noticed very quickly, indeed in 'real time', that this was not the case; in fact, performance art *can* be documented and saved, and, confirming the state security's greatest fear, performance is never a singular action by any means. They noticed very early on that it was exactly the reenactment potential that represented the greatest threat to socialist state order. It was also clear that performances or their documentation had nothing to do with dematerialization or the documentation of so-called dematerialized events either, a fact that had already been a prominent mantra of performance theoreticians from the 1970s to the 1990s.

A wave of new research focuses on reenactments in recent years, showing that performance is never a 'singular' or 'dematerialized' event. Rebecca Schneider, for example, invites us to think about 'performance as a medium in which disappearance negotiates, becomes materiality'.[13]

This 'disappearance becoming materiality' is grounded in the vast amount of physical material on performance art in in hundreds of thousands of handwritten and typed pages in state security archives, documents that constantly re-act and reenact scenarios, 'legends', and operative measures. Nevertheless, reenacting is also manifest in writing the endless reports and measure plans. Thus, operative reenactment

---

12   This is claimed by Peggy Phelan in *Unmarked: The Politics of Performance* (London: Routledge, 1995), p. 146.
13   Schneider, *Performance Remains*, p. 106.

takes place not only in 'becoming the enemy' (in this case, an artist) but also on the archival level, as the reports and operative plans were triggering the urge to act and re-act constantly based on past events to prevent them in the future. This temporal dimension of reenactment in the interaction between state security and performance art provides a good illustration of how Schneider's concept of syncopated time is constructive for the theory on the interrelation between performance art and operative reenactment: nowhere is the non-linearity and in-betweenness of time more present than in the minutiae of the records, which, when read today, offer a new presence of the historicity of performance art in relation to state power.

When thinking about artists using these archives as artistic material or about researchers who use the archives for creating new histories of performance art, we can concur with Schneider when she says that the performative basis of the archive is 'that it is a house of and for performative repetition, not stasis.'[14] This is even truer in the case of state security archives.

No state security officer would have ever thought that the archive of the archive based on their reenacting strategies would become one of the sources of research on performance art and theory. As one secret agent training manual states: 'The reconstruction of the past is the task of historians and not agents.'[15] Today's art historians have to be alert not to unwittingly perpetuate the narrative set up by fictionalized facts in state security records.

As we now live in a thoroughly performative world, one that is more and more focused on presence, and where the mediatized notion of 'live' surveillance has political urgency, the reconsideration of operative reenactments in state security is not only relevant for art practices but for the overall understanding of citizens' power of presence and its relation to state power.

---

14   Ibid., p. 108.

15   'Az információs munka elméleti és módszertani kérdései [The Theoretical and Methodological Questions of Information Work], Állambiztonsági Szolgálatok Történeti Levéltára Budapest [Historical Archive of the State Security Services Budapest], 2 vols. (1977), I:ÁBTL A-3005/30/1, p. 38.

The Collection of Jane Ryan & William Saunders

Reconstruction as 'Democratic Gesture'

PIO ABAD

The Collection of Jane Ryan & William Saunders is an ongoing project that I started in 2012. It focuses on the role that a collection of artefacts has played in the recent history of the Philippines, specifically on the cultural legacy of Ferdinand and Imelda Marcos, who ruled the country as a conjugal dictatorship — or what they preferred to call 'constitutional authoritarianism', and what I would prefer to call a kleptocracy — from 1965 to 1986.

Through a combination of wilful obfuscation and political convenience, this collection has been largely unavailable to the public. What has been recovered of the so-called Marcos Collection, a seemingly arbitrary assortment of old masters, Georgian and Regency-era silverware, and even one of the largest collections of Grandma Moses paintings, was sequestered by the government shortly after 1986. Some pieces were hidden away in storage, a few were displayed in government offices, and most were auctioned off. Thirty years later, a huge number of works of art remain unaccounted for, their existence proven only by metal plaques on the walls where the works used to be displayed or on inventories on yellowing pieces of paper proclaiming them lost. Over the past six years, my project has aimed to make the

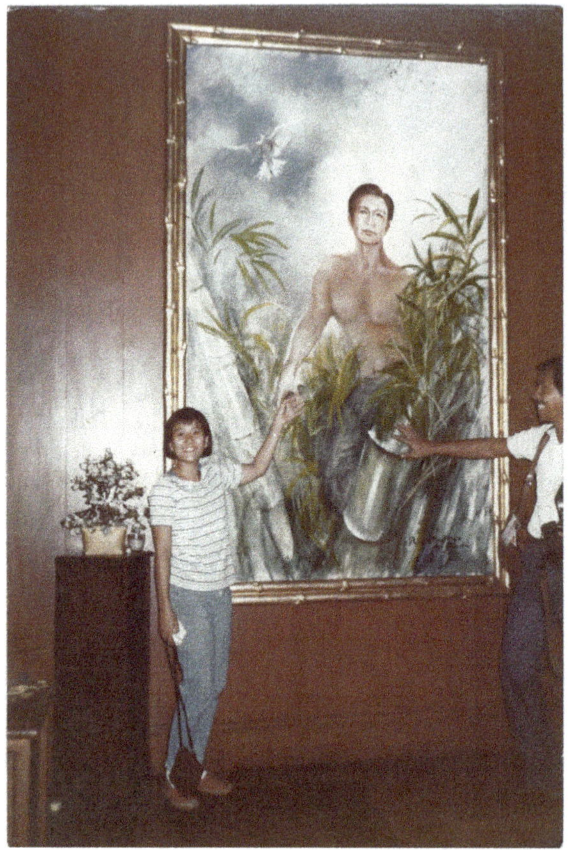

Figure 1. Photograph taken on 25 February 1986 in the Marcoses'
private chambers at Malacañan Palace (1986).

collection accessible to the public by recreating this inventory using
different strategies of reconstruction.

The genesis of this project can be traced to a family photograph.
'Genesis' is perhaps a particularly appropriate term given the subject of
the painting in the photo. It depicts Ferdinand Marcos as the mythical
figure Malakas. According to popular legend, Malakas (The Strong
One) and Maganda (The Beautiful One) were the first Filipinos, who
entered the world fully formed when a magical bird split a single stalk
of bamboo in half, revealing the pair cradled inside. The Marcoses de-
ployed this myth as the iconographic representation of their conjugal

rule. Edenic images of the couple were fed into the propaganda machine and proliferated as murals and sculptures throughout the city. In assuming the personas of Malakas and Maganda, the Marcoses sought to mythologize the progress of history and present themselves as the originators of the circulation of cultural and political power.[1]

This photograph was taken by my mother on the evening of the 25 February 1986. A few hours before, Ferdinand and Imelda were chased out of the presidential palace and boarded one of Ronald Reagan's helicopters for a reluctant Honolulu exile. My mother and father, the figure on the right, were two of the first protesters to enter the private chambers. This photograph, I believe, is one of the earliest documentations of that exact moment when the public façade of Malakas and Maganda collapsed, and the people they had been oppressing for two decades suddenly had access to the sordid private life behind these misrepresentations. The Marcoses' modernist myth came at the cost of 3,257 lives, the torture and incarceration of 34,000 more — my parents among them — and the systematic ransacking of the national treasury, one of the largest thefts in history that exploited the then nascent system of offshore havens and shell companies.

At this historical juncture, replacing Malakas and Maganda with another set of alter egos will be more instructive. Jane Ryan and William Saunders, the characters from which this project takes its title, were the false identities used by Imelda and Ferdinand Marcos to register their first Swiss bank account at Credit Suisse Zurich in March 1968, and it was presumably through this dummy account and many others that the couple purchased art and property, skimmed off Japanese World War II reparations, donated a million dollars to each of Richard Nixon's presidential campaigns, and transformed foreign aid to private wealth. By the time they left office, investigators estimated their wealth at about ten billion US dollars[2].

The scale of the Marcoses' loot is so vast and so astonishing in range that it is often only referred to in collective terms such as 'loot',

---

1   Vicente Rafael, 'Patronage and Pornography: Ideology and Spectatorship in the Early Marcos Years', *Comparative Studies in Society and History*, 32.3 (1990), pp. 282–304.

2   Nick Davies, 'The $10bn Question: What Happened to the Marcos Millions', *Guardian*, 7 May 2016 <https://www.theguardian.com/world/2016/may/07/10bn-dollar-question-marcos-millions-nick-davies> [accessed 22 February 2021].

'plunder', and 'ill-gotten wealth'. So much so that over time, it has assumed, in its status as a collective noun, an almost abstract singularity — a single object that is subsequently easier to disregard, trivialize, and contain within one of Imelda's stilettos. One of my main objectives behind this project was to wrest this loot from that collective singularity and confront the public with its unwieldy scale and its terrifying range.

Over the past few years, I have used a number of strategies to reconstruct this collection. In 2012, when I was researching for the project's first iteration at Gasworks in London, I came across catalogues of two Christie's auctions held in New York on 10 and 11 January 1991. Acting on behalf of the Philippine Commission on Good Government (PCGG), the agency tasked with the sequester and the liquidation of the Marcoses' wealth, Christie's auctioned off seventy-eight lots of Georgian and Regency-era silverware, at the time the largest collection of silverware from a single collection, and seventy-eight Renaissance paintings of inconsistent quality (and, as discovered later on, dubious provenance). In addition to these, twenty-five old masters paintings of arguably superior quality, which were confiscated from a yacht owned by the Saudi arms dealer Adnan Kashoggi, were being sold by the US Federal Government. It was alleged that Kashoggi was hiding these works for Mrs. Marcos.

These images became the basis for exploring the idea of exhibition making as medium — museological display as armature for creating photographic installations and sculpture. It also served as a way of restaging my earliest memories of a museum, an experience irrevocably tied to the fall of the Marcos dictatorship.

The hastily constructed museum of personal effects is a post-revolutionary trope in freshly liberated autocracies, and for a number of years after the revolution the basement of the presidential palace was turned into a provisional museum. At six years old, I vividly remember walking through rows and rows of mahogany shelves and table tops, each one filled with various items: paintings, ornaments, perfume bottles, bulletproof brassieres, and the infamous pairs of shoes.

Unfortunately, the fragile democracies that follow revolutions are accompanied by another trope: the systemic failure to institutionalize collective acts of remembering that displays such as these were meant to engender. By 1990, the political compromises of the new govern-

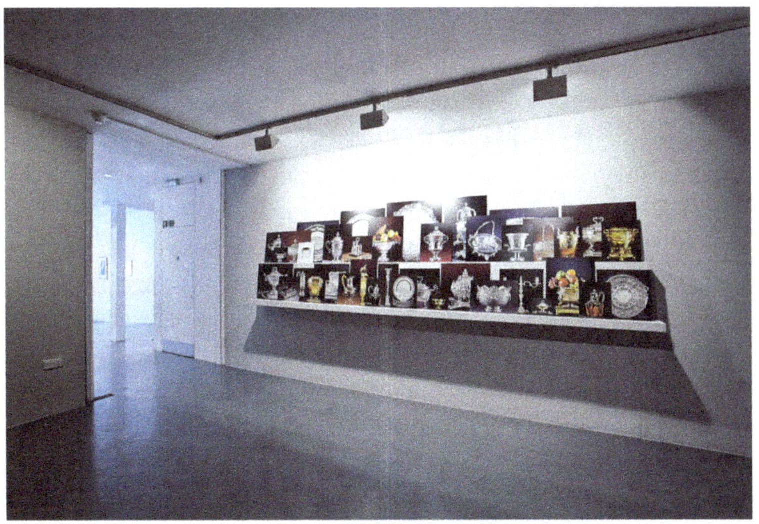

Figure 2. *The Collection of Jane Ryan & William Saunders* (2014),
Thirty-eight archival inkjet prints on Epson semi-gloss paper, mounted
on aluminium, installation view (Gasworks, London).

ment and the convenient shifts in allegiances by many of the Marcoses'
cronies meant that, by the time this museum was packed away, the
clamour for political accountability by an exhausted and disillusioned
public seemed to have gone with it.

I was interested in using the auction catalogues as the basis for
excavation for a number of reasons. Firstly, the Christie's catalogue
provides such a crisp and extensive visual accounting of the Marcos
Collection that even the PCGG uses it as one of its primary points of
reference. Before coming across the catalogues, a lot of the documentation I had found, if I could access it, was of poor quality. The rest I had
imagined as buried under the bureaucratic and legal entanglements of
the past thirty years.

Another reason for my interest was the timing of the event itself, taking place in between two defining, if unfortunate, episodes. A
few months prior to the auction, Imelda Marcos was indicted by the
Federal Court in New York City for fraud and racketeering charges.
Imelda's tearful performance as a naïve widow during the trial was
sensational. It was a performance that also proved convincing. After a

four-month trial, the jury decided that the late Ferdinand Marcos had looted the Philippine treasury without the explicit knowledge of his wife. On 3 July 1990, Imelda was acquitted of all charges. Immediately after the verdict, she headed to St. Patrick's Cathedral and proceeded to creep down the entire aisle to the altar on her knees.

A few months after the auction and as a result of the acquittal, the Philippine government decided that there were no longer any legal impediments to bar Imelda's return to the Philippines. On 4 November 1991, an unrepentant Imelda returned home and would eventually be elected back into political office, along with two of her children. In the recent 2016 presidential elections that saw the rise of Rodrigo Duterte, Ferdinand Marcos, Jr., nicknamed 'Bongbong', nearly captured the vice presidency. In November of that same year, the newly installed President Duterte fulfilled a personal promise to the Marcoses by allowing the body of the dictator Ferdinand to be secretly interred at the National Hero's Cemetery.

Viewed in the context of these events, the auction, by dispersing the Marcos Collection and recirculating it back into the market, also served to launder these objects, silencing the historical narrative by which they are tainted. The museological installation and its accompanying text became a means of reconstituting this collection and reiterating its complicity to this history of corruption.

In his writings on art during the Marcos regime, the Filipino art historian Patrick Flores uses the term 'democratic gesture' in relation to the development of avant-garde practices in the Philippines during the 60s and 70s.[3] As 'the connoisseur of the new, a patroness of the avant-garde, and an arbiter of experiments in the arts',[4] Imelda favoured conceptualism, as she did not see any conflict between its aesthetics and the American-coddled authoritarianism of her and her husband's government. As an art form, it served as a sophisticated retort to the more activist inclinations of social realist painting, reiterating the regime's idea of ethno-modernity and development and fitting perfectly with the rhetoric of progress that the Marcoses brazenly

---

3   Patrick Flores, 'Total Community Response: Performing the Avant-Garde as a Democratic Gesture in Manila', *Southeast of Now: Directions in Contemporary and Modern Art in Asia*, 1.1 (2017), pp. 13–38.

4   As described by the writer and Philippine National Artist Nick Joaquin.

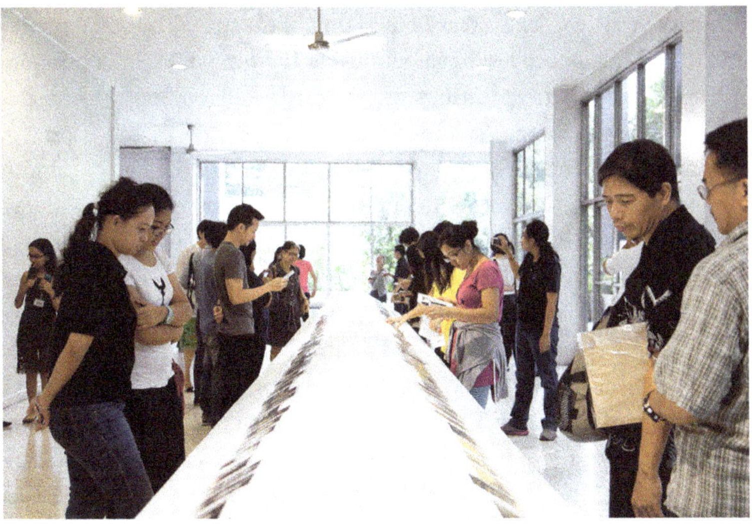

Figure 3. *The Collection of Jane Ryan & William Saunders* (2014),
97 sets of postcards, unlimited edition, installation view
(Jorge B. Vargas Museum, Manila).

asserted. The Cultural Centre of the Philippines, a Brutalist building that Imelda constructed on reclaimed land along Manila Bay, became the main edifice for arts and culture during the regime, serving as the institutional site for experimental performance, installations, and film. It did not seem to matter that all of this was taking place under martial rule and amidst the repressed bodies of its citizens.

The weaponized nature of the term 'democratic gesture' in relation to the Marcoses' support of avant-garde and conceptual practices has become central to the development of *The Collection of Jane Ryan & William Saunders*. Central to the project is the desire to reclaim this definition of a 'democratic gesture' from Imelda's perverted appropriation.

The Gasworks exhibition was shown concurrently with my first museum presentation in Manila at the Jorge B. Vargas Museum at the University of the Philippines. For a Filipino audience, it became important that the work was participatory. For most, if not all, of the visitors to the exhibition it would serve as their most extensive encounter with the Marcos loot. Deploying participation as a conceptual strategy in the work also served to highlight the muted political agency in avant-garde practices prevalent during the time of the dictatorship.

I presented the paintings as postcards laid out on a ten-metre long white plinth that spanned the length of one of the rooms in the museum. The idea was to present an installation in an almost forensic fashion — a monumental body of incontrovertible evidence neatly arranged for scrutiny. On the back of each postcard is a series of seven different texts lifted from various sources, tracing the fraudulent history of this collection and implicating an expansive network of players from the worlds of art and politics.

The democratic gesture is performed by inviting the public to take ownership of the artworks and create their own personal collection of paintings from the postcard reproductions — a symbolic restitution of a collection purchased with the hard-earned money of, but never enjoyed by, the Filipino public.

The final part of this project concerns the collection of jewellery seized by US Customs from the Marcoses when they entered Hawaii in 1986, appropriately referred to in courts as the Hawaii Collection. The collection includes an extremely rare 25-carat pink diamond worth five million dollars and a tiara with twenty-five pearls in a diamond frame seized from the Russian Tsar's family in 1918.

Shortly after their seizure, the collection was turned over to the PCGG. Since then, they have languished in the vaults of the Central Bank, hidden from public view, amidst legal challenges from the Marcos family. In February 2016, the PCGG announced that all legal impediments had been cleared for the pieces to go to auction with a planned public exhibition to precede the sale. The victory of Rodrigo Duterte in May 2016 put these plans on hold. His administration announced plans to begin dismantling the PCGG with its responsibilities being transferred to the Office of the Solicitor General, a position currently held by a Marcos loyalist.

In collaboration with jewellery designer Frances Wadsworth Jones, we have digitally reconstructed the collection from photos obtained from the PCGG in early 2016 and created 3D printed replicas out of translucent resin. This iteration of the project was recently exhibited in Hawaii as part of the second Honolulu Biennial. Returning to the site of the Marcoses' short-lived exile, the jewellery

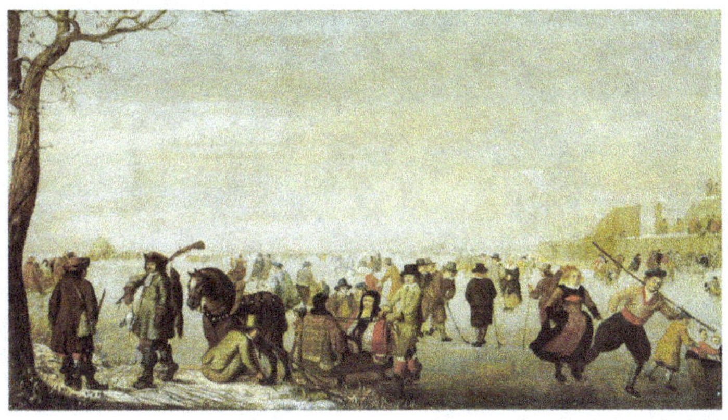

The Marcos Collection: Fortune and Folly
Artnews Magazine, October 1990

Investigators say that just as the Marcos government was toppling, someone, or some group, emptied the 66th Street town house, the Olympic Towers apartment, and the other Marcos residences of much of their most valuable contents before the properties were seized.

Nothing on the record indicates where the 38 paintings Khashoggi bought were kept during the interim, but investigators did pick up their trace in the person of Khashoggi's sometime Manhattan chauffeur, Ernest Sabatino.

On May 19, 1986, Sabatino testified, he got a call from a Khashoggi aide who told him to rent a small truck 'and wait for a call from someone named Irene.' Something had to be delivered to Khashoggi's private plane, a Boeing 727, then parked at the Butler Aviation Terminal at Newark Airport. 'Irene' called, Sabatino continued, and he was told to drive to a mall in DOuglaston, Queens, and turn the truck over to two men while he waited in a parking lot. When the two men returned with the truck, he was to drive it to Khashoggi's plane.

Everything went according to plan, said Sabatino, adding that he never learned the identity of the men nor the contents of the truck.

When the men asked him to sign a receipt, what 'looked like names and titles,' said Sabatino, he refused. 'I didn't load the truck,' he said. The two men told him not to worry about it, Sabatino continued. 'So I just signed *Mickey Mouse*.'

'You signed *Mickey Mouse*?' roared Judge F. Keenan in astonishment when he heard the testimony.

'I literally signed *Mickey Mouse*,' Sabatino replied, adding that on his way to Newark Airport, he had parked the truck unattended on a Manhattan side street while he stopped to get some Chinese food.

Figure 4. *The Collection of Jane Ryan & William Saunders* (2014),
97 sets of postcards, unlimited edition (detail).

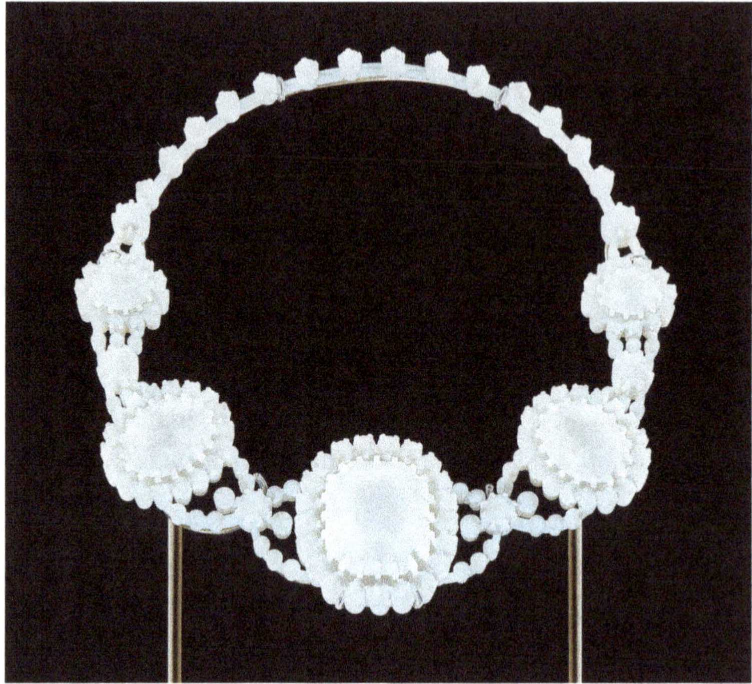

Figure 5. *The Collection of Jane Ryan & William Saunders* (2019).
3D printed plastic, brass and dry-transfer text (detail).

reappears not as a collection of luxurious objects but as effigies — ghosts of a history condemned to be in a perpetual state of irresolution.

Over the course of working on *The Collection of Jane Ryan & William Saunders*, the Philippines has moved from a democracy, however flawed and chaotic, to once again being on the precipice of a much more violent dictatorship. This has made continuing with this project a difficult, if not perilous, endeavour, but it has also intensified the urgency to reconstruct this collection at a time when the cost of forgetting is too great a price to pay.

Insistence
The Temporality of the Death Fast and the Political

ÖZGE SERIN

> Whoever stays with the story penetrates
> into something opaque that he does not
> understand, while whoever holds to the
> meaning cannot get back to the darkness of
> which it is the telltale light. The two readers
> can never meet; we are one, then the other, we
> understand always more or always less than is
> necessary. True reading remains impossible.
>
> Maurice Blanchot, 'Reading Kafka'

On 23 January 2007, the Death Fast of prisoners affiliated with out-lawed Marxist-Leninist organizations in Turkey came to an end after 122 deaths. This mass hunger strike — 2286 consecutive days long, which the participating organizations extended for more than six years by launching new teams almost continuously — began as a prison resistance against the introduction of high-security penal institutions as part of the larger restructuring of the Turkish penal regime in the new millennium.[1]

---

[1] The text that follows is based on my long-term ethnographic work on the Death Fast in Turkey and is a continued meditation written in the margins of that experience.

The introduction of high-security penal institutions, known as 'F-type' prisons, had its legal basis in Article 16 of the Anti-Terror Law (1991), which stipulated that the sentences of those convicted and awaiting or standing trial on charges under the provisions of this law would be served in 'special penal institutions' built on a system of cells holding one or three inmates, explicitly prohibiting any open visitation and any communication and interaction between the inmates.[2] The construction of the new celled prisons, along with the alteration of the remaining seventy-five prisons into a similar architectural plan, provided the Turkish state with the infrastructural capacity to abolish the prison commune as an economic and political entity and reestablish punitive sovereignty over the prisoners in the service of coercive individualization.

The first and only irrevocable demand of the hunger strike was the immediate abolition of the F-type prison project. In the view of prison organizations, the F-type prison entombed the prisoner in the cell; by naming the cell-type prison *tabutluk* (coffin), they insisted that isolation was no different than being buried alive.[3] Isolation killed the subject without killing; it annihilated the subject but conserved life. Such individualized and separated life, the organizers argued, was at best only a hollowed-out life, a brutal and oppressive attempt to extend the condition of alienation and abstraction under capitalism by destroying the inmates' communal life in the prison. Instead of appealing to the fundamental and inalienable right to life as a (legal) value in and of itself, which would have had disquieting similarities with the very discourse of the state authorities that they sought to challenge, the political organizations reaffirmed each prisoner's right to death, a right that was absolute to the extent that each death faster made a sovereign decision about their own fate.

What Maurice Blanchot says of reading Kafka can equally be said of reading the Death Fast, since the main source of the self-questioning paradoxes of the Death Fast is the incompatibility between the political

---

2   For the full text, see Terörle Mücadele Kanunu (Anti-Terrorist Law), Law No. 3713, 12 April 1991 <http://www.mevzuat.gov.tr/MevzuatMetin/1.5.3713.pdf> [accessed 15 November 2017].

3   'F Tipi Tabutluk Gerçeği' (Truth of the F-Type Coffin), *Ekmek ve Adalet*, 5 June 2002, p. 5.

and extrapolical elements of the hunger strike itself.[4] Whatever is singular in a radical sense — and every right to death is so singular — offers resistance to the conventions of language, the instituted order of meaning, and the historical record. By making the motives or interests, messages or arguments, demands or ends generally communicable, the hunger strike *form* renders this singular resistance representable and thus visible in the first place.[5] At its extreme, the motives or interests, messages or arguments, and demands or ends would have to be capable of being universalized in order for the hunger strike to be recognized as the same form of political action across social, cultural, and linguistic space. Every death, by contrast, at its extreme would be so singularized that it would elude universal communicability, withdraw from what is generally called the 'scene of politics', and be accessible only as an entirely untranslatable, extrapolitical idiom.

The Death Fast, far from facilitating mediation, had the effect of intensifying the discord between the communicable content of the prison movement and the incommunicable sovereignty of the prisoners. The declared aim of prisoners gave way to a state of suspension, overwriting the conclusiveness of demands with an abstract insistence that was symptomatically reflected in the duration of the prison resistance. The duration of the resistance was extended by means of an ostensibly inexhaustible reserve of volunteers, but the actual substitutability of hunger strikers was achieved not by effacing their singular relation to death but by accentuating it, not by denying the differences between the volunteers, but by recognizing their irreducibility. This internal economy of recognition had as its own paradoxical outcome: the abstraction of self-starvation. Such deliberate abstraction ultimately foundered on the scandalous disproportion between human loss and paltry gains, revealing an indelible residue that threatened to overwhelm political instrumentality.

---

4   Maurice Blanchot, 'Reading Kafka', in Blanchot, *The Work of Fire*, trans. by Charlotte Mandell (Stanford, CA: Stanford University Press, 1995), pp. 1–11 (p. 4). One of Franz Kafka's final stories, 'A Hunger Artist', may be said to engage the aporia addressed in the following reading of the Death Fast.

5   Jacques Derrida often insists upon the universalizability of the singular. See, for example, his *Demeure: Fiction and Testimony*, trans. by Elizabeth Rottenberg (Stanford, CA: Stanford University Press, 2000), p. 41.

In considering the repeatability of death as a dramatization of this tension between the incommunicable and the communicable, I will deploy the concept-metaphor 'event' in order to explore the divide between the space of dying and the space of politics, which are incompatibly distinct yet inextricably linked.

Gilles Deleuze, borrowing from the distinctive vocabulary of Blanchot's *The Space of Literature*, offers death as the ultimate example of the event in order to mark its double structure: 'Death and its wound are not simply events among other events. Every event is like death, double and impersonal in its double.'[6]

No longer synonymous with worldly affairs, the event is necessarily irreducible to historical factuality; indeed, effects are so radically disjoined from causes that the event is affirmed as that which breaks with a linear or expressive causality. More importantly, the event is never simply 'present', but instead takes place repeatedly, though always differently, in an open-ended movement of spatiotemporal differentiation. It is grammatically associated with the substantival infinitive *mourir* (dying) inasmuch as death corporealizes itself only in singular bodies, and yet it always exceeds all its possible corporealizations. An unrepresentable excess that is never present in itself, but only as a perpetual movement of self-differentiation, death is always already at least two, simultaneously singular and 'impersonal and pre-individual, neutral'.[7]

I propose reversing the current of concept-metaphor here against a certain performance theory of sovereignty and ask, not what the concept-metaphor *death* does for the thought of the event, but what the concept-metaphor *event* does for the thought of death on the hunger strike, in order to distinguish the infinite reserve of the event from sovereignty.

Giorgio Agamben determines the structure of sovereignty in terms of an oppositional identity between actuality and potentiality.[8]

---

6   On 'double death', see Maurice Blanchot, *The Space of Literature*, trans. by Ann Smock (Lincoln: University of Nebraska Press, 1989), pp. 153–55; Gilles Deleuze, *The Logic of Sense*, trans. by Mark Lester and Charles Stivale (New York: Columbia University Press, 1990), pp. 148–53 (p. 152).

7   Ibid., p. 151.

8   See Giorgio Agamben, *Homo Sacer: Sovereign Power and Bare Life*, trans. by Daniel Heller-Roazen (Stanford, CA: Stanford University Press, 1998), pp. 46–47.

Such identity is evidently both performative and 'afformative' for his astute readers in anthropology.[9] Sovereignty, Allen Feldman maintains, grounds itself in the body as pure effective power inasmuch as it could construct itself as 'an archic center and reserved site of power' — both visible and invisible, tangible and intangible, secret and public — only through reenactments of violence in an open seriality that necessarily thwarts a final closure or a determinate form. He writes, 'In its desistance from violence, sovereignty puts off from itself any configurable essence of violence; desisted violence persists as a formless force in its nonbeing and promissory phenomenality.'[10] Thus, as an 'evental' site of sovereignty, the temporal body cannot be subjectivized; the subject loses its relation to itself as possibility or propriety and dissipates to a point of extremity, where it becomes a double of sovereign self-identical indifference. Nevertheless, despite or even because of the sheer exteriority of its body, Feldman further asserts that the subject has the chance of recovering self-identity in death. In Feldman's account, the state of impropriety turns unaccountably into one of propriety in a mimetic reversal of expropriation.[11]

Though Feldman contests desubjectivation as absolute sovereign effect in Agamben's thought; essentially instrumental, Feldman's notion of 'subjectivization of power as exteriority' depends upon the bifurcation of the self and the active objectification of the body as an instrument of violence in a desire for the proper body and body politics. Accordingly, Feldman construes the 1981 Irish Hunger Strike as a deathly purification of the self, a 'sacrifecal' expulsion of state violence by means of eating the very body that has become infested with it — in other words, consuming the enemy by consuming the self.[12] Similarly, Banu Bargu's reading of the Death Fast is organized largely by the same logic of counter-subjectivation, taken in the first instance from Feldman's locution 'weaponization of the body' and displaced in

---

9   See, respectively, Allen Feldman, *Formations of Violence: The Narrative of the Body and Political Terror in Northern Ireland* (Chicago: University of Chicago Press, 1992), and *Archives of the Insensible: Of War, Photopolitics, and Dead Memory* (Chicago: University of Chicago Press, 2015). For the exposition of the term 'afformative', see Werner Hamacher, 'Afformative, Strike', *Cardozo Law Review*, 85 (1991–1992), pp. 1133–57 (p. 1139).

10 Feldman, *Archives of the Insensible*, p. 163.

11 Feldman, *Formations of Violence*, p. 178.

12 Ibid., p. 236.

such a way that the weaponization of life comes to signify the sacrifice of life in the name of a life that would, in the end, be worth more than life.[13] However, counter-subjectivation is not 'counter-actualization'; the margin of freedom does not consist in mimetic subversion but, on the contrary, concedes to the radical impropriety of the event and becomes equal to it in reenactments that actively incomplete its full actualization.[14]

It is precisely this suspended relation to death that distinguishes death fasting from self-immolations and suicide attacks. Despite all the emphasis on the instant of decision, the death fast does not necessarily precipitate death and its actual consummation in the immediacy of an ecstatic moment; rather, the political efficacy of the death fast depends on the prolongation of the interval that separates 'death' as finality from 'dying' as impersonal event and keeps the coincidence of two deaths in perpetual reserve.[15] What is essential in death fasting is that the irreducible anachrony between two deaths — the passage of time that separates dying as pure potentiality from death as a radically contingent event that comes either too early or too late — is not resolved or equalized, and that this interval of time that passes between the two is itself maintained at the limit of bodies. Accordingly, the suspension of death (or life) is less in the service of mastery than of an endless contestation bearing witness to someone, or someones, that can only communicate or affirm itself in this interim state, belonging neither to life nor to death: the undead and the unborn.

The clandestine memory and belief of the space of dying that may never be relinquished are expressed in the temporal structure of the Death Fast. In the form of a potentially infinite series of reenactments, the participating organizations invested in a structure of temporal return that set in motion a strange oscillation between eventfulness ('already happened') and suspension ('still to come'). In addition to this structure of temporal return that paradoxically potentialized the limit between life and death through the very actualization of death,

---

13   Banu Bargu, *Starve and Immolate: The Politics of Human Weapons* (New York: Columbia University Press, 2014), pp. 14–18.

14   Deleuze, *The Logic of Sense*, pp. 150–52.

15   The following reading is much indebted to Blanchot's reflections on 'double death'. See also Jacques Derrida, *Aporias*, trans. by Thomas Dutoit (Stanford, CA: Stanford University Press, 1993).

which was itself rendered possible by the multiplication of hunger strikers, the organizations advanced a temporal suspension in the form of a constant deferral between life and death. This deferred death (or life) was as much a result of the intake of vitamin B1 as of the Turkish state's policy of forced feeding after the loss of consciousness. Deferral and repetition, extraordinarily long self-starvation periods (up to 558 days), and serial introduction of teams resisted the idea of ending in the interest of maintaining the constant possibility of the end until their ends were achieved.

The space of dying that haunted the representational space of politics was consigned to obscurity by a phantasm of immortality that repressed the difference between two forms of repetition: (1) reproduction of heroic death as an exemplary model, and (2) the repeated return of the difference that suspends the distinction between the act and citation and the instant and instance. The longevity of the Death Fast, maintained by the exceptional perseverance of death fasters who had succeeded each other uninterruptedly over the course of six years, was presented by the organizations as proof of their exteriority to law. Far from being beyond the law, however, they had instead fallen hostage to it, with the repeated negation of the law by the return of death necessarily confirming the law as a limit. As a result, the relation to the limit of law began to resemble the limitlessness of time, a limitlessness that gave rise not to another law but to the endless succession of teams and deaths that resisted designation as events, if only because they were bound to the future as the coming of victory. As Ç., one of my interlocutors, recapitulated their slogan, 'To the End, To Eternity, To the Last', each death faster was the penultimate, but never the last, in an infinite but closed series, a series of absolutely singular yet substitutable placeholders: 'Every volunteer, every death faster is a last man, but they are not the last point. There is no last man until victory.'[16]

The organizational command invoked the endlessness of the Death Fast only to abstract a sacrificial Subject from the uninterrupted continuity of its teams, and it did so by subsuming the singular acts of dying within a totalizing unity and closure.[17] Though they now ap-

---

16   Private communication, 12 July 2006.

17   'Büyük Direniş 2000–2007 Ölüm Orucu' (Great Resistance 2000–2007 Death Fast), *Yürüyüş*, 12 October 2008, p. 10.

peared, by a fetishistic inversion, to be the embodiments of a self-same immortal Subject, it was the singular acts of dying that had in fact given rise to this ideal and unchanging self-identity by their possibility of repetition. The organizations revisited the possibility of repetition itself as a new tactic on the second-year anniversary of the Death Fast by exploiting the iterability of the calendar to radical effect. Henceforth, the ninth and subsequent teams were named after exceptional martyr-death fasters, and these commemorative teams were introduced on the anniversaries of their deaths.[18] In this manner, the inaugural series duplicated itself to constitute a new series of death fasters, who repeated the past events as if they were anticipating their future repetition for completion. By turning toward the past events to recall them, despite and even because of the irreversibility of the past, the singular acts of dying severed their relationship with the law to inscribe the event itself as a timeless instant within time. That the organizational command sought to capitalize upon, or at least to recuperate, this repeated return of death by tethering it to a rival code of values could not efface its unanswerability. As far as the outside gaze was concerned, the unanswerability of this insistent repetition was perhaps the one that was the most disturbing, for at the very moment that the Death Fast lost its political force and justification, its own repetition of itself divided the presence of the present and denied the seeming closure of the event. From an outside view, this repetition could only appear as mechanical repetition, which was why, in turn, it was mediatized as political religion; nevertheless, it was an event which knew no negation.

Crucial to the difference between sovereignty and event is their opposing relationship to time; while sovereignty is the 'eternal present', Deleuze argues that the actor, on the other hand, exists in relation to another time: that is, the time of the 'mobile and precise instant'.[19]

---

18   The ninth team was named after Zehra Kulaksız, a member of TAYAD (Solidarity Association for the Families of Detainees and Convicts) who had died on the death fast outside the prison in Küçükarmutlu in June 2001. The tenth was named after Gültekin Koç who died in a suicide attack against a police headquarters in January 2001. The eleventh team was named after Sevgi Erdoğan who had continued to fast in Küçükarmutlu after her release and died in July 2001. The twelfth team was named after Fidan Kalşen, a female prisoner who had set herself on fire in Çanakkale Prison during the prison operation. The last team was named after Cengiz Soydaş, the first death faster to fall martyr in Sincan F-type Prison in March 2000.

19   Deleuze, *The Logic of Sense*, p. 150.

'Aion', unlike 'chronos', has the curious property of existing only as an 'empty present' that reflects an unlimited past and future. This is why, as Deleuze puts it, counter-actualization is an impersonal reenactment of events 'perpetually anticipated and delayed, hoped for and recalled', but also why the negation of death (objective genitive) is intimately bound to the 'substitution' of the self by 'the figure which the most singular life takes on'.[20]

Deleuze, in his implicit dispute with Blanchot, insists on the difference between 'consciousness dying' and an 'empty consciousness', teeming with a virtual multiplicity that vacillates between the self's finitude and the infinitude of the event and inflects the sense of the impersonal. Hence, for Deleuze, the impersonality of dying, no longer only designating the absence of a fixed subject, indeed resembles more affirmatively a place of communication that he terms 'the fourth person'.[21]

Only such a 'figure' would interrupt the narrow sense of 'death' — if it has a sense at all — and bring out the mediality of the hunger strike as political medium. I argue that, in this radically different understanding of 'death', the body of the hunger striker is neither the material ground for the production of law nor the expressive sign for self-sovereignty, but the anonym, which 'comprehends all violence in a single act of violence, and every mortal event in a single Event'.[22]

---

20   Ibid, p. 153.
21   Ibid., p. 152.
22   Ibid.

'Interrupting the Present'
Political and Artistic Forms of Reenactments in South Africa

KATJA GENTRIC

A sense of things *repeating* themselves, or that of some unfinished business, pervades contemporary South African political and cultural debate. Conflicts arising in South Africa today need to be addressed, while simultaneously keeping in mind the conflicts of the past. This remark systematically comes forward in analyses of the renewed student protests receiving media attention since March 2015; the same observation is also relevant in reference to the crises of what is referred to as 'xenophobic' attacks attaining national proportions in 2008.[1] Today's student movements parallel several features of the South African resistance and liberation movements, most importantly the 1976 student uprisings.[2] Likewise, it can be argued that contemporary questions of migration (and the linked xenophobic attacks) have to be viewed in the context of the 1952 Pass Laws Act and the artificially imposed migrant labour system under apartheid, which led to severe conflicts in South Africa as early as 1960.[3] At a pivotal position between these moments

---

1   Marietta Kesting, *Affective Images: Post-Apartheid Documentary Perspectives* (New York: State University of New York Press, 2017), note 21, p. 205.

2   Kylie Thomas, 'Decolonisation Is Now: Photography and Student-Social Movements in South Africa', *Visual Studies*, 33.1 (2018), pp. 98–110 <https://doi.org/10.1080/1472586X.2018.1426251>.

3   Kesting, *Affective Images*.

of political struggle stands what has been referred to as the 'miracle' of the peaceful transition in 1994, helped along in an almost administrative way by the process of the Truth and Reconciliation Commission (TRC) hearings from 1996 to 2001.

THE TRUTH AND RECONCILIATION COMMISSION AND ITS MEDIATIZATION

The TRC was intended to be a forum where the wrongs of the past were to be brought into the open, and the nation would henceforth be able to proceed as though a shared memory bridging segregated apartheid legacy had come into existence.[4] With this goal in mind, much attention was given to media coverage. All hearings were transmitted by radio broadcast; national television dedicated a weekly analytical programme to the TRC, the minutes of the hearings have since been made available on dedicated websites,[5] and the proceedings have been published in five volumes in 1998.[6]

In his introduction to these proceedings, the chairperson of the commission, Archbishop Desmond Tutu, acquiesces that there would necessarily be controversy regarding the TRC process, but he points out that, in his opinion, the most important legacy of the hearings would be the archives they produced, allowing further research to start taking place. Today, more than twenty years after the last hearings, analyses from a wide spectrum of perspectives have become available.[7]

One incident became a widely recognized representation of the TRC in public imaginaries. It is the demonstration of the 'wet bag

---

4   Historical Papers (The Library, University of the Witwatersrand) and South African History Archive, *Traces of Truth: Documents Relating to the South African Truth and Reconciliation Commission* <http://truth.wwl.wits.ac.za/about.php> [accessed 6 April 2018].

5   Truth and Reconciliation Commission, *The TRC Report* <https://www.justice.gov.za/trc/report/index.htm> and *Traces of Truth* <http://truth.wwl.wits.ac.za> [accessed 6 April 2018].

6   Truth and Reconciliation Commission, *Truth and Reconciliation Commission of South Africa Report*, 5 vols (London: Macmillan, 1999). Prior to this international edition, the Report was published in South Africa in October 1998 (Cape Town: Juta, 1998).

7   Historical Papers (The Library, University of the Witwatersrand) and South African History Archive, 'Traces of Truth: Select Bibliography of the South African Truth and Reconciliation Commission (TRC)', *Traces of Truth*, 2008 <http://truth.wwl.wits.ac.za/TRCBIB.pdf> [accessed 9 April 2021].

method' by a former special branch detective, Jeffrey Benzien.[8] This rudimentary reenactment was set up spontaneously because the victim had asked to see what had been done to him.[9] The press photographs taken during the hearing show the former special branch detective crouching over a handcuffed man lying facedown on the floor. A bag is pulled over his head. The TRC proceedings note Benzien's explanation of his torture method, which consisted of the repeated near-suffocation of the interrogated detainee until his testimony was obtained.[10]

While it remains debatable whether the TRC produced the hoped-for benefits within South African society at large, it has inspired several forms of artistic practice and led to more and more astute analyses of photographs produced in this context.[11] During Documenta 11, curated by Okwui Enwezor, one platform explored commissions set up to investigate human rights violations under military regimes from the early 1980s onward. Rory Bester contributed an analysis of the South African TRC and the polemical contradiction arising when giving an account of intimate and traumatic experiences in an atmosphere of spectacle within the staged circumstances of a public hearing: 'In the space between memory and amnesia, between the trauma of memory and the comfort of forgetting, how do we *re–present* the TRC without turning it into a spectacle?'[12]

THE CENTER FOR HISTORICAL REENACTMENTS, JOHANNESBURG

Within this set of circumstances, a group of curators, artists, and writers — Gabi Ngcobo, Kemang Wa Lehulere, and Donna Kukama

---

8   'Twenty Years of Democracy, Truth and Reconciliation Commission', image by George Hallet <http://www.specialcollections.uct.ac.za/20-years/truth-reconciliation-commission> [accessed 22 November 2020].

9   Rory Bester, 'Trauma and Truth', in *Experiments with Truth: Transitional Justice and the Processes of Truth and Reconciliation: Documenta 11_Platform 2*, ed. by Okwui Enwezor (Ostfildern: Hatje Cantz, 2002), pp. 155–73 (p. 167).

10   The Truth and Reconciliation Commission, *Truth and Reconciliation Commission of South Africa Report*, ii, pp. 188–90.

11   Kylie Thomas, 'Exhuming Apartheid: Photography, Disappearance and Return', *Cahiers d'études africaines*, 230 (2018), pp. 429–54.

12   Bester, 'Trauma and Truth', p. 173.

amongst others — formed a collective named Center for Historical Reenactments (CHR) in 2010. Two of the key actions performed by artists later to become CHR members happened before this date.

The first of these, planned as a three-day intervention, was performed in a backyard in Gugulethu in 2008. Accompanied by a sound recording of the artist combing his hair, Kemang Wa Lehulere dug a hole in the ground using an afro-comb as a digging tool. Titled *uGuqul'ibhatyi* ('to turn a coat inside out', an expression linked to race reclassification under apartheid), the action was meant to be a gesture of unearthing erased personal stories and traumatic questions of identity. At about one meter in depth the digger hit upon bones, which turned out to be part of a rib cage. The incident and the unravelling of the uncanny situation following the discovery are retold in an interview with Gabi Ngcobo.[13] Wa Lehulere has since performed a number of such digging actions, never knowing what 'historical rubble' he might unearth.

The second is an action by Donna Kukama, performed in 2009 on the site of Kwa-Mai-Mai, a traditional healer's market in central Johannesburg. *The Swing (after after Fragonard)*[14] is hung under the gigantic concrete structure of the highway bypass bridging the market. The artist, daintily dressed in white, swings several meters above the shoppers, throwing bank notes into the crowd and provoking a commotion. In mid-action the wooden seat of the swing accidentally snapped, and the artist fell several meters to the ground, breaking her right leg. In later projects the CHR revisits this scene and the socio-economic underpinnings of this action.[15]

---

13 Gabi Ngcobo and Kemang Wa Lehulere, 'Unearthing Skeletons in History's Shallow Graves', in *PASS–AGES, References & Footnotes*, ed. by the Center for Historical Reenactments and the Johannesburg Workshop for Theory and Criticism (Johannesburg: Center for Historical Reenactments, 2010), p. 10.

14 The performance referenced two earlier artistic uses of a swing: Jean–Honoré Fragonard, *The Swing*, 1767, oil on canvas, 81 x 64.2 cm, The Wallace Collection, London, and Yinka Shonibare, *The Swing (After Fragonard)*, 2001, installation, 330 x 350 x 220 cm, Tate Modern, London.

15 *After–after Tears: Wie sien ons?* (2013, video commissioned by the New Museum, New York). Kukama's action was not only a comment on the neo-liberal South African society of today but also a protest to a recent aggression against a female commuter, who had been a victim of 'corrective' methods used by the taxi drivers at Noord Taxi Rank.

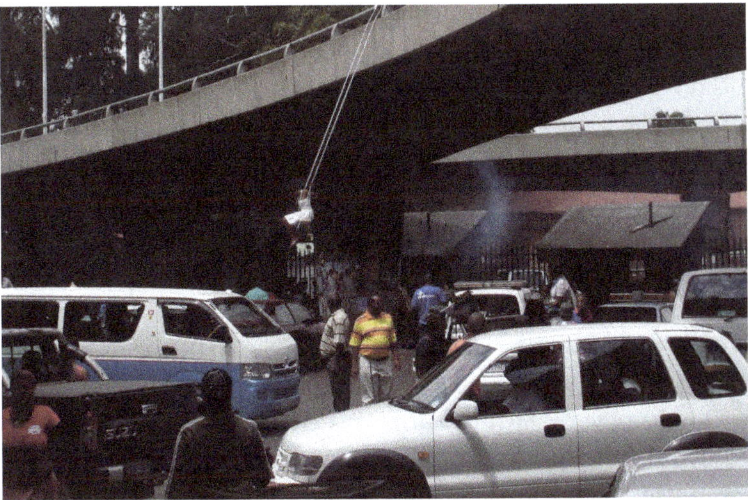

Figure1. Donna Kukama, *The Swing (after after Fragonard)* (2009),
performance and video, 4:54 mins, Photos courtesy: Matthew Burbidge
and the artist.

The uncanny link between these two precursory interventions is
the coincidence that the actions, both referencing events of the past,
were each 'interrupted' by unforeseen circumstances. The interruptive
element became the reason for these actions to be revisited again and
again by the CHR.

Apart from Kukama's *Swing*, CHR actions do not resemble under-
standings of reenactment in other contexts[16] — very few of the interventions are staged in any way. Instead, the collective may publish
newspapers, referring to the past in visual quotations. The members

---

16   Here, I would like to briefly mention two texts teasing out differences between popular
      and artistic forms of reenactment and their relationships with history. Both authors
      think of the final product of a reenactment as a film. Caillet speaks of a revision of
      an aspect of the past in the present and for the present, with the intent of question-
      ing official history, while simultaneously pointing at compulsive behaviour in certain
      repetitions (p. 72). Leeb's interest lies not only in the utopic quality of politically
      motivated reenactments but also in a form of concretized sense of the possible (Mög-
      lichkeitssinn), which extends both to the future and to the past but unfolds in the
      present (pp. 36, 39, 42, 43). Susanne Leeb, 'Flucht nach nicht ganz vorn, Geschichte
      in der Kunst der Gegenwart', *Texte zur Kunst*, 76 (December 2009), pp. 28–45. Aline
      Caillet, 'Le Re-enactment: Refaire, rejouer ou répéter l'histoire?', *Marges. Revue d'art
      contemporain*, 17 (2013), special issue *Remake, reprise, répétition*, pp. 66–73 <https:
      //doi.org/10.4000/marges.153>.

of the collective may invest in sites, search through archives, repeat quotes, host communal meals, play word games, or propose repetitive public readings of texts. They may conduct seminars, exhibitions, residencies, and community work, and engage in transversal research processes, subversion and mediation, or counterarchival responses. In short, they seem to avoid acting in any theatrical sense; rather, they *enact*, putting concepts into praxis.

A routine of carrying out the same gestures time and again, thereby providing the circumstances for difference to set in,[17] became the modus operandi of the CHR. In this spirit, the CHR established itself in a cyclical appropriation of space in different historically laden sites — for example, N° 80 Albert Street in the basement of the former Pass Office, the site that controlled a central aspect of the South African apartheid system: the policing of freedom of 'migration' under the segregated pass laws.[18] However:

> The documents that may have served as testimony to the site's activities have been destroyed, this denied their roles as witnesses and spared the interrogation of the Truth and Reconciliation Commission. Ironically, it is this very emptiness that creates a space for us to call upon our abilities to remember and inject memory (unreliable and slippery as it may be) to the site.[19]

A few months later, the CHR invested in a workspace in another significant location, August House, at the heart of Doornfontein in central Johannesburg. A photograph of the western window and the view from this third-floor vantage point was one of the first posted on the CHR Facebook page. This same window makes a reappearance in sev-

---

17   Thierry Davila, 'Endurance de la répétition, surgissement de l'invention: Le *Remake* et la fabrique de l'histoire', in *Remakes* (Bordeaux: CAPC-Musée d'art contemporain, 2003), pp. 26–46 (pp. 41–42). Davila speaks of repetition in order to observe the differences induced by mnemonic activity — creativity becoming evident in these differences).

18   The building at 80 Albert Street formerly housed Johannesburg's Pass office. After 1994 the building was re-used and housed social projects of a different nature. Khwezi Gule commences his essay about *PASS–AGES* by evidencing the layers of history this building stands for. Khwezi Gule, 'Center for Historical Reenactments: Is the Tale Chasing its Own Tail?' *Afterall: A Journal of Art, Context and Enquiry*, 39 (2015), pp. 88–100.

19   *PASS–AGES: References & Footnotes*, p. 2.

eral later installations.[20] Ngcobo draws a web of interrelated thoughts through the gesture of 'looking out' of the confined art space.[21] The window indeed looks out onto the neighbouring streets, with their international bus terminals and 'occupied' buildings, a polyglot social tissue formed by inhabitants coming from all parts of the world. Metaphorically, the CHR addresses this question in an experiment entitled 'Xenoglossia' (the condition where a subject, for an unexplained reason, can speak or write in a language with which he has had no contact). For lack of other evidence, this condition is connected to the possibility of reincarnation. By preferring the (paranormal) state of Xenoglossia to the notion of translation, the CHR chose to address questions of language difference without imposing the foreclosure that equivalence of meaning has to be the only possible outcome of speech acts. One telling experiment with reflexive and partly abstruse forms of language-use was the performance 'Does a mirror have a memory?' The participants engaged in conversation while looking at each other via the mediation of a mirror. Taking its cue from the technical detail that every rear-view mirror has a blind spot,[22] this exercise was referred to as a 'setup for failed communication'. During the two-year course of the Xenoglossia project, the CHR has performed many such experiments and invited the public to partake in them.[23]

Another way of exploring 'how language has played a central role in some of the greatest historical misunderstandings that have been reincarnated in recent history'[24] is the visual/lexical quotation. In 2012, the CHR proposed reusing a protest banner, famous because of a photograph taken by Alfred Kumalo in Uitenhage in 1985, during a demonstration marking the twenty-fifth anniversary of the Sharpeville Massacre. The banner read: 'They will never kill us all.' The 1985 demonstration gave rise to new excesses on the part of the police, dur-

---

20   Recreated at the Lyon Biennale of Contemporary Art in 2011 and at New Museum of New York from 22 May to 7 July 2013.

21   Gabi Ngcobo, 'Does This Window Have a Memory?', *Other Possible Worlds* <http://www.otherpossibleworlds.net/?page_id=453> [accessed 6 April 2018].

22   Conversation with Donna Kukama, Johannesburg, 27 March 2017.

23   Mbali Khoza, 'What Difference Does It Make Who Is Speaking?' (unpublished master's thesis in Fine Art, University of the Witwatersrand, Faculty of Humanities, School of Art, 2016).

24   Ngcobo, 'Does This Window Have a Memory?'.

ing which twenty-five people lost their lives. To evoke the massacre of 21 March 1960, the members of the CHR reproduced, in March 2012, the banner of 21 March 1985.[25] Ngcobo refers to the works coming out of the engagement with the Alf Kumalo Archive as a way of 'interrupting the present'.[26] These interventions fissure the chronological order of events; they are a 'time–machine, [...] conceiving time as a tool, and setting it out of joint'.[27] Ngcobo not only thinks of the eerie foreboding wisdom carried by the banner of 1985, foretelling destiny, but also of a second futuristic work, titled *What happened Jo'burg 20*81*. Here, the CHR speculates about a reversal of time, imagining a world where Nelson Mandela, instead of aging towards his death, would begin to get younger every year — the CHR imagines Mandela in 2081 as a twenty-five-year-old[28].

On 12 December 2012, in a twelve-hour event, the CHR entered another phase of their cyclical project by staging their own suicide: '*We Are Absolutely Ending This*'. Their death marked a conclusion only to open up the possibility of staging their own afterlife, a second coming, in the exhibition 'After–after Tears'. Just as the CHR had started before its inception, it reached far beyond its suicide. Ngcobo, nominated as curator of the 2018 Berlin Biennale, uses phrases generated as part of the Xenoglossia research as titles of sub-sections of the Biennale; Kukama works in series of reiterations as chapters in a book; and Wa Lehulere engages with the work of fellow South African artists silenced under apartheid.[29] However, what Khwezi Gule interrogates as 'various acts of mutual cannibalism' between 'writing, art-making, historicising, teaching, archiving and curating', still begs the same question: 'How, then, to mobilize history in such a way that it becomes a truly transformative exercise?'[30]

---

25   *Rise and Fall of Apartheid: Photography and the Bureaucracy of Everyday Life*, ed. by Rory Bester and Okwui Enwezor (Munich: Prestel, 2013), pp. 528–29.

26   Gabi Ngcobo, 'Phantom(pain)', *Glossary of Common Knowledge*, May 2014 <https://www.youtube.com/watch?v=zqgLd_BdNmI> [accessed 6 April 2018].

27   Ngcobo, 'Phantom(pain)', [00:09:40] and [00:10:52].

28   A performance video was made during the project, which is mentioned on the CHR Facebook page on 20 Mai 2012 and by Gabi Ngcobo (in the text referenced in Note 41 of my text).

29   *Kemang Wa Lehulere, Bird Song*, ed. by Deutsche Bank AG, Art, Culture & Sports, Thorsten Strauß and Franziska Kunz (Berlin: Hatje Cantz, 2017).

30   Gule, 'Center for Historical Reenactments', pp. 91 and 99.

INTERRUPTING THE IM-MEDIATE PRESENT

A strikingly similar quest for true transformation is expressed by Frantz Fanon. In Fanon's case, this effort is paired with the struggle to overcome the inhibition inflicted by *ressentiment* in order to become *actionnel*, i.e., an individual taking action.[31] Fanon pursues his quest with both remedial care and revolutionary zeal.[32] A text by Ngcobo reiterates essential aspects of Fanon's thought, presenting it in parallel with the description of an enactment found in a text by Bessie Head: that of a person hiding. In a comic inversion of the process of hide-and-seek, the poses of hiding and/or seeking become confused. Ngcobo concludes, 'It is not that difficult for one to settle back into a position one tries to escape or reject'[33] — meaning, after Fanon, that in his quest of recognition and true change, the seeker must remain vigilant not to lose sight of his resolution to act.

The immediate urgencies arising during the recent student protests, with their very strong references to historical misunderstandings, are conducted under the sign of a Fanonian approach to the post-colonial situation. The phrase, 'immediate urgencies', carries two meanings in this context: instantaneous (not removed in time), and im-mediate (not yet mediated) — implying a sense of 'woke'-ness[34] in the process of becoming articulate. How can these urgencies be (self-)conducted into subjectivation — meaning the possibility of individual responsibility embedded in collective responsibility — a state of being which Achille Mbembe elaborates into a description of an 'ethics of becoming in reciprocal recognition'?[35] How does the storytelling taken on by the TRC restore individual dignity lost though historical misunderstanding?

---

31   Frantz Fanon, *Peau noire, masques blancs*, in Fanon, *Œuvres* (Paris: La Découverte, 2011), pp. 45–257 (p. 243).

32   Achille Mbembe, *Politiques de l'inimitié* (Paris: La Découverte, 2016) analyses Fanon's psychoanalytical and political thought and praxis as a *pharmakon*, that is, as both medicine and poison, thereby considering the possibility of creative violence. See p. 8, p. 10 and also pp. 91–140.

33   Gabi Ngcobo, 'Endnotes. Was It a Question of Power?', in *Condition Report: Symposium on Building Art Institutions in Africa*, ed. by Koyo Kouoh (Ostfildern: Hatje Cantz, 2013), pp. 65–67, also available at <http://historicalreenactments.org/documents/condition%20report/condition.pdf> [accessed 31 March 2019].

34   Thomas, 'Decolonisation Is Now', pp. 98–110.

35   Throughout *Politiques de l'inimitié*, Mbembe seems to describe what in later publications he will call 'l'éthique du devenir-avec-les-autres'.

Simultaneously mentioning the 'interruptions into the present' at the Alf Kumalo Archive, Ngcobo quotes Walter Benjamin, who, in his essay 'Excavation and Memory' stated:

> He [*sic*] who seeks to approach his own buried past must conduct himself like a man digging. Above all, he must not be afraid to return again and again to the same matter; to scatter it as one scatters earth, to turn it over as one turns over soil. For the "matter itself" is no more than the strata which yield their long-sought secrets only to the most meticulous investigation. That is to say, they yield those images that, severed from all earlier associations, reside as treasures in the sober room of our later insights.[36]

While reading what is translated here as 'matter itself', let us bear in mind that the word 'Sachverhalt' used by Benjamin in German communicates an awareness of 'how things exist in their relation to each other'. When Benjamin's text is read from within the art context, the final yield when digging would be an image ('Bild') gleaned from strata of yet unmediated 'historical rubble'. This image will represent these events in the collective imagination of the future.[37] These elementary mnemonic units can be carried either by a figurative image or by words, spoken or written. They are 'Denkbilder', as Benjamin liked to say: thoughts arising out of an image, visual or semantic, holding their own as concepts. Benjamin explains this process of coming-into-image by evoking the action of digging and scattering the dug-up contents around. In South Africa, digging can conjure up quite far-reaching associations; we might think of digging to find the remains of disappeared activists or other actively disremembered details of apartheid

---

36   Ngcobo quotes this translation in her text for *Fr(agile)*, a 2012 social sculpture and intervention at the Alf Kumalo Museum in Diepkloof, Soweto <http://historicalreenactments.org/blog_fragile.html> [accessed 6 April 2018]. For the German original see: Walter Benjamin, 'Ausgraben und Erinnern', in Benjamin, *Gesammelte Schriften*, ed. by Rolf Tiedemann and Hermann Schweppenhäuser, 7 vols (Frankfurt a. M.: Suhrkamp, 1972–91), IV.1: *Kleine Prosa, Baudelaire-Übertragungen* (1972), pp. 400–01.

37   Jean-Philippe Antoine, *Farces et Attrapes. Inventer les images* (Genève: MAMCO; Dijon: Les presses du réel, 2017). Antoine remarks (p. 12): 'Les conditions d'établissement de ce *faire image* concernent aussi bien des manières de faire de l'histoire que des manières de faire de l'art.' Even more to the point for the context of reenactments, a chapter is titled (pp. 117–37): '*La Reprise*: farce, occasion, extraction du nom d'art'.

past.[38] In a later text,[39] following the trail of a film by Michelle Monareng, Ngcobo will put into praxis the migration of imaginative content described by Benjamin. Ngcobo's text leads its readers from a contemporary historical moment (Mandela's burial) to a trip taken with friends today, a journey to a private home. It is a tale told through rumour and legend, a tale of forced removals and of unmarked graves, of objects that imbue people with special powers, of a bull appearing out of the mist to watch a man digging in ancestral soil. Be they speech-acts or reenactments, each of these elements participates in its own way in the common act of carrying on the migration of Ngcobo's '(Denk)bild'. In the context of the CHR, it is possible to claim that the migration of imaginative (i.e., image-making) 'Sachverhalte' can also show itself in the form of a xenoglossic leap,[40] by which the past or the future comes to disrupt the present, as a protester would, in order to undermine the usual.

Whether looking out of a window on the third floor of a building in polyglot-central Johannesburg, swinging in a back-and-forth motion high above a greedy crowd, digging in a backyard in Gugulethu, or standing on ancestral land with a bull as a solitary onlooker, the CHR is poised as a point of convergence. This point, ephemeral, transient, trans-cient or farsighted, and at the same time retro-futuristic, is a site where images are salvaged out of layers of forgottenness or disremembrance. The main questions explored by the CHR have lost none of their pertinence: how do readings of the past inform contemporary urgencies, and what are the political potentials of artistic interpretations of histories? How do they participate in the 'formation of new subjectivities'?[41]

---

38   On the importance of exhumations during the TRC process, see Kylie Thomas's 'Exhuming Apartheid'.

39   Gabi Ngcobo, 'Art in Context Africa, Part I: Sabelo Mlangeni's *No Problem*, and a Visit to the Site of Michelle Monareng's *Removal to Radium*', *Art Review*, 66.7 (October 2014) <https://artreview.com/features/october_2014_feature_art_in_context_i_gabi_ngcobo/> [accessed 6 April 2018].

40   The choice of the word 'leap' in this context should recall Fanon (*Peau noire, masques blancs*, p. 250): 'Je dois rappeler à tout instant que le véritable *saut* consiste à introduire l'invention dans l'existence.'

41   Cf. <http://historicalreenactments.org/index3.html> [accessed 6 April 2018].

Resounding Difficult Histories

JULIANA HODKINSON

In our imaginaries of historical events such as the Holocaust, the Cold War, the Vietnam War, and the Iraq War, what sounds come to mind, what voices, and what words?

Recordings of voices implicated in historical events are normally heard linked to visual footage. But we do not only live in a pictorial world. Through the growth of phenomena such as data sonification and sound archives, we are becoming more and more conversant in audio representations of our world.

Since the early days of recording technologies, it has been possible to introduce non-musical sounds seamlessly into artistic listening, and the scope for doing so was explored in every way possible during the twentieth century. Two developments in the mid-twentieth century — acousmatic composition and audio spatialization — began to take into account the consequences of the new situation for the listener, in which sounds' sources may appear literally and physically unconnected to their source. This separation could be obscured further through experimental editing and filtering. The contribution of technology to the disembodiment of sound led to new strategies in the abstract handling of voices and words. Nevertheless, a scepticism towards the compatibility of language and voice with highly abstract approaches to compositional technique and aesthetics meant that the use of voices and intelligible words remained largely the job of radio.

Consequently, the initiative for orchestrating the real world against aural fictions or reenactments, and the increasing use of aural technologies to bring audiences out of art buildings and into other listening contexts have often come from within the visual arts and theatre,[1] as well as from genres of sonic art distant from institutionalized music. Sound artist Brandon LaBelle has emphasized the physical attributes of sound, as relying for its existence on time and space, to underline the inescapably social properties of speech as something that is always moving through space and between bodies, making itself public.[2]

Three recent works in my artistic practice as a composer involve the mobilization and sonic framing of recordings of speaking voices to bring to mind moments of historical consequence. All three works involve, in differing ways, finding perspectives on historical and present political events and contexts in relation to one another. This involved taking up a position on why and how recorded audio, as historical artefacts or reenactments, may be incorporated into artworks today, as well as hopefully nudging to historical revision and political resistance through these reenactments.

SOUND AND DIPLOMACY

In 2012, I was invited to participate in a group exhibition on sound and diplomacy, 'Embassy Reconstructed', initiated by Åsa Stjerna. 'Embassy Reconstructed' was an arts-based exploration of the embassy as a phenomenon, inquiring how diplomacy can be interpreted and presented in sonic form, how the act of conflict management between nations could be interpreted through the arts, and what the sonic characteristics of the embassy might be. Operating within an expanded field — the special territory of the embassies as projection of nation —

---

1   Juliana Hodkinson, 'Creating Headspace: Digital Listening Spaces and Evolving Subjectivities', *Musicology Research*, 3 (Autumn 2017), special issue *Music on Screen: From Cinema Screens to Touchscreens, Part II*, ed. by Sarah Hall and James B. Williams, pp. 163–77 <https://www.musicologyresearch.co.uk/publications/julianahodkinson-creatingheadspace> [accessed 31 March 2018].

2   See Brandon LaBelle, *Background Noise: Perspectives on Sound Art* (London: Continuum, 2006).

the exhibition explored the embassy site partly as an ideal construction and partly as the source of a vocabulary serving as artistic material.

This strong and particular combination of contexts was the springboard for new pieces by Liv Strand, Susanne Skog, Brandon LaBelle, Jacob Kirkegaard, Åsa Stjerna, and myself, as well as a new adaptation of Alvin Lucier's *Memory Space.* For the exhibition, I created two pieces: a live electro-acoustic concert piece for four instrumentalists with quadrophonic playback of audio samples, and an eight-channel looped sound installation piece, installed in a large, semi-public open stairwell and running during the course of the building's daytime opening hours.

These two pieces — *Prompt, Immediate, Now / Very Vestrained and Cautious* (2013), and *Defending Territory in a Networked World* (2013) — draw on audio material freely available online. The audio sources ranged from radio and dictaphone archives to various publicly available communications, such as media broadcasts, press conferences, and interviews available mainly on YouTube, with the voices of presidents, foreign ministers, and foreign policy advisors of several countries, both past and present: Madeleine Albright, Hillary Clinton, Ahmed Aboul Gheit, William Hague, Dag Hammerskjöld, Christopher Hitchens, Richard Nixon, Condoleeza Rice, Donald Rumsfeld, Sushma Swaraj, Margaret Thatcher, and an unnamed German radio journalist broadcasting in the early 1940s. The speeches were mainly chosen for the ways in which they use language and vocal tenor in relation to the task of diplomacy and international relations; the selection ranged from formal restraint and extreme vagueness through public regret to national supremacy and open threat.

One opportunity offered by working with online sources is the possibility of transferring clearly recognizable voices, for example, to entirely different and obscure contexts. In *Prompt,* I brought the smoothness of these professional articulations alongside the controlled manoeuvres of instrumental chamber music, and in *Defending,* I bundled the voices alongside one another, confusing the individual clarity with which each was originally spoken.

Sound as a medium with a capacity to embrace time, space, and materiality — specifically, recorded sound as an opportunity to repeat words voiced in very particular contexts — generates ways of enacting these aspects so as to negotiate complex entities, such as, in this case, abstract territorial and performative notions of the embassy and of diplomacy.[3] In this way, artistic sonic material may be poised between the abstraction of the art form's matter and the potential for sonic artworks to represent the world and worldly (political) content.

PROMPT, IMMEDIATE, NOW / VERY RESTRAINED AND CAUTIOUS

Prompt, Immediate, Now / Very Restrained and Cautious was written for the opening of the group exhibition and first performed by Ensemble KNM on 27 January 2013, in the Danish building at the Nordic Embassies in Berlin.[4] In *Prompt, Immediate, Now / Very Restrained and Cautious,* all the documentation came from situations in which the words were originally spoken in publicly mediatized situations (i.e., radio broadcasts, press conferences, and fiction film). The Nixon dictaphone tapes are a breach of this categorization in the choice of audio samples. I opted to use excerpts from a telephone conversation between Nixon and the prominent evangelical Southern Baptist minister, Billy Graham. Like Roosevelt and other US presidents, Nixon installed telephone taps and concealed microphones to record his White House conversations. As such, the audio collected in this way stems from public office but breaches privacy in that Graham would presumably have been unaware that he was being recorded. Nevertheless, in the excerpts I chose, Graham's voice is only heard distantly giving short affirmations, while Nixon's voice carries all the political content and rhetorical drive.

Sourcing audio from the Internet — whether from online sound libraries or YouTube — entails a certain set of considerations related to intellectual property in the context of mass communication. Much easier and quicker than visiting archives, the kind of artistic material research that can be done online is increasing for all artists and ex-

3   The involvement of the sonic imaginary in embassy-centred international dramas has become particularly salient since 'Embassy Reconstructed', particularly considering the role of audio recordings in the gathering and exchange of intelligence on the murder of Washington Post journalist Jamal Khashoggi.

4   See Juliana Hodkinson, *Prompt, Immediate, Now / Very Restrained and Cautious* (Copenhagen: Edition Wilhelm Hansen, 2013).

panding the use of downloadable sonic vocabularies and experimental techniques for reworking them.

Many of the speeches used in this piece were topical and recent at the time of composition, such as the voice of Egyptian Foreign Minister Ahmed Aboul Gheit in 2011, pleading against the unhelpfulness of US pressure to legalize the Muslim Brotherhood: 'because when you speak about "prompt, immediate, now" — as if you are imposing on a great country like Egypt, a great friend that has always maintained the best of relationship with the United States, you are imposing your will on him'.[5] However, some are archival, such as the moderate voice of Dag Hammerskjöld talking of the need to by 'very restrained and cautious' in diplomatic relations.[6]

Against the background of a classical recorded music industry, which has reduced itself largely to reenactments of historical work (proliferating recordings of a canonic repertoire), I ask myself how contemporary instrumental art music can create relations between, on the one hand, sonic and listening practices which have grown up around historical instruments and, on the other hand, an artistic form of social currency that deserves the title 'contemporary'.

The instrumental music I constructed to surround these recorded voices aimed to parallel the diplomatic bind, full of nuances of intonation, small innuendos, and the attempt to remain benign and undramatic while also precise, with only occasional, strategically-chosen moments of rhetorical drama. The sonic relationship between the acoustic instrumental music and the speeches — in their varying recording qualities — shifts throughout the piece, with the instrumental writing initially 'following' the unmeasured rhetorical style of the voices, modelling instrumental sounds on the texture and rhythms of the speech. Later, the instrumental writing establishes itself as more autonomous, as a structure within which the voice samples are organized and manipulated according to musically rhythmic and timbral principles. Finally, percussive noise from a snare drum laiden with

---

5   'Egyptian Foreign Minister Tells U.S. Not to Impose Its Will', PBS NewsHour, February 2011, Youtube <https://youtu.be/TBXVHf_cIEM> [accessed 20 November 2020].

6   'Dag Hammerskjöld about "Quiet Diplomacy" (1955)', Dag Hammerskjöld Project, Youtube <https://youtu.be/2T4YrDCe5Yc> [accessed 20 November 2020].

metal objects alternates with intakes of breath amplified naturally through the clarinet and abrasive bowing in the viola and cello. This construction provides a quasi-military accompaniment to a noise-based filtering of William Hague's 2010 speech on the erosion of British post-imperial influence in the face of globalization and the rise of other growing economies, which also expressed the adjacent need for new diplomatic strategies in defence of British interests and territories.

DEFENDING TERRITORY IN A NETWORKED WORLD

In *Defending,* bundles of various meaningful diplomatic iterations on this topic are edited so that they appear in a way to be muttered simultaneously by a gentle and persuasive cacophony of (mainly polite and articulate) voices, cascading through space more or less out of the blue, before breaking off for several minutes of silence before the next bundle of iterations. While in *Prompt,* voices were framed by chamber music and presented one by one in order to be (initially, at least) clearly intelligible, in *Defending,* there is no musicalization at play, other than the pleasure of listening to the voices' natural musicality. As the piece was installed in the atrium of the Nordic embassies' public area — a non-art and non-work space — spectators (people crossing the atrium) experience the piece in an 'non-art-listening' mode; they are on their way up, down, or across, to lunch, to informal or formal meetings or tasks. Having only the political voices as sonic material and bringing them so closely into polylogue with one another might point more directly to diplomatic rhetoric as an overarching geopolitical tool. Particularly in Europe, the building and consolidation of nations and the formation of national identities has usually been tied to the unification of language throughout a territory. The use of audio reenactment, in this case, serves to point instead to structural modes in the operations of diplomacy, keeping in mind the fact that diplomacy often works through interventions of, alternately, silence (the unspoken) and gentle iterations of dynamic situations.

THE TRAIN DEPARTING AT 4AM

Afgang 04.00 (The Train Departing at 4am) (2017) is a vocal sound-theatre piece with text and concept by director Petra Berg Holbek, reflecting on events of the night of 12 October 1943 at Elsinore Station, Denmark, when 175 Jews were held captive in a waiting room overnight before being put on a train to Theresienstadt. *Afgang 04.00* draws on testimonies by victims and witnesses — both written reports from 1943 and spoken interviews filmed many decades later — re-framing the words of these accounts through the actors' voices. The piece was staged in 2017 on-site at Elsinore Station, with the audience wearing headphones and being immersed not only in the station environment but also interventional sounds from external loudspeakers and set designer Igor Vasiljev's video projections of palpitating colours. Holbek wrote text for the voice-actor recordings based on the archival reports and interviews uncovered during her research. During the development of the piece, it became clear, through Holbek's contact with the families of this group of people, that staging very personal accounts in the exact site of the historical events, in the town where many of these families still lived, might leave some individuals open to a kind of identification that could be problematic for them, even seven decades after the original events. These demands of sensitivity in the use of documentary material led Holbek to considerations of anonymity, with the text becoming increasingly fictionalized and abstracted from the original quotes as our work with the piece progressed. My task as composer was to create a relatively abstract sonic counterpart to the actors' voices. The composition was made up of vocal and instrumental music — for four singers and an accordion — and field recordings.

Not only does *Afgang 04.00* deal with a particular historical moment but the impetus for its sonic reenactment also came at a critical humanitarian moment in current affairs. Making the piece was, on all levels, an exploration of the challenge of letting difficult histories resonate in the present: more specifically, finding fitting modes of reenactment of the negotiations with sensitivity and anonymity as discussed above, as well as providing a present-day position on why and how these experiences might be incorporated in artworks today. During 2015, the year when the sudden rise in numbers of refugees and migrants heading for Europe came to the forefront of political and media attention, Holbek held an archive residency at the Danish Institute for International Studies, researching material related to the Holocaust in Denmark. This gave added relevancy, and even urgency, to the project of imagining experiences of flight lived through by others. Yet the historical accounts from 1943 were inescapably entwined with the fate of vulnerable subjects, some of whom only related their traumatic experiences toward the very ends of their lives, after having remained silent for several decades about their childhood experiences. There was no original sonic documentation to draw on whatsoever, and the spoken words were either originally documented in paraphrased, written form or related from memory at a distance of seven decades from their original iteration. Moreover, they were originally spoken in an enclosed private sphere of captivity in which basic human rights had been infringed upon, in advance of even worse to come.

How, then, to reenact this situation? Despite graphic witness reports, there remains so much silence surrounding that night that what could not be re-heard had to be invented. Holbek's choice of how to reconstruct and represent these voices — by writing a fictional script and recording it with actors in radio-play style — gave space for my task of constructing a non-verbal sonic framework within which the recorded actors' voices could be embedded. The production was created by a larger team of artists and sound engineers from Scandinavia, Germany, and Croatia.[7] This not only meant that a range of ethical and artistic positions coexisted in the development process with respect to the portrayal of this highly sensitive historical moment, but also that the communication between these positions, together with technical, practical, and budgetary factors, needed to be negotiated over considerable geographical and temporal distances, with translation between several languages providing further linguistic filters on the work.

---

7   Igor Vasiljev, set design and video; Petra Berg Holbek, text and directing; Amelia
     Kraigher, dramaturg; Juliana Hodkinson, composition; Andreas Borregaard and
     Phønix16, musicians; Kristian Hverring and Peter Weinsheimer, audio engineering,
     with binaural expertise from Technische Universität Berlin and Universität der Künste
     Berlin.

A phenomenological approach to the listening experience became an important complement to the director's work on reenactment of historical figures. In *Afgang 04.00,* the listeners' interaction with the space in its present-day form is eliminated as much as possible, with only the train platform being activated as a direct reference (the sight and sound of a real train departing marks the end of the performance). One question we had for ourselves was to what extent different physical modes of audio playback would influence what was actually communicated to listeners. *Afgang 04.00* makes use of binaural recording techniques to evoke a heightened sense of the auditive presence of absent voices within a particular space, bringing imaginary and real spaces of the listening experience into play with one another. At the same time, techniques of sonic distancing or alienation are used, such as the diffusion of the singers' voices partly through megaphones in the recording studio, as well as the use of contemporary music idioms and vocal techniques. We worked primarily within a binaural headphone paradigm, but with added surround sound in external loudspeakers for a few key effects. This hybrid construction gave us a contrast between interior and exterior that aimed to fulfill the director's desire to explore psychological states of people held under the pressure of confinement. The underlying topic of discomfort transferred in many places to influence the playback levels of the external speakers. This is one very simple method of taking sound's visceral nature to various extremes in the service of referencing historical events through techniques of aural reenactment.

THE REPETITION OF CRIMES

As Pio Abad has pointed out regarding repeated crimes committed within an ongoing paradigm, historical revision is often impeded by the grouping of a huge number of individual criminal acts under singular terms.[8] The Holocaust is one such term. Even though the number of six million is readily attached to it, this figure counts 'only' the victims, which risks limiting the number of perpetrators and perpetrations to

---

8   Pio Abad, '*The Collection of Jane Ryan & William Saunders*: Reconstruction as "Democratic Gesture"', in this volume.

a handful of powerful individuals or orders given within a system that was designed to repeat the consequences of the orders, without blame newly attaching to those who carried them out each time.

In 1940, Denmark was more or less peacefully occupied by German forces, following an invasion that had lasted just two hours — after which the Danish government surrendered, judging that resistance was useless and hoping to work out an advantageous settlement. This Danish government stayed nominally in power, in a relationship of collaboration with the occupying forces. As the Second World War progressed, and the relationship between occupying forces, collaborationist government, and the general population hardened, one of the few courses of action that remained available to the Germans was a crackdown on Jews — both those of Danish nationality and those who had fled north as refugees from eastern Europe and the Baltic states. The plan to round up Jews was leaked a few days ahead of its implementation, and Danish history books are full of tales of civil courage on the part of ordinary Danish citizens who hid Jews, offered them refuge, or helped them to escape. On the night of the raid in October 1943, the Germans found only a few hundred Jews in Denmark, out of an estimated population of eight thousand. The main escape route was the sea to Sweden, with large and small fishing boats, rowing boats, canoes, and the regular ferry service being employed by both organizations and individuals to take Jews with and without payment across the ten-mile stretch of sea.

Because so many managed to escape, Denmark is rarely described, much less does it see itself, as a scene of Holocaust crimes. Nevertheless, five hundred people considered to be Jews were deported in four main deportations, by ship and by train, to concentration camps in Theresienstadt, Ravensbrück, and Sachsenhausen. If one defines scenes of Holocaust crimes as all the places in which crimes against humanity were committed against Jews, individually or systematically, thereby facilitating the Holocaust — such as restrictions on their freedom of movement within the country and violence directed towards them with the objective of injuring and terrorizing them — there are many places in Denmark that may be described as scenes of Holocaust crimes. Although the Gestapo bears the responsibility for initiating and executing this systematic plan, the round-up would never have been possible without the complicity of thousands of individual Danes. These people actively facilitated the transportations by betraying neighbours and hiding places, providing vehicles, turning a blind eye to terror and violence, and carrying out orders of the Gestapo without question, all the while imagining themselves to be passive bystanders. This is the reason that it is important not only for the victims but also the witnesses to hold up the experience of one large group of people against the national narrative.

Afgang 04.00 ultimately worked with a high level of fictionalization in the reconstruction of the events of the night in question, searching for the artistic mode in which lived experience from the past could be brought to the attention of present-day listeners. The creative process explored the gap between the past that can be accessed through archives and reports and the past as it has been popularly recounted in narratives that may be resistant to some events and experiences. The licence of fiction and psychological dramatization in *Afgang 04.00* opened up a space in which the pursuit of knowledge about a specific moment in the past was permitted to slip from the chains of sanctioned historical truths and explore deep insecurities, traumas, and secrets that lie beneath all of the past's constructions.

Afgang 04.00 is a case of bringing historical events out of the past and toward the present. *Prompt* and *Defending* were cases of drawing out, through the abstraction of working compositionally with the sound of familiar voices, the historical dimension of current and recent events. All three works addressed aspects of the cultural and social reverberation of sounding art and its sounding archaeologies.

PROMPTING, DEFENDING, AND DEPARTING

The pieces discussed above explore the challenge of letting difficult histories — whether recent or far in the past — resonate in the present, and of finding fitting modes of sonic reenactment and performance. All of them involve the listener in meeting articulations of private and public memory through the medium of sounding art. Each of them posed questions of how to introduce into an artistic listening situation the words spoken by people who shaped, witnessed, or were victims of crises of humanity in the twentieth and early twenty-first centuries.

This involved taking an ethically informed artistic position on the use of documentation involving people's spoken words. The positions turned out to be very different for each of the three works, but each of them appropriates others' verbal expressions — and, at times, their silences — in order to create or dismantle identification, affiliation, and influence through artistic reiteration.

Archival Diffractions
A Response to Le Nemesiache's Call
GIULIA DAMIANI

In the following text, I will outline three scenes read through a psycho-analytical and theatrical lens. After a short introduction, I will use these scenes to suggest that scripting and diffractive writing can be innovative methodologies of archival enquiry. Each scene will be a way to succeed or 'come after' work of the feminist collective Le Nemesiache from Naples, responding to 'their call' to continue their legacy. Each scene will be described through an image, a sound, or a gesture. This presentation is part of my research project and broader practice focusing on feminist epistemologies and archival diffractions.[1] I borrow the concept of diffraction from Donna Haraway to define the methodology used in my work on Le Nemesiache's archive. In the context of her epistemological project of 'situated knowledges', Haraway defined diffraction as an optical metaphor that:

> [records] the history of interaction, interference, reinforce-ment, difference. Diffraction is about heterogeneous history, not about originals. Unlike reflections, diffractions do not displace the same elsewhere, in more or less distorted form,

---

1   I am completing a PhD funded by the AHRC at Goldsmiths University in London, with the working title *Porous Places, Eruptive Bodies: The Feminist Group Le Nemesiache in 1970s and 1980s Naples* (2020).

> thereby giving rise to industries of [story-making about origins
> and truths]. Rather, diffraction can be a metaphor for another
> kind of critical consciousness.[2]

Diffraction can account for the intricate relationship between past and present, alongside the complex desires of different generations of feminists that are triggered in a researcher's consideration of an archive. Going against the idea of the authenticity of the archive and its authority as expressed by Jacques Derrida, among others, diffraction speaks of the material, metaphorical, and embodied effects of encountering an archive as a meaning-making tool in itself.[3] My desire is not to 'give voice' to Le Nemesiache's nearly forgotten actions, but to show how these can be active co-creators of feminist epistemologies. My research, at once theoretical and embodied, displaces Le Nemesiache's archival material to encourage innovative associations and disassociations, while simultaneously reinforcing some of the nuances of their work. This displacement happens by retelling and re-siting Le Nemesiache's archival traces in the present in different languages and locations.

Le Nemesiache are a group of women who have been part of the feminist struggle in Italy since 1970.[4] In that year, this separatist group was initiated by the artist and philosopher Lina Mangiacapre in her hometown, the city of Naples. Although its composition has varied throughout the decades, the collective has been said to have been animated by up to twelve women at times, the core of the group consisting of at least five people. From the late 1980s onward, the collective transformed into a loose association called 'Le tre ghinee' (The Three Guineas), which preserves the legacy of Le Nemesiache's ideas and

---

2   Donna Haraway, *Modest−Witness@Second−Millennium.FemaleMan−Meets−OncoMouse* (London: Routledge, 1997), p. 273, quoted by Karen Barad in Rick Dophijn and Iris van der Tuin, 'Matter Feels, Converses, Suffers, Desires, Yearns and Remembers: Interview with Karen Barad', in Dophijn, van der Tuin, *New Materialism: Interviews & Cartographies* (Ann Arbor, MI: Open Humanities Press, 2012), pp. 48–70 (p. 51) <https://dx.doi.org/10.3998/ohp.11515701.0001.001>.

3   Jacques Derrida describes the archive principle as a 'paternal and patriarchic principle [that] only posited itself to repeat itself and returned to re-posit itself only in the parricide'. Jacques Derrida, *Archive Fever: A Freudian Impression*, trans. by Eric Prenowitz (Chicago: University of Chicago Press, 1996), p. 95.

4   The following information is the result of my PhD research and ongoing work on Le Nemesiache's archive, which started in 2013. See first note.

actions. After the premature death of Lina Mangiacapre in 2002, their meetings and presence have been reduced. Le Nemesiache's women have dedicated themselves to the arts and in particular to cinema and theatre. Their feminist stance lies in their belief that women's liberation can only be achieved through women's creative self-determination. In 1977, the collective wrote the 'Manifesto for the Appropriation of Our Creativity', in which they reaffirmed the intention behind their practice. In a cyclostyled leaflet dotted with the signatures of the women, they claimed: 'Creativity is political, it is life, routine, erotic, in harmony with nature and the cosmos.'[5]

Cycles, nature, and the cosmos introduce another aspect of Le Nemesiache's preoccupation: their passionate use of mythology to overturn men's patriarchal rationality. Lina Mangiacapre adopted the mythological name 'Nemesis' after the Greek goddess of justice against hubris: excessive arrogance as conceived by the Greeks. The Neapolitan group considered hubris to be a quality inherent in men's behaviour. The collective Le Nemesiache, followers of Nemesis, strained against patriarchal arrogance. Other members were inspired by the legendary nymphs, such as the naiads of the fresh water, the dryads of the trees, and the oreads of the mountains. Medea, Helen of Troy, Niobe, and Cassandra were among the mythological figures with which the group identified.

Following their desire to rethink women's subjectivities through art, Le Nemesiache worked on theatre performances, films, poetry happenings, video art, music, and paintings, but they also staged protests and occupations of buildings to trigger a new conception of their location, Naples, and of the spaces for women's creativity that the city might offer. As a collective, they produced five performances, three films, four music concerts, and seven video works. In 1976, they initiated one of the first feminist film festivals in Europe, called Rassegna del Cinema Femminista. It ran in Sorrento until 1994.

---

5   Le Nemesiache, 'Manifesto per la riappropriazione della nostra creatività' (Manifesto for the Appropriation of our Creativity), trans. by Giulia Damiani (2020), available in the pamphlet from the exhibition *From the Volcano to the Sea: The Feminist Group Le Nemesiache in the 1970s and 1980s Naples*, Rongwrong, Amsterdam (2020).

SETTING UP A SCENE FROM THE ARCHIVE

'The scene is the principal form of reminiscence: a kind of memory cut off from its origins and access routes, isolated and fixed, and reduced to a trace.'[6] In this quote, theorist Jane Rendell reflects on what psychoanalyst Jean Laplanche conceived as a scene. Laplanche believed the scene to be the primary fragmented and repeated trace of the process of translation-repression happening between conscious and unconscious. I am interested in appropriating this notion of scene as it expresses the encounter between several boundaries: past and present, original and trace, and self and other, where 'other' can be a being or an object. Laplanche defined the unconscious as an 'internal foreign body', and even as one put inside the self by an alien.[7] These scenes are traces of aliens; better still, they are ghosts appearing on the frontier between translation and feminine repression, inner and outer worlds, and past and present enactment. They are fleeting sites of encounter with Le Nemesiache's practice reduced to a trace, or 'glimpses'. In the writing of the philosopher Georges Didi-Huberman, glimpses are apparitions whose traces last longer than the apparition itself.[8] Glimpses are beings half-seen and already loved. They require a form of investment.

Although scenes are glimpses without a visible origin, the origin of the term 'scene' reinforces the ideas of encounter and displacement of the trace. From the Greek *skene*, the word 'scene' originally indicated a tent or booth, something that gives shade or a shadow.[9] Scenes mark the shadows of sites of encounter, stretching over into the present and future through their trace. In this sense, the scene points to its own excess, to what exists beyond it — the event projecting the shadow. In

---

6   Jane Rendell, *Site-Writing: The Architecture of Art Criticism* (London: I. B. Tauris, 2010), p. 117.

7   Jean Laplanche, 'The Unfinished Copernican Revolution', in Laplanche, *Essays on Otherness*, ed. by John Fletcher, trans. by Luke Thurston, Leslie Hill, and Philip Slotkin (London: Routledge, 1999), pp. 53–86 (p. 65).

8   Georges Didi-Huberman, *Glimpses*, online video recording of a public open lecture for the students of the Division of Philosophy, Art & Critical Thought at the European Graduate School EGS, Saas-Fee, Switzerland, 26 May 2015 <https://egs.edu/lecture/ georges-didi-huberman-glimpses-2015/> [accessed 25 February 2018].

9   John Oswald, *An Etymological Dictionary of the English Language* (Philadelphia, PA: Key & Biddle, 1836), p. 385.

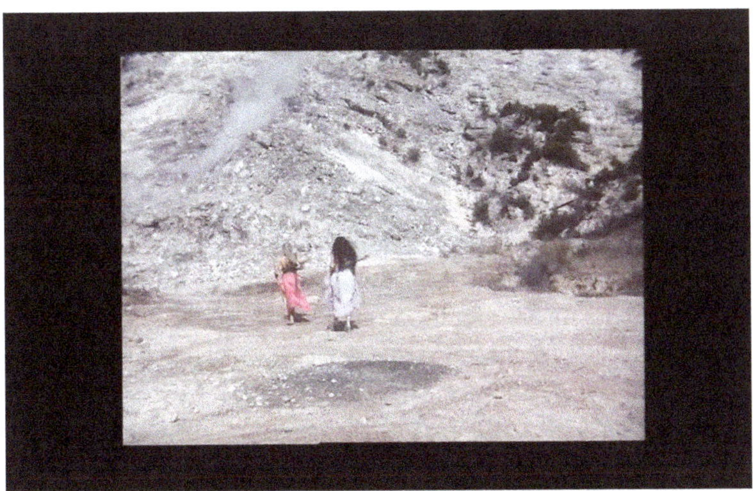

Figure 1. Screenshot from the film *Didone non è morta* (Dido Is Not Dead), dir. by Lina Mangiacapre (1987). Courtesy of Le Nemesiache.

this case, it is the encounter with a past feminist struggle; however, this can only be experienced differently, through retelling and re-siting — through the trace of the shadow itself. The scene is transformed into a new site for analysis calling for a response: for new incisions. According to Rebecca Schneider, this is what happens to an original event when it is narrated through a trace: the retelling and re-siting become the event itself.[10] The origin is lost. But the scene is also a theatrical event, both spatial when intended as the setting of the scene and temporal when the scene is a moment in a longer narrative. The scene is located in front of an audience. Audience members' shadows are marked on the scene throughout this process.

WRITING SCENE-SITES: SCENE NUMBER ONE IS AN IMAGE SHOT AT *CAMPI FLEGREI*, THE PHLEGREAN FIELDS

Shadows grow in the encounter with Le Nemesiache's artistic work. In the 1970s, their experience began overlapping with their environment — the natural volcanic phenomena present in the region of Naples

---

10   Rebecca Schneider, 'Solo Solo Solo', in *After Criticism: New Responses to Art and Performance*, ed. by Gavin Butt (Oxford: Blackwell, 2004), pp. 23–47.

(such as the sulphur fumes from the crater in this image) with the ancient myths that were located there. Their site was one of many repetitions: retranslations of something atavistic and repressed. Although I, the viewer, recognize this feeling, I cannot name it.

The black frame around the image indicates that it was filmed on a Super 8mm camera. This format was widely used by amateur filmmakers throughout the 80s. It is a frame from another time and from a longer feature, a still of something already in movement. In this shot, one woman is following another. The viewer participates in this chase. I understand this scene as a message of the desire to come after, to follow someone else's steps. The two characters are Dido, the legendary queen of Carthage, and her sister Anna. Dido is the oldest and the most celebrated in the family because of her tragic suicide. Anna walks behind her, ready to accompany Dido in her fate, but her final trajectory will be different. In this 'coming after', one after the other, their image will never coincide. A fracture can be expressed through an image still. We are following their steps; we come after. We can rewind and repeat. In telling this story, what is my position in this repetitive structure? Am I acting out something unconscious through the repetition of this trace-scene?

Laplanche's term 'afterwardsness' can be lifted from his psychoanalytic theory to become something different here.[11] Afterwardsness indicates a deferred action — a repetition with difference — that provokes the release of repressed ideas. This occurs through the relation with something from the past that is retranslated in the present. It can be a conscious process but not necessarily a knowing one.[12] Can this scene be the site of a personal and collective feminist investment? Retelling, displacing this trace onto other countless sites to begin again, to grasp something anew?

NUMBER TWO IS A SCENE OF 'VULCANIZATION'

The rumble of the volcano (see fig. 2) reverberates in the recording. Volcanoes are objects of scientific studies, subjects of paintings and

---

11   Jean Laplanche, 'Notes on Afterwardsness', in Laplanche, *Essays on Otherness*, pp. 264–69.

12   Rendell, *Site-Writing*, p. 63.

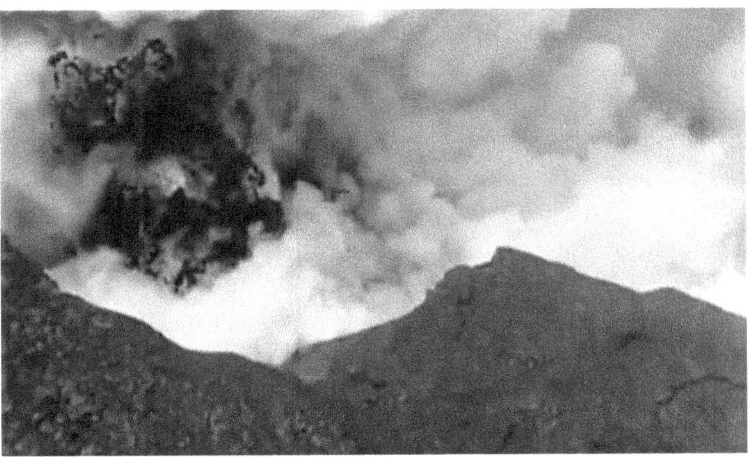

Figure 2. A recording of the rumble of the Vesuvius is available from
'Vesuvius in Eruption', filmed by British Movietone News on
29 July 1929 <https://youtu.be/-7W6BAV0wmw>
[accessed 21 November 2020].

poems, and background phenomena in contemporary art installations. Philosophers such as Didi-Huberman describe volcanoes as 'nothing but nature' when they exist outside of human intervention. They are certainly present, but they are not yet sites.[13] Le Nemesiache possessed the rumble of Mount Vesuvius, the renowned volcano near Naples. The volcano infiltrates their practice, which can be said to, in a metaphorical sense, cannibalize the potentially destructive but also generative force of Mount Vesuvius. For Le Nemesiache, women's stories were present in the lava. Throughout the 1970s, they said that history was written in their blood, the blood of women. They waited for the explosion of their veins. They would walk in the world splashing their story like lava. 'Lava, vulcani e sangue' ('Lava, Volcanos, and Blood') was the title of an article by Mangiacapre, published posthumously in the magazine *Il paese delle donne* in 2004.[14] In an almost mystical language, Mangiacapre discussed how a conception of humanity based on the individuality of the single man as a fundamental basis has produced a

---

13   Georges Didi-Huberman, *The Man Who Walked in Color*, trans. by Drew S. Burk (Minneapolis, MN: Univocal, 2017), p. 73.

14   Lina Mangiacapre, 'Lava, vulcani e sangue' ('Lava, Volcanos and Blood'), *Il Paese delle donne*, May 2004.

society that celebrates straight lines, rigidity, and phallocentric towers. Lava, volcanoes, and blood would make the world start from naught again; naught was intended as a necessary destruction to achieve a new harmony with the cosmos, a new unity with the natural elements, with the volcanoes. This destruction would be led by women. The blood of women, of past witches, and the lava of the volcano are thus interpreted as prophetic actors coalescing the historical suffering of women into the promise of a future regeneration.

The volcano is revealed as a site of investment. The group's actions did not aim at depicting or altering the functioning volcano. Their intention was, rather, to bring the volcano away from being a separate place and into the city — to recognize the lava in themselves and to see how the alien-ness of the volcano finds a shadow in the self. Thus the volcano has the potential to actualize unconscious structures but also material and patriarchal relationships: for example, in the ruins from the eruption of Mount Vesuvius, which authors such as Freud and Derrida have used.[15]

Embracing artist Andrea Fraser's definition of enactment as that which brings into focus 'the structures of relationships that are pro- duced and reproduced in all forms of activity', can the volcano be exploded into a performance of such conscious and unconscious struc- tures?[16]

In doing so, the performance is made into a volcanic bomb, which is the moment when volcanic lava turns into rocks of different shapes. By leaving the volcano and changing temperature, lava is shaped in flight and can land several kilometres away from its point of origin. Claiming again the power to imagine women's action as a burning prophecy, we are left with an unforeseeable promise of eruption des- cending from the rims of Mount Vesuvius.

---

15   The ruins of Pompeii became a model for Sigmund Freud's analogy between arche- ology and psychoanalysis, the ruins representing what is repressed and preserved in the unconscious. The relief of a female figure Gradiva is famously used by Freud to analyse memory and repression. On this subject, see Griselda Pollock, 'The Image in Psychoanalysis and the Archeological Metaphor', in *Psychoanalysis and the Image: Transdisciplinary Perspectives*, ed. by Griselda Pollock (Oxford: Blackwell, 2006), pp. 1–29.

16   Andrea Fraser, 'Performance or Enactment', in *Performing the Sentence: Research and Teaching in Performative Fine Arts*, ed. by Carola Dertnig and Felicitas Thun- Hohenstein (Berlin: Sternberg Press, 2014), pp. 122–27.

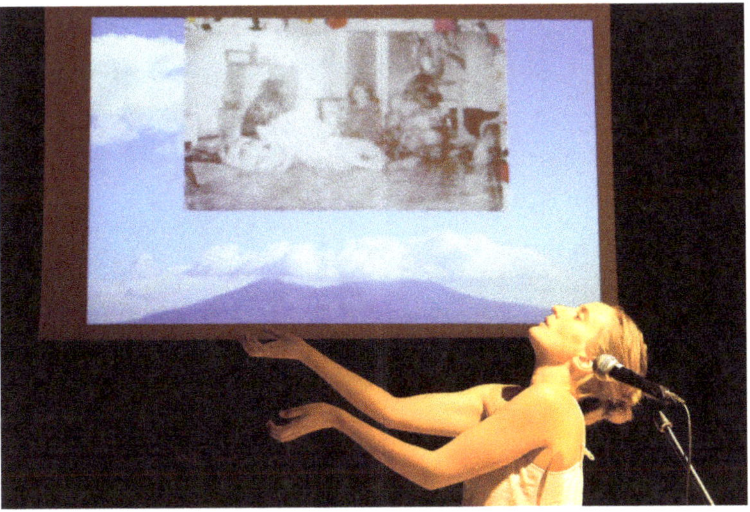

Figure 3. *How to Sing a Prophecy*, scripted and dir. by Giulia Damiani,
with performer Helena Rice (2017).

NUMBER THREE IS THE SCENE OF A PROPHETIC GESTURE

Can we recognize this prophecy now? The root *phēmi* belongs to
the Greek word for prophecy, *prophēteia*. *Phēmi*, in its proto-Indo-
European origin, is cognate with *fabula*, meaning story or fable.[17] The
other component of *prophēteias* is the prefix 'pro', meaning 'before'; in
this case, moving one's hands forward. Prophecy is the putting forward
of a fable, held in arms and pushed ahead. It is fabulation from other
times carried into sites that are always different. Constantly displaced,
it can only be noticed by shifting the gaze, in a glimpse.

---

17   *Chamber's Etymological Dictionary of the English* Language, ed. by James Donald (Edinburgh: William Chambers, 1868), p. 403.

Archival Reenactement and the Role of Fiction
Walid Raad and the *Atlas Group Archive*

ROBERTA AGNESE

Talking about the dialectical image, Walter Benjamin borrows an illuminating comparison from the French historian André Monglond. In the fragment that Benjamin quotes, Monglond describes the resemblances between the ability of a literary text to show and introduce meanings that appear mysterious to contemporary readers and the way that photographic images are impressed on a photosensitive plate and then revealed:

> The past has left images of itself in literary texts, images comparable to those which are imprinted by light on a photosensitive plate. The future alone possesses developers active enough to scan such surfaces perfectly.[1]

The concept of the 'dialectical image', of the image that is 'dialectics at a standstill',[2] is at the core of Benjamin's materialist thought of history, a concept that explores and reveals the dialectical relationship between the *what-has-been* and the *now*. For Benjamin, this relationship is deeply different from the temporal relationship between the

---

1   Walter Benjamin, *The Arcades Project*, ed. by Rolf Tiedemann, trans. by Howard Eiland and Kevin McLaughlin (Cambridge, MA: Harvard University Press, 1999), p. 482.

2   Ibid., p. 463.

past and the present, because it is 'not temporal in nature, but figural (*bildlich*)'.[3] The image is, in this sense, the moment when 'what has been comes together in a flash with the now to form a constellation'; it is the 'perilous critical moment' of the now of recognizability.[4] Thus history, in this perspective, has to be conceived as a construction, a montage made of different temporal layers in which the historical images are those moments (*Augenblicke*) of recognizability, through which the past as *what-has-been* can be known and recognized in an unpredictable way, in a constellation of times and meanings that appears understandable only at a particular moment. This montage is what Benjamin calls the 'historical index' of images, which creates the possibility to recall the past in the present through images that can be read or that become readable at a specific moment in time.[5] The image as 'dialectics at a standstill' is thus a figural crystallization of disjointed temporalities: the past deposes itself, and the future can reveal it, but only in their collision in the flash of the now of recognizability can the past be reactivated, shaped, and reshaped. Consequently, the dialectical image works as a sort of photosensitive plate of history: the past leaves its images on it, but only the future has developers active enough to show and reveal all the details.

A meaningful example of shaping, reactivating, and questioning the past through dialectical images is the vast project *The Atlas Group Archive*[6] by the Lebanese artist Walid Raad, who acts, in a Benjaminian sense, as a materialist historian and a political artist at the same time. Through his work, I would like to consider the reenactment in visual artistic practices as a way of reactivating the past in the present, not as a repetition or a restaging, but as a specific way of questioning that past by 'fictioning' a disregarded history through images.[7]

---

3   Ibid.

4   Ibid., pp. 462–63.

5   Ibid., p. 462.

6   To see a selection of the works that constitute the project: *The Atlas Group*, (1989–2004), artist website <https://www.theatlasgroup1989.org/> [accessed 20 January 2021].

7   Throughout this chapter, I use this term according to the English translation of the French neologism, '*fictionner*', which Michel Foucault introduced in the text 'Les Rapports de pouvoir passent à l'intérieur des corps', interview with Lucette Finas, *La Quinzaine littéraire*, 247 (January 1977), pp. 4–6 (p. 6) (repr. in Foucault, *Dits et écrits*, ed. by Daniel Defert, François Ewald, and Jacques Lagrange, 4 vols (Paris: Gallimard,

The Atlas Group Archive is a composite artistic project that presents itself as 'established to research and document' contemporary Lebanese history, especially the history of the fifteen-year long Lebanese Civil War. This war officially ended in 1991, when a General Amnesty Law was enacted by the Lebanese parliament. This law, which was largely controversial, granted amnesty for the crimes committed during the war and passed with the aim of a quick restoration and pacification of the country. Instead, it contributed to the instauration in post-war Lebanon of what has been defined by several specialists and scholars as 'a state-sponsored amnesia'.[8] It produced a 'collective forgetfulness' for those who lived the war, who were the 'victims of a lacuna between personal memory and collective amnesia', and the war therefore lingered in a state of latency and the past came to 'appear unreal'.[9]

For a past that seems to have become unreal, what form does an archive of such dematerialized events have to assume? In a context where a growing opacity covers the past, where — as it has been observed — 'amnesty and amnesia were [...] conscious policies',[10] how can one manage to shape a historical discourse that is missing but necessary? How can one build a collective memory, when the 'interdiction to remember' is taken as the basis for a renewed public life?

The Atlas Group tries to cope with these kinds of questions. *The Atlas Group Archive* is thus an archive, but a weird one: it is made up of documents as well as artefacts, presented in a digital mixed-media form, documents that are found but also produced and attributed to 'named imaginary individuals or organizations', 'anonymous individuals or organizations', and the Atlas Group itself.[11] These archives look

---

1994), iii: *1976-1979*, pp. 228–36 (p. 236)); in English as 'The History of Sexuality', in his *Power/Knowledge: Selected Interviews and Other Writings, 1972–1977*, ed. by Colin Gordon (New York: Pantheon Books, 1980), pp. 183–94 (p. 193). I think that the use of this neologism is particularly meaningful here, since it underlines the fiction as being not only a result or a goal, but a process, a method, an operation in itself, which is at the same time a technical and an artistic one. See also note 11.

8   Samir Kassir, 'Dix ans après, comment ne pas réconcilier une société divisée?', *Monde Arabe Maghreb Machrek*, 169 (2000), pp. 6–22, quoted in Sune Haugbolle, *War and Memory in Lebanon* (Cambridge: Cambridge University Press, 2010), p. 71.

9   Haugbolle, *War and Memory*, p. 72.

10   Ibid., p. 71.

11   Walid Raad, *Miraculous Beginnings* (London: Whitechapel Gallery, 2010), p. 23.

immediately ambiguous: they do not collect historical documents; instead, they contain visual artefacts created by Raad, who worked on the project from 1989 until 2004.

As a counterpoint to the institutional and historical fiction enacted by the amnesty, a fiction that has a performing influence on past and present, where we politically act as if something never occurred,[12] Raad decides to build a *fictional* archive of a past that becomes 'unreal', with the aim to question the limits and the possibilities of writing the history of contemporary Lebanon and to experience the possibility to reactivate in the present a rejected past.

> These colours, lines and forms are all borrowed from different documents. […] I produce an image by borrowing historical facts. I always work from facts but some of these facts can only be experienced in a place we call fiction.[13]

With this project, Raad manufactures and 'fictions' historical materials by establishing an archive, not to assert their truth, but to make these fictions function in a necessary discourse of truth. He does not search for factual or historical knowledge of the events he collects in this strange archive; rather, he displays those events by 'fictioning' their truth potential. As Michel Foucault affirms:

> [T]he possibility exists for fiction to function in truth, for a fictional discourse to induce effects of truth, and for bringing it about that a true discourse engenders or 'manufactures' something that does not as yet exist, that is, 'fictions' it. One 'fictions' a politics not yet in existence on the basis of a historical truth.[14]

---

12   As a historical and political fiction – since we pretend that something never happened – amnesty has a performative impact on the past and on time by posing oblivion as a founding act to renew our life as a community. French historian Nicole Loraux, in her book *The Divided City: On Memory and Forgetting in Ancient Athens*, trans. by Corinne Pache and Jeff Fort (New York: Zone Books, 2006) reminds us that amnesty acts "as if the present were thinkable only in the past, on condition, however, that the past, stripped of all potentially subversive value, only be used as an edifying model. To disarm, one by the other, the present and the distant past: this is political memory's great strategy for forgetting the most recent past" (p. 261). This legal, temporal and historical fiction takes the form of an erasure, of an " institutional obliteration of those chapters of civic history that the city fears time itself is powerless to transform into past events". (p. 145). On political and historical consequences of the civil war see also Giorgio Agamben, *Stasis: Civil War as a Political Paradigm*, trans. by Nicholas Heron (Stanford, CA: Stanford University Press, 2015).

13   Walid Raad, *Miraculous Beginnings*, p. 14.

14   Foucault, 'The History of Sexuality', p. 193.

The Atlas Group Archive is therefore not intended to preserve the memory of the past, because they are not based memory — but *amnesia*. These archives are useful in deconstructing contemporary Lebanese history into pieces and reshaping it, or reenacting it, by creating fictional documents that work as dialectical images or as fictional politics able 'to induce effects of truth' in the present that they address.

I would like to end by briefly considering a specific section of this archive, *Secrets in the Open Sea*.

> *Secrets in the open sea* consists of 6 large photographic prints that were found buried 32 meters under the rubble during the 1992 demolition of Beirut's war-ravaged commercial district. The prints were different shades of blue. […] In late 1994, The Atlas Group sent the prints to laboratories in France and in the United States for technical analysis. Remarkably, the laboratories recovered small black and white *latent* images from the prints, and the small images represent group portraits of men and women. The Atlas Group was able to identify all the individuals represented in the small black and white prints, and it turned out that they were all individuals who had been found dead in the Mediterranean sea between 1975 and 1990.[15]

The six plates that comprise this section appear to be monochrome representations of six different shades of blue. Raad says, 'I have rarely considered monochrome paintings I have encountered as empty screens, but rather as surfaces too much filled […] by their own material.'[16] Upon closer viewing, we discover that those plates are in fact not monochrome paintings, but six digital photographic colour prints filled with another fundamental element: in addition to the big blues, we can observe, in the bottom right, a faded black and white photograph, which is supposed to be the latent image discovered by the laboratories.

The blue of the Mediterranean Sea thus becomes a material and symbolic layer that hides latent images. The blue becomes a *documentary colour*, as Raad observes:

> I have the impression to document a colour that is not yet available as a referential element, as documentary. […] [B]y

---

15   Raad, *Miraculous Beginnings*, p. 61.
16   Ibid., p. 17.

Figure 1. Anonymous, The Atlas Group, Secrets In the Open Sea
(1994-2004), Color digital print, 111.76 x 175 cm/1, Courtesy of the
artist and Sfeir-Semler Gallery, Beirut / Hamburg.

> documenting this colour, I feel I become the recipient of a letter
> that I have to save for a future addressee.[17]

The latency of images addresses future recipients who will have to explore all the layers of this faded memory and will be able to reactivate Raad's gesture, because only the future has developers active enough to reveal the details. This latency is a state of apparent inactivity but also a delay, an expectation, a wait in the *camera obscura* for an image to reveal itself, to discover the fate of those 17,000 women and men kidnapped during the war and still missing.

These black and white photos come from Lebanese newspapers of the 1990s. They are not the 'real' portraits of those who are missing; they are only possible — not to say *fictional* — portraits that stand in as faces and bodies of anonymous victims of the war. This intermedial superimposition questions all kinds of testimony and narration, all kinds of documentary truthfulness, not by fostering an iconoclastic position, but by waiting for a figuration in the present. The viewer is always required to reactivate the gesture that leads to the creation of

---

17　　Ibid., p. 14.

Figure 2. Anonymous, The Atlas Group, Secrets In the Open Sea
(1994-2004), Color digital print, 111.76 x 175 cm/3, Courtesy of the
artist and Sfeir-Semler Gallery, Beirut / Hamburg.

Raad's documents, because the present that looks at this history is the very subject of Raad's work and has to recognize itself in those dialectical images for the process to be complete.

In this sense, Raad's gesture acquires a specific political value: which relationship does the present forge with history and memory, in the critical and perilous moment of recognizability?

By fictioning a disregarded history, Raad makes it emerge and work in our present, he opens up the possibility for configuring a 'politics not yet in existence'[18] by inventing documents, in an etymological sense — that is to say, by finding and discovering them, and at the same time by creating something new. Raad discovers and finds the testimonies he displays in this sense; he invents his documents by excavating and searching in a specific space and time. But he also borrows facts and shapes them, integrating them in an aesthetical and fictional operation. Archives are no longer closed within a classificatory order, and documents are no longer shut away within them; instead, both are

---

18   Foucault, 'The History of Sexuality', p. 193.

Figure 3. Anonymous, The Atlas Group, Secrets In the Open Sea
(1994-2004), Color digital print, 111.76 x 175 cm/3, Detail, Courtesy of
the artist and Sfeir-Semler Gallery, Beirut / Hamburg.

renewed by Raad's gesture and they can, in this way, continue to have
effects in the present. As Raad says:

> The story one tells oneself and that captures ones attention and
> belief may have nothing to do with what happened in the past,
> but that's the story that seems to matter in the present and for
> the future.[19]

---

19   Quoted in Kassandra Nakass, 'Double Miss: On the Use of Photography in the Atlas
     Group Archive', in *The Atlas Group (1989–2004): A Project by Walid Raad*, ed. by
     Kassandra Nakass and Britta Schmitz (Cologne: Walther König, 2006), pp. 49–52 (p.
     52).

II. AESTHETIC FORMS OF REHABILITATION

Unintentional Reenactments
Yella by Christian Petzold

CLIO NICASTRO

> And I thought: where did all the girls from the former East Germany go? Which dreams do they have? What kind of fortune hunters are they?
>
> Christian Petzold,
> quoted by Jaimey Fisher

Yella (Nina Hoss) is a young woman who grew up in Wittenberg, a town in East Germany. After the fall of the Wall, she lost both her job and her husband Ben (Hinnerk Schönemann), from whom she separated following a crisis in their relationship, perhaps caused, certainly aggravated, by the failure of Ben's business. Yella has now returned to her father's house and, in the first scene, we see her packing her suitcases to move to Hanover, where she seems to have found a job as an accountant. After breakfast with her father, a nasty surprise awaits her in front of the house: her ex-husband insists on giving her a lift to the station, despite her being protected by a restraining order. His insistence is such that she is eventually forced to accept. The conversation is very tense from the start: Ben blames her for not being there for him, for not supporting him at a critical moment, for wanting to start a new life elsewhere without him... The car is approaching a bridge over the river beyond which the station is located. The dialogue becomes increasingly heated, and Ben deliberately swerves off the road. The car breaks through the guardrail and plunges into the water. A few minutes after the violent impact, the two bodies are miraculously carried face down onto one of the banks, the woman first. Yella opens her eyes. The leaves of a large tree stir over the two motionless bodies. The woman gets up from the ground and, with a dazed look, walks away from her ex-husband's unconscious body towards the station. Her hair and clothes are wet, but not a single scratch is visible.

It was only after reading a review of *Yella* (2007) that Christian Petzold realized that his film was an 'unintentional' remake of one of his favorite movies, *Carnival of Souls* an American low-budget horror film the German filmmaker was obsessed with in the 1980s.[1] *Carnival of Souls*, too, opens with a car crashing into a river, taking with it the protagonist Mary (Candace Hilligoss), an organist who is about to leave her small town and move to Salt Lake City for work — a place that will turn out to be a limbo between the world of the living and the ghosts. In an interview, Petzold pointed out how in that very moment he became aware of the role of the subconscious in filmmaking,[2] or more precisely, of the difference between 'staged quotations' and those that re-emerge through the unconscious reenactment of the same gestures and circumstances:

> [W]hen I wanted to make a quotation, it was a disaster. At the beginning of making *Yella*, I'd seen Hitchcock's *Marnie* again. We ordered very expensive tracks that stretched one hundred meters on a train platform, and Nina Hoss had to stand on this platform like Tippi Hedren. It looked great, but I knew in that moment it was total shit because it had nothing to do with our story—it was just a quotation. It cost 65,000 euro and we threw it out. So I hate quotations. A movie might open a door for you, but to go through that door you don't have to make quotations.[3]

---

1   *Carnival of Souls*, dir. by Herk Harvey (Harcourt Production, 1962).

2   Hillary Weston, 'Missed Connections: A Conversation with Christian Petzold', *The Current: An Online Magazine Covering Film Culture Past and Present*, 7 December 2018, hosted by The Criterion Collection <https://www.criterion.com/current/posts/6088-missed-connections-a-conversation-with-christian-petzold > [accessed 20 February 2021].

3   Ibid.

(Expensive) quotations apparently cannot reawaken ghosts, or at least not those wandering creatures that no longer belong anywhere and that populate Petzold's *Ghosts Trilogy* (*Gespenster-Trilogie*). The trilogy is composed of *The State I Am in*, *Ghosts*, and *Yella*.[4] In the first film, the ghosts are a wanted couple part of the RAF group which is on the run across Europe with their teenage daughter. *Gespenster* follows the wanderings of Nina (Julia Hummer), an orphan girl who lives in a foster home, entrusted to social services, and who spends her daily life on the fringes of Berlin, in those areas that turned into a no man's land after reunification. Petzold's ghosts are not evanescent, frightening creatures, but characters who have lost their place, who are no longer useful, because they have slipped out of history — "They are not needed anymore and fall out of history / the story."[5] — and are confronted with 'marginal temporalities': that time 'on the run' which is eventually interrupted by the irruption of adolescence in *The State I Am in*, the search for an identity in *Ghosts*, and the temporal loops of the repetition compulsion in *Yella*. These people, who are being pushed out of society and do not know where to go, end up in 'transitional spaces, transit zones where nothingness looms on one side and the impossibility of returning to what existed in the past on the other'.[6] Together with the other filmmakers belonging to the so-called Berlin School,[7] namely Thomas Arslan and Angela Schanelec, Petzold has always reflected on the social, economic, and urban transformations that Germany underwent after reunification, which coincides with the period in which he studied at the German Film and Television

---

4   *The State I Am In* (*Die Innere Sicherheit*), dir. by Christian Petzold (Schramm Film Koerner & Weber, 2000); *Ghosts* (*Gespenster*), dir. by Christian Petzold (Schramm Film Koerner & Weber, 2005); *Yella*, dir. by Christian Petzold (Schramm Film Koerner & Weber, 2007).

5   'Sie werden nicht mehr gebraucht, fallen aus der Geschichte': Christian Petzold, 'Interview: Christian Petzold: "Gespenster irren herum"', *Rheinische Post, RP Online*, 12 September 2005 [my translation, C.N.] <https://rp-online.de/kultur/film/christian-petzold-gespenster-irren-herum_aid-17041845> [accessed 20 February 2021].

6   Marco Abel, 'The Cinema of Identification Gets on My Nerves: An Interview with Christian Petzold', *Cineaste*, 33.3 (Summer 2008) <https://www.cineaste.com/summer2008/the-cinema-of-identification-gets-on-my-nerves> [accessed 20 February 2021].

7   See Marco Abel, *The Counter-Cinema of the Berlin School* (Rochester, NY: Camden House, 2013) and Jaimey Fisher, *Christian Petzold* (Urbana: University of Illinois Press, 2013).

Academy of Berlin (DFFB) to become a film director. As Benjamin Heisenberg — whom Marco Abel recognizes as a member of the Berlin School's second wave — has pointed out, this generation of filmmakers had to deal with the question of identity (both as an impossibility and as a rejection) and therefore with the need to account for the sudden changes of the country. Beneath the surface of an ostensible stasis, the Berlin School scrutinizes mundane movements and gestures which are not external revelations of a secret essence but rather survival strategies: 'It's not really about how people are hiding something; rather, it concerns how they become economic.'[8]

Among the protagonists of the trilogy, all women, it is Yella who is the 'real' ghost, doubly embodying Petzold's fascination with the ghost as the cinematic figure par excellence, since cinema can restore life to those who have lost a space for action. Yella no longer belongs to the GDR, she has not been given the opportunity to reclaim her history. She has no future unless she undergoes a process of assimilation in which she will learn and repeat the gestures of a 'new' economic system and its strategies. In Petzold's terms, cinema tells the stories of people who no longer belong anywhere, but who claim their right to belong to a history — to interact, to love, to desire; people who want to be there once again, in a space of transition (which, in *Yella*, becomes a metaphor both for German reunification and for the continuous reworking of the unconscious), even when this attempted redemption turns out to be an illusion, the enactment of a repetition compulsion.

Once in Hanover, Yella discovers that the job position was actually a scam and finds herself alone in her hotel room, having only her father's savings to rely on. Sitting on the edge of her bed, worried and looking for a solution, she is assaulted by Ben for the first time (is this a hallucination?). The man will continue to torment and attack her, making more than one attempt on her life. On more than one occasion she will ask for help from Philipp, a manager whom Yella meets in the hotel bar and with whom she will begin to work, learning the techniques and tricks of the negotiations of the marketing world. Although coming from a completely different context, Yella will immediately understand that the power of capitalist structures is based above all on

---

8   Fisher, *Christian Petzold*, p. 1.

the introjection and reproduction/reenactment of gestures, attitudes, poses, and tricks of the trade. After agreeing on the meaning of certain postures (leaning back in the chair with hands on the nape of the neck, certain words whispered in the ear), Yella and Philipp sit at the table of long negotiations, in front of their clients. Here Petzold — who always developed the scripts for his films together with the German documentary filmmaker Harun Farocki (until Farocki's death in 2014) — accurately reenacts parts of the two-hour negotiation session between the developer and the risk company that Farocki had documented in *Nothing Ventured*.[9]

One night at the hotel where the two continue to stay, after being attacked again by Ben, Yella takes refuge in Philipp's room, with whom she now begins a relationship. The morning after their first night together, Yella finally experiences a moment of domesticity, the only one, as she watches Philipp peel an orange with the same technique and attention as her father, but in fact the comfort of this image immediately becomes, once again, a sign that precedes the return of the repressed. Just as at the beginning of the film the affection with which her father peels the orange at breakfast is the last reassuring familiar gesture before Ben drives the car into the river, the second appearance of the orange, with Philipp's hands carefully removing the peel, anticipates a variation of the motif. Philipp confesses to Yella that he cheated to raise money to start a new business for which he still needs two hundred thousand euros. Determined to not repeat the same 'mistake' she made with Ben, Yella tries to avoid their downfall by blackmailing Dr Gunthen (Burghart Klaußner), seemingly rich (but actually broke) client who is already involved in Philipp's intricate plan. While waiting for the man to hand over the money sitting at the table with other clients, Yella has a strange, vivid vision: the soundscape disappears, the voices of the men sitting opposite her fade away, replaced by a piercing sound. She sees a tree shaken by the wind, a pond, and the image of Dr Gunthen with his hair and clothes soaked in water. She runs to the blackmailed man's house and, together with his wife, finds him face down in the lake in the lush garden. In the meantime, Philipp arrives and accuses Yella

---

9   *Nothing Ventured (Nicht ohne Risiko)*, dir. by Harun Farocki (Harun Farocki Filmproduktion, 2004).

of having driven the man to suicide with her threats. As she sits alone in the backseat of a cab, weeping silently with her head leaning against the car window, Yella finds herself back in Ben's car, just a moment before Ben deliberately swerves off the road. Just a 'minimal variation' occurs:[10] this time Yella does not react, does not try to steer the wheel in the opposite direction. She stares at the man, the car crashes into the water.

The Wittenberg police pulls Ben's car out of the water and finds the bodies of Yella and Ben inside. They lay them on the riverbank, covering them with a silver cloth. The foliage of a large tree stirs over their bodies.

This story never took place: it reveals itself as a circular dream fallen into the river. Petzold mixes up past, present, future, and their oneiric re-elaboration to question the memory of a past, that of the GDR, vanished and *nachlebend*, which in his view has never really been constituted as history. Yella's story is a series of events we see but which never actually becomes memory, because it is a false future. Who is the subject who dreams it? Understanding the past archaeologically, in particular its moments of transition and transformation, as well as its relationship to the present, means staging its future possibilities, even those that were never actualized, even those that failed. This becomes possible only by conjuring up the minor voices, the ghosts on the margins of history that otherwise would not have had the strength to reappear. Yella is an involuntary dreamer, not free to alter reality through phantasy, but rather forced to confront the past reality inscribed in her unconscious in the constant work of *Durcharbeiten*, in the sense proposed by Sigmund Freud for the first time in 'Erinnern, Wiederholen und Durcharbeiten'.[11] Freud, after all, was a constant reference for Petzold both during the development of the screenplay and

---

10   Here I refer to Harun Farocki's notion of 'minimal variation'. Minimal variation consists in presenting the same fact or the same argumentative process more than once in the same film, every time slightly changed. According to Farocki these different layers together bespeak new problems and critical questions since they gradually undermine the spectator's faith in the previous image. See Harun Farocki: '"Minimale Variation" und "semantische Generalisation"', *film. Eine deutsche Filmzeitschrift*, 7.8 (August 1969), pp. 10–11.

11   Sigmund Freud, 'Weitere Ratschläge zur Technik der Psychoanalyse: II. Erinnern, Wiederholen und Durcharbeiten', in Freud, *Studienausgabe*, ed. by Alexander Mitscherlich, Angela Richards, James Strachey, and Ilse Gubrich-Simitis, 11 vols

during the filming of *Yella*.[12] In the short 1914 essay, Freud describes the transition from the hypnosis method, which aimed to trigger an abreaction (i.e., an emotional discharge with a cathartic reaction), to free associations to discover what the patient could not remember, thus trying to let resistances emerge. If, under hypnosis, remembering produced a clear distinction between past and present and the patient never confused the previous situation with the present one, the psychoanalytic setting allows to re-enact, to re-actualize patterns and memories through the mechanisms of transference.

> [W]e may say that the patient does not remember anything of what he has forgotten and repressed, but acts it out. He reproduces it not as a memory but as an action, he repeats it, without, of course, knowing that he is repeating it.[13]

The patient does not remember having had a certain behaviour and certain reactions but re-actualizes and re-enacts them in the relationship with the therapist. Freud observes that this repetition, which he defines as repetition compulsion, is the primary way of remembering that the patient develops and maintains during therapy. The greater the resistance, the greater the extent to which remembering is replaced by enacting. The transference process is obviously not linear, but in turn encounters a great deal of resistance: the patient repeats past gestures and behaviours instead of remembering, or rather remembers by translating memory into gesture. So, according to Freud, the question is: what does the patient repeat or re-enact? The therapist must be able to observe symptoms and inhibitions in order to bring to the surface the repressed, which is enacted in the repetition compulsion, whose morbidity, far from ceasing with the beginning of therapy, rather becomes more acute. These symptoms are not to be treated 'as an event of the past, but as a present-day force'.[14] Therefore, the task of the therapist is to carefully lead back into the past in which the patient

---

(Frankfurt a.M.: Fischer, 1969–75), *Ergänzungsband: Schriften zur Behandlungstechnik* (1975), pp. 205–15.

12   Ficher, *Christian Petzold*, p. 104

13   Sigmund Freud, 'Remembering, Repeating and Working-Through', in *The Standard Edition of the Complete Psychological Works of Sigmund Freud*, ed. and trans. by James Strachey, 24 vols (London: Hogarth, 1953–74), XII (1958), pp. 145–57, (p. 150).

14   Ibid., p. 151.

experiences these symptoms as something real and present. Freud insists on emphasizing that hypnosis, a laboratory experiment, artificially suspends the struggle between past, present, and future, while the repetition compulsion that occurs in transference exposes the subject to the danger and vertigo of the clash between the different temporal dimensions. Precisely for this reason, as the treatment progresses, new forces can emerge that risk undermining the recovery. In this sense, the doctor's challenge is to keep all the impulses that the patient would like to move into the motor field within the psychic field.

> We render the compulsion harmless, and indeed useful, by giving it the right to assert itself in a definite field. We admit it into the transference as a playground in which it is allowed to expand in almost complete freedom and in which it is expected to display to us everything in the way the pathogenic instincts that is hidden in the patient's mind.[15]

The transference creates a transitional space between illness and life, in which the repetition compulsion is transformed by the *working through*, which eventually allows the patient to open new unforeseen scenarios. For the analyst this in-between space allows her to partake in the reenactment of the illness, its symptoms, gestures, and language in the peculiar intersubjective context of the psychoanalytic setting. Over time, when the repetition compulsion is successively transformed by the *working through*, the space changes accordingly.

But in which way can the psychoanalytic setting be compared to the space unfolding in *Yella*? Would the analogy lead to the conclusion, that the analyst is the director, feeding the patient/audience with suggestions how to think? Or does it turn the audience into the role of the analyst, dissecting the psychic material of the director? Both ideas are misleading. Both setting and film create an imaginary and intermediary space in which the magmatic material can be looked at without the necessity to react to it as in real life. The director proposes an understanding of a conflict by re-enacting the conflict, shaping and framing it. That is of course different to the technique of free association — the film, on the contrary, presents a highly edited and thought-through result of phantasies related to a specific conflict, not necessarily by

---

15   Ibid., p. 154.

becoming consciously aware of the content of the conflict. If the film were to resolve the conflict, as it is the aim of psychoanalytic work, the film would collapse into banality. Petzold situates the subjects and objects that populate his stories in a setting constructed at the crossroad between a protected environment where the reenacted events are sheltered by the temporal and spatial coordinates of the plot and a place weathered by the unpredictable atmospheric agents of the present. The wind blowing on the treetops in *Yella*, as well as Yella's hallucinations, become the 'material' trace of the clash between the past and the present — or rather the future that in fact never happened.[16] Both *Barbara* and *Transit* are, in this respect, two emblematic examples of the temporal clash the German director aims to stage.[17] By filming the characters of *Transit* (Franz Rogowski) — a story that takes place during the Nazi occupation of Paris — in the present-day streets of the French capital and in Marseille, Petzold intensifies the disorientation of the protagonist as well as their desperate yet failed attempt to support each other.

Petzold recounts that he once was struck by a sentence of François Truffaut's in which the French director, commenting on *La carosse d'or*,[18] criticized Jean Renoir for not having shot his historical films in a studio. If, in this film genre, the wind blowing in the images is the real one, the actual one, the scene simply does not work, because the story is substantially altered, interfered with. According to Truffaut, a completely artificial dimension must be created for historical films to be convincing and effective: 'And I believed that for a good while thinking that I could not make a historical drama because I simply cannot bear to be in the studio', Petzold confesses in an interview.[19] At

---

16   Interestingly, Harun Farocki — in his video installation from 2012, *Parallel* — also shows an image of the wind blowing on a tree to reflect on the different ways in which films, on the one hand, and computer animation, on the other, (re)produce reality: 'animations are currently becoming a general model, surpassing film. In films, there is the wind that blows and the wind that is produced by a wind machine. Computer images do not have two kinds of wind.' <https://www.harunfarocki.de/installations/2010s/2012/parallel.html> [accessed 20 February 2021].

17   *Barbara*, dir. by Christian Petzold (Schramm Film Koerner & Weber, 2012); *Transit*, dir. by Christian Petzold (Schramm Film Koerner & Weber, 2018).

18   *La carosse d'or* (*The Golden Coach*), dir. by Jean Renoir (Panaria Film, 1952).

19   Jaimey Fisher and Robert Fischer, 'The Cinema is a Warehouse of Memory: A Conversation Among Christian Petzold, Robert Fischer, and Jaimey Fisher', *Senses of Cinema*,

a certain point, however, the question arose as to whether Truffaut was wrong: whether the task of directors, of narrators, is not precisely that of reflecting on the past by exposing the characters to the atmospheric agents of the present in such a way as to reenact the past, inverting the relationship between what has been written, said, experienced and its present traces.

> The question is not what does [Friedrich] Schiller have to say to us today, but rather what do we mean to Schiller? And I agree with this: the question is not what the GDR [East Germany] in 1980 means to us, but rather what do we, in the future, mean to the people in the GDR in 1980, who were living in a system in utter collapse.[20]

The temporal circularity of *Yella*, or rather the series of events that will eventually turn out never to have happened — as in Petzold's latest work *Undine* (2020), whose themes are a direct continuation of the 2007 film — becomes an open question about the relationship between natural, mythical, and historical time. Particularly water becomes the *topos* in which hopes for happiness and stability are drowned and that pushes the characters back into the time of a repetition compulsion. Thus, Petzold is not afraid to go beyond the visible connections and rather uses the supernatural to counteract an idea of nature as a return to the origin, to open a critical breach in a reality that is too often content with faithful reproductions.[21] However, the metaphorical level on which the film operates cannot and must not obscure the event around which the entire story unfolds and on which its circular structure insists: a collapsing economic and political system and a reflection on what it means to put back together the pieces of a country like Germany, avoiding the dynamic of a repetition compulsion on a historical scale. Beneath, within, at the beginning, and again at the end of this macro-analysis that makes use of small 'supernatural' interventions to explore the realm of the possible, of what could have happened, of what should not have happened, the film stages

---

84 (September 2017) <https://www.sensesofcinema.com/2017/christian-petzold-a-dossier/christian-petzold/> [accessed 20 February 2021].

20   Ibid.

21   Clio Nicastro, 'Undine', *Filmidee*, 24 (October 2020) <https://www.filmidee.it/2020/10/undine/> [accessed 20 February 2021].

a murder, a feminicide. Ben's envy towards his former wife's search for independence, his failing strategy to bind her to himself through coercing love turns into misogynistic rage and hatred. To allow other levels of filmic discourse to attenuate Ben's inability to accept that his ex-wife's life will flourish without him would marginalize what *Yella* puts right before our eyes, at the beginning and at the end of the film, once again. But at the same time, the powerful role of the violent act unfolds precisely in its ambiguous presence and distorted perception. Murder is the center of the film both historically and emotionally, but Petzold would take away the analytic process from the beholder if he were to reveal it. The audience, though, is lured into taking on Ben's deceptive perspective: he does not murder Yella since he kills himself *together* with her, perceiving her as a part of himself. This process of assimilation resonates with Petzold's attempt to crack the celebratory narrative of German reunification. The only character who is able to transform the compulsion to repeat is Yella. Through the *Traumarbeit* in her ghostly dream she is at least able to slightly change the order of events in a minimal variation: but paradoxically what differs in the final scene, when we witness the murder one more time, is the lack of any reaction to Ben's sudden swerve off the road.

Everyday Aesthetics and the Practice of Historical Reenactment
Revisiting Cavell's Emerson

ULRIKE WAGNER

Today, we know Ralph Waldo Emerson as a thinker of transition, as someone who regards human life as a ceaselessly revising process. His renowned epigrammatical exclamations suggest that the individual 'in the right state' needs to be 'Man Thinking' and to respond to life's insecurities and 'slippery sliding surfaces' with an always active, alert, and self-corrective mind.[1] Drawing on an eclectic body of works of others, he appropriates, reworks, and reenacts his sources, thereby performing his core concern of keeping the mind in a restless state, in a 'moment of change, say of becoming' rather than 'being'.[2] His writing practice, aimed at gearing the trajectories of the mind toward a fluid stream of transformation, leads to a fascinating de-hierarchization and pluralization of objects of aesthetic experience. Breaking with artistic norms and introducing a new voice into aesthetic discourses of his

---

1   Ralph Waldo Emerson, *The Collected Works of Ralph Waldo Emerson*, ed. by Alfred R. Ferguson and others, 7 vols to date (Cambridge, MA: Belknap Press of Harvard University Press, 1971–), I: *Nature, Addresses, and Lectures* (1971), p. 53, III: *Essays, Second Series* (1984), p. 28.

2   Stanley Cavell, 'Being Odd, Getting Even (Descartes, Emerson, Poe)', in Cavell, *In Quest of the Ordinary* (Chicago: University of Chicago Press, 1988), pp. 105–30 (p. 111).

time, he turns to the low and common, calling on his readers to see and appreciate the value and beauty of the everyday.

According to Stanley Cavell, it is Emerson's preoccupation with the significance and value of the ordinary that is vital to understanding and appreciating the originality of his philosophical work. Drawing attention to and elevating ordinary matters — 'The meal in the firkin; the milk in the pan; the ballad in the street; the news of the boat; the glance of the eye; the form and the gait of the body' —[3] Emerson advances his philosophical approach in conversation with, and in contradistinction to, the German philosophy of idealism and England's empirical tradition.[4] In *Transcendental Etudes*, Cavell locates a place for Emerson's penchant for the low and common on the philosophical map of his time while also bringing into view how his thinking and aesthetics anticipates that of J. L. Austin, Wittgenstein, Heidegger, and Nietzsche.[5]

The eclectic composition of Emerson's works and their cross-cultural impact call for such transnational examinations focused on his place in the history of philosophy. However, while the 'philosophicality' (to use Cavell's term) of his ordinary aesthetics and technique of writing have been explored widely, their historicity is understudied. To be sure, it is well known that the reception of German classical scholarship and historical Bible criticism played a major role in the development of Transcendentalism, America's first major cultural movement, and that historical research had a formative impact on Emerson's work. In this context, the names of young students from New England who learned German and went to study at the University of Göttingen keep cropping up, as well as references to the works of Johann Gottfried Herder, Ludwig Heeren, Johann Gottfried Eichhorn, Wilhelm de Wette, Friedrich Schleiermacher, Friedrich August Boeckh, Cornelius Conway Felton, George Ripley, James Marsh, George Bancroft, and Robert Bridges Patton.[6] Needless to say, I am

---

3   Emerson, *Collected Works*, I, p. 67.

4   Stanley Cavell, 'An Emerson Mood', in Cavell, *Emerson's Transcendental Etudes* (Stanford, CA: Stanford University Press, 2003), pp. 20–32 (p. 25).

5   Cavell, 'The Philosopher in American Life (Toward Thoreau and Emerson)', in *Emerson's Transcendental Etudes*, pp. 33–58 (pp. 34–36).

6   For the most recent comprehensive overview, see Kurt Mueller-Vollmer, *Transatlantic Crossings and Transformations: German-American Cultural Transfer from the 18th to the End of the 19th Century*, Interamericana, 6 (Frankfurt a.M.: Peter Lang, 2015).

deeply indebted to the meticulous recoveries of these multiple strands of cross-cultural transmission and transformation by other scholars; however, my own assessment of the significance of these transatlantic travels of intellectual history differs from existing analyses.

Most critical writings concerned with the role of German historical criticism in early to mid-nineteenth-century New England focus their enquiries on identifying what sources, translations, and modes of transmission contributed to the hallmark of the Transcendentalist movement, which is often referred to as a subjective turn.[7] A question that rarely gets sufficiently addressed in this context, however, is exactly how this trafficking of critical techniques and ideas translated into activities supporting this turn toward the project of empowering the subject. How did people's engagement with past civilizations contribute to strategies of authorizing the individual? And what qualities distinguish such authorized individuals? These questions call for a broad reassessment of this vital period of intellectual history and a review of Transcendentalist writings and translations other than those of Emerson. Given the scope of this paper, however, I focus only on him. More specifically, I ask how the historico-critical discourse of Emerson's time contributed to what Cavell calls his practice of 'aversive thinking.' From a philosophical vantage point, Cavell examines how Emerson renews common thinking, citations, and fragments by means of aversive thinking: his way of turning writing back upon itself and away from conformity and conventional frames of reference.[8] A ques-

---

7   Most works that focus on the reception of German Biblical criticism in New England
     demonstrate how the translations and reviews of German theological texts by Transcendentalist critics such as James Marsh or George Ripley transfer the idea of divine
     authority from the letter into the interior world of the subject. Under the influence of
     German historical criticism, American critics begin to treat religious texts no longer
     as infallible testimonies of divine revelation, but as historical records giving diverse
     accounts of human experiences of the spiritual world. Against the backdrop of their
     reception of German critical efforts, Transcendentalists install the subject's soul as the
     resource we ought to tap in order to develop an intuitive understanding of religious
     truth. See Philip F. Gura's chapter 'Reinvigorating a Faith' in his *American Transcendentalism: A History* (New York: Hill and Wang, 2007), pp. 46–68.

8   See Cavell, 'Aversive Thinking: Emersonian Representations in Heidegger and Nietzsche', in *Emerson's Transcendental Etudes*, pp. 141–70 (p. 145): '[A] guiding thought
     in directing myself to Emerson's way of thinking is his outcry in the sixth paragraph
     of "Self-Reliance": "The virtue in most request is conformity. Self-Reliance is its aversion." I gather him there to be characterizing his writing, hence to mean that he writes
     in aversion to society's demand for conformity, specifically that his writing expresses

tion that arises here is how Emerson's concern with detaching meaning from commonplace contexts and treating life as a restless stream of contingent events relates to, and is formed by, the scholarly discourse that was unfolding in the related fields of religious criticism and classical studies. His engagement with and contribution to these debates is illuminating, I suggest, because they cast light on why he came to treat sources of various origins as sites for the continuous breaking and remaking of customs and aesthetic norms. In fact, a friend of his highlights the importance of the latest developments in humanist research for Emerson's thinking and writing.

When his correspondent Herman Grimm first comes across his writings in the mid-nineteenth century, he compares reading Emerson's essays to the discovery of a new continent.[9] Without understanding much initially, the originality and liveliness of Emerson's style captivates the son of Wilhelm Grimm (the younger of the two Grimm brothers). Thoughts that have crossed his own mind multiple times appear fresh, and his thinking seems to renew itself through Emerson's formulations. In trying to explain how and why he developed such an unparalleled mode of composing, Grimm goes beyond suggesting that Emerson's style is simply a testament to his native genius. Interestingly, he links his writing technique to the direction that American nineteenth-century scholarship took. He argues that the ways in which Emerson's contemporaries practice research provides the broader intellectual historical context for his success, bringing the thoughts of past generations into conversation with his love and enthusiasm for the present without letting the cultural legacies of others inhabit and stifle him:

> [H]ow much Emerson's doctrine has become second nature to today's America shows the condition of its budding scholarly life. Among us, we take our point of departure from what *Wissenschaft* demands of itself (certainly the higher point of view), while in America it benefits the learner — in many cases

his self-consciousness, his thinking as the imperative to an incessant conversion or refiguration of society's incessant demands for his consent — his conforming himself — to its doings, and at the same time to mean that his writing must accordingly be the object of aversion to society's consciousness, to what it might read in him.'

9   Herman Grimm, *Fünfzehn Essays. Erste Folge*, 3rd rev. and enlarged edn (Berlin: Dümmler, 1884), p. 438.

the more practical and better path toward the goal. The living should take priority.

> [W]ie sehr jene Lehre Emersons dem heutigen Amerika in Fleisch und Blut übergegangen sei, zeigt die Beschaffenheit des dort sich regenden wissenschaftlichen Lebens. Bei uns geht man aus von dem, was die Wissenschaft für sich verlange — gewiss der höhere Standpunkt; in Amerika von dem, was den Lernenden dienlich sei — in vielen Fällen der praktischere und besser zum Ziele führende. Zuerst sollen die Lebenden zu ihrem Rechte kommen.[10]

According to Grimm's assessment, it is the humanist orientation that distinguishes American research practices and resonates with Emerson's approach to writing. German scholarship, by contrast, appears compartmentalized, fractured, and detached from the flow of everyday life in Grimm's eyes. What he misses in Germany is the strong link between *Wissenschaft* and the project of *Bildung* that he finds in New England's educational institutions and reverberating in the writing of the Transcendentalists' best-known figurehead. Ironically, however, while Grimm recognizes the crucial role of *Wissenschaft* in Emerson's style, he overlooks that it was precisely his discovery of a humanist impulse in scholarly practices that drew him to German research in the first place.

Emerson highlights figures whose works express what he considers pioneering treatments of tradition and suggests that their creative fashioning of the works of others is bound up with contemporary historical criticism. In the second lecture on 'Literature' (1839) of 'The Present Age' series, he discusses the 'new epoch in criticism' dating from the ways 'ancient history has been dealt with by Niebuhr, Wolf, Müller, and Heeren', and in particular from 'Wolf's attack upon the authenticity of Homeric poems'.[11] He demonstrates that their research reveals in different ways the openness of ancient history; issues we thought we had settled appear inconclusive in light of their findings.

---

10 Herman Grimm, 'Ralph Waldo Emerson – Ein Nachruf', in *Der Briefwechsel Ralph Waldo Emerson / Herman Grimm und die Bildung von Post-mortem-Gemeinschaften*, ed. by Thomas Meyer, trans. by Helga Paul, Europäer-Schriftenreihe, 14 (Basel: Perseus, 2007), pp. 67–68 (my English translation).

11 Ralph Waldo Emerson, 'Literature [Second Lecture]', in Emerson, *The Early Lectures of Ralph Waldo Emerson*, ed. by Stephen E. Whicher, Robert E. Spiller, and Wallace Williams, 3 vols (Cambridge, MA: Harvard University Press, 1959–1972), iii: *1838–1842* (1972), pp. 224–37 (p. 225).

The new insights about the lack of unity and fragmentary nature of the Homeric poems lead Emerson to draw a number of interesting conclusions relevant to the functions of past legacies in his own time:

> Out of histories written in so narrow a mind as most of our histories are, laborious indeed but without a pious and loving eye to the universal contributions of nature to a people, nothing can come but incongruous, broken impressions, unsatisfactory to the mind. But the views obtained by patient wisdom studious of facts and open to the permanent as well as partial causes would give an analogues impression to the landscape. As it studies history, so it looks at the sciences in a higher connection than before [...] Our own country, I may remark, shares largely in whatsoever is new and aspiring in thought. Our young men travel in foreign countries and read at home with hungry eyes foreign books. Wishful eyes are cast to Germany [...] but here is Germany or nowhere.[12]

The most significant shortcoming of the method of history writing customary in Emerson's own country is that it leaves the mind with 'broken impressions'; it provides a potpourri of collected data but no coherent interpretation. What would become the hallmark of Emerson's view on how the modern individual ought to approach history is already evident in his early lecture: for history to be of any value, the interpreter needs to take on an active role as a shaper of facts. There are obvious resonances between this lecture and the essay on Shakespeare, in which Emerson calls him the 'father of German literature' because of his ability to bring the past back to life in a loving manner.[13] In the lecture on 'Literature', he also gestures at the important role that a 'loving eye' plays for viewing the significance of historical materials in broader contexts. More than that, he suggests that a subject who has learned to exercise his 'loving eye' will also begin to see the landscape differently. What Emerson gains from studies of cultural history, in other words, has a formative impact on his visual capacities to draw fragments together in a new field of vision. His way of turning the transnational rise of new approaches to assessing and relating to past civilizations into an occasion for a pervasive recasting of aesthetic

---

12   Ibid., p. 228.
13   Emerson, *Collected Works*, IV: *Representative Men* (1987), p. 117.

categories marks one of the most interesting aspects of his delving into cultural and literary history.

These passages from Emerson's early lecture provide merely a small glimpse into his comprehensive and nuanced engagement with the German critical tradition throughout his work. We can see, however, that his unconventional reenactment of forms of cultural expression flows naturally from the scholarly discourse into which he was tapping. The use of history and books lies in what they can do for the living generation. Regardless of whether Emerson turns to Friedrich August Wolf, Barthold Georg Niebuhr, or Johann Gottfried Herder, the question of interest to him is how they manage to put their findings into the service of the individual's development and present-day cultural renewal. He regards ancient texts as models for man's constant attempt to give expression to experience, and believes that the way to engage with them is by generating new modes of expression: 'They say much of the study of the Ancients, but what else does that signify than, direct your attention to the real world and seek to express it, since that did the ancients whilst they lived.'[14]

Emerson, I suggest, uses this perspective on history as a springboard to corroborate and authorize what he would work into a fully-fledged practice of writing and recasting of aesthetic norms. Man needs to break with traditions and conventions as much as he needs to experiment with and cultivate new forms of life and expressions, such as 'the low, the common [...] the philosophy of the street', rather than what is traditionally considered 'sublime and beautiful'.[15] Emerson's concern with the historical debates of his time shows clearly that leaving old forms behind is as important to him as creating new ones. For him it is the right balance between letting go and appropriating new habits of thinking and living that indicates the health and happiness of individuals and societies alike. While Cavell has designated Emerson's place in the history of philosophy, his place in the historical discourse as it developed in the related fields of classicism and religion has yet to be determined. Such examinations of his voice in debates over techniques

---

14   Ralph Waldo Emerson, *The Journals and Miscellaneous Notebooks of Ralph Waldo Emerson*, ed. by William H. Gilman and others, 16 vols (Cambridge, MA: Harvard University Press, 1960-1982), v (1965), p. 290.

15   Emerson, *Collected Works*, I, p. 67.

of historical enquiry and their humanist value will show that Cavell's
approach to treating his work 'less as an object of interpretation than as
a means of interpretation', and as a nodal point for placing his 'writing
in conjunction with the writing of other writers', is not only a viable
option but truly in the spirit of Emerson's own practice of historical
reenactment.[16]

---

16   Stanley Cavell, *Emerson's Transcendental Etudes*, 'Introduction', pp. 1–9 (p. 5).

Speculative Writing
Unfilmed Scripts and Premediation Events
PABLO GONÇALO

WRITING AS A MEDIUM OF TIME: ARCHIVES BETWEEN FOSSILS AND PROBABILISTIC EVENTS

This essay will investigate some key issues concerning writing: not the act of writing in its traditional meaning, but writing as a technological process in constant change following new standards of tools for expression. Since typewriters and old editing practices have lost their central role, writing has been undergoing fundamental transformations. Less mimetic than before, it has been interacting with alphanumeric codes and has also been dealing directly with potential open futures, rather than with representations of past facts.

From the work of Plato to that of Jacques Derrida, writing has been conceived (or deconstructed) as an act aimed at the representation of past facts and events. It could be constructed as an ideal event based on 'reality', or a gesture that involves metaphysical doubles, voices, and concepts; every future event, in this particular concept and tradition of writing, is related to something created, experienced, or represented in a past time. Even in performing arts such as music and theatre, someone (an 'author') creates an aesthetic environment and lays out plans that will become reality on stages, pages, or screens, realities that generate the outlines of further events. If reenactments produce differences and repetitions, it bears investigating what kind of temporality (as well as subjectivity) an alphanumeric writing paradigm has been conceiving up to this point. If writing is indeed a medium of time, what might be the duration of an alphanumeric reenactment? Is it possible to claim that some of these alphanumeric reenactment events might conceive durations that are beyond the capacity of human subjects experiences?

By proposing the concept of 'speculative writing', a notion that I am still developing, I am dealing directly with a new kind of dramaturgy. It consists of a writing practice that looks at artificial intelligence, chaos, and new relations between subjects and objects as alternative means of creating events and potential infinities in a new and not so clear aesthetic context. These potentialities raise several questions: first, how is writing altered when dealing with ontologically oriented objects, and second, what kind of discontinuity has digital writing been creating?

ALAN TURING AND THE ARCHIVE

Turing's ideal machine has not only altered our relationship with writing but also inaugurated another historical period. Alan Turing believed that a computer could mimic anything that humans have already created, experienced, and even conceived. Therefore, some objects may be able to imitate everything that — and even produce something beyond what — a human has programmed it to imitate. If this claim is correct, it leads us to another issue: can technical objects write? In fact, an alphanumeric representation does duplicate mimesis: humans have become spectators of some mimetic representations that have been performed or even written by computers and softwares. Thus, what would be the difference between human-automatic writing and machine-automatic writing?

Let us look at, for example, Derrida's conception of an 'archive fever' that emphasizes the *arché* as a place and institution that conceives truth, authority, and classical metaphysical processes for the receiving subject.[1] If one looks carefully at the ontology of alpha-

---

1   Jacques Derrida, *Archive Fever: A Freudian Impression*, trans. by Eric Prenowitz (Chicago: University of Chicago Press, 1996).

numeric writing, this archival problem does not match it or fit so precisely. Digital archivals are more like a metaphor for empty and virtual places, for imaginary architectures, than for physical spaces. Even the production processes of mechanical and digital machines are completely different from one another, and such a distinction can illuminate the writing shift that this essay seeks to highlight.[2]

It is through these distinctions pertaining to archivals that we may come closer to a speculative writing historical period. Consider, for example, the concept of *arche-fossil*, proposed by the French philosopher Quentin Meillassoux, which indicates 'the existence of an ancestral reality or event; one that is prior to terrestrial life'.[3] For Meillassoux, the 'arche-fossil' perspective may reveal some event archivals (or archived events) that happen before (and beyond) the human and the subject. They do conceive of a metaphysical event, but it is a strange one, because it reveals a metaphysics without subject. This kind of speculative and material realism is of particular interest to my problem and question, as it is a speculative method in which corelationism is not a key aspect and might even gradually disappear.

When examining Meillassoux's reflections, it is worth considering and developing his distinction between potentialities, virtualities, and actualizations, a process which identifies the core issue with speculation as resting upon the provisional aspect of scientific laws and philosophy's need to deal with probabilistic aberrations. In each of those biases — of chance, potentialities, and virtualities — there is a notable preoccupation with restoring a very specific metaphysics that must refute any totalizing, fixed aspect that is blind to inevitable transformation and mutation processes.

> Potentialities are the non-actualized cases of an indexed set of possibilities under the condition of a given law (whether aleatory or not). Chance is every actualization of a potentiality for which there is no univocal instance of determination on the basis of the initial given conditions [...] and virtuality (is) the property of every set of cases of emerging within a becoming

---

2   Mario Carpo, *The Alphabet and the Algorithm* (Cambridge, MA: MIT Press, 2011), p. 5.

3   Quentin Meillassoux, *Après la finitude. Essai sur la nécessité de la contingence* (Paris: Seuil, 2006), p. 26.

which is not dominated by any pre-constituted totality of possibles.[4]

Therefore, a speculative writing may flirt with those aberrations, by which chance, chaos, virtuality, and potentiality would occur in between subject and object durations. In other words, it points to a temporality of writing as a medium that 'breaks with the fixity of potentialities' and inaugurates other aesthetic durations by which objects might be subjects (and vice-versa), and by which aesthetic (and reenactment) experiences generate events beyond past archival procedures.[5] In the following pages, I investigate some of this temporality's aspects through examination of unfilmed scripts as well as some specific 'premediated events'.

UNFILMED SCRIPTS

Taking into consideration that screenwriting is an ever-changing practice, I want to highlight some aspects of it that make up an alternative approach to film theory, film history, and what has been called 'media archaeology'. The first aspect concerns *unfilmed scripts.* In the course of my doctoral research, I came across several unfilmed scripts that aroused my curiosity. At that time, my genealogical bias favoured writers transitioning from literary writing into properly imagistic writing, and the discovery of these unfilmed scripts sparked a number of questions. For example, was it possible to talk about a negative history of film, a history that did happen but failed to become fully realized? Would not those unfinished strokes by writers and screenwriters from the twentieth century serve as an invitation to conceive of an imaginary history of films that never actually reached the screens? Lastly, what kinds of archivals are unfilmed scripts?

During my research, the most interesting and wide-ranging example of this kind of bias was the French publication *Anthologie du cinéma invisible. 100 scénarios pour 100 ans de cinéma (Anthology of Invisible Cinema: 100 Scripts for 100 Years of Cinema)*, compiled by

---

4   Quentin Meillassoux, 'Potentiality and Virtuality', trans. by Robin Mackay, in *The Speculative Turn: Continental Materialism and Realism*, ed. by Levi Bryant, Nick Srnicek, and Graham Harman (Melbourne: re.press, 2011), pp. 224–36 (pp. 231–32).

5   Ibid., p. 233.

Christian Janicot.[6] Released in 1995, the book is the product of an almost archaeological type of research. Its authors introduce a hundred projects, ideas, and scripts by famous authors, intellectuals, and artists, such as Georges Bataille, Italo Calvino, William Burroughs, Louis-Ferdinand Céline, Max Frisch, Federico García Lorca, André Gide, Allen Ginsberg, Graham Greene, Hugo von Hofmannsthal, Antonin Artaud, Georges Pérec, Stefan Zweig, René Magritte, Antoine de Saint-Exupéry, Vladimir Mayakovsky, and E. E. Cummings, among dozens of other key twentieth-century figures.

Standing as possible movies, the unproduced scripts, more than just hidden archivals, show us how twentieth-century writers and artists imagined and flirted with film. These writers were writing texts that would no longer be restricted to books or the stage; they were intended for a forthcoming screen. Pier Paolo Pasolini defined scripts as texts that do not want to remain texts[7]. I would like to add that scripts might also be paper archivals that would like, someday, to turn into audiovisual archivals. They are situated on a boundary. Unfilmed scripts, however, are very special cases, because they demand time (an interval) before the metamorphosis of the script into film. Unfilmed scripts are archivals that present an incomplete and open ontology, pointing to a sort of speculative archaeology. They are potential films, and they refer to imaginative events that one may never comprehend but only speculate about.

More than claiming a waiting period, unfilmed scripts can really be slotted into a dynamics of undefined and pendulum-like oscillation between potentialities and virtualities. Would the drafted films be, if taken as a whole, possible, virtual, and speculative narratives that failed to transform into the most applicable form of archival (that of film) in the history of cinema? Are they multiple stories, denying the totality of predetermined *possibles*?

If we focus on the archival as open and incomplete, unfilmed scripts reveal an archival that oscillates between a reader and a film

---

6   *Anthologie du cinéma invisible. 100 scénarios pour 100 ans de cinéma*, ed. by Christian Janicot (Paris: Jean-Michel Place, 1995).

7   Pier Paolo Pasolini, 'The Screenplay As a "Structure That Wants to Be Another Structure"', in Pasolini, *Heretical Empiricism*, ed. by Louise K. Barnett, trans. by Ben Lawton and Louise K. Barnett, 2nd edn (Washington, DC: New Academia Publishing, 2005), pp. 187–96 (p.187).

audience, the latter being, of course, absent. In some ways, unfilmed scripts are archivals that approach what Graham Harman calls as an 'ontologically-oriented object', which is something between a real and a sensory object. For Harman, they 'are autonomous forces in the world, existing even if all observers sleep or die', while sensory objects 'exist only insofar as a perceiver is occupied with them. These perceivers need not be human.'[8] Unfilmed or speculative scripts could, one day, be perceived by cameras, screens, or even readers and spectators. As they are incomplete and multi-natural, unfilmed scripts are part image and sensory objects and part potential real objects, so they remain almost fugitive events. Through aesthetic speculation alone, they truly become possible and upcoming events. Consequently, unfilmed scripts reveal certain aspects of writing that have left the mimetic paradigm, that flirt with media technologies and new events by pointing to new archivals. Their incompleteness translates as an open archive that may be the basis of an interaction between human perceivers and machines, the latter of which might in turn, under some circumstances, write.

WHAT MIGHT A SPECULATIVE WRITING BE?

Beyond the challenges that unfilmed scripts face, a speculative writing aims at approaching more precisely the interfaces between literature, narrative, and the dramaturgies of the 1970s onward. On the other hand, its historical, laboratorial, and experimental combinations are now interacting with the extended area of artificial intelligence. It is important to remember here the literary experiments of the Oulipo group, in which Raymond Queneau and Georges Pérec participated, along with a number of other French writers. Additionally, one should also include in this genealogy the first experiments with fictional dialogues between human beings and computers, of meta-novels — in the wake of *Tale-Spin* and the creation of Alternative Reality Games — examined within the scope of transmedia narratives.[9] There are many

---

8   Graham Harman, 'Seventy-Six Theses on Object-Oriented Philosophy', in Harman, *Bells and Whistles: More Speculative Realism* (Winchester: Zero Books, 2013), pp. 60–70 (p. 60).

9   Noah Wardrip-Fruin, *Expressive Processing: Digital Fiction, Computer Games, and Software Studies* (Cambridge, MA: MIT Press, 2011), p. 6.

writers and computer scientists (or artificial intelligence engineers) already treading this path.

In addition, upon carefully looking into an ontological object history, one may include Gilbert Simondon's seminal concepts of the mode of existence of technical objects. For Simondon, a technical object leads directly with three different aspects, such as the element, the individual, and the ensemble.[10] Looking over the relations between writing and artificial intelligence, one may consider how objects interact with human subjects and how this ensemble conceives of a new writing and reading-gaming experience. Therefore, genuine speculative writing opens up an experimental phenomenon that triggers an inversion, where objects offer experience to humans in a random (programmed, but also not controlled) manner.

It is also important to consider Claude Shannon's entropy information theory, which was a pioneering perspective. Shannon argued that compression and coding programs might be aware of the constant probability of information loss and noise. Applying this inversion ensemble to the context of writing, one may also realize that noise and entropy would play a key role between a writing object and a human receiver, gamer, or reader. What escapes in these potential entropies triggers unthinkable events, which are essential to a speculative sublime experience. Therefore, every reenactment of an instance of speculative writing should appear as an entropic aberration: that is, something that was thought of as predetermined but will, however, be revealed to be occurring again, even if it originally seemed that it was happening for the first time.

It is interesting, at this point, to recapture the ontological characteristics of new media as favoured by Lev Manovich in his pioneering book on the subject, which synthetically introduces the concepts of 'numerical representation', 'modularity', 'variability', 'automation', and 'codification'.[11] At first, what stands out is a mode of writing that has more than just the algorithm and the numeric digital fusion as its (im)material basis, as it is also changeable, modular, and extensive.

---

10   Gilbert Simondon, *Du mode d'existence des objets techniques*, 3rd edn (Paris: Aubier, 1989), p. 15.

11   Lev Manovich, *The Language of New Media* (Cambridge, MA: MIT Press, 2002), p. 27.

More than mere imitators and simulators of human behaviour like by-products of Turing's machine, new computational media would engender new products, new grammars with codes and languages that would also generate other interface syntaxes.

Following Manovich, Mario Carpo has claimed that variability has turned into the key element of writing and expressivity of digital tools. This variability conceives of a distinct paradigm, whereby the copying reality ceases to be the main goal of writing and representation. For screenwriting history and practice, for example, digital (and speculative) writing may appear too distant from the blueprint metaphor, which claimed that the film should be a copy of what was written on the script. More recently, scripts have been interacting intimately with edition software, collaborative workers, and animation characters, so they are closer to animation aesthetics and videogame languages than they are to the work of a classic screenwriter, who would be struggling alone with the blank page, his typewriter, and his textbook writers' block:

> Digital technologies inevitably break the indexical chain that, in the mechanical age, linked the matrix to its imprint. Digital photographs are no longer the indexical imprint of light onto a surface; digitally manufactured objects are no longer the indexical imprint of a mold pressed into a metal plate; and digital variability may equally cut loose the indexical link that, under the old authorial paradigm, tied design notations to their material result in an object.[12]

Thus, one could claim that speculative (and aesthetic) writing produces events that appear to happen again, although they have never actually happened. By means of archivals, they point to the return of something that is potential but has never been experienced or even conceived. It is a sort of probabilistic aberration by which human beings remain fragile spectators of creatures that have emerged beyond their dreams, imagination, and even nightmares. So far, speculative writing points to writing and reading practices that are far removed from a mimetic tradition as well as all the anti-mimetic aesthetic experimentations that have taken place over the past century.

---

12   Carpo, *The Alphabet and the Algorithm*, p. 43.

AN ABSTRACT REENACTMENT: SPECULATIVE WRITING AND PREMEDIATED EVENTS

What kind of *scene* could a speculative writing procedure conceive? Though unanswered and still in need of development, this will certainly be a key question for all premediated events, pointing also to what I propose to call an 'abstract reenactment'. Let us look at an example: designed by Daedalic Entertainment, the game *Long Journey Home* conceived of its algorithm based on NASA's map of the universe, which is always expanding and tends to infinity. Because the tale-spinning possibilities are not randomized, every gamer will have a unique and unrepeatable experience, as they do in life. Aligned with other contemporary game designers, a method called procedural generation, which is based on the geometric patterns of fractals, was used to build *Long Journey Home*.[13] These patterns open up new logics and experiences between storytelling, repetition, and differentiation of events. If it faces infinite possibilities, can we still conceive of it as form of reenactment?

An answer to such a complex question may be directly related to premediated events. According to Richard Grusin, premediation leads with a set of possible events. It is connected to the idea of the ubiquity of media and claims that the future is also produced by a previous remediated event. With a focus on political events such as the 2001 terrorist attack on the World Trade Center, Grusin perceived that this event had already been 'premediated' by films, books, and other fictional narratives.[14]

---

13   Richard Cobbett for Daedalic Entertainment, *Long Journey Home* (2017), Microsoft Windows.

14   Richard Grusin, 'Premediation', *Criticism*, 46.1 (Winter 2004), pp. 17–39 (p. 29).

Reenactment in Theatre
Some Reflections on the Philosophical Status of Restaging

DANIELA SACCO

Theatre, because of its ability to represent or present through restaging, would seem to be the quintessential platform for reenactment, which is so widespread recently in a variety of artistic endeavours, especially in the performing arts. Indeed, 'to enact' means 'act out (a role or play) on stage' or 'put into practice': 'to reenact' means the repetition of the acting out.

Since the 1990s, reenactment has moved from the context of historical reconstruction to artistic and curatorial practice. It emancipated itself from the phenomenon of Living History where it functioned as a revival, or as a reenactment, of its historical antecedent. As an art form, it has changed meaning not by strict adherence to the original model but by highlighting its difference while maintaining respect for the original.

As noted by André Lepecki, reenactment as an art form is an interpretative gesture that never produces a real repetition but always an opening of meaning, a variation that denies the action of merely

---

*   A different version of this article has been published in Italian as 'Re-enactment e replica a teatro. Riflessioni sullo statuto filosofico della ri-presentazione', *Materiali di Estetica*, 4.1 (2017), pp. 340–51.

copying.[1] The concept of reenactment enters fully into performative practice when the rule that prevented repetition is disregarded: that is, when the performance, which asked for the absolute authenticity of the *hic et nunc*, has, for example, accepted the practice of preserving and repurposing props, or using the documentation itself as an art form.[2] The most relevant case is the transition that Marina Abramović made from considering 'no rehearsal, no repetition, no predicted end' as the laws of performance to taking the act of reenacting her life and work as the only means of creating distance after her break-up with Ulay, her former partner in art and life.[3] The most mature and well-known outcome of this change in perspective is *Seven Easy Pieces*, a performance in which Abramović reenacted seven famous perform-ances previously realized by her and the precursors of Body Art in the 60s and 70s. Performed in 2005 at the Guggenheim Museum in New York, this reenactment took place over the course of seven days.

Even if the concept of reenactment is tied to performance and is widespread in other artistic fields, precisely because of the great importance that performance art has developed in recent years, a re-flection on the sense of restaging as reenactment can also be made in reference to the most traditional form of theatre. Even though the prin-ciples that support traditional staging differ considerably with respect to the performative event and performance art, and the main objective of performance artists has historically been its difference with respect to theatre, the comparison is enough to observe the mechanism of repetition in theatrical practice itself. This mechanism exists in several forms, not least of which is the repetition of the 'same' theatrical event (at least as intended) in different contexts and times. These attributes of repetition can thus serve to widen the reflection on reenactment to theatre considered in its entirety.

---

1   André Lepecki, 'The Body as Archive: Will to Re-enact and the Afterlives of Dance', *Dance Research Journal*, 42.2 (Winter 2010), pp. 28–48 <https://doi.org/10.1017/S0149767700001029>.

2   Cf. Domenico Quaranta, 'RE:akt! *Things that Happen Twice*', in RE:akt! *Reconstruc-tion, Re-enactment, Re-reporting*, ed. by Antonio Caronia, Janez Janša, and Domenico Quaranta (Brescia: LINK Editions, 2014), pp. 43–52.

3   Ibid.

This can also be observed where the theatrical staging does not make specific use of the medium, the use of which has historically favoured not only the phenomenon of reenactment but also reflection upon it. The use of the theatre medium must, in fact, be considered as a component of the larger whole of the reproductive phenomenon: that is, theatre in itself.[4]

Consequently, one could say that repetition is specific to theatrical art, but, as Antonin Artaud teaches us: 'theatre is the only place in the world where a gesture, once made, can never be made the same way twice.'[5] Theatre resides in the dialectic tension between these two aspects, which are co-present, and it feeds on this paradox. Artaud, who anticipated the principles later embodied by performance speaks in the name of the vital and creative principle he wants recognized in the theatrical medium. It is no coincidence that in France the great theorists of the relationship between identity, difference, and repetition such as Jacques Derrida and Gilles Deleuze, have found in Artaud an important interlocutor. Thus, the reflections that are valid for works in which the reenactment is expressly practiced — as for example, in today's perhaps more recognized and effective case of the staging by Swiss director Milo Rau[6] — can be applied at the same time to works of which we can observe a simple restaging, a simple replication.

A significant example is the restaging of *Orestea (una commedia organica?)* by Romeo Castellucci and Socìetas Raffaello Sanzio on December 2015 in Paris, at the Odéon-Théâtre on the occasion of the

---

4   On this topic, see also Samuel Weber, *Theatricality as Medium* (New York: Fordham University Press, 2004).

5   Antonin Artaud, *The Theater and its Double*, trans. by Mary Caroline Richards (New York: Grove, 1958), p. 75.

6   Here we simply recall Milo Rau's plays: *The Last Days of the Ceausescus* (Teatrul Odeon, Bucharest / HAU Berlin, 2009), *Hate Radio* (Kunsthaus Bregenz / Memorial Centre Kigali / HAU Berlin, 2011), *Brevik's Statement* (Deutsches Nationaltheater Weimar, 2012), the trilogy *The Civil Wars* (Beursschouwburg Brussels / Theaterspektakel Zurich, 2014), *The Dark Ages* (Residenztheater, Munich, 2015), *Empire* (Theaterspektakel Zurich / Schaubühne Berlin, 2016), and *Five Easy Pieces* (Sophiensæle Berlin, 2016); on this theme, see also Priscilla Wind, 'L'art du reenactment chez Milo Rau', *Intermédialités / Intermediality*, 28–29 (2016) <https://doi.org/10.7202/1041080ar>; and Enrico Pastore, 'Intervista a Milo Rau', *PASSPARnous Teatro*, 22 (September 2014) <http://www.psychodreamtheater.org/rivista-passparnous-ndeg-22---teatro---intervista-a-milo-rau---a-cura-di-enrico-pastore.html> [accessed 24 November 2017].

Festival d'Automne, twenty years after the play's 1995 world premiere in Prato, Italy.[7]

In this restaging, the play, at the director's will, remained unchanged. It featured only two of the original actors from the 1995 debut, and the original composer, Scott Gibbons, created new musical tracks, since those from twenty years prior have been lost. The restaging of this work stimulates some observations on the value of the collision of the same form with different historical and cultural contexts, and therefore additional observations on its recontextualization, which always implies new meanings.

With *Orestea (una commedia organica?)*, Castellucci and the company overturn a consolidated interpretation of Aeschylus's work. It is no longer the work that tells of the end of myth and the birth of tragedy, and, with tragedy, the beginning of the heroic path of man in the construction of Western civilization. This previous understanding of civilization was based on the institution of the court — the Areopagus — on the *logos*, the reason of the law, which laid the legal foundation of the city against the violence of personal revenge, the justice of *genos*. The director, instead, construes the *Orestea* as a sign of the defeat of the values that, in the development of Western civilization, are believed to have historically had supremacy. He refuses to conclude the Aeschylean tragedy with the foundation of the judicial system, the institution of a patriarchal and spiritual system destined to win, over the centuries, on the *ius naturale*. For this purpose, Castellucci stages the violence, the life, and the matter, represented by the pre-tragic power of the matriarchal order. He stages this by the presence of heavy female figures and animals: Clytemnestra, Cassandra, and Electra are powerful figures representing the dominant matriarchy. Along with the female presence is also that of the animal, with real horses, donkeys, and monkeys populating the stage.

The pervasive presence of female figures and animals symbolizes the overthrow of a destiny that seems to have marked the development of Western civilization: the Olympians are not gods to win over the previous deities, and it is not the masculine principle that

---

7   See also Daniela Sacco, 'La Jetztzeit del teatro. L'Orestea della Societas Raffaello Sanzio/Romeo Castellucci venti anni dopo', *Biblioteca Teatrale*, 119–120.2 (2016), pp. 65–84 <https://doi.org/10.1400/256739>.

prevails but rather the most archaic Mediterranean worship of the Mother Goddess, who marked the ancient origins of Greek culture. If this interpretation of *Orestea* was radical in 1995, it turned out to be even more so in the Parisian staging of December 2015. Castellucci re-proposes the piece, accepting the invitation that the Festival d'Automne gives to the artist in order to dedicate a portrait — in this case the *Portrait Romeo Castellucci* — to the theme of the tragic.

Not only does the piece remain essentially unchanged, but Castellucci also distances himself from his poetry of twenty years prior. He considers his work a foreign object that no longer belongs to him. He later stated that 'it was like working with ghosts', and he compared the show to a 'stone', found on earth and collected 'as an unknown object', 'made and thrown by an unknown man, a lifetime ago'.[8] In Paris, the work is therefore 'moved' and 'relocated' to another environment, different from Italy, which had welcomed it. It is no longer tied to the reasons that had generated it, not only the need for the company to affirm its poetry against a theatre tied to a repertoire but also its resonance with the corruption of Italian political power and the rampant power of the mafia, which was very strong at the time. In Italy, since 1992, we have witnessed the phenomenon of 'Tangentopoli', a term used to define the widespread system of political corruption and, linked to it, the operation 'Mani pulite' — meaning 'Clean Hands' — to indicate the series of judicial investigations meant to check this corruption. Italy was the theatre of the massacres carried out by mafia terrorism, culminating in the assassinations of Sicilian magistrates Giovanni Falcone and Paolo Borsellino. The work no longer reflects the great distrust of political power and justice, which in the 1990s were revealed to be corrupt, and it no longer resonates, even with the violent power of the mafia that, following the first major anti-corruption trial, responded to the sentences with massacres.

Twenty years later, in Paris, the historical context changed. It was no longer national but international, and the most relevant event was the terrorist attack, which struck the French capital shortly before the staging of the play. On 13 November 2015, Paris was brought to its

---

8   Cf. Romeo Castellucci, 'Il silenzio dell'eroe', interview by Anna Bandettini, *La Repubblica*, 29 September 2016 (my translation).

knees by a series of terrorist attacks claimed by the armed militia of the self-proclaimed Islamic State (IS) in Syria. It was an event that caused disarray, terror, and military repression culminating in the bombing, in support of France, by the United States and Russia of the Syrian cities inflamed by jihadist fury.

In tune with those dramatic Parisian events, the play turned out to be even more effective; it was a representation of tragedy where tragedy had actually taken place. The organizers at the Odéon had to prepare the audience to avoid public alarm: for example, by warning, shortly before the start of the show, that eight loud shots would be heard.

The overturning of the consolidated interpretation of Aeschylus's work by the Socìetas Raffaello Sanzio appears even more poignant. *Orestea* does not represent the birth of Western civilization from the ashes of myth but the persistence of myth and of archaic culture, as well as the possibility, always lying in wait, of its re-emergence in the uncontrolled form of violence. Thus, the idea that man has heroically emancipated himself through his power, for better or for worse, is revealed to be an illusion. Tragedy then clearly shows its origins, which are inseparable from myth, that is, its 'pre-tragic' nature.

In the unrepeatable moment of staging the *Orestea* in Paris, an intersection occurred between what had been — the play staged twenty years before — and the present. This relationship generated a new constellation of meaning. The evidence of this new meaning is favoured by the exceptional nature of the events that have occurred. It is a macroscopic case, but it is always valid for the uniqueness and unrepeatability of the *hic et nunc* which characterizes every theatrical action.

Benjamin's philosophical concept of *Jetztzeit*, as it emerges in his 1940 'Theses on the Philosophy of History', can help elucidate this phenomenon of collision between past and present.[9] The synchrony of the image of the past caught in the instant, namely, the *Zeit*, is the time that is given in the *Jetzt*, the 'now'. The *Jetztzeit* clarifies that it is always the urgent priority of the present to appropriate the past in

---

9   Walter Benjamin, 'On the Concept of History', trans. by Harry Zohn, in Benjamin, *Selected Writings*, 4 vols (Cambridge, MA: Harvard University Press, 1996–2003), IV: *1938–1940*, ed. by Howard Eiland and Michael W. Jennings (2003), pp. 389–400 (pp. 396–97).

order to re-interpret it. It is precisely the need, the current necessity, and above all, Benjamin warns us, the danger, that dictates the sense of its appropriation. As appropriation will inevitably determine its transformation, the past does not come back as an unalterable datum but is accepted in the new sense that the present attributes to it. Therefore, every appropriation is significant in an unprecedented way. This collision between past and present creates an event, with the novelty of a form identical to the past but in relation to 'the now', which has the originality of an occurrence.

We can observe the same mechanism in the act of quotation: a text unchanged is extracted from a context of origin and relocated, through montage, into a new context. Relocation is always a source of transformation of the original meaning of the quoted text. The same thing could also be noted regarding the operation of translation, where between the original and translated versions there is never a relationship of faithful reproduction but, as Benjamin called it, a 'relationship of life'.[10] It is a relationship that always requires a dialectical polarity of the translation compared to the original, where the tension and the difference are played out with respect to the original. On the other hand, reenactment can be thought of as a form of quotation; it is comparable to an act of appropriation. As Domenico Quaranta observes in the context of performance art, 'art is always a linguistic fact, even when it turns into an event', and the event, once transformed into a fetish, 'becomes an object to be found in the sea magnum of cultural chaos'.[11] Quotation, moreover, goes hand in hand with the act of repetition; that is, we repeat what is quotable.

Benjamin understands the particular value of quotation and repetition in the context of Bertolt Brecht's epic theatre, confirming that theatre is the ideal place to observe the mechanism of repetition. As Samuel Weber observed, Benjamin notes the value of repetition in the text he dedicates to Brecht's epic theatre more than in any other writings.[12] Benjamin understands that what is quoted on the stage of epic

---

10   Cf. Walter Benjamin, 'The Task of the Translator', trans. by Harry Zohn, in Benjamin, *Selected Writings*, I: *1913–1926*, ed. by Marcus Bullock and Michael W. Jennings (1996), pp. 253–63.

11   Quaranta, 'RE:akt! Things that Happen Twice', p. 47.

12   Samuel Weber, *Benjamin's -abilities* (Cambridge, MA: Harvard University Press, 2008), pp. 95–96; see also Weber, *Theatricality as Medium*.

theatre happens first through gesture, or *gestus* as Brecht sometimes called it, using a German term with Latin origins. The gesture — that is, as Brecht intends it, the 'overall attitude' (*Gesamthaltung*) assumed in front of other people, therefore, the socially connoted act — turns out to be the oxymoronic core of the relationship between identity, difference, repetition, translatability, and untranslatability which quotation reveals. *Haltung,* in fact, is the German word for both 'attitude' and 'posture', which Brecht uses in combination with *gestus.*

The gesture — the performative act par excellence — becomes quotable through the estrangement technique (*Verfremdungstechnik*), because of the interruption that is created with respect to the flow of action and the context in which it originally belongs. According to Benjamin, interruption is one of the 'fundamental methods of all form-giving';[13] it is the same concept put forth by Artaud when he states that the actor 'does not make the same gestures twice, but he makes gestures, he moves; and although he brutalizes forms, nevertheless behind them and through their destruction he rejoins that which outlives forms and produces their continuation'.[14] Artaud states that 'to break through language in order to touch life is to create or recreate the theatre'.[15] His observations confirm the relationship of this kind of performance to life, the vital principle that lies in the revolutionary act of destroying a traditional form and relating the original to the destroyed tradition, a relationship also present in the work of Benjamin.

On the other hand, the vital mechanism of continuation, of the survival of forms through their betrayal and destruction, is also a theme addressed by Aby Warburg, who coined the terms *Pathosformel* and *Nachleben.*

The Brechtian *gestus* could enucleate the concept of *Pathosformel* coined by Warburg. *Pathosformeln,* or *pathos formulae,* which by their nature consist of a durable element — the *Formel* — and a malleable element — the *Pathos* — are energy vehicles of ancient forms, which change in relation to their function in different historical contexts.

---

13   Cf. Walter Benjamin, 'What Is Epic Theatre? [First version]' and 'What Is Epic Theatre? [Second Version]', in Benjamin, *Understanding Brecht,* trans. by Anna Bostock, intro. by Stanley Mitchell (London: Verso, 1998), pp. 1–22.

14   Artaud, *Theater and its Double,* p. 12.

15   Ibid., p. 13.

Pathosformeln do not remain identical to themselves but are transformed in transmission. Only the contact with 'the selective will of an age',[16] which welcomes the formulae through the creative act of the artist, causes them to polarize and transform, to imply a radical inversion of meaning. It is the contact, the new relationship created between the two elements in question, which makes the difference and determines the content of the object, rather than any alleged objectivity or substantiality in itself. This contact guarantees the invariance of the content: the original. Instead, the invariant is the relationship, the contact.

Furthermore, the survival of the *Pathosformeln* in this relationship of repetition and variation gives life to the *Nachleben* — another functional concept of Warburg —, which refers to the posthumous life of motifs, of images of art that maintain a relationship with the originals as if they were echoing them. From this perspective, a Warburgian idea of memory emerges as a reenactment. In the same way, for Castellucci's *Orestea* it is the contact with the new historical context in which it is located that determines its re-semantization.

In every repetition, there is a tearing away from the original and the creation of the new at the time of its reproduction; this is a contrastive mechanism that pertains to the theatre. The distancing from a form — which is intended to be an emotional control — is followed by a creative principle, which is a reinstatement into the *pathos* of a form. This reinstatement, in turn, implies its re-appropriation. On the other hand, emotional control is a fundamental aspect observed in the context of psychoanalysis by Freud in the mechanism of 'repetition compulsion', which is also a reflection on repetition and reconstruction.[17]

Milo Rau, expressly using reenactment, states that 'theatre is something that starts all over again every day. It's terrifying but at the same time it's something that awakens you', because it demands that performers 'face each other everyday with something new and different', and the actors act in a different way every evening.[18]

---

16   Aby Warburg, 'Grundbegriffe, I, Notizbuch, 1929' (p. 26), quoted in Ernst Gombrich, *Aby Warburg: An Intellectual Biography* (London: Warburg Institute, 1970), p. 249.

17   Cf. Sigmund Freud, *Beyond the Pleasure Principle*, trans. by James Strachey (New York: Liveright, 1989).

18   Enrico Pastore, 'Intervista a Milo Rau'.

What makes repetition so crucial in theatre, distinguishing it from other forms of art, is presence, including the physical presence of the actor, the spectator, and the communication that such interrelationship implies. Presence is the condition of the relationship, of the contact from which a change of meaning always arises. And the gesture is the embodiment of presence.

For this reason, gesture is a sign of presence as well as a quotable act. The presence, the actuality of the contact that is given in the symbolic relationship of the theatrical medium is the guarantor of a vital relationship that determines form and content of the work of art, always an event loaded with novelty.

According to Amelia Jones, the true event is presence; it is the 're-iteration as the presence that can never be full in/to itself'.[19] Or rather, it is the meaning of presence that the French philosopher François Jullien explored in relation to theatre. In his opinion, Greek theatre was invented as a repository to save presence from corruption, to restore presence to its purity by preserving it in its intensity. The stage is the place of presence: the place where, in the alternation between entering and leaving the scene, presence is torn from loss, from opacity, from the excess of reality from which it is destined to be returned instead to transparency. Theatre realizes and authenticates presence 'through its flaunted unreality, to experiment again (artificially) that a presence is (indeed) possible; to cleanse and purge the ordinary presence through the organized semblance of theatre, freeing it from sinking into the realism that it itself produces'.[20]

Theatre thus acts as a filter in the relationship between scene and audience, to purify the presence and subtract it from opacity. This is the contribution of theatrical mimesis, which has little to do with reproduction or mere copying. Instead, it has to do with the paradox of the mingling of both presence and absence, which theatre, as an ephemeral art, is able to express.

---

19   Cf. Amelia Jones, 'The Artist Is Present: Artistic Re-enactments and the Impossibility of Presence', *TDR: The Drama Review*, 55.1 (Spring 2011), pp. 16–45 (p. 34).

20   François Jullien, *Près d'elle. Présence opaque, présence intime* (Paris: Galilée, 2016), p. 44 (my translation).

Re-search, Re-enactment, Re-design, Re-programmed Art

SERENA CANGIANO, DAVIDE FORNARI, AND AZALEA SERATONI

At the end of the 1950s, Bruno Munari and Umberto Eco both worked for the Italian publishing house Bompiani. Munari had just shown *Direct and Polarized Light Projections* at the Museum of Modern Art in New York, and his *Travelling Sculpture* at Bruno Danese Gallery in Milan. Thus, he was investigating the dematerialization of the artwork as well as its portability, thinking about artefacts that speculate on multiplication rather than authorial action without foreseeing the geo-political and geo-cultural expansion of our hypermodernity — or perhaps just anticipation of what would have happened later on. Eco had not yet become the acclaimed author of *The Name of the Rose* (1980) and other successful novels. He had not yet written his crucial text, *The Open Work* (1962). He was the pre-semiotic Eco, once defined as 'an aesthetician with antennas'.[1] He was then working at the national radio and television public broadcasting network in Milan. Situated on the second floor, his office was the studio of musical phonology, directed by Luciano Berio and Bruno Maderna, the two pioneering inventors of electronic music.

---

1   Giovanni Anceschi, 'How Programmed Art Was Born', in *Arte riprogrammata. Un manifesto aperto. Reprogrammed Art: An Open Manifesto*, ed. by Serena Cangiano, Davide Fornari, and Azalea Seratoni (Milan: Johan and Levi, 2015), pp. 74–79 (p. 77).

Together with Munari, Eco was curating the editorial contents of *Almanacco Letterario Bompiani*, an annual publication dedicated to what was considered a crucial and future-oriented issue. The name 'Arte Programmata' (Programmed Art) was coined on this occasion. The expression appears in the table of contents on page 3, and it was used to define a group of works, of 'drawings and paintings', as specified below, by Giovanni Anceschi, Davide Boriani, Enrico Castellani, Gianni Colombo, Gabriele Devecchi, Karl Gerstner, Enzo Mari, Munari, Dieter Roth, Jesús Rafael Soto, and Grazia Varisco. However, they were not really drawings and paintings.

The *Almanacco*, published in 1962 but edited already in 1961, was titled 'Applications of Calculators to Moral Sciences and Literature'. The terminology sounds rather clumsy and antiquated. The words that are now so necessary for describing the contemporary age — 'computer', 'digital', 'virtual' — were quite out of the remit of the common lexicon of the early 1960s. The title appeared on the cover designed by Munari, who was in charge of the graphic design for the entire publication. In the background, there is a coloured photo provided by IBM — who, together with Olivetti, gave their support for this initiative — between a stripe of perforated cards and an artwork by Colombo: a programmed graphic.

Colombo, together with Anceschi, Boriani, and Devecchi, had founded Gruppo T just three years prior: Varisco joined the group immediately after. Indeed, the works by Gruppo T, among the other authors involved in this publication, are those waiting for the technology to mature to be implemented.

While Eco was gathering the content for *Almanacco*, he turned to Munari and said: 'For literature, we're good: there is *Tape Mark One*, the electronic poem invented by Nanni Balestrini. But for the arts, we've got nothing.' To which Munari is said to have replied: 'Look, I've just met a group of young artists, Gruppo T, that I think are on-the-ball and available. Let's try asking them.'[2] This led to a meeting where the proposal was put forward to create works 'built according to cybernetic criteria.'[3]

---

2   Ibid., p. 75.

3   Davide Boriani and Giovanni Anceschi's oral testimony, given to the authors.

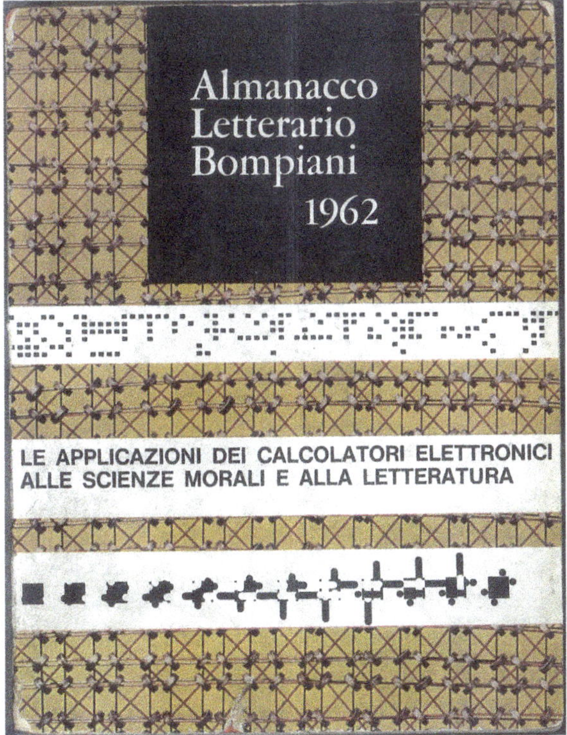

Figure 1. Cover of Almanacco Letterario Bompiani, 1962.
From Giovanni Anceschi Archive.

In other words, the idea of programmed graphics was, so to speak, 'commissioned' by Munari and Eco for the members of Gruppo T to execute. The idea was then presented on the pages of the *Almanacco*, accompanied by an extraordinary essay by Eco called 'The Form of Disorder'.

Munari and Gruppo T had met just before the exhibition 'Miriorama 1' (1960). The story of this first exhibition by Gruppo T deserves a retelling, since it is not yet considered as paradigmatic in the history of twentieth-century art exhibitions as it should truly be. First of all, the name 'miriorama' means 'infinite visions' (from the Greek *orao*, 'see', and *myrio*, which means 'ten thousand', that is, a virtually infinite amount). Moreover, 'miriorama' also refers to an optical toy that was quite popular in the nineteenth century, involving the display and rearranging of a set of illustrated cards depicting, for example, a landscape. 'Miriorama 1' would be the first 'manifestation' — a term that the artists preferred to 'exhibition' — in a series of such events numbered from 1 to 14, in order to stress the continuity of this collective program that would orient their artistic efforts for several years. The fourteen 'Miriorama' exhibitions were accompanied by graphically impeccable catalogues, more like a series of published books, with essays by Munari, Lucio Fontana, and Shuzo Takiguchi (one of Japan's leading cultural figures, who had introduced Surrealism to Japan), a combinatory poem by Nanni Balestrini, and, naturally enough, writings by the artists themselves.

'Miriorama 1' was a group show and consisted of four highly experimental works by Gruppo T. *Pittura in fumo* was a transparent display board on which an image produced by carbon dioxide fumes was altered by puffs of air. *Superficie in ossidazione* consisted of a copper surface on which haloes of variable colours appeared, due to the polarization caused by a heat source. *Superficie in combustione* involved an electric burner at the back of the work, which heated a sheet of polyethylene with a geometric grid printed on it; the sheet gradually became deformed, and an ulceration formed on the surface. Under the effect of the heat, the plastic melted and then started to burn, until the work literally fell apart. Gruppo T members enjoyed telling the joke that the work had gone from Vasarely to Burri. Lastly, *Ambiente a volume variabile*, nicknamed '*Grande oggetto pneumatico*' by Munari, consisted of seven pipes made of transparent plastic, forty centimetres in diameter and six to eight meters long, which, jerking into action due to the compressed air inside them, expanded into the environment, arranging themselves into different patterns. Air was alternately pumped into the pipes and sucked out, making them jerk forward or recoil and forcing the audience out of the room. *Ambiente a volume variabile*, designed and mounted between late 1959 and early 1960, and frequently restaged, was Gruppo T's first environment.

The artists' research on environment, through which they developed and matured the ideas found in their initial works, would resume in 1964, when a new form of collaboration was launched that would commit two or three of the artists in the group at a time to a specific project. The formula would persist even after 1968, the final year that the group produced a collective artwork, their *Percorso dinamico ad ostacoli programmati*, in Grenoble.

The four works by Gruppo T constituted the second part of the exhibition. The first part consisted of texts, reproduced images, and original works by those artists whom the group considered their precursors, forming a virtual genealogy of the topic of time in contemporary art: a kind of essay in images.

The words of this essay were taken from the writings of historic avant-garde manifestoes (by the likes of Paul Klee, Wassily Kandinsky, Umberto Boccioni, Lucio Fontana, Giacomo Balla, and Fortunato Depero), while the images were borrowed from artists who were para-kinetic or proto-kinetic, such as Alexander Calder, Constantin Brancusi, Naum Gabo, Nikolaus Pevsner, and Marcel Duchamp. This theoretical and critical background was rounded out by the original works of friends of the group, all of which hinged on the notion of time: *Concetto spaziale* by Fontana (the 'gestural time' of execution), *Meta-Malevich* by Jean Tinguely (time being mechanically modified), *Specchio rotto* by Enrico Baj (the time represented by the viewer's interaction), *Linea* by Piero Manzoni (time frozen in the concept), and lastly, *Macchina inutile* by Munari ('varying spaces in time'). For this initial part of the exhibition, the members of the group seemed to wear two hats: that of the artist and that of an eclectic figure who acted as critic, theoretician, cultural organizer, and curator all at once. An artist who was first and foremost an intellectual.

At that time, the members of Gruppo T were not personally acquainted with Munari, and they went to his studio to borrow his *Macchina Inutile* for 'Miriorama 1'. He was pleased to lend the work and found out only during the opening of the exhibition that he was a role model for these artists. From that day on, Munari's collaboration and friendship with Gruppo T grew stronger and resulted in many collaborative exhibitions, up until the show 'Arte Programmata', which featured works by Enzo Mari, Gruppo T, Gruppo N, and Munari himself, and was organized at the Olivetti showroom in Milan in 1962.

As Eco wrote in the catalogue, 'it takes years to understand the significance of an event, it is all part of the logic of history. Time itself creates its own legends and perspective is what sharpens the outlines

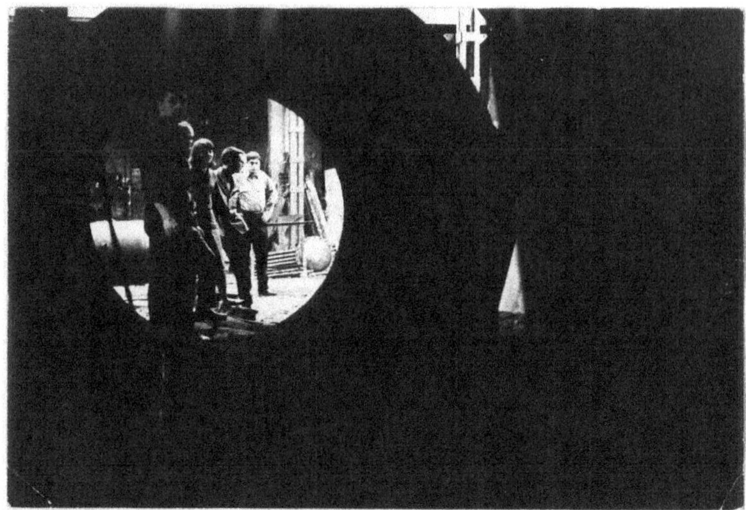

Figure 2. Gruppo T at work in Varisco's workshop, Milan 1962.
Courtesy of Grazia Varisco Archive.

of things and takes their measures.'[4] To understand why Gruppo T was
ahead of its time, we have had to wait for the advent of the IT revolution
and the emergence of concepts such as immersivity and interaction, as
well as the use of increasingly refined technologies by artists. In this day
and age, it is the very notion of time that has become urgent. After all,
it is clear how difficult it must have been for contemporary audiences
to read, understand, and accept Gruppo T. Gruppo T had set itself up
as an entity that superseded the romantic idea of the individual artist
who acts alone. Instead, Gruppo T's behavioural model was more akin
to that of scientists carrying out research projects: sharing the results
with the public but responsibly acknowledging its role.

Gruppo T offered artworks to the audience that moved, works
that represented the continuous flow of the world. We can define these
works as fields of happenings. They rejected the passivity of contemplation in favour of active participation by the viewer; for example,
in *Scultura da prendere a calci* by Gabriele Devecchi (1959), several
modules of synthetic sponges, which formed a regular square shape,

---

4   Umberto Eco and Bruno Munari, *Arte programmata. Arte cinetica. Opere moltiplicate.*
       Opera aperta (Milan: Officina d'Arte Grafica Lucini, 1962), p. 5.

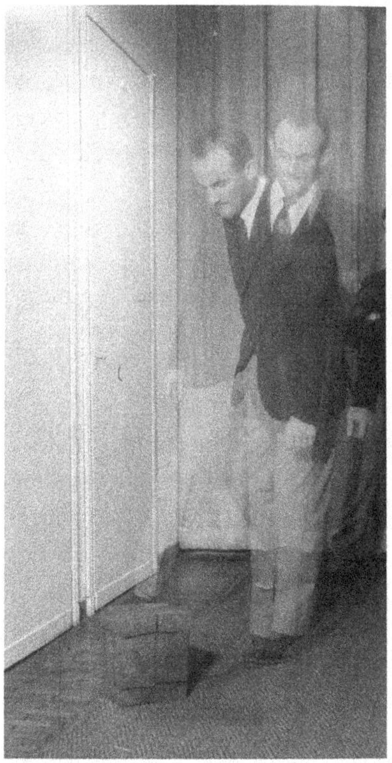

Figure 3. Gabriele Devecchi and *Scultura da prendere a calci*, 1959.
Courtesy of Gabriele Devecchi Archive.

were connected to each other and a base by elastic bands. They could be kicked at so that they broke up in the air and composed an unpredictable new plastic configuration in a different spatial arrangement: a sculpture that was not meant for contemplation by any means. Instead, its distinctive aesthetic features were the interaction with the body of the beholder and the fate of being worn out over time by usage.

At the time, it was difficult to accept an aesthetic activity that urged the viewer to 'move, touch and feel'. Gruppo T said, 'We shall shape the viewer along with the work.'[5] The group championed the production of

---

5   Preliminary manuscript version of *Dichiarazione Miriorama 1* (Miriorama 1 Declaration), Archivio Giovanni Anceschi, Milano.

artworks that triggered the experience of the audience, using devices that involved their bodies and their behaviour. The group's enthusiasm for technology was ironic and provocative. It was instrumental in achieving the effect they sought: in reminiscence of Baroque Art, a sort of enchantment in front of an unexpected phenomenon that endlessly regenerated itself.

Their artworks were designed to be serially produced. Their oeuvre was light years away from the commodity fetishism of the art market. The idea underlying their work was that these were objects that anyone should be able to construct and reproduce at any time. Gruppo T imagined 'aesthetic creations that anybody could build'.[6] One particular episode exemplifies this concept: when Anceschi saw Colombo's *0 ↔ 220 Volt* for the first time — an extraordinary work made of two opaque incandescent light bulbs, of which the brightness is steadily alternated from a minimum to maximum intensity to create a sort of continuous counterpoint — it was love at first sight and he begged Colombo to give one to him, to which Colombo replied: 'Make it yourself!'[7]

As it turned out, Gruppo T was written out of the official history of art until the dawn of the new millennium. It is only now that an international cultural reappraisal is taking place and Gruppo T is being rediscovered, as is Programmed and Kinetic Art in general, and the debt of the present-day art scene to these precursors is being acknowledged. It is not only the art world that has sought out the group after such a long time. Our own mobile, hyper-connected reality, variable and metamorphic as it is, has rediscovered them. The reappraisal of the art and these artists who used words like 'time-space', 'becoming', 'relation', 'variation', and 'participation' as part of their 1960s vocabulary can also be explained by the emergence of a new art and design scene that was born with these same concepts in mind. Precisely in this erratic temporality that complicates linear and teleological models, we can include 'Reprogrammed Art: An Open Manifesto'.[8] In this case,

---

6   Gabriele Devecchi, *A proposito delle ipotesi Miriorama, Arte programmata e cinetica 1953/1963. L'ultima avanguardia*, ed. by Vergine Lea (Milan: Mazzotta, 1983), p. 168.

7   All quotations by Giovanni Anceschi from conversations with the present authors.

8   'Re-programmed Art: An Open Manifesto' is a project coordinated by Serena Cangiano and Davide Fornari, with the collaboration of Azalea Seratoni, promoted by the

the 're' of the title does not indicate a repetition but a form of return that interweaves materials from different disciplines, including design, art history, and interaction design. The conceptual framework evolves around words such as 'interaction', 'reproducibility', 'memory', 'multiplication', 'reflection', 'reenactment', 'conservation', 'action-research', and 'open source technologies'.

The group of artists and designers involved in the project had the task of reprogramming a number of works by Gruppo T. The concept of 'reprogramming' is about more than just reconstructing the original works, understanding how they were made, and mastering the algorithms used to incorporate an element of chance. It means bringing them to life again, using new materials and technology. Starting from the works of Gruppo T, new open artworks were realized, new prototypes of kinetic and programmed works inspired by their creations. These new artefacts would translate the main principles of Programmed Art into the codes of contemporary culture, following the tenets of peer production, namely open source hardware, software, and digital fabrication technologies. They can now be reproduced, expanded on, and completed by other users.

The project 'Re-programmed Art: An Open Manifesto' was originated exactly from the idea that art can be interactive, shared, and reproduced, as well as from the ephemeral and experimental features and the fragility of the works by Gruppo T. They cannot be photographically reproduced in their becoming. Their fragility is constantly disclosed by the failure of mechanisms. The artists were forced to narrate, to describe the effects that they would have shown if the mechanisms had worked.

Laboratory of visual culture of SUPSI – University of Applied Sciences and Arts of Southern Switzerland, in partnership with Museo Alessi, Archivio Gabriele Devecchi, Archivio Gianni Colombo, Arduino, ECAV – Ecole cantonale d'art du Valais, SGMK – Swiss Mechatronic Art Society, and WeMake. The project was developed in the context of 'Viavai – Contrabbando culturale Svizzera-Lombardia', a program of binational exchanges promoted by the Swiss Arts Council Pro Helvetia and realized in partnership with the Cantons Ticino and Wallis, the City of Zurich, and the Ernst Göhner Foundation, and under the patronage of the Arts Councillorships of the Region Lombardy and of the Municipality of Milan. The project is supported by Migros Culture Percentage.The entire project is documented at <http://www.reprogrammed-art.cc> [accessed 20 November 2020] and through *Arte riprogrammata. Un manifesto aperto. Reprogrammed Art: An Open Manifesto*, ed. by Serena Cangiano, Davide Fornari, and Azalea Seratoni (Milan: Johan and Levi, 2015).

By thinking about the difficulties in practice, conservation, technology, and market, which confined Gruppo T for far too long to the margins of mainstream art history, and through the methodological tool of reenactment, 'Re-programmed Art: An Open Manifesto' elaborates on a crucial episode of the twentieth-century history of art.

The project proposed not only a *re*-staging or a superficial *re*-construction, but a *re*-design, *re*-thinking and *re*-programming of the experience of Gruppo T, which seemed outside the bounds of any pre-existing scheme and any possible definition, because of the group's remarkable foresight in deliberately choosing to operate on this particular and difficult frontier between art, science, and design.

In the Beginning There Is an End
Approaching Gina Pane, Approaching
Discours mou et mat

MALIN ARNELL

The lecture room at ICI Berlin is darkened. I place myself with a microphone on a stand behind the seated audience. I read the text below from an iPad. On the large screen in front of us, a fifteen-minute long excerpt from the documentation of my action *Reflect Soft Matte Discourse* (2011)[1] is projected parallel to the documentation of the French-Italian artist Gina Pane's (1939–1990) action *Discours mou et mat* (1975).[2]

> Here I am — Now — And then
> In front of you
> Within History

---

1   The action *Reflect Soft Matte Discourse* was performed together with Clara López Menéndez, who featured as 'the body of an unknown woman' listed in the score, and Ulrika Gomm, who documented the action with a video camera. The action was part of 'LIKA — A Performance Evening' at KAMARADER, Stockholm on 24 May 2011.

2   This text is an excerpt from a longer script, which was part of the performance lecture *AFTER, REHEARSAL AFTER*, first performed as a praxis session during the conference 'PSi19: Now Then: Performance and Temporality!', 26 to 30 June 2013, Stanford University, Stanford, CA., and which later became part of my dissertation 'Avhandling / Av handling (Dissertation / Through_action, 2016)' at Stockholm University of the Arts/Lunds University <http://dissertationthroughaction.space/avhandlingav_handling-dissertationthrough_action/after-rehearsal-after-4/> [accessed 20 February 2021].

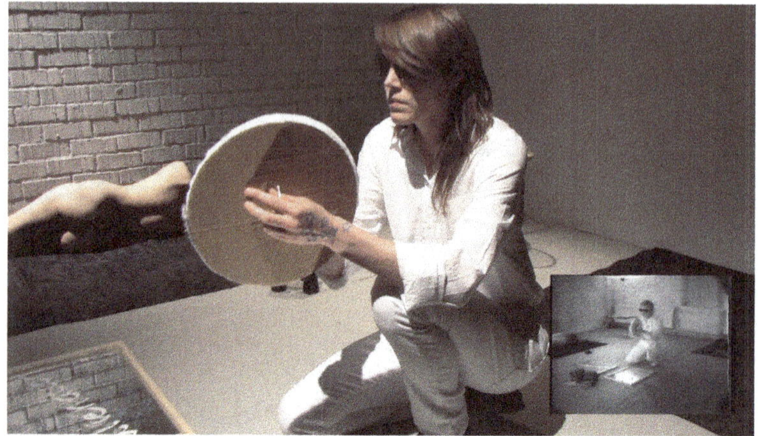

Figure 1. Malin Arnell, still from video documentation of *Reflect Soft Matte Discourse*, 2011, combined with a video still from Gina Pane's performance *Discours mou et mat*, 1975. Courtesy of the artist and of the Galerie Kamel Mennour, Paris.

Over time — In time — Right here
Colliding
In love — By love and uncertainties

With documentations
Others and mine
Ours
Together
In Difference

Action — Enacted — Re-enacted — Later rehearsed.

(This is what I desire.)
We ask: 'Is your body mine?'[3]

She said: 'This is a mobilization of aesthetics against anaesthesia.'

'I am the others.'[4]

On 28 June 1975, Gina Pane performed the action *Discours mou et mat* (*Soft Matte Discourse*) at De Appel in Amsterdam. Following her

---

3   Gina Pane, *Lettre à un(e) inconnu(e)*, ed. by Blandine Chavanne, Anne Marchand, and Julia Hountou (Paris: École nationale supérieure des beaux-arts, 2004), p. 85: 'ton corps est-il le mien?'. Quoted and translated in Frédérique Baumgartner, 'Reviving the Collective Body: Gina Pane's *Escalade Non Anesthésiée*', *Oxford Art Journal*, 34.2 (June 2011), pp. 247–63 (p. 258).

4   Ibid. p.85: 'Je suis les autres'.

instructions, I realized the action *Reflect Soft Matte Discourse* in May 2011 in Stockholm.[5]

> In the beginning there is an end.
> Slipping between position of power and passivity, between control and subservience.
>
> Back to the fall of 2010.
> *This is a beginning.*

I had the film documentation of *Discours mou et mat* sent to me as a DVD.[6] I played it on my computer: twenty-two minutes and thirty-four seconds. I had help in translating the words spoken, but not clearly audible, in the action: *Te Souviens-tu des seins de ta mère?* In English: *Do you remember your mother's breasts?* And the response: *Yes, they were soft and matte as snow.* Up to this point, I had not been aware that the action contained a dialogue about the mother, that the mother was present in the action, that the naked body could be understood as the mother. I hadn't known and I really didn't want to know. It was important to me not to know. I didn't want to know about Gina Pane's relationship to the various objects or to the different activities. I wanted to learn, to learn by doing, by putting *Discours mou et mat* into motion, by putting my body into dialogue with the objects and activities of which *Discours mou et mat* is composed. I wanted to be able to relate to and understand *Discours mou et mat* through a physical interaction with the materials. I wanted to use *Discours mou et mat* to allow the pain, the wound, to take its place.

There is a distinct difference between my body here and now in this room (or then and there in 2011) and Gina Pane's body in Amsterdam in 1975. There are similarities.

I imagine a lesbian continuum or a continuum of homosocial desire. My body. Gina Pane's body. The lesbian body. Gina Pane firmly

---

5   The action *Reflect Soft Matte Discourse* was performed together with Clara López Menéndez, who performed as 'the body of an unknown woman' listed in the score, and Ulrika Gomm, who documented the action with a video camera. Duration: 58 minutes. The action was part of 'LIKA – a performance evening' at KAMARADE, Stockholm on 24 May 2011.

6   From The Netherlands Media Art Institute. Gina Pane, *Discours mou et mat*, 1975, videorecording, 22:32 min, available from LIMA, the international platform for sustainable access to media art <http://www.li-ma.nl/site/catalogue/art/gina-pane/discours-mou-et-mat/2848> [accessed 2 February 2020].

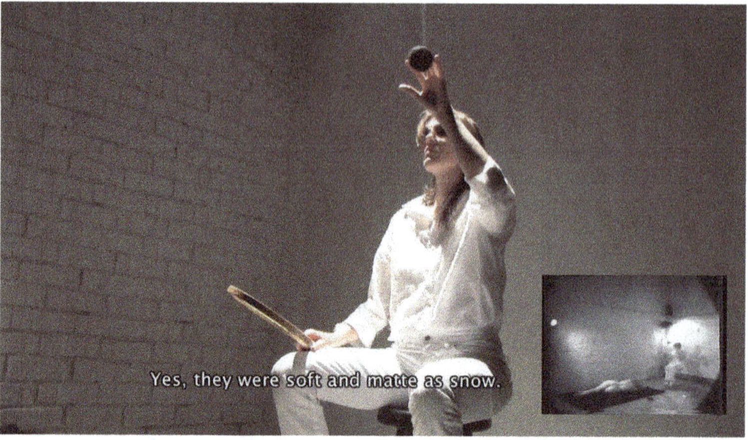

Figure 2. Malin Arnell, still from video documentation of *Reflect Soft Matte Discourse*, 2011, combined with a video still from Gina Pane's performance *Discours mou et mat*, 1975. Courtesy of the artist and the Galerie Kamel Mennour, Paris.

asserted that her attitude was 'absolutely not autobiographical'.[7] By using Gina Pane's instructions, I am firmly asserting that my attitude is autobiographical (but not authentic). Is that possible?

I follow the score to create experience through my body, along with an audience in a given place in a limited time span. Not to put forward the truth concerning *Discours mou et mat*, but instead in an attempt to take responsibility for what I do not know through doing, through action, through performance.

'I lose my identity to find it again in others, back and forth, balance between the individual and the collective, the transindividual body,' Gina Pane writes.[8]

THIS IS A MUTUAL ACT

There are different versions of the score for *Discours mou et mat*. I will now read the one available in the archive of De Appel in Amsterdam:

---

7   Pane, *Lettre à un(e) inconnu(e)*, p. 40: 'Attitude absolument pas autobiographie'. Quoted and translated in Baumgartner, 'Reviving the Collective Body', p. 263.

8   Pane, *Lettre à un(e) inconnu(e)*, p. 40: 'Je perds mon identité en la retrouvant chez les autres, va-et-vient, équilibre de l'individuel et collectif, le corps transindividuel.'

In order to enter the performance space, visitors first had to sidestep a motorcycle that blocked the entrance. In the room, several objects had been placed as the scenery of the forthcoming performance: a safety helmet, boxing gloves, knuckledusters, a gold-painted golf ball and razor blade, red and white roses, plus a naked woman whose back had been decorated with blue stars.[9]

The first scene lasted fifteen minutes. Pane entered the performance space, dressed in white pants, a white blouse, and high heels of the same colour. She wore sunglasses and had drawn blue stars on her left arm and hand. On the floor had been placed two mirrors, with sheets of glass on top. On the right mirror (from Pane's point of view), stars had been drawn, and the word 'aliénation' had been written on the glass. The left mirror was blank, but on the sheet of glass on top, the portrait of a person wearing shades had been drawn. The sunglasses reflected a mill and a field of tulips. Pane kneeled down behind the mirrors and played two cymbals of cardboard, with cotton wool on the insides. After this silent concert several slides were projected.

During the second scene of five minutes, Pane smashed the sheets of glass with her fists.

The next ten minutes Pane sat down on a stool, playing tennis with a ball that hung from the ceiling. She hit the ball with a racket and stopped it with her forehead.

During the fourth scene, Pane crawled to the shattered sheets of glass to hit them once again, meanwhile gasping into a microphone.

For scene five, that also took ten minutes, Pane cut a vertical incision in her upper and under lip with a razor blade.

During the final scene, Pane laid down next to the naked woman and looked at the ceiling through binoculars. Meanwhile music by Brahms was played in slow-motion and some slides were shown.

There is also a clear difference between the political situations in Paris and Amsterdam in 1975 and the one in Stockholm in 2011. During the thirty-nine years that have passed since *Discours mou et mat* was performed, any number of political battles have been fought. Some of them are familiar, and some are not, probably different for all of us.

---

9   Gina Pane, *Discours mou et mat*, performance, Brouwersgracht, 28 June to 17 July 1975 <https://deappel.nl/en/events/gina-pane-discours-mou-et-mat> [accessed: 2 February 2020].

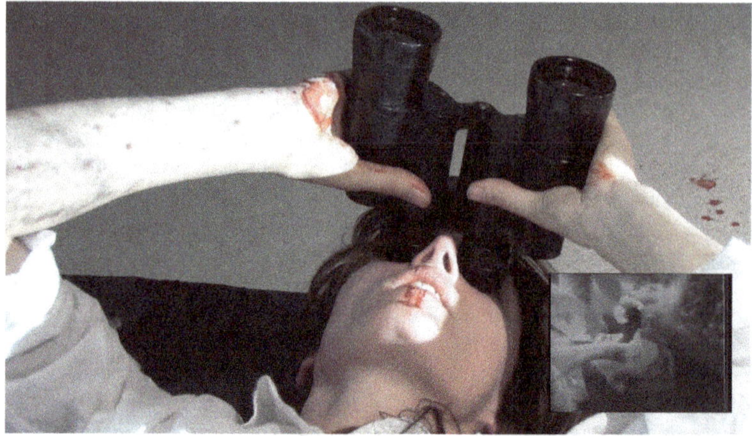

Figure 3. Malin Arnell, still from video documentation of *Reflect Soft Matte Discourse*, 2011, combined with a video still from Gina Pane's performance *Discours mou et mat*, 1975. Courtesy of the artist and the Galerie Kamel Mennour, Paris.

Then, in 1975: I was five years old. I was hiding in the woods, making up my own reality. Out there was the New Left, the Black Power movement, the war in Vietnam, the African independence movements, gay liberation movement, the situationist movement, the May 1968 revolt in Paris, the French structuralist feminism movement. Monique Wittig published *Les Guérillères and Le Corps Lesbien* (translated as *The Lesbian Body*).

Now: I have nowhere to hide. It's all around. It's inside. The inexorable growth of financial neoliberalism and concentration of wealth in fewer hands, the war on terror, the environmental catastrophe, the struggle to get through pessimism, the Arab spring, the Occupy Movement, Tiqqun in France, the revolts in Brazil and the deaths and confusion in Ukraine, the criminalization of homosexuality in Russia, and a Nordic region where xenophobia and racism are rampant, and the dismantling of the Swedish welfare state is at its peak.

And here we are. What battles are taking place right here right now? What is at stake?

In 1977, Gina Pane wrote:

> Before May 68, all living forces in Paris were working intensely to be able to get beyond the 'Social Criticism Theory' in order

> to be at peace with 'real life.' In this broken, upset environ-
> ment, creativity was emerging everywhere. The confrontation
> of mine with the post-1968 public, benefited from a relation-
> ship that I could define as 'active' and my work was not only
> looked at, but lived.[10]

Gina Pane's actions, including her self-inflicted wounds, were motiv-
ated by her ambition to promote an idea of the body as a communal
entity. Indeed, for her, this was the condition for a collective de-
anesthetization.

> If I open my 'body' so that you can see your blood therein, it is
> for the love of you: the Other.[11]

There is a religious, spiritual aspect in Gina Pane's work. In this respect,
her actions can be seen as a direct attempt to create a link between her
own body and the spilling of blood associated, in Christianity, with
redemption. The tone of Gina Pane's words is sometimes biblical, and
she seems to be referring to an almost Christ-like wound when she cuts
herself, when she opens the wound through her actions. When she
cuts her lips, her eyelids, her abdomen, her tongue and upper arms.
The wound stands for a state of the body's extreme sensitivity; it is a
sign of suffering, a sign of external aggression. The wound recalls the
situation of being the object of aggression, of always being exposed to
violence.[12]

Gina Pane often used the word 'aggression.'[13]

Gina Pane once said that she had to perform *Discours mou et mat*
to 'get her father and mother's relationship under control'. I thought

---

10   'Avant Mai 68, toutes les forces vives de Paris travaillaient intensément pour parvenir
       à dépasser la "Théorie de la Critique Sociale" afin d'en assumer son "vécu". Dans ce
       climat éclaté, renversé, la créativité émergeait de toutes parts. La confrontation de
       la mienne avec le public d'après 1968 bénéficiait donc d'un rapport que je pourrais
       définir "d'Actif" et mon travail n'était pas seulement regardé mais vécu"' (Pane, 'Avant
       Mai 68', *Lettre à un(e) inconnu(e)*, p. 45. Written on 12 December 1977. Translated in
       Baumgartner, 'Reviving the Collective Body', p. 254).
11   Gina Pane, 'Lettre à un(e) inconnu(e)', in *ArTitudes international*, 15–17 (October–
       December 1974), pp. 26–35 (p. 34). 'Si j'ouvre mon "corps" afin que vous puissiez y
       regarder votre sang, c'est pour l'amour de vous: l'autre' trans. by Gina Pane.
12   See Mary Richards, 'Specular Suffering: (Staging) the Bleeding Body', *PAJ: A Journal
       of Performance and Art*, 30.1 (January 2008), pp. 108–19.
13   See Paweł Leszkowicz, 'Gina Pane — Self-Inflicted Pain Is You! Today Photographs
       Are All That Remain. We Can Only Imagine the Hurt', trans. by Timothy Williams,
       Czas Kultury (Time of Culture), 20.1 (2004), pp. 42–55 (p. 50).

I finally had that part under control.[14] And here I am, back in the middle of the psychoanalytic drama. Between consideration, offering, and acceptance.

The same year that Gina Pane performed *Discours mou et mat*, Hélène Cixous wrote *The Laugh of the Medusa*, in which she states:

> Woman must write herself: must write about women and bring women to writing, from which they have been driven away as violently as from their bodies — for the same reasons, by the same law, with the same fatal goal. Woman must put herself into the text — as into the world and into history — by her own movement.[15]

Gina Pane never claimed to be a feminist, never firmly positioned herself as a lesbian, or dyke. In many of her works, she took a firm anti-bourgeois and anti-imperialist standpoint, and her fight was against the anesthetized society. She was neither an activist nor belonged to any political party, but she expressed a desire to challenge, through her work, 'the internal determinism' propped up by 'the regulatory systems'.

BETWEEN YOU AND ME

'Gina Pane's blood could not provide affirmation and succor for spectators, instead it demanded action.'[16]

When I decided to reenact *Discours mou et mat*, I tried to be very concrete in my approach to the material. I did not want to relate my actions to a predetermined narrative. I wanted to admit not knowing. Creating another narrative. Making a path. Following one. I wanted to point out the daily occurrence of violence. To point out that violence is always present.

Gina Pane wrote:

---

14   Gina Pane, paraphrased in Antje von Graevenitz, 'Then and Now: Performance Art in Holland', *Studio International*, 192 (July–August 1976), pp. 49–53 (p. 52).

15   Hélène Cixous, 'The Laugh of the Medusa', trans. by Keith Cohen and Paula Cohen, *Signs: Journal of Women in Culture and Society*, 1.4 (Summer 1976), pp. 875–93.

16   Inge Linder-Gaillard, 'Stigmata, Icons and Reliquaries', in *Gina Pane* (Southampton: John Hansard Gallery, 2002) pp. 43–54 (p. 47).

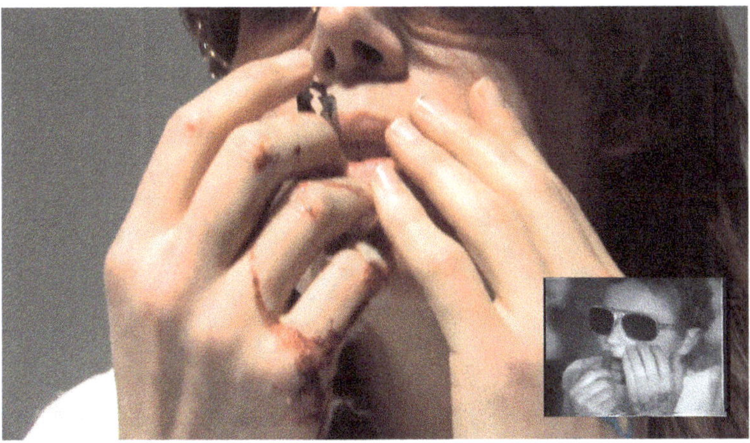

Figure 4. Malin Arnell, still from video documentation of *Reflect Soft
Matte Discourse*, 2011, combined with a video still from Gina Pane's
performance *Discours mou et mat*, 1975. Courtesy of the artist and the
Galerie Kamel Mennour, Paris.

(The body is) the irreducible core of the human being, its most
fragile part. This is how it has always been, under all social
systems, at any given moment of history. And the wound is the
memory of the body; it memorizes its fragility, its pain, thus its
'real' existence. It is a defense against the object and against the
mental prosthesis.[17]

---

17 Ezio Quarantelli and Gina Pane, 'Travels with St. Francis: A Rare Discussion with
the French Artist Who Is One of the Premiere Practitioners of Body Art', *Contemporanea*, 1.4 (November–December 1988), pp. 44–47 (p. 46). Quoted in Kathy O'Dell,
Contract With the Skin: Masochism, Performance Art, and the 1970s (Minneapolis:
University of Minnesota Press, 1998), p 27.

Performance Art in the 1990s and the Generation Gap

PIERRE SAURISSE

> [T]he saddest thing you could possibly imagine
> – you could just cry right away – is to see '70s
> performances repeated in the '90s. It can be so
> sad, so displaced, so completely out of time.
>
> Hans Ulrich Obrist, 'Talk-
> ing with Marina Abramović,
> Riding on the Bullet Train to
> Kitakyushu, Somewhere in Japan'

In the 1990s, the reenactment of historical performances was becoming a marked phenomenon. Although on some occasions artists re-performed their own works from the past, this trend was mostly the doing of younger artists looking at art history. In the context of an understanding of performance being largely based on visual documentation, this tendency allowed works often previously known through no more than a handful of iconic images to be put back in the spotlight of live presentations.

The 1990s saw the question of the legacy of early performance being posed in fresh terms, and with a particular sense of urgency. Reenactments not only reproduced past works but positioned artists within the history of performance. The example of Marina Abramović is particularly significant in that she took charge of the recreation of her own works in a theatrical production mounted in 1992, whereas the cases of Takashi Murakami and Oleg Kulik are illustrations of artists engaging with the history of performance at the beginning of their careers. Underlying these echoes of historic performance in the 1990s is the awareness of the passage of a generation and the constitution of the genealogy of performance.

Performance appeared on the art scene with a sense of utter newness. Events such as the festivals organized in Paris by Jean-Jacques Lebel from 1964 or the Destruction in Art Symposium that took place in London in 1966 revealed the strength of this nascent art form and its multiple facets. The feeling prevailed that a new form of artistic expression was coming into existence. Allan Kaprow explained in 1966 that it was 'in the midst of a young activity' that he wrote his book on what he then called 'happenings'.[1]

Performance enjoyed unprecedented exposure in the 1970s while it found a linguistic anchor in the term 'Performance Art'. This recognition of performance was a remarkable achievement for its creators. It could be argued that these pioneers developed a specific consciousness of a generation — not as a mere age cohort but as a group distinct from others 'within the same actual generation which work up the material of their common experience in different specific ways'.[2] In a seminal essay, the sociologist Karl Mannheim describes this social phenomenon as a 'generation unit, which represents a much more concrete bond than the actual generation as such'.[3] Distinguishing themselves from other artists for their involvement in live art, the pioneers of performance art formed a 'generation unit' of their own.

The generation of artists who propelled performance centre stage redirected their activities fairly quickly to the making of objects. By the end of the 1970s, Vito Acconci was concentrating on design and

---

1   Allan Kaprow, *Assemblage, Environments & Happenings* (New York: Abrams, 1966), p. 150.

2   Karl Mannheim, 'The Problem of Generations', in Mannheim, *Essays on the Sociology of Knowledge*, ed. by Paul Kecskemeti (London: Routledge, 1952), pp. 276–322 (p. 304).

3   Ibid.

architecture, and in 1981, Gina Pane opted for partitions instead of live actions. As Abramović commented retrospectively, 'the originators of the medium were no longer young, and [performance] work was very hard on the body.'[4] In one of his last performances before he definitively converted to sculpture, Chris Burden played with his own history and mythology as performance artist by inviting the audience to look at the scar left on his arm after he was shot in his 1971 piece *Shoot* (*Show the Hole*, 1980).

The withdrawal of key artists from live art created a gap in the history of performance, and this gap consigned the once young medium to history. Soon after the early phase of performance ended, the period around 1970 came to embody the 'golden years' of this art form, as they were dubbed by RoseLee Goldberg in 1984.[5] Around the same time, Wayne Enstice commented on the liberation of performance from object-making as the 'coming of age' of performance and referred to this evolution in terms such as 'performance in its adolescence' and 'its mature phase'.[6] This rhetoric unwittingly suited the evolution of performance and also of its very protagonists, who tended to move away from live art as they aged.

Among the protagonists of historical performance, only a few confronted the question of the preservation of the live component of past works. While most pioneers eventually retired from live art, Kaprow presents a notable exception, as his involvement in performance never waned. Early in his career, he had laid the groundwork for the future of his works by ensuring that they could be repeated. For example, on the occasion of the exhibition 'Precedings', held in Arlington in 1988, he put on a number of new versions of his performances, among them *18 Happenings in 6 Parts* (1959), from which the term 'happening' originated. These new iterations authorized some degrees of interpretation, thus allowing the works to morph and to adapt to new situations and

---

4   Marina Abramović and James Kaplan, *Walk through Walls: A Memoir* (London: Penguin, 2017), p. 119.

5   RoseLee Goldberg, 'Performance: The Golden Years', in *The Art of Performance: A Critical Anthology*, ed. by Gregory Battcock and Robert Nickas (New York: Dutton, 1984), pp. 71–94.

6   Wayne Enstice, 'Performance's Art Coming of Age', in *The Art of Performance*, ed. by Battcock and Nickas, pp. 142–56.

performers. 'By deciding in favour of reinventions rather than reen-actments,' writes Stephanie Rosenthal, 'he was guiding his work in a direction that could be sustained even in his absence.'[7]

Like Kaprow, Abramović's commitment to performance was sustained throughout her career. From 1981 to 1987, her practice was dominated by *Nightsea Crossing*, a performance that she presented with Ulay across the globe. After the two artists separated as both life and work partners in 1988, the afterlife of her performances became a central concern of hers. This question materialized in *The Biography*, a work first presented in Madrid in 1992 and then elsewhere until 1994. Conceived in collaboration with Charles Atlas, this new live piece adopted theatre conventions, signalling a dramatic departure from what had been Abramović's precepts up until that point. Presented on a stage, it did not adhere to the real time (and space) principle that her original performances had followed. Unorthodxly, it was recounting her past.In *The Biography*, Abramović's life was narrated year by year, and, for the first time, past performances were partially reenacted. Works were recreated in shorter versions focusing on key moments: for example, the cutting of a star on her belly with a razor blade in *Thomas Lips* (1975). When it came to performances originally conceived with Ulay, such as *Relation in Time* (1977), during which the pair had their hair tied together for seventeen hours, Abramović recreated them with the help of slides projected onto two screens, one performer displayed on each side. The show was, the artist explained, a 'theatre piece in which I [was] actually playing myself'.[8]

While *The Biography* told the story of Abramović's existence, it also staged the very process of accounting for the past. As pivotal moments of her career were narrated by her own recorded voice coming from offstage, she presented herself as taking responsibility for cataloguing, and ultimately historicizing, her career. The fact that she assumed the roles of both artist and historian was also reflected in the title of the piece. Since a biography implies a second party undertaking

---

7   Stephanie Rosenthal, 'Agency for Action', in *Allan Kaprow: Art as Life*, ed. by Eva Meyer-Hermann, Andrew Perchuk, and Stephanie Rosenthal (London: Thames & Hudson, 2008), pp. 56–71 (p. 62).

8   Marina Abramović in Thomas McEvilley, 'Stages of Energy: Performance Art Ground Zero?', in *Marina Abramović: Artist Body: Performances 1969–1998*, ed. by Emanuela Belloni (Milan: Charta, 1998), pp. 14–25 (p. 17).

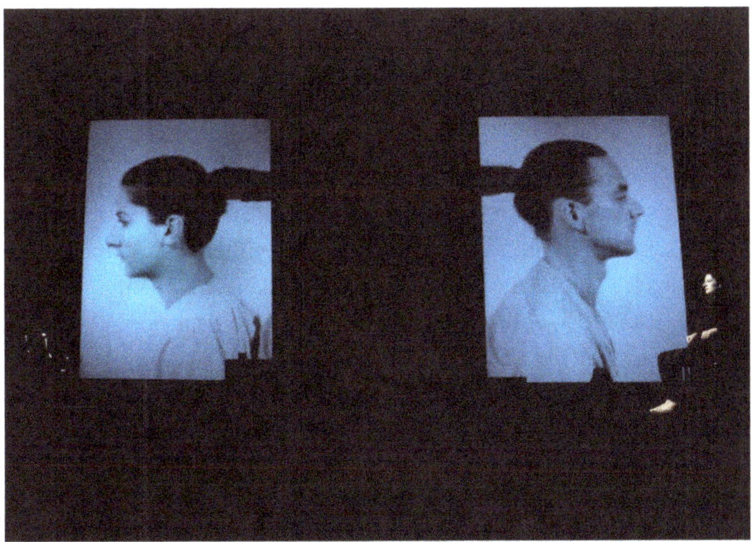

Figure 1. Marina Abramović, *The Biography*, Theatrical performance,
Kunsthalle, Vienna, Austria, 1992. Courtesy of the
Marina Abramović Archives.

the job of an historian, the title is tellingly inaccurate for what is, in effect, an autobiography.

By setting the ground for the future of performance, *The Biography* made the problem of the transmission of the memory of past performance very explicit. Mannheim has explained that, although cultural heritage is usually incorporated in the present unconsciously and unnoticed, patterns of behaviour can also be adopted consciously as models, as a 'guide for action'.[9] He writes, 'We are directly aware primarily of those aspects of our culture which have become subject to reflection; and these contain only those elements which in the course of development have somehow, at some point, become problematical'.[10]

Reenactments did not just place Abramović's past works at the core of *The Biography*; they also explored the very possibility of their continuation in the future. In fact, Abramović's intention at the time

9   Mannheim, 'The Problem of Generations', p. 295.
10   Ibid., pp. 295–96.

was to continue presenting *The Biography*, in regularly updated versions, for the rest of her life (in 2004 she would present a piece, *The Biography Remix*, conceived in the same vein). In addition, she gave unprecedented credence to the possibilities of reenactment with the idea, formed shortly after putting on *The Biography*, of interpreting performances by other artists.[11] This project would only materialize in 2005 in the seminal *Seven Easy Pieces*, at the Guggenheim Museum in New York, where she reenacted works by Bruce Nauman, Vito Acconci, VALIE EXPORT, Gina Pane, and Joseph Beuys. By making the legacy of her own work and that of others 'subject to reflection', Abramović tackled the question of the memory of live performance, which was often swept under the carpet by the existence of documentation.

Young artists emerging in the 1990s were confronted, Abramović asserted in 1997, with 'so much mystification about the 1970s and also a short historical memory'.[12] Not only was the history of performance galvanized by its utter radicality, but it was still relatively fragmentary, with the book *Performance: Live Art, 1909 to the Present*, written in 1979 by Goldberg, being one of the only comprehensive accounts of the subject.[13] In addition, while in 1993 Peggy Phelan insisted on the 'maniacally charged present' of performance, documentation of past events such as photographs, films, and relics remained the staple of exhibitions on this topic.[14] Young artists engaging with the legacy of performance grappled with a history which was exposed to both idealization and ossification. However, this history could be key to their own appearance as artists. For example, Tania Bruguera's art education culminated in her exhibition 'Ana Mendieta/Tania Bruguera', held at Centro de Desarrollo de las Artes Visuales in Havana in 1992. In this exhibition, Bruguera performed works by Mendieta, such as *Body Tracks* (1974), and came into existence as an artist through the persona of the Cuban-American artist.

---

11   See, for example, Guy Hilton, 'Fifty Is Just the Beginning', *Make*, 73 (December 1996–January 1997), pp. 3–5 (p. 4).

12   Marina Abramović in Guy Hilton, 'Fifty Is Just the Beginning', p. 4.

13   RoseLee Goldberg, *Performance: Live Art, 1909 to the Present* (London: Thames & Hudson, 1979).

14   Peggy Phelan, *Unmarked: The Politics of Performance* (London: Routledge, 1993), p. 148.

Takashi Murakami began reenacting past performances in 1992, at the outset of his career. After he trained in painting, his practice was at a crossroads; in the same year he created Mr. Dob, a character who would be emblematic of the spectacular take-off of his career a few years later. The works repeated by Murakami were originally presented by his namesake Saburō Murakami, from the group Gutai, in 1956, and by the Hi Red Center in 1964. In appropriating these works, he claimed the legacy of artists who embodied the 'golden years' of performance in Japan. This kind of appropriation of past performances, notes Catherine Wood, is akin to a 'rite of passage', which would punctuate the career of a number of artists in the 2000s. Alluding to Tino Sehgal and Rabih Mroué, among other examples, Wood notices that these artists making past works their own 'are not just pointing to past work, they are speaking from a subject position'.[15]

The performance by Saburō Murakami, *Breaking Through Paper Screens*, which was reenacted by Takashi Murakami, involves the artist walking through large sheets of paper mounted on frames, resulting in large holes. To perform this brief and intense action, the younger Murakami took great care to resemble the older Murakami, mimicking his round-framed glasses and distinctive haircut. With this reenactment, not only does Murakami make his artistic trajectory meet that of his forebear, but he also operates a close identification with him. This episode took place at a time of uncertainty in Murakami's nascent career, during a 'process of transformation, going from *nihonga* [Japanese painting] to contemporary art'.[16] He explains, 'I came up against this problem: gradually, as I made more and more works, I realized that I didn't really have an identity'.[17] Such a 'problem' is exposed in the overlap of identities that was enacted in his reiteration of *Breaking Through Paper Screens*: not only does he appropriate a work but also a persona. Crucially, this reenactment specifically cements an artistic filiation with the young artist that Saburō Murakami had himself been in the heydays of Gutai.

---

15   Catherine Wood, 'Re-make, Re-model', *Frieze Masters*, 1 (October 2012) <https:// frieze.com/article/re-make-re-model-0> [accessed 27 September 2019].

16   Takashi Murakami in Hélène Kelmachter, 'Interview with Takashi Murakami', in *Takashi Murakami: Kaikai Kiki*, ed. by Hélène Kelmachter (Paris: Fondation Cartier pour l'art contemporain, 2002), pp. 72–105 (p. 73).

17   Ibid.

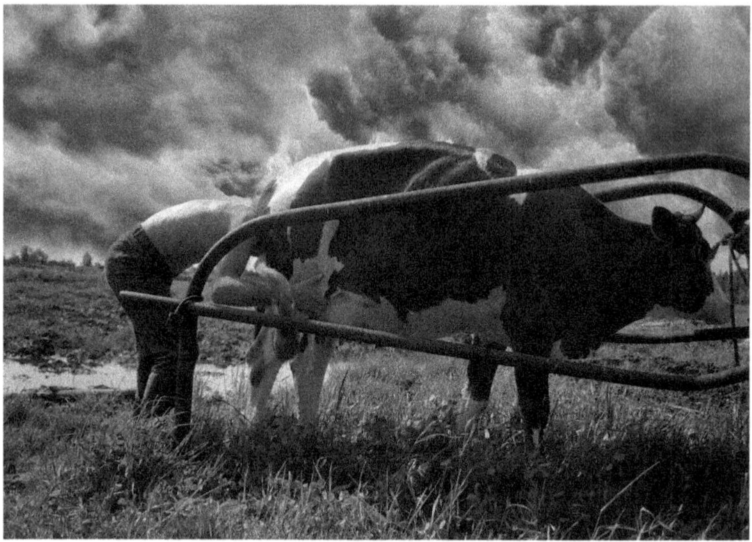

Figure 2. Oleg Kulik, *Deep into Russia*, 1993. Courtesy Oleg Kulik.

A rite of passage also marks Oleg Kulik's early career, before he started doing the dog performances that propelled him to fame. In *Deep into Russia* (1993), Kulik's head, in his own words, 'penetrated the vagina of a cow in an attempt to be born anew'.[18] Although this action, which evokes a return to the womb, is comparable to an act of regression, it also suggests the act of being born. Kulik's early work is very much, he has explained, a 'reaction to Moscow Conceptualism, with its sectarian exclusiveness',[19] and this episode enacts his birth as a radical performance artist as much as it denies the legacy of his artistic milieu.

With *Deep into Russia*, Kulik claims his own artistic filiation by possibly making a reference, however obliquely, to Joseph Beuys. The German artist continuously emphasized the importance of reconnecting with a primitive state of being after his plane crashed in Crimea in 1944, and he was brought back to life by Tartars. Insisting on a lin-

---

18   Oleg Kulik, 'Artist's Notes on Performances from the Zoophrenia Programme', in *Oleg Kulik: Art Animal*, ed. by Deborah Kermode and Jonathan Watkins (Birmingham: Ikon Gallery, 2001), p. 72.

19   Oleg Kulik, 'Return Tickets', in *Live: Art and Performance*, ed. by Adrian Heathfield (London: Tate Publishing, 2004), pp. 50–57 (p. 56).

eage linking him to Beuys, Kulik's 1996 performance *I Love Europe but Europe Doesn't Love Me Back* is an obvious nod to *I Like America and America Likes Me*, which was performed by Beuys at the René Block Gallery in New York in 1974. When Kulik presented *I Bite America and America Bites Me* in the following year, he imitated the German artist by living in a cage set up for him in the exhibition space; however, in stark contrast to Beuys' interaction with a coyote in the original work, he impersonated a dog, in this way marking the performance as his own.

By taking ownership of the history of performance, artists demonstrated a specific awareness of their temporal relation to this history. This question was posed in not so dissimilar terms for art historians. 'I was not yet three years old, living in central North Carolina', writes Amelia Jones in 1997, 'when Carolee Schneemann performed *Meat Joy* at the Festival of Free Expression in Paris in 1964; three when Yoko Ono performed *Cut Piece* in Kyoto; eight when Vito Acconci did his *Push Ups* in the sand at Jones Beach' (the list carries on with other examples.)[20] Running through a number of performances in parallel with her own age development, Jones stresses the particular subjectivity with which the appreciation of past performance is pregnant. She adds, 'I was thirty years old — then 1991 — when I began to study performance or body art from this explosive and important period, entirely through its documentation.'[21] Jones wrote these lines when the history of performance was the object of new and unprecedented scrutiny among scholars. More recently, performance caught the attention of a wider audience with Abramović's exhibition 'The Artist Is Present' at the Museum of Modern Art in New York in 2010. By then the designation 'grandmother of performance' had been adopted by the popular media, suggesting a longing for the family tree of performance to be drawn.

---

20   Amelia Jones, '"Presence" in Absentia: Experiencing Performance as Documentation', *Art Journal*, 56.4 (Winter 1997), pp. 11–18 (p. 11).
21   Ibid.

III. RESISTANCE AND RECONCILIATION IN THE MUSEUM

Re-Presenting Art History
An Unfinished Process
CRISTINA BALDACCI

In recent years reconstructing and reenacting art history has become habitual for artists and curators alike. On the one hand, via restaged exhibitions and remakes of artworks, often temporary, unfinished, never to be completed, leaving room for new presentation and hence interpretation. On the other hand, performances that reembody gestures and impermanent objects, where the impermanence or unfinished state hints at a possible return.

From the 1970s onwards, as a postmodernist aesthetic principle,[1] the idea of 'different repetition' ran parallel with the output of artists engaged in Institutional Critique, exploding the (modernist) 'con' of art being authentic only when 'original'. Museums, historians, sometimes artists themselves had perpetrated that 'con' in their common endeavour to find and supply certification of originality — primarily

---

1   The reference is to the exhibition 'La ripetizione differente' (the title itself is a reference to Deleuze's famous 1968 *Difference and Repetition*) curated by the Italian art critic Renato Barilli at the Studio Marconi, Milan in 1974 and then repeated in 2014 by the same curator, in what has today become the Marconi Foundation. On the idea of repetition as a postmodernist art strategy, see, e.g., Andreas Huyssen, 'The Search for Tradition: Avant-Garde and Postmodernism in the 1970s', *New German Critique*, 22 (Winter 1981), pp. 23–40 and Benjamin H. D. Buchloh, 'Allegorical Procedures: Appropriation and Montage in Contemporary Art', *Artforum*, 21.1 (September 1982), pp. 43–56.

for business considerations. Thus, working backwards from classicism, one came to realize the copy as the *underlying condition of the original*.[2] This point has been hammered home in the last decade by a series of well-received exhibitions put on by the Prada Foundation in Milan and Venice: *The Small Utopia: Ars Multiplicata* (curated by Germano Celant, 2012), *Serial Classic* (curated by Salvatore Settis and Anna Anguissola, 2015) and *L'image volée* (curated by Thomas Demand, 2016).[3] I mention these as typically exhaustive in their treatment, but they are far from the only instances.

Though long devalued until postmodernism, especially from Romanticism on, repetition has always been part of art practice. It is intrinsic to the very idea of originality — as argued by Rosalind Krauss and also Douglas Crimp in the early 1980s.[4] For that matter, as early as the mid-1930s Walter Benjamin produced the insight that 'in principle a work of art has always been reproducible' (before photography, other techniques had enabled copies to be made, albeit more slowly).[5] But instead of the fixation on the new and avant-garde at all costs, 'repetition restores the possibility of what was, renders it possible anew', creating a continuous dialogue with memory and the past. Not, as Giorgio Agamben puts it, that it 'give[s] us back what was, as such: that would be hell. Instead memory restores possibility to the past'.[6]

Agamben's note of clarification is fundamental (it comes in an essay on the cinema of Guy Debord that is close to Benjamin's idea of messianic time). Repetition is rife nowadays in all that begins with 're-': the digital media have spread and accelerated such contemporary

---

2   Cf. Rosalind Krauss, 'The Originality of the Avant-Garde: A Postmodernist Repetition', *October*, 18 (Autumn 1981), pp. 47–66 (p. 58). See also Douglas Crimp, 'The Photographic Activity of Postmodernism', *October*, 15 (Winter 1980), pp. 91–101.

3   *The Small Utopia: Ars Multiplicata*, ed. by Germano Celant (Milan: Progetto Prada Arte, 2012); *Serial / Portable Classic: The Greek Canon and its Mutations*, ed. by Salvatore Settis, Anna Anguissola, and Davide Gasparotto (Milan: Fondazione Prada, 2015); *L'image volée*, ed. by Thomas Demand (Milan: Fondazione Prada, 2016).

4   Cf. references in footnote no. 2.

5   Walter Benjamin, 'The Work of Art in the Age of Mechanical Reproduction', in Benjamin, *Illuminations: Essays and Reflections*, ed. by Hannah Arendt, trans. by Harry Zohn (New York: Schocken, 1968), pp. 217–51 (p. 218).

6   Giorgio Agamben, 'Difference and Repetition: On Guy Debord's Films', trans. by Brian Holmes, in *Guy Debord and the Situationist International: Texts and Documents*, ed. by Tom McDonough (Cambridge, MA: MIT Press, 2002), pp. 313–19 (p. 316).

practice to the point, one might say, of a proper 're-turn',[7] and this goes for artwork, curatorship, and hence also history and criticism. But such repetition is not to be seen as some (reactionary, revisionist) historicizing revival akin to 'Living History' or a sense of nostalgia. Nor is it the rebirth of some prior style, taste, or code, as one gets with movements beginning with 'neo-'. No: the term 'reenactment' — here taken to embrace a miscellany of practices, though in the awareness that all such classifiers must be arbitrary —[8] has nothing to do with harking back to the past, creative exhaustion, sterile quotation for quotation's sake. It does of course have roots in a precise historiographic tradition (see Sven Lütticken's preface to this book), but in this case the focus is on contemporary art and its idioms, first of which is performance.[9]

When one is confronted with present-day art practice picking up from the past or past tradition, one tends to resort to a lexical jungle hinging on the idea of copying.[10] Thus one has 'processes of quotation, excerption, framing, and staging' at the core of postmodern strategy — beginning with the Picture Generation as posited by Crimp, where the photograph stands as the intermedial idiom par excellence. Yet such a lexis, to an art historian or critic, does not imply the search for an origin or original. It is, rather, a mode of defining 'structures of signification', given that 'underneath each picture there is always another picture' (the noun 'picture' is here deliberately used because of its non-medium specificity).[11]

---

7   My current research project focuses on the various 're-' practices in the visual arts and the turning point they marked in image production, affording constant comparisons with the contemporary iconosphere and visual culture.

8   Cf. *The Routledge Handbook of Reenactment Studies: Key Terms in the Field*, ed. by Vanessa Agnew, Jonathan Lamb, and Juliane Tomann (London: Routledge, 2020).

9   Cf. *The Oxford Handbook of Dance and Reenactment*, ed. by Mark Franko (Oxford: Oxford University Press, 2017).

10 Salvatore Settis draws up a small but exhaustive list of the most frequently used terminology: "'allusion", "appropriation", "citation", "influence", "inspiration", "manipulation", *"pastiche"*, "borrowing", "reference", "usage"'. One might also add: "'comparison", "theft", *"spolium"*, "homage", "paraphrase", "taking", "resumption", "transfer" and so on'. See Salvatore Settis, *Incursioni: Arte contemporanea e tradizione* (Milan: Feltrinelli, 2020), p. 17 [translation of this passage by Ralph Nisbet].

11 Douglas Crimp, 'Pictures', *October*, 8 (Spring 1979), pp. 75–88 (p. 87 and 75). In another famous essay, published shortly thereafter, in which he outlines postmodernism in photography, Crimp states that 'against the pluralism of originals, I want to speak of the plurality of copies'. See Crimp, 'The Photographic Activity of Postmodernism', p. 91.

So when one connects the concept of reenactment to art practice, as well as museum practice, curatorship, and art history — activities to do with producing, circulating, receiving, and preserving artworks and images —,[12] one is bound to acknowledge that this is an act of critical appraisal. An act that challenges a whole range of apparently 'antithetical' relations between past and present, original and copy (cf. originality, copyright), repetition and variation, authenticity and auraticity, presence and absence, canon and appropriation, *durée* and transience.

From the art critic/art historian's angle, a distinct cultural value attaches to reconstructing and reactivating past artworks/images, gesture/action, events/shows in our present setting, ensuring they survive, are protected and known about for the future. Dieter Roelstraete gives a clear idea of the educational scope of this:

> Both remake and re-enactment represent a type of renegade art history in action, anxious to keep in living memory that which is always in danger of being forgotten, marginalized, swept aside […]. Remakes and reenactments, then, perform a reconstructive educational role that ensures the perpetuation of an 'other' art history outside the confines and constraints of canon and mainstream alike — one that truly is written by the (remaking, reenacting) artists firsthand.[13]

On such a view, the prefix 're-' may provide a keystone for building a different relationship with the past, one that does not entail any preestablished art-historical or art-critical methodology. The reverse: that 're-' tends to hover between *back* and *again*, giving rise to complex patterns in space and time that elicit some unexpected resonances and correlations.[14] It serves as an effective tool decanonizing a certain mode of interpretation and provides new hermeneutic

---

12   In this regard, see my previous 'Reenactment: Errant Images in Contemporary Art', in *Re-: An Errant Glossary*, ed. by Christoph F. E. Holzhey and Arnd Wedemeyer (Berlin: ICI Berlin Press, 2019), pp. 57–67, and the volume I am currently co-editing with Susanne Franco *On Reenactment: Concepts, Methodologies, Tools* (Turin: Accademia University Press, forthcoming).

13   Dieter Roelstraete, 'Make it Re-: The Eternally Returning Object', in *When Attitudes Become Form: Bern 1969/Venice 2013*, ed. by Germano Celant (Milan: Fondazione Prada, 2013), pp. 423–28 (p. 424).

14   Francesco Giusti, 'Passionate Affinities: A Conversation with Rita Felski', *Los Angeles Review of Books*, 25 September 2019 <https://lareviewofbooks.org/article/passionate-affinities-a-conversation-with-rita-felski/> [accessed 25 February 2021].

tools for what Nicolas Bourriaud called 'altermodernity', namely, 'a modernity specific to the twenty-first century, a modernity to be constructed on a global scale, through cooperation among a multitude of cultural *semes* and through ongoing translation of singularities'.[15] This is what the French philosopher and curator suggests in response to postmodernism and the contemporary overuse of the prefix 'post-' (e.g., post-history/human/conceptual/Internet…), which, according to him, has undermined the foundations of modernism without offering a true alternative in the present.

Although any prefix that historians or critics use to shake off a prior mode of interpretation inevitably sets up a new canon, the beauty of 're-' is that it can be repeated again and again in a process of framing and unframing that leaves no room, or time, for conceptual closure.

This brings me to the core question of this essay, namely: can reenactment be like image reactivation — an art practice — or exhibition rebuilding — a curator's practice — in that it can be seen as a viable critical approach or method of rereading art history by experiencing or reexperiencing a past object, gesture, or event in an ever-different here and now? Apart from anything else, such a method would imply the gesture of presenting anew instead of representing, where shortening the perceptual space-time distance enables the one experiencing or reexperiencing (be they interpreter or public) to take part in a 're-presencing' (not so much rewriting) of art history.[16] The gesture of restoring visibility to something no longer present — an absence —, reactivating or reembodying it as an object/image *in* and *for* the present, is a (political) act of restitution and historical recontextualization.

In reappraising the negative connotation Michael Fried gave to 'presentness' — and hence, from the late 1960s on, to the extending of typical theatre notions of temporality and presence to the world of visual arts (see the 'theatricality' of minimalist sculpture) — Crimp

---

15 Nicolas Bourriaud, *The Radicant*, trans. by James Cussen and Lili Porten (New York: Lukas & Sternberg, 2009), p. 39.

16 Gabriella Giannachi, 'At the Edge of the "Living Present": Re-enactments and Re-interpretations as Strategies for the Preservation of Performance and New Media', in *Histories of Performance Documentation: Museum, Artistic, and Scholarly Practices*, ed. by Gabriella Giannachi and Jonah Westerman (London: Routledge, 2018), pp. 115–31 (p. 117).

commented that representation should not be seen as '*re*-presentation of that which is prior, but as the unavoidable condition of intelligibility of even that which is present'.[17] Which makes presence tantamount to absence, in the sense of an 'unbridgeable distance from the original, from even the possibility of an original'.[18]

At this point one may advance a first definition of reenactment as: (1) the act of (re)appropriation or *Aneignung*, in Paul Ricoeur's words 'the process by which one makes one's own (*eigen*) what was initially other or alien (*fremd*)';[19] (2) an exercise of (re)interpretation in the sense of working-through or *Durcharbeitung* (from the verb *Durcharbeiten*), to use Freud's famous expression, which Jean-François Lyotard later exhumed;[20] (3) a process of (re)construction, given that the event or object to be reactivated is often chosen precisely because it was left unfinished, or got lost or altered as an artefact or memory; (4) a gesture of (re)mediation in the sense of the term given by Jay Bolter and Richard Grusin,[21] that is, reworking and transposing not just from one time and/or setting to another, but also from one support, idiom, or medium to another; (5) the act of (re)circulating images across time, space, the media, and later (re)contextualizing them.[22]

What happens to images (nowadays that includes digital images) and their formal and semantic values when, more or less unawares, they migrate from place to place or culture to culture in our globalized

---

17   Crimp's views particularly relate to photography and the Picture Generation. See Crimp, 'Pictures', p. 77.

18   See Crimp, 'The Photographic Activity of Postmodernism', p. 94. A bit later on in the text, Crimp insists on this point: 'A group of young artists working with photography [i.e., the Picture Generation, C. B.] have addressed photography's claims to originality, showing those claims for the fiction they are, showing photography to be always *representation*, always-already-seen. Their images are purloined, confiscated, appropriated, *stolen*. In their work, the original cannot be located, is always deferred; even the self which might have generated an original is shown to be itself a copy". Ibid., p. 98.

19   Paul Ricoeur, *Hermeneutics and the Human Sciences: Essays on Language, Action, Interpretation*, ed. and trans. by John B. Thompson (Cambridge: Cambridge University Press, 2016), p. 140.

20   Jean-François Lyotard, *The Inhuman: Reflections on Time*, trans. by Rachel Bowlby and Geoffrey Bennington (Cambridge: Polity, 1991), p. 26.

21   Jay D. Bolter and Richard Grusin, *Remediation: Understanding New Media* (Cambridge, MA: MIT Press, 1999).

22   See my 'Recirculation: The Wandering of Digital Images in Post-Internet Art', in *Re-: An Errant Glossary*, ed. by Christoph F. E. Holzhey and Arnd Wedemeyer (Berlin: ICI Berlin Press, 2019), pp. 25–33.

world? Do they still stand as vectors of memory and 'afterlives' in the Warburgian sense (cf. his concept of *Nachleben*)?

As an artist's or curator's practice, reenactment entails a series of issues largely concerning the link with institutional contexts and the socio-political structures that artworks are situated in; the process of selecting them; the differences that occur between 'original' and copy in the process of repetition or adaptation/revising. Let me briefly try to summarize these issues.

The first might be formulated as: What kind of change is produced in the interval of time that separates the 'original' from its reenactment from a historical-critical, cognitive-perceptual, linguistic-formal, as well as exhibition display perspective? To elaborate on this point, it is important to consider that reenactment in itself is an anachronistic action, inasmuch as two different temporalities — past and present — coexist in it. Most of the time, the interval is a short period of time, which allows those who already saw or experienced the 'original' to experience it again in a new here and now. Whereas, for those who do not have any memory of the previous event (be it a gesture, work, or exhibition), it is a unique opportunity to see it in the present, although a replicated event cannot be the same anymore. Repetition always implies variation, which depends, first of all, on the different moment and context in which it takes place, and, secondly, on the act of interpretation that is part of the process of reenactment.

The second question runs as follows: What does reenactment mean for the historian, critic, curator, and artist who establish a comparison either with their own work or with the work of someone else? What does it mean for the collector or museum that owns and re-displays the work/exhibition, for the gallery that acts as a sponsor, and — last but not least — for the viewer?

And the third and last main question: What kind of relationship between oneself and one's own history is revealed by the contemporary enthusiasm for replicas and replication processes, for appropriation and postproduction as artistic strategies, for the diffusion of notions such as repetition (vs. representation), double (vs. copy), and restaging (vs. interpretation)?

Though not an artwork or an art exhibition, one emblematic example here is the minute reconstruction — and later restaging, in significantly different forms, at the ZKM–Zentrum für Kunst und Medientechnologie, Karlsruhe in 2016 and at the HKW–Haus der Kulturen der Welt, Berlin in 2020 — of the Warburg *Bilderatlas* on the part of an art historian, Roberto Ohrt, and an artist, Axel Heil, primarily because Aby Warburg's cognitive method was based on the repetition and recurrence of archetypal images or *Pathosformeln*, from ancient to contemporary, high culture to low, and on the duplicability of images via photography. And additionally, Ohrt and Heil put so much effort into producing a formally and philologically exact copy of the *Bilderatlas*.[23] On a 1:1 scale, they reconstructed all the plates from the last version, which Warburg left unfinished in 1929, hunting down (in the field and in the extensive Warburg Institute archives) and rephotographing the thousand or so 'original' images he used, one by one. That is why they insisted on the originality of the undertaking — an insistence that might otherwise seem quite out of place.[24] It is emblematic both for Warburg's intentions and methodology, and because the *Bilderatlas* remained a fragment of a much more extensive design and hence an unfinished work open to variation and interpretation: something to be viewed as an intellectual and research task, or at most a historical artefact, and definitely not an object for aesthetic contemplation. And again because, being based on reproductions of images, as a corpus it is hypothetically replicable without end — indeed was intended to be just that, since the form Warburg had wanted for its circulation was a printed atlas, i.e., a publication.

---

23   As many of the examples treated in this section of the book show, various kinds of reconstruction exist, especially in the case of exhibitions. By way of a tentative initial classification one might single out: philological reconstruction (as in the case of *Bilderatlas: The Original*, or *When Attitudes Become Form 1969/2013*, at the Venice Fondazione Prada, 2013); temporal extension (as with *The Pictures Generation, 1974–1984*, at the Metropolitan Museum of Art, New York in 2009, which recently extended to *Pictures, Revisited*, 2020, or else *Other Primary Structures*, at the Jewish Museum, New York in 2014); archive reactivation (as with *Les Magiciens de la terre, retour sur une exposition légendaire*, at the Centre Pompidou, Paris in 2014, or the recent restaging of the Venice Biennale story via its archive, *The Disquieted Muses*, Central Pavilion, Venice Biennale, 2020). Archives are obviously a central tool in each of these forms of reconstruction and in the method of reenactment in general.

24   Aby Warburg, *Bilderatlas Mnemosyne: The Original*, ed. by Roberto Ohrt and Axel Heil, in cooperation with the Warburg Institute and Haus der Kulturen der Welt (Berlin: Hatje Cantz Verlag, 2020).

After an initial *damnatio memoriae* due to its complexity and the mishaps befalling Warburg's archive and library after his death, the *Bilderatlas* nonetheless continues to be studied nearly a century later and taken up with enthusiasm by art historians and image theoreticians, as well as artists. The reason certainly is that it paved the way for an alternative, inclusive cultural methodology quite distinct from hierarchies or canons that lay down a law. And equally because he chose images and image/photo-montage to be the tools of knowledge, anticipating the latest way of relating to, and 'surfing' among, images as practiced today. But above all because to Warburg, as Salvatore Settis neatly sums up:

> 'artistic tradition' dictates the historical and social space within which artworks of the past, reappreciated in a rhythmic sequence of deaths and rebirths, become agents of innovation, essential ingredients in experience that reflect ever-changing emotional horizons and cultural tensions. This goes for the artist's job, but also for that of the historian of art and culture; it involves a figurative gamut embracing all kinds of image (not necessarily 'artistic') that represent social memory. It implies an expressive mechanism whose core lies in the conventional expression ('formula') of an emotional content ('pathos'), and is transmitted historically in an intermittent process.[25]

Such 'survivals' from artistic tradition, that ideal image store and concrete image repository upon which to draw, influence the artist's work and likewise that of the art historian, critic, and curator.

In thinking of reenactment as a curator's and historian's method, the greatest risk is that it be used for economic rather than cultural ends, making it into a way of turning out ersatz likenesses and multiples that fuel the production of consumer objects and collectors' pieces. This aspect has been spotlighted by two artists (clearly not unique of their kind) who are often deemed controversial: Jeff Koons and Damien Hirst. Their less-than-scrupulous repetition of pop culture has led, in the former, to kitsch sensationalism, and in the latter to an obsession with archaeology and necrosis. Hirst took this to extremes with *Treasures from the Wreck of the Unbelievable*, his 2017 exhibition at Venice's Palazzo Grassi, in which he used repetition and fakes to

---

25   Settis, *Incursioni*, p. 30 [translation of the passage by Ralph Nisbet].

'throw' the viewer, undermining the authentic, iconic, original quality (or aura) of the artwork, as well as the nature of the creative process itself. He thus rubs the viewer's nose in the working of a particular system — that of globalized contemporary art with its often vacuous and pompous rhetoric — and likewise the West's number-one cultural obsession: archiving and museumizing, which is to say lavishing care on one's own memory and identity.[26]

TRANSLATED FROM THE ITALIAN BY
RALPH NISBET AND THE AUTHOR

---

26   Cf. my essay 'For the Future: The Archive as an Artistic Gesture of Resilience', in *Present Archives: Reflections from a Collection of Prints*, ed. by Beatrice Zanelli and Ersilia Rossini (Foligno: Viaindustriae Publishing, 2019), pp. 53–58.

Reconciling Authenticity and Reenactment

An Art Conservation Perspective

AMY BROST

Conservators are responsible for the care and long-term preservation of works of art. They not only treat artworks but also apply their knowledge of art history, artists' methods and techniques, properties of materials, non-invasive analysis, and mechanisms of aging and deterioration to manage change in the artworks under their care. Traditional conservation theory, established in the nineteenth century, equated ethical conservation practice with the preservation of the physical integrity of the unique art object, which included minimizing losses of original material.[1] The object itself was thought to possess the special quality of authenticity, derived from its endurance over time and its accrual of meaning.[2] In contemporary practice, conservators preserve that meaning by taking non-material as well as material aspects into account when they intervene in the life of an object to bring it to a

---

1   Pip Laurenson, 'Authenticity, Change and Loss in the Conservation of Time-Based Media Installations', *Tate Papers*, 6 (Autumn 2006) <http://www.tate.org.uk/download/file/fid/7401> [accessed 17 July 2019].

2   Benjamin, Walter, 'The Work of Art in the Age of Mechanical Reproduction', in Benjamin, *Illuminations: Essays and Reflections*, ed. by Hannah Arendt, trans. by Harry Zohn (New York: Schocken, 1968), pp. 217–51 (p. 221).

desired state through conservation treatment.[3] The physical and conceptual consequences of any intervention (repairs, additions, erasures, or even cleaning) are carefully considered.[4]

Postmodern and contemporary art present conservators with an added challenge: the artwork as defined by the artist may not consist of a unique object to preserve. In this case, physical changes to the work are not analogous to the changes and losses undergone by traditional art objects.[5] Terms related to re-creation, including 'reenactment', 'reconstruction', 'restaging', and so on, suggest that an artwork has a vital connection to a past event but also a meaningful difference, often a physical one. Curators, conservators, and art historians have attempted to categorize these kinds of artworks and develop appropriate approaches to their preservation. The term 'variable media' was coined to describe artworks with medium-independent aspects and behaviours that may be more important to preserve than the original physical media.[6] Elements of these works can be replaced, refabricated, reformatted, or reprogrammed in a way that is acceptable to the artist, because the artwork itself is not compromised by these material changes. The term 'time-based media' describes artworks with a durational element, and it includes moving-image, performance, and interactive artworks. These works often exhibit variability from one instantiation to the next, ideally within parameters set by the artist.

For conservators, installing variable media and time-based media artworks over and over again necessitates making decisions on each occasion that affect the appearance and experience of the work. Developing conceptual models, ontology, and terminology to undergird this decision-making process is an ongoing effort within the conservation field. What follows is an overview of some approaches and ideas that have been central to this effort, as well as a suggestion: viewing the mu-

---

3   Barbara Appelbaum, *Conservation Treatment Methodology* (Lexington, KY: CreateSpace, 2010), pp. 14–16, pp. 65–119.

4   Brian Castriota, 'Meditating Meanings: Conservation of the Staffordshire Hoard', *Postmedieval*, 7.3 (2016), pp. 369–77 <https://doi.org/10.1057/s41280-016-0003-5>.

5   Laurenson, 'Authenticity, Change and Loss', p. 4.

6   Jon Ippolito, 'Accommodating the Unpredictable: The Variable Media Questionnaire', in *Permanence Through Change: The Variable Media Approach*, ed. by Alain Depocas, Jon Ippolito, and Caitlin Jones (New York: Guggenheim Museum Publications, 2003), pp. 46–53 (pp. 48–50) <http://www.variablemedia.net/pdf/Ippolito.pdf> [accessed 05 February 2018].

seum as a ritual setting can shed new light on the practice of preparing these artworks for public display. While 'variable media' and 'time-based media' are relatively new terms applied to recent art, a ritual model evokes behaviours with longer histories.

SCORE/PERFORMANCE MODEL

In a wide-ranging article stemming from the seminal 2000 United States symposium 'TechArchaeology', conservator William Real suggested that perhaps performance could provide a model for caring for time-based media installations, since both have dimensions of experience, movement, sound, and time.[7]

Pip Laurenson, a pioneer in the conservation of time-based media art at the Tate, put forth a score/performance model in 2006.[8] She looked to the work of the philosopher Stephen Davies, who had examined the notion of authenticity in the performance of music. In discussing the tradition of Western music, he wrote that 'a performance of a given work is authentic if it faithfully instances the work, which is done by following the composer's work-determinative instructions as these are publicly recorded in its score'.[9]

Laurenson adapted Davies's thinking to the conservation of time-based media installations, suggesting that the 'work-defining properties' of an artwork must be maintained to ensure authenticity, but other properties of the work could change.[10] She showed how variability and change of the original material elements of time-based media installations could occur over time without compromising the authenticity of the artwork. Rather than thinking of an artwork as an object in a particular material state, she suggested using the concept of 'identity' to describe 'everything that must be preserved in order to avoid the loss of something of value in the work of art'.[11]

---

7   William A. Real, 'Toward Guidelines for Practice in the Preservation and Documentation of Technology-Based Installation Art', *Journal of the American Institute for Conservation*, 40.3 (2001), pp. 211–31 <https://cool.culturalheritage.org/jaic/articles/jaic40-03-004_indx.html> [accessed 05 February 2018].

8   Laurenson, 'Authenticity, Change and Loss', pp. 4–6.

9   Ibid., p. 5.

10   Ibid., pp. 7, 9.

11   Ibid., p. 12.

Conservator Joanna Phillips subsequently noted that artists might alter the 'work-defining properties' and create new conditions for display as part of the evolution of the work, so conservators should not attempt to define those properties prematurely.[12] Instead, at any given moment while the work is being exhibited, conservators should document the essential characteristics, conditions, and team decision-making processes of the artist, studio, and museum staff, so that over time a complete picture of the identity of the artwork can emerge.[13]

ALLOGRAPHIC AND AUTOGRAPHIC WORKS

One conclusion Laurenson drew from applying the score/performance model to time-based media art installations is that they are allographic in nature. Seeking to resolve fundamental questions about authenticity in art, philosopher Nelson Goodman created a distinction between autographic and allographic works. Goodman stated that 'a work of art is autographic if and only if the distinction between original and forgery of it is significant; or better, if and only if even the most exact duplication of it does not thereby count as genuine.'[14] Goodman defined allographic works, on the other hand, as those for which authenticity hinges on the faithful performance of the 'score' of the work, such as a musical score, script, or blueprint expressed in a standard notation system.

Allographic works cannot, by definition, be forged. While the score/performance model suggests that perhaps time-based media artworks are allographic, there is no standard notation system for them. Moreover, some artists' practices, such as editioning or creating certificates of authenticity, create a significant distinction between the artwork itself and unauthorized identical copies that are not the

---

12   Joanna Phillips, 'Shifting Equipment Significance in Time-Based Media Art', in *The Electronic Media Review*, 1 (2012), pp. 139–54 (p. 152) <http://resources.conservation-us.org/emg-review/wp-content/uploads/sites/15/2016/07/Vol-1_2010_Ch-6_Phillips.pdf> [accessed 12 February 2020].

13   Joanna Phillips, 'Reporting Iterations: A Documentation Model for Time-Based Media Art', *Revista de História da Arte*, 4 (2015), pp. 168–77 <http://revistaharte.fcsh.unl.pt/rhaw4/RHAw4.pdf> [accessed 25 September 2017].

14   Nelson Goodman, *Languages of Art: An Approach to a Theory of Symbols* (Indianapolis, IN: Hackett, 1976), p. 113.

work.[15] By Goodman's definition, then, whether variable media and time-based media artworks are autographic or allographic depends on the artist's intention and instructions.

ITERATION, RECOLLECTION, AND REPETITION

Art historian Tina Fiske rejects allographicity and prefers Jacques Derrida's notion of iteration, which in the context of literary theory is related to citationality. Unlike mere repetition, citation connects a text to its source but also introduces contextual differences.[16] In this way, an artwork is to an exhibition as a literary quotation is to new writing in which it is embedded.

Fiske, drawing from Derrida, writes of 'tethering' an iteration to its 'source'.[17] Perhaps this 'tether' can also extend into the future; Kierkegaard believed that repetition was actually memory, working forward. He wrote, '[R]epetition and recollection are the same movement, but in opposite directions.'[18] This statement could be true for variable and time-based media artworks that are exhibited many times. Perhaps they are not reenactments, but simply enactments.[19]

Consider the celebration of a birthday, in which a child is the central performer. Some material elements are always present, such as the cake and candles, but every birthday is a personally defined authentic iteration, not a reenactment (Fig. 1). His future birthday celebrations will be just as authentic as the ones in his past — an example of repetition and recollection as one movement in opposite directions.

---

15   Amy Brost, 'From "Certificates of Authenticity" to Authentic Iterations in Variable Media Art' (unpublished master's thesis, New York University, 2016), p. 34, presented on 22 March 2017, online video recording, Vimeo <https://vimeo.com/211559056> [accessed 11 April 2017].

16   Tina Fiske, 'White Walls: Installations, Absence, Iteration and Difference', in *Conservation: Principles, Dilemmas and Uncomfortable Truths*, ed. by Alison Richmond and Alison Bracker (Amsterdam: Elsevier, 2009), pp. 229–40 (pp. 232–33).

17   Ibid., p. 232.

18   Søren Kierkegaard, *Fear and Trembling/Repetition*, ed. and trans. by Howard Hong and Edna Hong, (Princeton, NJ: Princeton University Press, 1983), p. 131.

19   Martha Buskirk, Amelia Jones, and Caroline A. Jones, 'The Year in "Re-"', *Artforum*, 52.4 (December 2013), pp. 127–30 (pp. 127–28, 130).

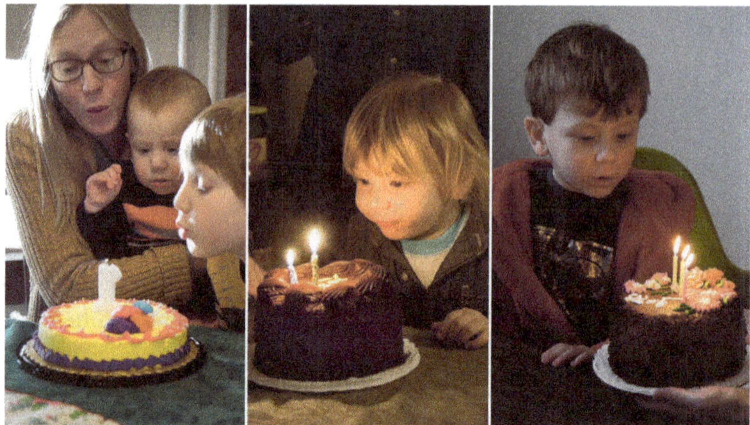

Figure 1. Birthday ritual at age 1, 2, and 3. Photographs of the author and
her son. Courtesy Harvey Wang.

AUTHENTICITY AS A PRACTICE

Authenticity can also be viewed as a practice. Dr. Vivian van Saaze, a
social scientist, used ethnographic research methods to study collaboration in realizing artworks in museums. By experiencing multiple
installations of the work *One Candle* (1988) by Nam June Paik, she
observed that authenticity could be seen as 'an enactment or performance' and showed how it was more related to continuity than to the
maintenance of a fixed state.[20]

She was struck by how institutions perpetuate the notion of the
static, unchanging original to the public, while the reality is that 'doing
artworks' as a team results in far more variety, conflict, and transformation than is apparent to the casual viewer.[21] She asserted, then,
that authenticity 'is not something out there waiting to be discovered.

---

20   Vivian van Saaze, 'Authenticity in Practice: An Ethnographic Study into the Preserva-
      tion of *One Candle* by Nam June Paik', in *Art Conservation and Authenticities: Material,*
      Concept, Context, ed. by Erma Hermens and Tina Fiske (London: Archetype Publica-
      tions, 2009), pp. 190–98 (pp. 192, 197).

21   The title of Vivian van Saaze's 2009 PhD dissertation for Maastricht University
      and the Netherlands Institute for Cultural Heritage was 'Doing Artworks:
      A Study into the Presentation and Conservation of Installation Artworks'
      <https://cris.maastrichtuniversity.nl/en/publications/48896dc1-48e5-4691-
      9d6f-6d2e5f045916> [accessed 25 November 2020].

Rather, it is part of practice and can be studied as being "done".[22] She suggested that the way in which museums label these works could acknowledge, and make more transparent, the social activity of museum staff.[23]

Sociologist Howard Becker similarly observed that the decision-making process that informs the installation of these artworks is shared, and that the artist's voice, while critically important, is but one in a chorus of voices. According to Becker, works of art are 'joint products of all the people who cooperate via an art world's characteristic conventions to bring works like that into existence'.[24]

Conservator Glenn Wharton and sociologist Harvey Molotch suggest that the role of the conservator could evolve to that of a coordinator — one who can marshal the expertise of a network of specialists to sustain these works. In this way, they write, 'The museum itself becomes less a collector of things and more a mechanism of collaboration and an arranger of experiences'.[25]

RELIGIOUS AND SECULAR RITUAL ACTION

Theatre and music are not the only practices with similarities to variable media and time-based media artworks. Religious practices demonstrate how authenticity, repetition, and community participation are reconciled within a ritual context.

One such example is the Jewish ritual of the Passover Seder. Rabbinic guidelines determine what makes the Passover Seder authentic, or *kosher*. These requirements are like the 'work-defining properties'.[26] There is a set of material elements that are required, some reused and

---

22   Vivian van Saaze, 'From Singularity to Multiplicity? A Study into Versions, Variations, and Editions in Museum Practices', *The Electronic Media Review*, 1 (2012), pp. 87–96 (p. 94) <http://resources.conservation-us.org/emg-review/wp-content/uploads/sites/15/2016/07/Vol-1_Ch-12_VanSaaze.pdf> [accessed 12 February 2020].

23   She adds to the argument put forth by Jon Ippolito in his paper 'Death by Wall Label' in *New Media in the White Cube and Beyond: Curatorial Models for Digital Art*, ed. by Christiane Paul (Berkeley: University of California Press, 2008), pp. 106–33.

24   Howard Becker, *Art Worlds* (Berkeley: University of California Press, 1984), p. 35.

25   Glenn Wharton and Harvey Molotch, 'The Challenge of Installation Art', in *Conservation: Principles, Dilemmas, and Uncomfortable Truths*, ed. by Alison Bracker and Alison Richmond (Amsterdam: Elsevier, 2009), pp. 210–22 (p. 220).

26   Laurenson, 'Authenticity, Change and Loss', p. 7.

some procured every year. These material elements are arranged in clockwise order on a Seder plate — *Chazeret* (lettuce), *Karpas* (vegetable), *Beitzah* (roasted egg), *Zero'ah* (roasted bone), *Charoset* (nuts and dates) — with *Maror* (bitter herbs) at the centre. The table must have three pieces of unleavened bread (*matzot*), specially arranged and covered, and a bowl of salt water. There is a time requirement (the Seder cannot begin until sundown) and a sequence of words and actions, organized into fifteen steps that the leader must perform. Seders are incredibly varied, because once the requirements are fulfilled, the remainder of the decisions are open for interpretation. If artworks are performed as a practice or ritual, then they are authentic every time.

Of course, in human history, ritual action preceded formal religion, so it is not surprising to find this long-established aspect of our humanity intersecting with contemporary art. In her book *Civilizing Rituals*, Carol Duncan argues that Western art museums are ritual structures that are not only physically modelled after temples and palaces but also provide a stage setting upon which visitors enact ritual behaviours — including pilgrimage, procession, and contemplation — with the goal of achieving a transformative or enlightening experience.[27] Duncan says of the ritual nature of a visitor's experience of the art museum:

> Once we question our Enlightenment assumptions about the sharp separation between religious and secular experience — that the one is rooted in belief while the other is based in lucid and objective rationality — we may begin to glimpse the hidden — perhaps the better word is disguised — ritual content of secular ceremonies.[28]

Duncan focuses her analysis on the visitor's experience, but the corollary suggests that museum staff, like the temple priests or Seder leaders, program the ritual site for the pilgrim or guest. Some of the recent art practices that appear to challenge us in wholly new ways may in fact have deep histories, connecting us to behaviours that are fundamentally human.

---

27   Carol Duncan, *Civilizing Rituals: Inside Public Art Museums* (London: Routledge, 1995), pp. 1, 2, 7, 12–13.
28   Ibid., p. 8.

RITUAL MODEL

Using ritual as a conceptual model for continually presenting and re-presenting artworks takes more aspects of doing these artworks into account than the score/performance model does. Both models incorporate the notion that variable media and time-based media artworks have work-defining properties, multiple allowable interpretations within limits defined by the artist, and programmed spectator experiences. However, the ritual model also accounts for diverse instruction systems beyond the idea of a 'score', which suggests a formal notation system.

With ritual settings, physical space is a part of meaning creation, physical objects may be required and their placement may be specified, certain gestures and recitation may be required, and participation may be required and even welcomed. This model allows a series of defining elements without which the entire iteration would not be authentic, and, perhaps most importantly, it provides a conceptual basis for the iteration as an authentic enactment, without necessitating the addition of the prefix 're-'.

Moreover, the defining elements become the core structure of the installation, around which collective participation and interpretation come into play as positive social activity, just as curators, exhibition designers, preparators, conservators, and others play their roles in realizing iterations of works of art in the museum.

These ideas represent an ongoing effort to reconcile various viewpoints and realities, as conservators strive to present variable media and time-based media artworks in an authentic manner over and over again. In conservation practice today, understanding the complete identity of an artwork is central to understanding what is needed to preserve it for the future.

These models help explain why the museum keeps a set of specific televisions for one video artwork but not for another, or why one artwork must be shown on a film projector while another, which also originated on film, can be shown on a video screen. They explain why conservators repeatedly interview artists to better understand the lives of artworks, why repeatedly installing artworks is critical for their survival, and why documentation models and strategies figure so prominently into their care.

With so many artworks now combining traditional media and new technologies, it is essential for conservators to continue to develop and test models for preservation that are built upon the shared foundation of conservation ethics and methodology that has been established for all cultural heritage. Only through collaboration, across the conservation field and beyond, can long-term preservation of these artworks be achieved.

UNFOLD
The Strategic Importance of Reinterpretation for Media Art Mediation and Conservation

GABY WIJERS

The conservation of media art is one of the greatest challenges for the future of our digital culture. Time is slowly erasing the work of entire generations of media artists from any future art history. This loss is irreparable, and urgent action is needed.

Since the mid-1990s, the ephemerality and immateriality of much of these time-based artworks has demanded the configuration of a new set of techniques to ensure their future presentation. Media art challenges existing forms of conservation and documentation not only because of ever-changing technology but also because of their unique nature: digital art, media art, live art, and performances are different from other art genres. They are dependent upon practices, not objects, and upon the performative role of the spectator. These kinds of works are experienced through media, browsers, networks, documentation, and forms of storage. Most of today's digital works of art are processual, ephemeral, interactive, multimedia, and, fundamentally, context dependent. However, most of these issues have been centred on technical responses to rapid technological obsolescence, the deterioration of materials, or varied installation requirements. Together with the need to preserve long-term custody of all forms of recorded material, it is therefore also necessary to continue researching beyond the object:

to look at the medium of an artwork and, more urgently, beyond the medium, to focus instead on the creator and user.

The following strategies are normally used to keep our media artworks available for future generations: (1) Storage: The acquisition and storage of the physical media equipment such as DVD players or computers used in multimedia or digital artworks, has proven a short-term tactic at best, as hardware can either quickly become obsolete or 'stale' in storage.[1] Storage itself is also notoriously bad at capturing the contextual and live aspects of works, such as Internet art, performance art, and live electronic music. (2) Migration: To migrate a work of art means to upgrade its format from an aged medium to a more current one, e.g. from VHS to DVD, accepting that some changes in quality may occur while the integrity of the original is maintained.[2] This strategy assumes that preserving either the content or the information of an artwork trumps concerns over fidelity to the original look and feel, despite its change in media. (3) Emulation: The process of simulating an older operating system (or, by extension, other supporting infrastructures) on a newer software or hardware platform. In migration, the impetus behind emulation is to keep a work alive, even though its original media may become obsolete. Unlike migration, however, emulation of computer-based art preserves the original code that underlies the artwork. Emulation software is currently used in various stages of development and efficiency. (4) Reinterpretation: The most powerful, but also most risky, preservation strategy for new media art is to reinterpret the work each time it is recreated. Reinterpretation may require rewriting the code for a completely different platform, either following site-specific instructions regarding the installation or recasting a work in a contemporary medium with the metaphoric value of an outdated medium. Reinterpretation can be a dangerous technique when not expressly permitted by the artist, but it may be the only way to recreate performed, installed, or networked art that is designed to vary with changing contexts.[3]

---

1   'Variable Media Glossary', in *The Variable Media Approach: Permanence Through Change*, ed. by Alain Depocas, Jon Ippolito, and Caitlin Jones (New York: Guggenheim Museum Publications, 2003), pp. 123–37 (p. 129) <https://www.variablemedia.net/e/preserving/html/var_pub_index.html> [accessed 12 March 2021].

2   Ibid., p. 126

3   Ibid., p. 128.

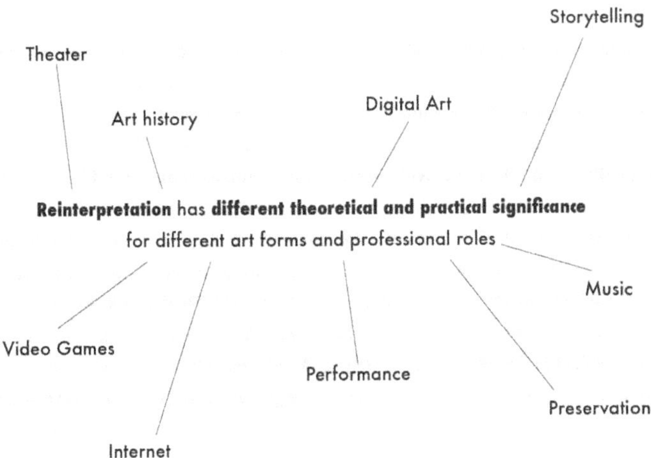

Figure 1. UNFOLD design by Pier Taylor

While the first three strategies are amply used, the fourth is, remarkably enough, seldom professionally applied to media art. Reinterpretation is traditionally used in other performative art disciplines, such as music, dance, and theatre, but it is almost new in the fields of media art and digital art, although it both tells a lot about a work and gives space for creativity. On the whole, reinterpretation can be seen as a way of keeping the work alive. Presenting and preserving media artworks is undeniably related to issues of technological obsolescence, networked connectivity, and the interactive nature of digital art. The variable nature of this art form stretches the boundaries of traditional preservation methods and requires insights from both the artist and curator to determinate the future viability of restaging the piece. How do we deal with the changes of digital or media artworks over time, and how can the performative aspect of a work be preserved and mediated? Reinterpretation is a method that brings us perspective on the potential of media articulations to live a 'life' beyond the medium that generated them.

With these issues in mind, the platform in the Netherlands for media art, new technologies, and digital culture, LIMA, has responded to the need for looking further and beyond the object and medium of an artwork.[4] This is how the project UNFOLD: Mediation by Reinterpretation was born.[5] In the course of one year (March 2016 to March 2017), LIMA investigated reinterpretation as an emerging practice for the conservation of media artworks. To facilitate this research, LIMA brought together international professionals, artists, art curators, archivists, conservators, choreographers, musicologists, and theatre and performance scholars, as well as those whose practices traverse several of these disciplines.[6] The aim was to provide greater insight into the challenges related to media art conservation beyond technology and, ultimately, to create a consortium for a future collaborative, interdisciplinary, and international project to conduct further research on this topic.

UNFOLD studies processes of documentation and conservation of performance, post-net, and digital art in relation to dance, theatre, and music, which have ensured their survival and transmission through live actions. Bearing in mind that media and digital art share a number of related characteristics with performance art, the project's main research questions were: (1) Can reinterpretation as a creative act be seen as a preservation strategy for media artworks? (2) Is it possible to develop new standards and techniques within media art preservation strategies by using reinterpretation to capture the hybrid, contextual, and live qualities of the original piece, rather than proposing an ongoing process of changing platforms and operating systems?

By analysing how a work is mediated and how it is performed (again) it may be possible to come to a different — and perhaps more relevant — core of the media artwork. Reinterpretation could ensure the continual presentation of art happening in the 'now'.

The project's point of departure was the definition of reinterpretation as presented in 'Permanence Through Change: The Variable Media Approach', which in turn resulted from the research undertaken under the project The Variable Media Initiative. Thanks to this groundbreaking project, a flexible approach to the preservation of a

---

4   See LIMA's webpage at <http://www.li-ma.nl/> [accessed 7 December 2019].

5   The final report and manifesto can be found online at <http://www.li-ma.nl/site/article/unfold-mediation-reinterpretation> [accessed 19 July 2018].

6   Gaby Wijers (director), Lara Garcia Diaz (researcher), Christian Sancto (assistant researcher), and many others. See the whole team at <http://www.li-ma.nl/lima/about> [accessed 7 December 2019].

range of creative practices was introduced, and the notion of variable media started to be taken seriously. The project introduced a whole new vocabulary, opening up and challenging traditional notions of preservation. Within its framework, reinterpretation is defined as 'the most radical preservation strategy', since it implies 'reinterpret[ing] the work each time it is recreated'. For the Variable Media Initiative, reinterpretation is 'a dangerous technique when not warranted by the artist, but it may be the only way to recreate performed, installed, or networked art designed to vary with context'.[7] Considering the research already undertaken, and through the organization of three network meetings, one expert meeting, three public events, and one workshop, UNFOLD aimed at configuring a project that would continue and reinforce a line of research in which the possibilities and potential consequences of reinterpretation could be addressed in debates concerning media art mediation, transmission, and preservation.

Even if ensuring the transmission of knowledge from one generation to another is an ancient cultural activity, it is critical to instigate new conversations around knowledge transmission. In the case of media art, this includes exploring possibilities of preservation beyond a permanent process of constantly changing operating systems. Thus, UNFOLD proposes to conceptualize and practice preservation as an interpretative act, in which the hybrid, contextual, or live qualities of the original piece can be captured through its reinterpretation or reenactment. In this way, it is possible to look beyond the medium and see the work's capacity to generate networks of relations that interconnect different versions of the same work.

Through UNFOLD, traditional paradigms of conservation that regard objects as fixed and static entities were rethought, and reinterpretation as a process became better understood — mainly the process through which it is feasible to understand another creative process and how this process originally emerged. Reinterpretation proposes a rearticulation of artistic thought as it unfolds in the original work: can we conceive of artworks in terms of their temporal duration — as events, performances, and processes?[8] Can artworks, which include

---

7   'Variable Media Glossary', p. 128.

8   Unpublished interview with Nicolle Beutler by the UNFOLD team, 2016. See also Hanna Hölling, 'An Aesthetics of Change: On the Relative Durations of the Imper-

both the most recent and traditional forms of artistic production, be reconsidered in terms of time and their intrinsic temporalities? Why and how would this matter for their conservation?[9]

UNFOLD's multidisciplinary research group met three times for discussion, and a public presentation followed the debate. For each session, a different set of questions was addressed, with our overall questions acting as anchors: how can different strategies and technologies be used to archive, share, and understand? Can reinterpretation as a creative act be seen as a preservation strategy? Can other methodologies of preservation, like those of theatre, music, and dance, be integrated into the preservation of media art and performance? What are the paradigms for the preservation of an ephemeral artwork? How can staging, repertoire, remake, enactment, reenactment, and reinterpretation be used as different strategies for the preservation of cultural heritage? How does one negotiate conservation ethics and the pressure of institutional protocols when reinterpretating media artworks, and how can one be transparent about that process?

The group explored the idea of reinterpretation as an instrument, as a kind of artistic method that makes it possible to zoom in on specific aspects of a work in its previous set-ups and explore to what extent these can be used in a new digital context. The conclusion to which such a reinterpretive discussion led stayed far away from any conclusions about the materiality of the digital; in fact, it partly contradicted the concept. Reinterpretation cannot be seen as a substitute for thinking about materiality, but rather as an addition.

For his UNFOLD commission #67, artist Joost Rekveld was asked to select and reinterpret a work by video artist duo Woody & Steina Vasulka: he chose *Telc* (1974) and *Reminiscence* (1974). Both works belong to the Vasulkas' series of experiments with the Rutt/Etra Scan Processor.[10] In *Telc*, this device is used to transform Portapak images of a trip to a town in Southern Bohemia; similarly, *Reminiscence* (1974) is

---

manent and Critical Thinking in Conservation', paper presented during the symposium 'Authenticity in Transition', Glasgow School of Art/University of Glasgow, 1–2 December 2014, documented online at <https://seminesaa.hypotheses.org/7948> [accessed 16 December 2019].

9   Ibid.

10   Cf. 'Rutt/Etra Scan Processor', in Yvonne Spielmann, *Video and Computer: The Aesthetics of Steina and Woody Vasulka* (Montreal: The Daniel Langlois Foundation, 2004)

based on footage that Woody recorded during his visit to a farmhouse in Moravia.

For his intervention, Rekveld focused on exploring the works as experiments with different modes of perception. He first investigated the possibilities of wearable devices that would give a different kind of sensory access to the environment. The aim was to make a work that also strongly conveyed the impression of navigating through a space — a visualized space that does not derive from visual information. Later on, this led Rekveld to develop an interest in the Rutt/Etra Scan Processor and to eventually build one himself. If there is an emergent 'preservationist' ethic in Rekveld's work, one might conclude that it consists of reworking the concerns of earlier works and technologies through contemporary artistic preoccupations.[11]

For Vera Sofia Mota's and Fransien van der Putt's UNFOLD commission concerning the reinterpretation of artworks by Nan Hoover, time will tell what kind of artistic process will be executed. UNFOLD was also the starting point for the text Gabriella Giannachi wrote, who is a professor of performance and media art studies at the University of Exeter: 'At the Edge of the "Living Present": Re-enactments and Re-interpretations as Strategies of Preservation of Performance and New Media Art'.[12]

The research group's next steps address the questions how to deal with digital artworks as they change over time and how to maintain their performativity. It is essential to ensure that such artworks can still be experienced in the future, which goes beyond maintaining physical availability; it is about keeping the works accessible, intelligible, and relevant. Reinterpretation is a suitable complementary approach that requires — and gives — insight from both the artist(s) and the

---

<https://www.fondation-langlois.org/html/e/page.php?NumPage=456> [accessed 12 March 2021].

11   Cf. *UNFOLD #3 Reinterpreting the Digital + Workshop presentation by Joost Rekveld*, LIMA, Amsterdam, 1 December 2016 <https://www.li-ma.nl/lima/news/unfold-3-reinterpreting-digital-workshop-presentation-joost-rekveld> [accessed 12 March 2021].

12   Gabriella Giannachi, 'At the Edge of the "Living Present": Re-enactments and Re-interpretations as Strategies of Preservation of Performance and New Media Art', in *Histories of Performance Documentation: Museum, Artistic, and Scholarly Practices*, ed. by Gabriella Giannachi and Jonah Westerman (London: Routledge, 2018), pp. 115–31.

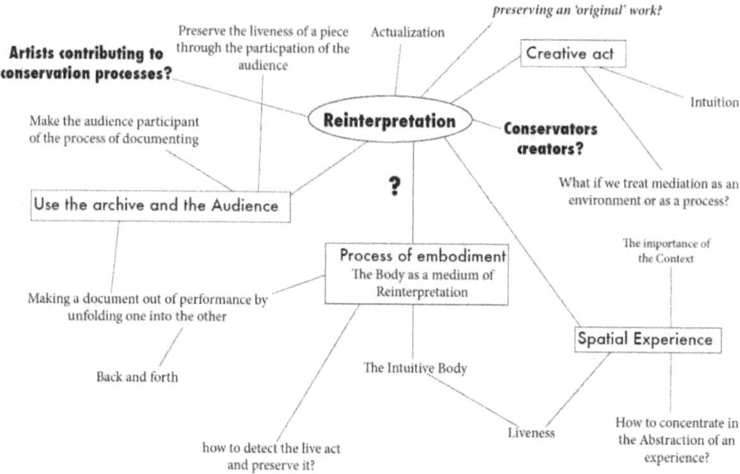

Figure 2. *Questions and Topics* by Lara Garcia Diaz for UNFOLD

curator(s) on the future viability of either reinstalling or repairing the work. It is known that every new presentation of a work contains a certain element of reinterpretation; this element is often seen as a disturbing noise to be reduced as much as possible in order to minimize the risk of deviating from or clouding the artist's original intentions. Resistance to this reinterpretation is traditionally centred on ideas of authenticity.

Reinterpretation as a preservation strategy has been around for twenty years, but it is still controversial. The most interesting developments, however, are the challenges that arise when reinterpretation is actively, rather than implicitly, implemented and seen as more or less undesirable. Dealing consciously and openly with reinterpretation yields a wealth of insights and skills. Instead of suppressing reinterpretation as part of a custodial relation to an artwork, we advocate embracing reinterpretation as a vital and dynamic element in this chain, as an important force for further artistic developments of the lifecycle of artworks. Reinterpretation has great potential for maintaining the relevance of works of art for present and future audiences, as well as to activate collections and archives and to unfold creative and curatorial processes and role patterns.

Starting from the initial question — can reinterpretation as a creative act be seen as preservation strategy? — the project ultimately led to what was perhaps its inversion: can preservation be understood as a creative act, and therefore include reinterpretation as one of its strategies? The duality between, on the one hand, the idea of conservation as a creative act and, on the other, artists reinterpreting and contributing to conservation processes has pivoted the LIMA group's focus. With no clear ground as yet, the group has nonetheless used such a position to frame reinterpretation within a temporality that does not obey linearity but rather follows the network form. It was, in fact, possible to confront the idea of the origin suggested by classic art historian discourses, and the rhizome was used as a research plane to investigate preservation, not just as a practical necessity but also as a creative space. Thereafter, reinterpretation was reframed as a tool to rethink, to rearticulate, or — as Giannachi suggests by taking up Giorgio Agamben's idea of repetition — to be able to live what has perhaps been unlived: that is, reinterpretation as the exploration of the past from the present that equally permits the questioning of our contemporaneity and the devising of other futures.[13] However, in order for us to use this tool effectively, many discourses on authorship and conservation ethics need to be challenged and opened.

Jon Ippolito has highlighted that the importance of social impact lies in what the object is by briefly presenting his research on indigenous media and its mode of preserving culture. He has discussed the case of a Malangaan sculpture, and how anthropologist Marilyn Strathern has shown that natives of Papua New Guinea sell that sculpture after a public display, only to then destroy it so that the new caretaker must have it recreated from memory.

For Ippolito, a Malangaan figure carved from wood and shells is not nearly as ephemeral as a *lamak* made of palm leaves — or indeed, a website made of HTML and Perl. But each generation recreates Malangaan sculptures because they value such 'proliferative preserva-

---

13   Cf. *UNFOLD: Mediation by Re-interpretation – Annual Project Review Report, March 2016–March 2017*, ed. by Gaby Wijers, Lara Garcia Diaz and Christian Sancto (Amsterdam: LIMA, 2017), p. 15 <https://www.li-ma.nl/lima/sites/default/files/Unfold_verslag_excl.pdf> [accessed 12 March 2021].

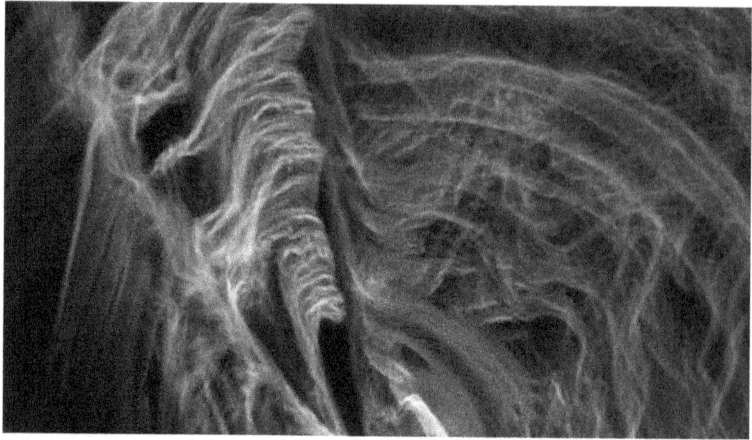

Figure 3. Joost Rekveld, #67, 2017, still from video

tion' as a mechanism for forging interpersonal bonds across clans and generations.

Ippolito concludes by pointing out the necessity of examining preservation models and traditions in different contexts, detecting their constraints and limitations when it comes to aspects of heritage and ownership. What Ippolito is proposing could be applied within a critical examination of conservation's complex theoretical and methodological approach, due to the existence of new artistic processes that, for example, are not built to last. It is precisely this ephemeral status that frames the conceptual meaning.[14]

In conclusion, the complexities of integrating reinterpretation within debates of cultural heritage preservation necessitates going beyond the art piece or its author and incorporating gallerists, private collectors, conservators, archivists, historians, lawyers, or even economists, to name just a few of the possible actors. By doing so, one could, for example, really question how institutional policies would need to change if reinterpretation is to be practiced as a preservation strategy. Here, further research will be needed to 'unfold' the layers of institutional practices while simultaneously reevaluating current attitudes and methodologies of practical conservation.

---

14   Ibid.

Moreover, such attitudes should also be confronted with the idea that some artworks are not built to last, and that it is precisely their ephemeral status that frames their conceptual meaning. In the UNFOLD project, reinterpretation as a conservation strategy has been put on the international and interdisciplinary agenda, a conceptual framework has been developed for reinterpretation, and a manifesto has been written, both with shared support. Reinterpretation must and can now be further tested in practice in art institutions and museums. Now that the theoretical layer has been explored in the multidisciplinary international network of experts and institutions comprising UNFOLD, the project ventures to further launch a number of experiments in reinterpretation.

The strategic dimensions of reinterpretation will be further explored in terms of artistic yield, degrees of necessity with respect to different types of works, required new ways of documenting works, and the redeploying of various contexts. To take the next step toward fulfilling these objectives, IMA, LIMA, Ars Electronica, and other affiliates have begun writing an application in the scope of Horizon 2020.

To be continued…

Thanks to all the participants and special thanks to UNFOLD researcher Lara Garcia Diaz.

Unfold Nan Hoover

On the Importance of Actively Encouraging a Variable
Understanding of Artworks for the Sake of their
Preservation and Mediation

VERA SOFIA MOTA AND FRANSIEN VAN DER PUTT

INTRODUCTION

The variable, ephemeral aspects of a work of art can pose problems
for those who want to preserve it. On the one hand, questions need
to be answered, including whether the desired preservation relates
to issues of presentation, heritage, or trade, and if the work in its
current state can be identified and justified as 'the' work. On the
other hand, there is artistic work that speculates on variability. For
instance, new media and digital art tend to travel platforms or manifest
themselves by generating new form and content in the course of,
or 'as', their existence. Theatre has a very different attitude towards
preservation and lacks the obsession with an original object and thus
also the consequent sense of loss so common to visual art.

In the performing arts, if preservation is considered at all, professionals often use audio-visual (AV) recordings to document a practice
or a performance. Formal compositions are instead kept in scores, ranging from personal notes to shared scoring systems to official music
and dance notations or textbooks. Instructions or ideas about how and

why to perform a certain work are often preserved in personal archives, which are rarely published.

In music it is common to publish audio recordings and, although it is radically less common, in opera, dance, and theatre AV recordings are sometimes published. In the performing arts the work is also preserved by a (cross-generational) transfer through practice and routine through trainings, workshops, and rehearsals. A recent trend in dance adds to this tradition by shifting interest from AV recordings documenting individual works to publications that reflect more broadly on artistic method and aesthetics — this is the case with choreographers such as William Forsythe, Boris Charmatz, Emio Greco|PC, Jonathan Burrows, Meg Stuart, and Anne Teresa de Keersmaeker.[1]

One could say that in theatre the work 'itself' or 'as such' is a matter of interpretation and reinterpretation. When created, performed, performed again, or restaged, even the original authors and performers have to make new decisions each time. This is not only due to the variability of conditions and contexts but also because the work itself develops in the course of its coming into being or its existence. The practice of creating and performing 'it' extends into the history of particular reenactions by original authors and all those who have been reinterpreting this 'it' as repertoire.

One might conclude that in the performing arts, instability and variability are foundational aspects to a trade in which an original work can only exist as a result of a process of numerous forms of interpretation and transfer. Whether a work is totally set on agreements between people or has a certain number of formal features to be repeated via scores, notations, or captures both in AV and in the current digitally enhanced 3D capturing, it always remains a matter of interpretation, or — as the prefix 're-' emphasizes — a continued process of translation into substantiation.

---

1   See: Boris Charmatz and Isabelle Launay, *Entretenir: A propos d'une danse contempo-raine* (Dijon: Les presses du réel, 2003); William Forsythe, *Improvisation Technology: A Tool for the Analytical Dance Eye* (Ostfildern: Hatje Cantz, 1999); *Capturing Intention: Documentation, Analysis and Notation Research Based on the Work of Dance Company Emio Greco|PC*, ed. by Scott deLahunta (Amsterdam: AHK-Amsterdam University of the Arts, 2007); *Are We Here Yet*, ed. by Jeroen Peeters and Meg Stuart (Dijon: Les presses du réel, 2010); Jonathan Burrows, *A Choreographer's Handbook* (London: Routledge, 2010); Anne Teresa De Keersmaeker and Bojana Cvejić, *A Choreographer's Score: Fase, Rosas danst Rosas, Elena's Aria, Bartók* (Brussels: Mercatorfonds–Rosas, 2012).

Variability also has consequences for notions of ownership and authorship. The original work resides in a mix of prescribed and reenacted aesthetics. The work, as understood by its authors and performers, is depending on an ongoing choice-making process and on notions of improvisation. Any degree of improvisation gives the performers co-auctorial power, or at least the responsibility that goes with it. Formal instructions, individual processes of actualization, and conventions and traditions in production and presentation accumulate in a process shared between many different practitioners, generations, and disciplines.

Firstly, original authors within the different performing art traditions choose what part of the work needs to be prescribed and what part is left to the discretion of the people responsible for performing it.[2] Secondly, many theatre works become part of a repertoire. Repertoire is available to a multitude of practitioners, not only due to the publication of recordings, scores, notations, or documentations but also because of a widespread engagement with the work through popular culture and amateur practice.

Needless to say, convention is what keeps the performing arts together, as much as its artistic development or 'progress' depends on breaking the rules of that same convention. This is the exact point where dramaturgy comes in as a way to understand and investigate the process of designing the rules and the functionality for the usage of materials in a specific work that has to be presented in a specific way.

In the performing arts, notions of authenticity, finality, and ownership are being challenged. These challenges typically occur through dramaturgy, because in the course of creating a work — either staged or performed live — dramaturgical features implicitly specify the ways and the reasons through which matters and actions are related, not only with respect to each other but also with respect to other works, conventions of art, and to society and the historical world at large. It is often the specific form of variability through which a work creates an

---

2　In general, artists that stage and design are also considered authors. Performers tend to be excluded from this, although for instance in Belgium and the Netherlands since the 1960s, theatre groups of all kinds (text, object, visual, music, dance, and mime) have developed ways of working in which authorship is shared, and auctorial and performative roles are combined or vary per project.

alignment with — as much as it breaks away from — common systems of signification and regimes of perception, that mark the work's specific form.

UNFOLD NAN HOOVER

Since 2015, we have been researching the oeuvre of Nan Hoover (born in New York in 1931, died 2008 in Berlin), a pioneer in performance and video art and among the most prominent artists in the LIMA Collection.[3] As a choreographer (Mota) and a dramaturge (van der Putt), who have been collaborating since 2011, we were invited by LIMA to prepare a new work, which could be based on either one or several of Hoover's works. The context of the commission was the research project, UNFOLD: Mediation by Reinterpretation, organized by Gaby Wijers and Lara Garcia Diaz in 2016–17. The project undertook a comprehensive exploration of reinterpretation as a cross-disciplinary archival strategy from different levels of practice, positions in the field, and disciplinary backgrounds, beyond the tradition of object-based preservation and literal reenactment widespread in the institutionalized visual art world.

Keeping a balance between practical and theoretical references, the project tried to both affiliate and cross notions and practices of scholars, institutional presenters, and preservationists with those of independent artists and researchers from different fields working with time based arts: i.e., video, film, installation, sound art, performance, and performing arts such as music, theatre, and dance.

VARIABILITY

In her contribution to the project, LIMA's director Gaby Wijers refers to the Variable Media Network, a Canadian initiative from the late 1990s, which proposed a flexible approach to the preservation of a

---

3   LIMA is a new media and digital art platform based in Amsterdam. Initiated by former staff members of the Dutch Media Art Institute (NIMk) when the latter lost its funding in 2012, the platform takes care of and distributes an impressive collection, which is kept up to date with new acquisitions but also clearly links back to the artist initiatives and organizations upon whose collective practice, artistic invention, knowhow, and activist mindset NIMk was built: Montevideo and Time Based Arts.

range of creative practices, challenging traditional notions of preservation and investing in the notion of variable media. Within this approach, reinterpretation is defined as 'the most radical preservation strategy', as it implies 'reinterpret[ing] the work each time it is re-created'.[4] For the Variable Media Approach Project, reinterpretation is 'a dangerous technique when not warranted by the artist, but it may be the only way to re-create performed, installed, or networked art designed to vary with context'.[5]

The variability of visual artworks normally concerns three different aspects: (1) forms of deterioration of the original object; (2) technology that carries (part of) the artwork turning obsolete; and (3) a lack of clarity about the 'rules' according to which the work should function, especially when works are already constructed to change or vary.

Nan Hoover's pieces collected at LIMA are video works. On the one hand, these seem to be rather stable objects, although they have been affected by deterioration and change due to the aging of materials, certain forms of video technology becoming obsolete, and the transfer of the work to digital formats for preservation and (online) mediation.

On the other hand, there are instances of variability that emerge from the collection's policy over the years. For instance, considering the way they are described in LIMA's online catalogue, it is hard to determine the dimensions in which Hoover initially presented her works. The digital files can be projected in any size, but originally Hoover chose a specific form of presentation: a monitor, a screen, or another type of projection tool with a specific projection-size. To change the size of the projection means to alter the work, at least in terms of its spatial and temporal qualities.

Thinking of devices, one could also be tempted to regard the original installation setting of certain works as crucial. How and where

---

4   *UNFOLD: Mediation by Re-interpretation – Annual Project Review Report, March 2016–March 2017*, ed. by Gaby Wijers, Lara Garcia Diaz, and Christian Sancto (Amsterdam: LIMA, 2017), p. 15 <https://www.li-ma.nl/lima/sites/default/files/Unfold_verslag_excl.pdf> [accessed 19 July 2019].

5   See the 'Variable Media Glossary', in *The Variable Media Approach: Permanence through Change*, ed. by Alain Depocas, Jon Ippolito, and Caitlin Jones (New York: Guggenheim Museum Publications, 2003), pp. 123–37 (p. 128) <https://www.variablemedia.net/e/preserving/html/var_pub_index.html> [accessed 10 March 2021].

devices were installed could be considered an important part of the 'original' work. None of this is mentioned in LIMA's catalogue. Does this mean that users of the archive are free to project the work in any size?

For whatever reason, the builders of the archive have added a new dimension to the work of Hoover, since information concerning the original equipment and set-up that she used for her exhibitions, installations, and events is left open.

One should not forget that Hoover herself opted for various systems when presenting a specific work during her lifetime. Not only was she working with the new medium of video, which meant that the device or format was changing constantly, but she also might have been changing the size of her monitor or projection because of new artistic choices, as a matter of artistic strategy, or as a form of improvisation during the installation of her work in each different display.

How do we present Hoover's work now, if she is no longer there to authorize its installation? How do we look at it now, even just in terms of size? Did Hoover care? Should LIMA care and everyone else approaching her work?

INTERMEDIA

Hoover's entire oeuvre consists of works in many different media. She produced paintings and drawings, videos, films and photographs, and performances and performative installations. In addition to prestigious institutions like Documenta in Kassel or the Museum of Modern Art in New York, Hoover also exhibited in small galleries or squats.

When looking into the personal archive of Hoover — as both her former assistant and artist Sandro Đukić and art historian Dawn Leach have done to organize her artistic inheritance and produce a catalogue raisonné on behalf of the Nan Hoover Foundation — it becomes clear that certain works exist in different versions, or are linked to a certain line of work. The many studies and sketches that are part of her inheritance attest to this.

The diversity of media and settings she worked with combines with a methodical approach that is overwhelmingly consistent. You will immediately recognize a Hoover when you see one. In lectures, writings and interviews, Hoover has commented on specific works and on her method. Critics and scholars have written about it. This kind of information often conjures the work as if it were present. But once the artist is no longer there, it becomes rather difficult to decide how to preserve, present, install, or remediate it in new settings or under new conditions — especially since, in her work, Hoover focused on the materiality of the medium, while questioning it at the same time. Her work is never just representational; it often alludes to issues concerning video, as well as painting, theatre, photography, and the specificity of each medium.

This not only renders the reinstalling, rehanging, or restaging of the work complex, but it also demands a certain responsibility from the archivists — that is, the curators of her archive — in the way they author or authorize her work after her. For instance, during the 2015 retrospective of Hoover's work at the Akademie-Galerie — Die Neue Sammlung in Düsseldorf, Đukić and Wijers decided that some of Hoover's works, which were originally presented on monitors, could be presented with beamers and be projected onto a wall in a size that was remarkably bigger than the average monitor used originally. Although the composition of the work does not really change, the material presence and the temporal experience of its pace changes considerably.

TO BRING ONE'S OWN BODY INTO PLAY

Often, if not almost always, Hoover included (parts of) herself in the video works she created. The complex relations she set up through playing with her own body in relation to perspective, proportion, pace and space, different sources of light, over- and underexposure, and overlapping shadows covering and uncovering the set-up, emphasize the materiality of the medium in relation to its representational functioning as much as the work obliterates these aspects to achieve a ghostly quality.

In Hoover's work, presence is a complicated and layered issue, often suspended by repetition, extreme forms of slowing down the motion, and disturbing the camera with over- and underexposure, to the point of exhausting the representational. Here, from the surface of the canvas to the moving image in video to the time and space of a performative event, conventions of different artistic traditions are being intersected.

In this way, different forms of spectatorship are being addressed. Hoover's experimental approach questions representation not only in relation to the materiality of the medium but also in relation to the corporeality of the spectator, very much speculating on perceptual flaws and hence enchantment. She hardly ever used montage to cut from one perspective to another. Instead, she would use (part of) her body to interfere with several light sources and the depth of field to break the stable perception of the objects in front of the camera.

Hoover's notion of time and space and use of light relate to theatre and dance, as her sense of colour and composition relates to the tradition of painting and sculpture. By putting herself in the work, she turns her sober videos and installations into a rather wild theatre of gestures: object and subject collapse, method and machine become protagonist, the abstract and the concrete compete, and a minimalist staging of different materials and devices causes a strange, ghostly form of interdisciplinary fiction to appear.

REINTERPRETATION AND DRAMATURGY

We realized that reinterpretation as a strategy has much to do with the postmodern rethinking of modernism, with the postdramatic theatre van der Putt grew up with in the Netherlands, but it actually goes back to a much older discussion about mimesis. As scholar Carlo Ginzburg beautifully described in an essay from 1980 that compares the house doctor, the detective, the hunter, and the fraudulent art dealer Giovanni Morelli, one has to imagine the truth to understand signs as traces or things in time.[6] Considering the broader definition of reinterpretation, the connection between the performing arts (restaging an opera or a play) and detectives calls for attention. Both have to collect and reread signs in order to stage past events.

To push the process of considering a work that is not yours as if it would or could be, as LIMA's invitation does — that is, to treat

---

6   Carlo Ginzburg, 'Morelli, Freud and Sherlock Holmes: Clues and Scientific Method', trans. and intro. by Anna Devin, *History Workshop*, 9 (Spring 1980), pp. 5–36.

Hoover's work as our material — constantly makes you surf the limit between actualizing things and rewriting them. Dramaturgy matches this interesting moment, as it researches and tries to pinpoint the kind of methodical logic a work demands during its making.

Interpretation traditionally refers to written scores in drama, music, and dance that are being restaged: it means to embody the score through translation, namely, to reinterpret in a different moment or from a different angle, with different instruments, with a different purpose or desire, or with a different dramaturgy.

GHOSTS, ARCHIVES AND EMPOWERMENT

In theatre we do not work with the idea of origin or of the original work as a stable object. We do work with the ghosts of these terms: for instance, when we speak about a specific authorship or the specifics of a certain work. A score can be an original score, just like a set design. Its author will be considered an original author, but still these artefacts do not give direct access to 'the' original work. It has to be created or manifested time and again, as theatre scholar Maaike Bleeker proposed in her contribution to an event at LIMA as part of the UNFOLD project.[7] One could even say that each performance is a speculative conversation about the reiteration of not only original ideas, concepts, plans, and scores but also of the latest decisions and deliberations about what has turned out to be the main material and formal base for the process of repeating a staged process — be it an age-old work or a brand new one still to be premiered.

In theatre, thus, the authenticity of an original object is a tricky thing, 'it' being produced in paradoxical, non-linear, or folding ways, which have to transcend a gap through forms of translation. When archiving variable or ephemeral forms of art, it seems imperative not to forcefully stabilize objects, but rather to try and map the different ghosts that constitute their core functioning.

---

7   Maaike Bleeker, 'Reenactment and the Lifeness of Media', keynote lecture, part of
     UNFOLD #3: Reinterpreting the Digital + Workshop Presentation by Joost Rekveld,
     LIMA, Amsterdam, 1 December 2016 <https://www.li-ma.nl/lima/news/unfold-
     3-reinterpreting-digital-workshop-presentation-joost-rekveld> [accessed 10 March
     2021].

This reminds us of the archival paradox: you have to allow the archive to have dark spaces and a messy genealogy, to let go of claims or promises for completeness and total transparency, in order for a certain transparency to be met. This means accepting archiving as a form of production, as a process of transfer, mediation, translation, and creation. To be more specific about how you produce in the archive in relation to purposes and political value systems means to do some dramaturgy, for dramaturgical reinterpretation, and archiving practices are closely related.

During another meeting of the UNFOLD project, curator Sarah Cook made an important contribution by pointing out that work redoings, such as reinstallation, reenactment, or reinterpretation, all suggest a certain set of fidelities.[8] We would like to add that the process of staging a redoing, in whatever form or frame, inevitably leads to forms of infidelity and betrayal — if not just to failure. It is exactly in these limit cases or moments of excess (which, by the way, result from being allowed access) that one can glimpse the original intentions or the former functioning of a work. Here the ghost of an original might appear.

Reinterpretation in relation to the dramaturgical question of (in)fidelity could be a way to map and deal with certain non-objective or transitory aspects of works of art, which are in need of some sort of strategy to survive the archive, the market, etc.

RESPONSIBILITY

Reinterpretation comes with a certain responsibility. Whatever the nature or grain of the reiteration is, reinterpretation always signifies a certain kind of respect or fidelity for a work or for the body of works you treat. Otherwise, the 're-' simply does not apply anymore.

When pushing the process of reconsidering to the fore or to the limit, a certain criticality is also being produced, not only in relation to the source material but also to one's own practice and work.

---

8   Sarah Cook, 'Good Artists Copy: Something Better, or At Least Something Different', lecture, 14 September 2016, as part of the workshop 'UNFOLD #2 Reinterpretation as Creative Act' <https://li-ma.nl/lima/news/unfold-2-reinterpretation-creative-act> [accessed 10 March 2021].

Thinking here of Jacques Rancière and his pivotal essay *The Emancipated Spectator*, one could say that reinterpretation is a form of empowerment or emancipation.[9] It grants a partial perspective and allows for a playful treatment and critical distance, undermining the patriarchal myth of the original, unique, and autonomous authorship, which so often stultifies both the presentation and the validation of artistic work in an institutional frame.

Considering the differences between the tradition of reenactment and of reinterpretation, it seems that the former is more about reconstructing or reconstituting a forgotten, lost, destroyed, censored, or misrepresented event as object. Many contributions to this volume try to locate and articulate historical gaps and lapses, to compensate for them, or even to restore the lost object to a truer meaning. Reinterpretation, instead, seems a different form of writing — geared towards an actualization of potential in terms of artistic method, means, and material — that permits one to move from one singular perspective to another. As in the case of our project on Hoover's video work, we go beyond the reconstruction or reenactment of the work, as Ðukić did with *Still Movement: Homage to Nan Hoover* (2012). We enter into a dialogue with artistic strategies and choices, while disclosing how the work is inherited, preserved, and mediated.

The original size of Hoover's works is not necessarily one of the most important features, at least not in our relation to them, but questioning the size reveals interesting gaps in how we deal with the artist's intent, artistic heritage, and actual inheritance.

HOW WE WORKED ON THE WORK:
AN EXPLORATION OF METHOD

While approaching Nan Hoover's work, we started intuitively with a close reading of it as it is available at LIMA.[10] We went from watching the whole body of video works to choosing individual pieces and specific aspects we found striking. From general qualities, like the

---

9   Jacques Rancière, *The Emancipated Spectator*, trans. by Gregory Elliott (London: Verso, 2009).

10   To visit the database at LIMA: <http://www.li-ma.nl/site/catalogue/work/list?classes=art%2Cdoc&agents=Nan+Hoover> [accessed 16 December 2019].

use of either black and white or colour, the slow pace of bodies in motion, or the repetition, variation, and duration of a work, we moved on to more specific features. We considered the kind of body that is appearing in Hoover's play with the obscuring and uncovering of spatial depth. She often turns her body or body parts into objects or surfaces via the manipulation of perspective, the depth of field, and pace in the videos.

During a residency at Amsterdam University Theatre in June 2016, we explored the videos, streaming them from the online LIMA database and beaming them onto a big screen on the stage of the theatre. We watched the videos for many days, either by ourselves or with invited guests, and discussed our impressions. We imagined how the work was actually created and then presented, how different elements worked out this or that way. We tried to consider what compositional choices were being made, in what context the work was done, what tools were being used, etc. We also imagined how the work would function today and, in contrast, how it had related to another time in art and society.

We then used imitation as a way of reading. Focusing on Hoover's appearing body or body parts, we read her movements, the specific timing and spacing, uses of light and dark, the consequences that the transition to colour has in her work, and the different camera settings she used. Using imitation, we started to mediate the work through new bodies, our bodies, which informed us about the work's limits, possibilities, and impossibilities. Our understanding of the work started to evolve around details, subtleties, hidden questions, or aspects that we would have never noticed by just watching the original videos. Reenacting some aspects of the work meant also becoming aware of the limits of imitating or redoing.

HOW TO CHOOSE?

The following step, which we have been developing since 2017 in several residencies in Amsterdam, Rotterdam, and Berlin, consisted in composing with varying materials or aspects we had picked from Hoover's work. Departing from the experience of watching, imitating, or redoing, we started to introduce new elements from our own practice.

Our choice of materials followed the process of getting to know Hoover's work. When watching her videos, we imagined how a live version would work, and which elements would be interesting or challenging to stage. Since we imagine our reinterpretation as a series of performative works, our considerations went towards the performative potential of Hoover's video work.

In the beginning we tended to do the most obvious: to go slowly and to start from variations in the body and movement, following our own expertise. We worked with space, time, the effects of black & white and colour, adjusting the number of bodies in play, and using the work as a score, projecting a video or just using its sound. At this point, our practice really began to detach from the 'original work'. Instead of relating to a work in its entirety, in terms of movement, light, sound, colour, etc., we chose to work only with one or maybe two elements.

For instance, when working with Hoover's *Direction of White Walls* (1978), we wondered whether we could repeat the sound and at what volume level we should play it. When introducing a second performer, adding a double into the work, we wondered how to organize the two performers in space. Should they be synchronized or desynchronized? Should we imitate the very typical walking of Hoover, in the sense of copying her posture? What would happen if we changed the pace of the walking and let every performer go at their own very slow pace? What would happen if we just reenacted the spatial trajectory and nothing else?

After these trials, which we used to open up the potential of Hoover's work for our practice and vice versa, we started to compose, finding ways for our practice to produce an interesting insight into her work.

STRATEGIES TO EXPLORE COMPOSITION:
EMERGENCE AND MIXING

To develop strategies and explore ideas for composition, we worked with emergence and mixing as compositional methods. Emergence, a concept often used by Mota in her own work, means that, instead of manipulating materials, one follows a slow process of intensification of the relation with the materials, which allows for compositional choices to emerge through the relation with the materials, rather than through preconceived ideas or plans. Following van der Putt's practice we were also mixing works, by putting Hoover's and Mota's work side by side, letting them contaminate and stress what happens in combinations, distortions, accumulation, superposition, variation, etc. At a presentation at Frascati Theatre in Amsterdam during the performance festival 'Come Together' (18–20 January 2017), we put a strobe light from Mota on Hoover's slow walks and used the sound of *Direction of White Walls* in one of Mota's performative works.

Emergence brings into focus and slows down the compositional process. It allowed us to get to know Hoover's work through adaptation, small changes, and discoveries. Mixing produces quite the opposite process. It allowed us to quickly see differences and similarities when comparing Hoover's and Mota's works; it allowed us to consider both aesthetic harmony and disharmony. Bringing together their works in a rather abrupt or radical way allowed for a fresh look and permitted us to realize how both bodies of work can be perceived.

The many subtle, ghostlike issues that arise from this extremely tangible, experimental practice embedded in artistic deliberations might inform people at LIMA about how to take care of Hoover's work in their collection. Reinterpreting and creating from her work, as well as showing works simultaneously, affects the way we read each of them. While being immersed in the process of (re-)reading, imitating, enacting small variations and recompositions, or composing new ones, the main question for us is: where does her work stop and ours begin?

Living Simulacrum
The Neoplastic Room in Łódź: 1948 / 1960 / 1966 / 1983 / 2006 / 2008 / 2010 / 2011 / 2013 / 2017 / ∞

JOANNA KILISZEK

The Neoplastic Room at the Muzeum Sztuki (Museum of Art) in Łódź was originally created by the avant-garde artist Władysław Strzemiński in 1948 and destroyed in 1950. Its various reconstructions since 1960 represent both a strategy to build a collection and a reflection on the meanings and values that define the past as a producer of a vision relevant to our time and to an (as yet) undefined future. Up to the present day, the restaging of the Neoplastic Room has included elements of performative bodily practice. The gesture of 're-curating' it should thus be understood as a performative movement that has been developed into a physically performative process by contemporary artists, such as Daniel Buren and Monika Sosnowska.

The work's reenactments at the Centre Pompidou in Paris (1983) and at the Reina Sofía in Madrid (2017) reveal a clear tendency to create quasi-bodily performative aspects. The aim of this paper is to emphasize their historical lineage from within the museum by focusing on the archive, the art object, and the curatorial strategy.

EXHIBITION SPACE AS A PERMANENT REENACTMENT

The Neoplastic Room was created especially for the International Collection of Modern Art in 1931 by the a.r. group (also known as

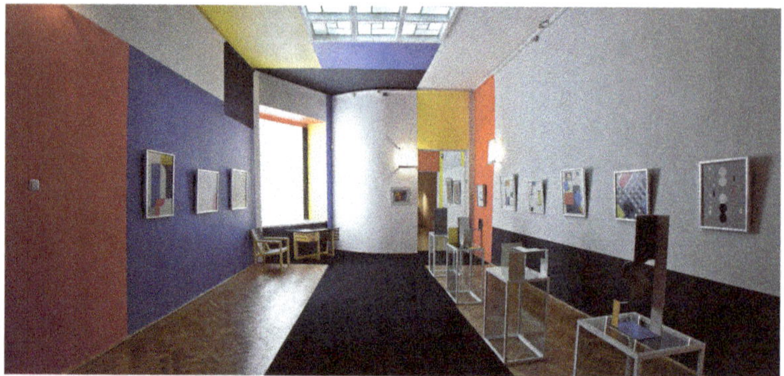

Figure 1: Władysław Strzemiński, *Neoplastic Room*, 1948/60.
Reconstruction by Bolesław Utkin; view of 2010. Archive of the
Muzeum Sztuki, Łódź, photo Piotr Tomczyk.

'revolutionary artists' or 'real avant-garde') initiated two years earlier
by the Polish artists Władysław Strzemiński, Katarzyna Kobro, Henryk
Stażewski, Jan Brzękowski, and Julian Przybos. The project of the
Room raised many questions: how should a homogeneous art complex
in a museum be ideally displayed? Should the museum create a special
space for a specific collection to reflect the assumptions and ideas of
the artists? To what degree can the artistic trend be legible for future
generations?

Marian Minich, who was appointed director of the Muzeum
Sztuki, Łódź, in 1935, continued this work in the postwar period
through his efforts to recover the remains of the Collection.[1] In 1945,
Strzemiński handed over his most important works to the museum.
Kobro donated to the museum some of her pre-war metal spatial
compositions. In 1946, Minich acquired a nineteenth-century neo-
Renaissance townhouse to serve as the new premises. In Poland, the
Second World War created a deep desire to rebuild lost cultural her-

---

1   About 75% of the works from the 'International Collection of Modern Art', donated
by the artists of the a.r. group, have survived (of the 112 works still present in the collection in 1939, nineteen were stolen or lost). See Jacek Ojrzyński, 'Historia Muzeum
Sztuki w Łodzi', in *Historia Muzeum Sztuki w Łodzi: Historia i wystawy*, ed. by Urszula
Czartoryska (Łódź: Oficyna Bibliofilów, Towarzystwo Przyjaciół Muzeum Sztuki w
Łodzi, 1998), pp. 6–39 (p. 17) <https://msl.org.pl/media/user/Czytelnia/muzeum-
sztuki-w-nnodzi-historia-i-wystawy-1998-1000dpi-pdf.pdf> [accessed 10 December
2019].

itage and to recover what remained after the material and cultural destruction of the war. The artistic and historical value of the donations by Kobro and Strzemiński — who in 1931 had also collected and given the works of various European avant-garde artists to the museum — convinced the museum authorities to create a special exhibition facility for them.

In one of the rooms of the palace, a neoplastic architectural interior was created, complete with paintings, sculptures, and furniture, forming a perfect space for the interpretation and understanding of these aesthetics. The work was entrusted to Strzemiński.[2]

The artist based his project on the manifesto he wrote, together with Kobro, in 1931, titled 'Composition of Space: Calculations of Space-Time Rhythm'. The rectangular room, with three entrances and a milky glass ceiling, was divided into planes based on strict mathematical calculations and painted with basic colours (red, blue, and yellow). These compositions were supplemented with a vertical and horizontal arrangement in neutral colours (white, grey, and black), thus achieving a balance and harmony of space. Kobro's curvilinear sculptures were displayed on pedestals and painted primarily in neutral colours, discretely located within the space of the room. There were also paintings of artists connected to the De Stijl group and painters focused on the neoplastic trend: Sophie Taeuber-Arp, Vilmos Huszár, Theo van Doesburg, Jean Hélion, Henryk Stażewski, and Georges Vantongerloo. The space created by Strzemiński exactly implemented the postulates contained in the *Composition of Space*:

1. Sculpture is part of space, its organic character is conditioned by its relationship with space.
2. Sculpture is not a composition of the form in itself but a composition of space.
3. The energy of successive shapes in space produces a space-time rhythm.
4. The source of the harmony of the rhythm is measurement, based on numbers.

---

2   Cf. Janina Ładnowska, 'Sala Neoplastyczna: z dziejów kolekcji sztuki nowoczesnej w Muzeum Sztuki w Łodzi', in *Muzeum Sztuki w Łodzi: Monografia*, ed. by Aleksandra Jach, Katarzyna Słoboda, Joanna Sokołowska, and Magdalena Ziółkowska, 2 vols (Łódź: Muzeum Sztuki w Łodzi, 2015), I, pp. 326–43.

> 5. Architecture organizes the rhythm of human movements in space, hence its nature as spatial composition.[3]

Opened on 13 June 1948, the Neoplastic Room soon became the museum's greatest attraction. It was the only place in Europe created as the result of a concurrent avant-garde vision referring to the model of exposition and museum experiment represented by the creation of El Lissitzky's *Kabinett der Abstrakten* at the Hannover Provincial Museum in 1927, which had been destroyed by the Nazis in 1937 and was recently reconstructed at the Sprengel Museum (2017). This exceptional display space had been commissioned by Alexander Dorner, the director of the museum.

The introduction of the doctrine of socialist realism to Polish art and museums in 1949, which was rejecting *a priori* the avant-garde artistic tradition, caused the closing of the Neoplastic Room in January 1950. The walls were painted over, and the paintings, sculptures, and furniture went into the storerooms.

Following the political thaw in the Soviet bloc after 1956, there was a return to universally recognized European artistic and aesthetic values. In 1960, Minich decided to recreate the Room.[4] Kobro had died in 1951 and Strzemiński a year later. There were no plans or designs of the Neoplastic Room in existence and only a few photographs of the interior. It was still possible to turn to Boleslaw Utkin, the pupil of Strzemiński who had assisted the artist in 1948. Documentation for the project based on research and his memories was created and the interior restored.

For the first time, plans were designed, which later became useful in updating subsequent installations. Kobro's sculptures were set on glass platforms, and on the walls behind pictures by Vilmos Huszár and Henryk Stażewski were hung. Strzemiński's furniture was placed opposite to them, and on these walls pictures by Theo van Doesburg and Jean Hélion were shown. In addition, director Minich proposed that

---

3   Katarzyna Kobro and Władysław Strzemiński, 'Kompozycja przestrzeni: Obliczenia rytmu czasoprzestrzennego', *Sztuka i filozofia*, 13 (1997), pp. 88–99 (p. 99) <https://monoskop.org/images/9/9c/Kobro_Katarzyna_Strzeminski_Wladyslaw_Kompozycja_przestrzeni_1931_1997_fragmenty.pdf> [accessed 20 October 2017].

4   On 21 October, the new exhibition of the Muzeum Sztuki in Łódź was opened to commemorate both the 30th anniversary of the Museum's founding and the 25th anniversary of the director's employment. Cf. Ładnowska, 'Sala Neoplastyczna', p. 341.

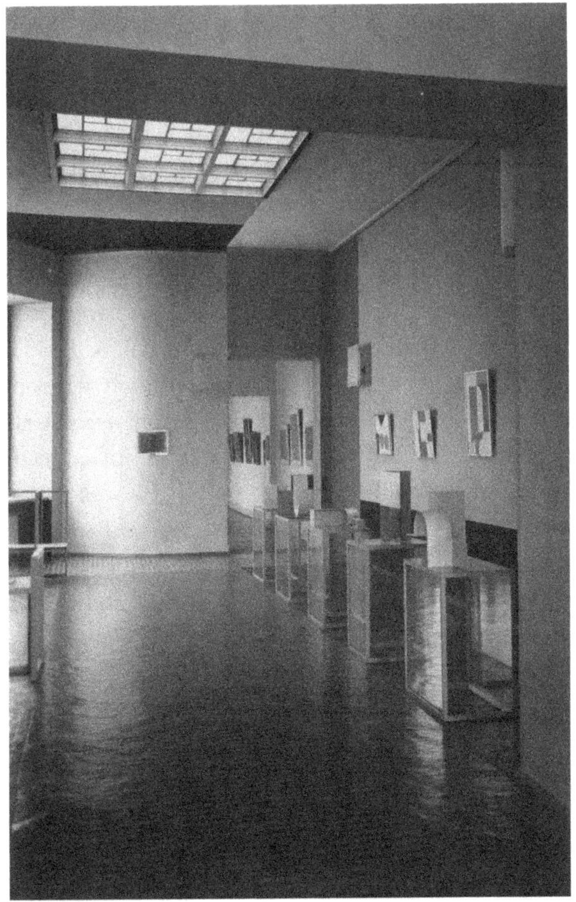

Figure 2. Władysław Strzemiński, *Neoplastic Room*, view of 1948–1950.
Archive of the Muzeum Sztuki, Łódź.

there should be an extension of the first Neoplastic Room to a second room, called the Small or Second Neoplastic Room, to increase the size of the display space and provide an opportunity to demonstrate the theory of Neoplasticism relating to the penetration of coloured planes and the functioning of their rhythm in infinite space.

The Neoplastic Room gained a symbolic dimension. Through its existence within the same space as the central and main part of the collection, from 1960 until today, it has become a link between the pre-war, avant-garde history of the collection and the present. It was shown in its original version but also in dialogue with new artistic works. The Room denotes the axis, a centre around which reflexive practice concerning the museum and collection is constantly focused. The material dimension is also important. In general, it can be said that the modern approach of reconstructing earlier works such as the Neoplastic Room became more elaborate in the twenty-first century. It seems safe to use the popular term 'reconstruction' or even 'simulacrum' here, which suggests that the reality of simulation can evoke reality itself.[5]

Over the years, the Room and furniture have been redesigned according to the pattern and plans developed by Utkin. The value of the a.r. group collection in Łódź has become widely known throughout the world since the early 1960s. The Neoplastic Room itself began to travel as an independent exhibition module. In 1983, it was reconstructed at the Centre Pompidou for the exhibition 'Présences polonaises'.[6] In this reconstruction, the collection of the a.r. group and the so-called *architekton* of Kazimir Malevich (with whom Kobro and Strzemiński worked in Vitebsk and Smolensk between 1919 and 1921) were exhibited. The Fyns Kunstmuseum in Odense, Denmark carried out another reconstruction of the Room in 1985. The last reconstruction was opened at the Reina Sofía Museum in Madrid in 2017.[7]

REFLECTIVE PRACTICE

Since the 1960s, there has been a slow change in the manner in which artworks are displayed. A new practice has emerged not only with respect to the presentation of art objects but also, and above all, in the process of creating them: that is, in the artistic process or the presentation of artistic gestures (i.e., actions, performances, and happenings)

---

5   Cf. 'Simulacrum', in *Lexico.com* (Oakland, CA: Dictionary.com, 2021): '1. An image or representation of someone or something. 2. An unsatisfactory imitation or substitute,' <https://www.lexico.com/definition/simulacrum> [accessed 11 July 2021].

6   The documentation of the exhibition, with photographs by Eustachy Kossakowski, is available at: <https://artmuseum.pl/pl/archiwum/archiwum-eustachego-kossakowskiego/2808> [accessed 21 October 2017].

7   Cf. the exhibition catalogue *Kobro & Strzemiński: Avant-Garde Prototypes*, ed. by Marta Alonso-Buenaposada (Madrid–Łódź: Museo Nacional Centro de Arte Reina Sofía–Muzeum Sztuki, 2017), available for download at <https://www.museoreinasofia.es/sites/default/files/publicaciones/textos-en-descarga/kobro_ing.pdf> [accessed 18 March 2019].

in a particular place and local context. For the Muzeum Sztuki, the post-communist transformations of 1989 provided the opportunity for a groundbreaking change in the organization of the museum by allowing the 2006 acquisition of a new building, a former weaving facility, the now reorganized Manufaktura. This site became the second headquarter of the museum. The new building was meant to house the main collection, which was to comprise a critical discourse with regard to its presentation of art history. Jarosław Suchan, the museum's director, finally decided to leave the Room in the old museum building, in the space originally designed by Strzemiński:

> We thought we could not ignore the fact that the Room was designed for a specific place and that this place was associated with over sixty years of history. Although its location has not changed, the context has changed: The Room is no longer part of the permanent exhibition. This involves a certain symbolic loss, but at the same time it provides the opportunity to [...] draw attention to its meaning that has so far remained in the shadows. For example, the 'economy of gift' became important for us: the fact that the artist created a space which was 'donated' to the works of other artists.[8]

The new museum building, however, would 'serve to present contemporary artistic phenomena, above all in relation, however, [to] those that would have some relationship with the context produced by the history and collections [...] of the Museum'.[9]

The new approach to the value of the Neoplastic Room became visible in 2006, with Julita Wójcik's action *The Museum as a Luminous Object of Desire* as part of the exhibition.[10] She asked Suchan to wear a sweater that she had knitted and to perform the opening ceremony wearing this costume. The patterning of the sweater made direct reference to Neoplasticism and to the colours and panels of the Room. The sweater 'responded' to the movement of the body it covered, and this

---

8   See Jarosław Suchan in Marta Skłodowska's interview, 'Czuła arytmetyka Muzeum Sztuki w Łodzi: Rozmowa z Jarosławem Suchanem', *Obieg* (2009) <http://archiwum-obieg.u-jazdowski.pl/rozmowy/9864> [accessed 10 November 2017].

9   Ibid.

10   Cf. the exhibition catalogue *Muzeum jako świetlany przedmiot pożądania/Museum as a Luminous Object of Desire*, ed. by Jarosław Lubiak and Maciej Świerkocki (Łódź: Muzeum Sztuki, 2007).

movement made the work itself a performance that was interpreting the opening of a new museum exhibition in an avant-garde institution.

Since the early spring of 2007, three preliminary versions of the future permanent exhibitions have been prepared. They were titled: 'Collection of Art of the Twentieth and Twenty-First Century — "Draft 1: Art and Politics"; "Draft 2: The Power of Formalism"; and "Draft 3: Beyond the Reality Principle".[11] During the first installation, the objects from the International Collection of the a.r. group were displayed. During the second one, objects from the so-called 'Unist Series', comprising several paintings from the following decade — such as a painting of Günter Uecker's *Untitled* (1988) — were exhibited in the Small Neoplastic Room.[12] The Neoplastic Room was treated as an architectural space and confronted with contemporary experiments in the sphere of space and architecture by artists such as Grzegorz Sztwiertnia, Igor Krenz, and (again) Julita Wójcik.

The transformation of the third project incorporated the 1980s' trend of emotional expressiveness; it became part of an exhibition titled 'Dreams'. Two expressive sculptures from an entirely different artistic tradition than the Room itself were placed on the passage that led through the empty Room: Piotr Kurka's *Sitting Man* (1988) and Mariusz Kruk's *Wolf* (1988) were displayed standing in a red triangle.

The exhibition explored the relationship between art and psychoanalysis; its title referred to Sigmund Freud's famous essay *Beyond the Pleasure Principle* (1920).

The reopening of the renovated old premises in 2009 highlighted three projects referring to the faithful reproduction of reality. One of them, Elżbieta Jabłońska's 'I Repeat Them to Reach Them', directly

---

11 The 'Collection of Art of the Twentieth and Twenty-First Century' was organized as follows: Project 1: 'Art and Politics', curated by Zenobia Karnicka, Maria Morzuch, and Jarosław Suchan, Muzeum Sztuki in Łódź (27 February–19 May 2007); Project 2: 'The Power of Formalism', curated by Jarosław Lubiak (6 September–24 March 2008); Project 3: 'Beyond the Reality of Principle', curated by Jarosław Lubiak (24 April–17 August 2008).

12 Unism (in Polish *unizm*) is a painting theory developed by Strzemiński in the years from 1923 to 1928. The artist postulated a homogeneous composition of a picture composed of abstract elements. The effect was the impression of a completely flat surface, deprived of depth and any dynamics. The main purpose of unism was to create a timeless image, working only with the concept of space. The idea comes from the spirit of constructivism.

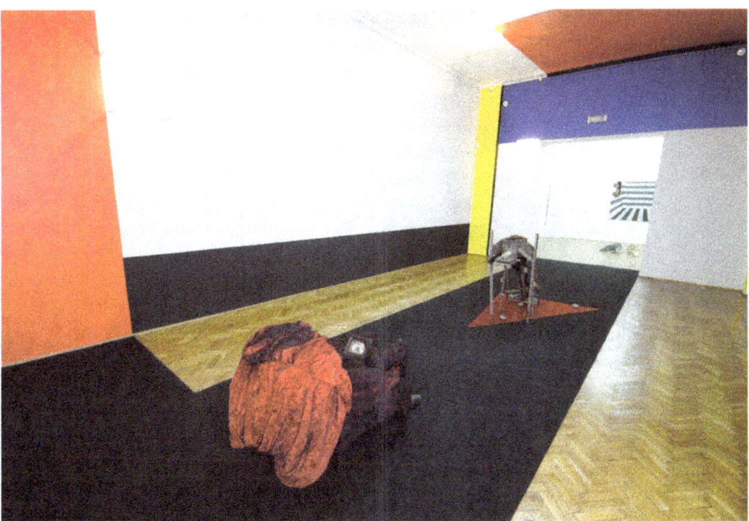

Figure 3. Exhibition view: Draft 3: 'Beyond the Reality Principle', 2008.
With works by Piotr Kurka and Mariusz Kruk Archive of the Muzeum
Sztuki, Łódź, photo Marian Stępień.

related to the history of the Neoplastic Room. The artist emptied the
Room of works of art, but in the middle she placed a long podium with
jigsaw puzzles consisting of large blocks, from which one could arrange
one's own Neoplastic Room.[13] Around it, she arranged a simulation
of painting and sculpture storerooms and presented inventory cards
and documentation. In the Room itself, films about Strzemiński and
Kobro were shown, as well as archival materials and commentaries on
the works of other artists. From the very beginning, Jabłońska prepared
a special spatial interactive game for visitors using abstract wooden
plywood shapes to allow each viewer to make a model of a neoplastic
composition. The Room provoked and implied new values, derived
from the assumption that art is a constant process.

Challenges are always present when particular situations arise,
such as when there are new works displayed in the Neoplastic Room
that start a dialogue with its architecture and the history of the mu-

---

13   Cf. Elżbieta Jabłońska's exhibition 'Powtarzam je by doścignąć', curated by Maria
      Morzuch at Muzeum Sztuki, Łódź, as part of the opening of the old venue after its
      renovation on 26 February 2009, <http://culture.pl/pl/wydarzenie/otwarcie-ms>
      [accessed 3 November 2017].

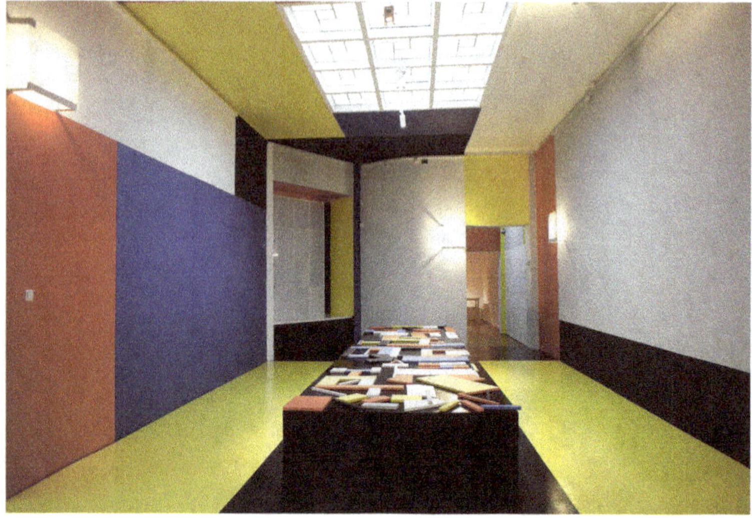

Figure 4. Exhibition with participatory elements: Elżbieta Jabłońska, 'I Repeat Them to Reach Them', 2009. Archive of the Muzeum Sztuki, Łódź, photo Marian Stępień.

seum. The first time this happened was in 2009, when a project was executed according to Daniel Buren's drawings, and that was the third version of the project (the first one had been mounted in 1985 at the Moderna Museet in Stockholm). He built the architectural and painterly installation *Hommage à Henryk Stażewski. Cabane éclatée avec tissu blanc et noir, travail situé, 1985–2009* for the exhibition, borrowing works by Henryk Stażewski from the Łódź collection. In a later project, 'Neoplastic Room, Open Composition', accomplished in 2010 by Suchan, the museum presented works and installations by a number of contemporary artists, including Jarosław Fliciński, the Grupa Twożywo, Krenz, Sztwiertnia, Jabłońska, and Wójcik. New works also appeared, such as Liam Gillick's prototype structures, as well as pieces by Monika Sosnowska, Céline Condorelli, and Nairy Baghramian.

CONCLUSIONS

In creating the Neoplastic Room, Władysław Strzemiński left the museum and its audience a a unique and valuable legacy in the context of contemporary art. It explodes every museum norm by being a utopian project. It preserves, as a result of successive reconstructions and the decisive approach of successive directors, and also serves as a witness to a monumental artistic, intellectual, progressive, and reflective effort. This progressive heritage has become the immanent and constitutive past, present, and future of the museum and its discursive programme. The prophetic nature of the mission of the new museum, with the power generated by artists and visionaries, has led to the creation of the Neoplastic Room, which has become a lasting feature and constitutes a reference point for subsequent discussions about values in art.

The current information chaos, the pressure of mindless consumerism, liquid reality, and the lack of any sense of constancy show that there is an urgent need for self-reflection. In times of uncertainty, times that question or break the past manners of analysis and extend beyond the possibilities of any planning, the museum turns again to the artists. This dialogue is currently taking place at the oldest museum of modern art in Europe. The museum (in fact, the people who preserve the traditions of the museum) trusts the talents of the artists and their ability to create a vision. However, questions remain: how smoothly will the museum adapt to the future? Will there be worthy successors to carry on this vision? The anticipation of the value of art and its development is the province of the most outstanding galleries and museums. This value characterizes outstanding institutions, and its practice shows that the Muzeum Sztuki in Łódź belongs to this leading group, currently heightening the expectations regarding the future work of the curatorial and conservation team.

'Repetition: Summer Display 1983' at Van Abbemuseum
Or, What Institutional Curatorial Archives Can Tell Us about the Museum

MICHELA ALESSANDRINI

> 'The world does not exist' – Faust concludes when the pendulum reaches the other extreme – 'there is not an all, given all at once: there is a finite number of elements whose combinations are multiplied to billions of billions, and only a few of these find a form and a meaning and make their presence felt amid a meaningless, shapeless dust cloud; like the seventy-eight cards of the tarot deck in whose juxtapositions sequences of stories appear and are then immediately undone.
>
> Italo Calvino, *The Castle of Crossed Destinies*

Italo Calvino's 1973 novel *The Castle of Crossed Destinies* can be considered both as an exploration of how meaning is created through words or images and as the expression of the several levels of interpretations and readings of a story.[1] Just like the tarots in Calvino's

---

1   Italo Calvino, *The Castle of Crossed Destinies*, trans. by William Weaver (New York: Harcourt Brace Jovanovich, 1977).

novel, archival images and documents can be used to do and undo equally valuable narrations and assist in layering them. Archives (curatorial and, in relation to the case presented here, especially institutional ones) are key places where multiple stories are produced and delivered. A plurality of sources often guarantees a plurality of choices: decentralizing the understanding of knowledge at the core of the archive creates the conditions for other stories to be told. Other stories can arise, for instance, from the replica of an artwork, or a past exhibition, in order to observe and critically analyse the product of a similar or different context than the one being considered.

According to Markus Miessen, the new curatorial urge to revise past exhibitions is indicative of a Western obsession with memory:

> The increasing number of exhibitions that remember past exhibitions attests to the importance of the exhibition phenomenon in today's societies and points to a growing interest in the history of exhibitions, collective exhibition memory, and intersections of past exhibition theory and practice with contemporary concerns [...] The emergence of the 'remembering exhibition' is a manifestation of Western culture's current fascination with memory as a modality for constructing individual or collective identities. How we remember exhibitions and our need to remember them are very much part of recent exhibition culture.[2]

Terry Smith reinforces this point too: 're-curating past exhibitions can be considered as the 5th paradigm of curating, and this may give a sense of how important the phenomenon has become, under its different definitions, in the art system and history.'[3]

So far, a number of historical surveys have included reconstructions of famous exhibitions, or rather bits of them. The reactivation of Rudi Fuchs's exhibition 'Summer Display' at Van Abbemuseum in Eindhoven serves as a crucial case study.[4] It is definitely one of the most interesting exhibition reactivations and one of the first, to our

---

2   Markus Miessen, 'Safe Haven', *Volume Magazine*, 15 (April 2008), n.p.
3   From an unreleased interview with the author on 11 February 2016.
4   'Summer Display of the Museum's Collection', Van Abbemuseum, curated by Rudi
     Fuchs, 2 July to 21 August 1983, with new works by Georg Baselitz, Alighiero Boetti,
     Daniel Buren, Gino De Dominicis, Luciano Fabro, Gilbert & George, Roni Horn,
     Anish Kapoor, Hermann Nitsch, Sigmar Polke, Lawrence Weiner, Fred Wilson.

knowledge, that does not consist of the reactivation of a single artwork or of a smaller part of an exhibition (for that has a longer history) but of a whole show as a system, with its own codes and autonomy.

Charles Esche has been the director of Van Abbemuseum in Eindhoven since 2004. Previously the director of Rooseum Center for Contemporary Art in Malmö (2000–2004), he has participated in the conception and development of a sociological and critical approach towards institutional dynamics, defined as New Institutionalism. 'My policy to combine radicalism with hospitality', he explained, 'is a way not to bend to populism but to show the most challenging and *avant garde* of contemporary art practice while building up a good and meaningful relationship with our audience.'[5] His directorship at the Van Abbemuseum has been inspired by a qualitative effort to understand the impact of the public on the institution and vice versa.

On its website, the museum describes its mission as follows:

> We challenge ourselves and our visitors to think about art and its place in the world, covering a range of subjects, including the role of the collection as a cultural 'memory' and the museum as a public site. International collaboration and exchange have made the Van Abbemuseum a place for creative cross-fertilization and a source of surprise, inspiration and imagination for its visitors and participants.[6]

The first years of Esche's directorship have been particularly linked to understanding the history and legacy of the institution by mining the archive and bringing it out of the closet. The archive of the Van Abbemuseum contains documentation about the history of the museum, its exhibitions, and the collection of artworks that was started in 1933 and continues to this day. Exemplary for raising awareness of the ways in which archives determine the writing of art history, the Van Abbemuseum's institutional archive has been at the core of many exhibition projects. One of them was the 'Living Archive' (2005–2009), which displayed works of art from the museum's collection in close relation

---

5   Charles Esche, museum director, unpublished papers, collected in the Van Abbemuseum's archives.

6   From the self-description of the Van Abbemuseum's on the publishing platform Art & Education (from *e-flux* and *Artforum*): 'Directory Entry Van Abbemuseum', Art & Eduction <https://www.artandeducation.net/directory/82357/van-abbemuseum> [accessed 11 March 2021].

— both conceptually and in terms of display — with the historical papers that documented their acquisition and management. As noted in *Folding the Exhibition*, a volume produced by the Museu d'Art Contemporani de Barcelona on archiving exhibitions, 'This active project of the archive functions to activate memory, giving new points of view on the exhibitions and offering a new way to access the documents that connect with the general public, and not only researchers.'[7]

The reactivation of Rudi Fuchs's 1983 exhibition 'Summer Display', part of the Play van Abbe project,[8] followed a similar approach and was a response to the challenges of various disciplines, including art, art history, cultural studies, and sociology:

> [It] investigates how to position a museum as a knowledge institution that tries to preserve a 'collective cultural memory'. It seeks to surprise and inspire a public while promoting critical, long term thinking about art's role in the contemporary world. [...] [T]he museum will focus on the stories of artists and exhibition makers. ['The Game and the Players'] is about positioning an art museum– today and in the past – and rethinking it as both a productive environment in which stories unfold and a site for presentation in which things are seen.[9]

What is particularly interesting about the reactivation of 'Summer Display' is that in 2009, twenty-six years after the 'original' show, it became a tool to physically compare the present and past directorships of the institution, as well as to question the codes and systems used by the museum. The reconstruction of the exhibition conformed as closely to the original as possible. The same works were displayed in the same rooms in which they were displayed in 1983. According to Reesa Greenberg, this has become a very common format in the making of exhibitions, namely the replica or 'remembering exhibition'. She explains:

---

7   Núria Gallissà, Maite Muñoz, and Marta Vega, *Folding the Exhibition* (Barcelona: MACBA–Museu d'Art Contemporani de Barcelona, 2014), p. 21 <https://www.macba.cat/en/learn-explore/publications/folding-exhibition> [accessed 11 March 2021].

8   'Part 1' of the exhibition, titled 'The Game and the Players', took place from 28 November 2009 to 21 March 2010 <https://vanabbemuseum.nl/en/programme/programme/play-van-abbe-part-1/> [accessed 5 July 2021].

9   Quoted from 'The Game and the Players', exhibition press release, Van Abbemuseum, museum website <https://vanabbemuseum.nl/en/programme/programme/play-van-abbe/> [accessed 11 March 2021].

> This approach seeks to re-assemble as much of the art work
> displayed as possible, either as originals or reproductions, in
> a stand-alone single exhibition or sequence of exhibitions that
> may or may not employ the initial installation schema and may
> or may not be held in the original location. In what I term
> a 'repeat remembering exhibition', all the original contents of
> an earlier exhibition are re-assembled in the same, unchanged
> space in the same arrangement as before.[10]

However, in the twenty-six years that passed between the two exhibitions, the venues changed slightly; the artworks travelled and were
displayed in different compositions and contexts. Some works became
world famous; others were forgotten. This discrepancy between the
'original' show and its reconstruction opens up several questions: what
story did the first curator want to tell, and how do we experience the
past exhibition in the present? What is the role of the archive in this
process?

Understanding the influence of the directorship on the Van Abbemuseum vision and strategies through examining the archive, especially the director's files that were used to reconstruct the exhibition,
is one of the main points upon which I have based my research on
personal and institutional archives at the museum. This practice seems
to diverge from the one adopted for the restaging of 'When Attitudes
Become Form' at Fondazione Prada in Venice in 2013, one of the
most often cited examples for the cultural phenomenon of exhibition
reconstructions. The goals and efforts made to reactivate 'Summer
Display' seem to be less about understanding the 'logical and creative
identity' of curators — as Germano Celant declared while curating,
together with architect Rem Koolhaas and artist Thomas Demand,
the reconstruction of Harald Szeemann's 1969 most celebrated exhibition at the Kunsthalle in Bern — but instead about discretely
revealing the logics of power and the non-objective value produced
by the subject/curator/director.[11] In fact, the restaging of 'Summer
Display' served as a witness to the ideology of the museum as a public

---

10   Reesa Greenberg, '"Remembering Exhibitions": From Point to Line to Web', *Tate Papers*,
       12 (Autumn 2009) <https://www.tate.org.uk/research/publications/tate-papers/
       12/remembering-exhibitions-from-point-to-line-to-web> [accessed 11 December
       2019].

11   Shortly after, Germano Celant adds: 'Like the public exhibition they organize, these
       people, called curators, have a logical and creative identity that it is time to study "from

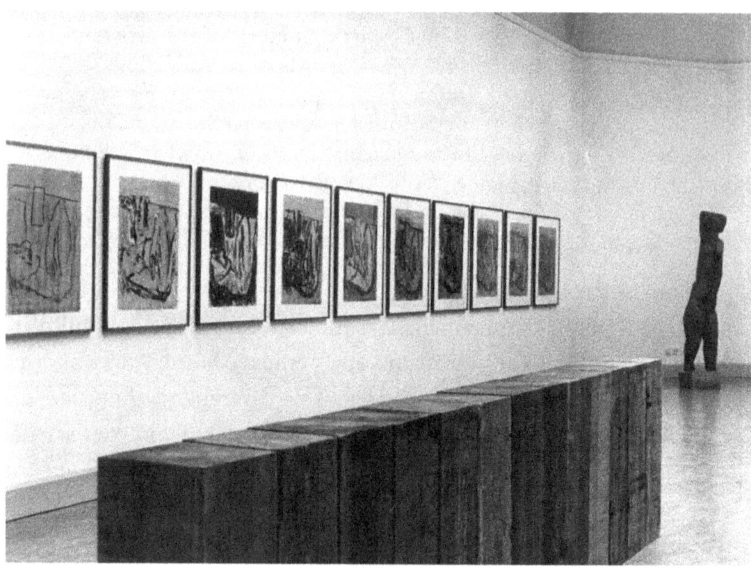

Figure 1. Installation view of 'Summer Display of the Museum's
Collection', curated by Rudi Fuchs, Van Abbemuseum, 1983.

institution and a critical reflection on the positions adopted by the
Van Abbemuseum throughout its history. By reconstructing the 1983
collection display, the Van Abbemuseum wanted to focus on the exhibition as an exhibition, in its performativity and repeatability, and,
eventually, on the exhibition as a story and system of codes. Diana
Franssen, former Curator of the Archive and Head of Research at the
Van Abbemuseum, remarked that it was a way to actually engage with
the past and the present on the same level and compare two directors
that were equally contested.[12]

Since Rudi Fuchs gradually distanced himself from the established
art scene and displayed unconditional loyalty to 'his' artists, his policy
in the 1980s received more and more criticism in the media. In a cer-

life", not just through documentation in photographs and films. This can be done only
by attempting to reconstruct and remake, as we are now trying to do at Ca' Corner in
Venice with a project of re-proposal, revisiting and recreating – "exactly as it was" – of
"When Attitudes Become Form," 1969. The intention is to re-examine the relations of
the show through its restaging'. Cf. Fondazione Prada Team, Journalists, and Friends,
'Why and How: A Conversation with Germano Celant', in *When Attitudes Become
Form: Bern 1969/Venice 2013*, ed. by Germano Celant (Milan: Progetto Prada Arte,
2013), pp. 393–421 (pp. 394–95).

12   Unpublished interview by the author, Eindhoven, summer 2017.

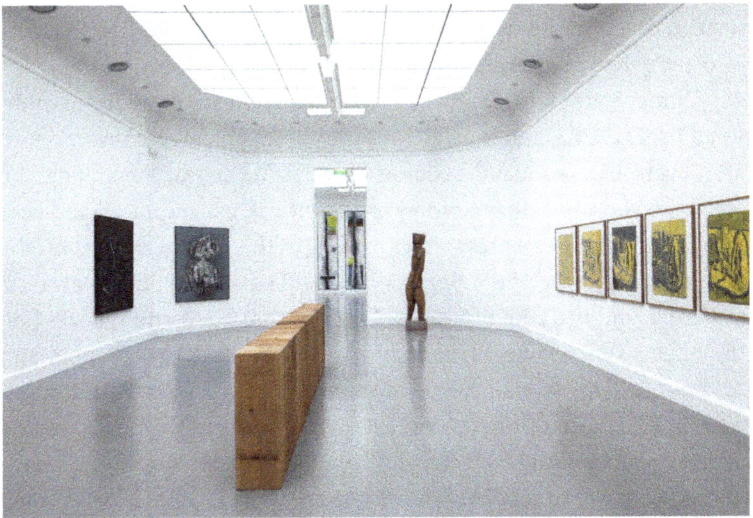

Figure 2. Installation view of 'The Game and the Players', curated by
Christiane Berndes and Rudi Fuchs, Van Abbemuseum, 2009.

tain sense, that was a logical consequence of his way of working. As
he affirmed in 1978, 'Partisanship is the issue in the art world. You
are for something or you are against something. When you are for
something you have to propagate it fervently, and the museum is an
instrument for this.'[13] Similarly, the current director, Charles Esche,
has used a radical approach at the Van Abbemuseum, which is probably
even more difficult for a wider public to accept than that of Fuchs. Actively engaging the public in a reconsideration of the entire historical
process underlying the museum and the construction of its tools (i.e.,
the collection and the archive) is a difficult effort that takes time, to say
the least. Franssen believed that having reactivated 'Summer Display'
and having added the concomitant exhibition 'Strange and Close' by
Esche to act in dialogue with it was a way to let differences between
their respective visions emerge, ultimately to recontextualize Esche's
approach to the museum. In general, the whole project revealed many
things about the strategies of the Van Abbemuseum, and was indeed a
strategy in itself. For Esche, showing the exhibition 'Strange and Close'

---

13   Cf. '1975–1987: Rudi Fuchs, Exhibition- and Acquisition Policy', Van Abbe-
      museum, museum website <https://vanabbemuseum.nl/en/about-the-museum/
      building-and-history/1975-1987-rudi-fuchs/> [accessed 11 December 2019].

next to one of the most important past displays of the collection was also a way to be confronted with Fuchs's past direction.

'Strange and Close' served as a counterpart to 'Repetition: Summer Display 1983' and showed how the geographical area that modern art covers has gradually become broader. As a way of linking the artworks and their story to the wider political, geographical, and economic context, Esche presented a reading of the history after 1989 (the year of the collapse of the Berlin Wall, the Tiananmen Square protests in China, and the end of Apartheid in South Africa) and reflected on the effects this historical moment had on the society we live in and in the museum we visit today. The artwork was no longer autonomous and disjointed from its context, as it had been in Fuchs's reading of the collection and its neutral display, immersed in a smooth container, deprived of tensions and conflicts. 'Strange and Close' worked as both a counterpart and an answer to the twenty-six-year gap occurring between the two curatorial manifestations. It demonstrated a shift in collecting and telling: from the autonomous artwork to an entangled variety of objects, archives, (documentary) sources, and stories. The exhibition permitted audiences to think of Fuchs's exhibition in different ways than they would have when it was originally installed; it helped to reflect on how much things had been changing within and outside the museum environment.[14]

The past becomes past very quickly, and exhibitions could be a way to prove it. Museum archives could serve as precious tools to bring back the past in a different time and context, serving not as providers of facts but as complex organisms that autonomously bring back as many tales as the questions these tales address. Reactivating exhibitions should be a way to deconstruct the history of institutions and, therefore, the role of art and exhibitions themselves in helping to understand the evolution of society and its codes and rules. As shown in Calvino's *The Castle of Crossed Destinies*, new histories are continuously built out of fragments of past histories. The critical task consists in being able to change perspective anew each time — this is perhaps what makes them worth being told.

---

14   Cf. 'Strange and Close: Play Van Abbe', project presentation, Van Abbemuseum, museum website <https://vanabbemuseum.nl/en/programme/programme/strange-and-close-1/> [accessed 16 December 2019].

'Political-Timing-Specific' Performance Art in the Realm of the Museum
The Potential of Reenactment as Practice of Memorialization

HÉLIA MARÇAL AND DANIELA SALAZAR

INTRODUCTION

Can reenactments be a way to create counter-narratives in and for the museum? This paper will explore the potential of reenactment as a practice of resistance in the museum. We will first interrogate the possibilities for the future of performance art, diving into the cases of artworks for which the potential for activating politics is particular in time and space — in brief, 'political-timing-specific'. We will then reflect on how those artworks unfold in the museum through various practices, referring to reenactments as sites of political action that multiply realities in time and space. This discussion will be illustrated by case studies from the Portuguese contexts that, by their mere existence, reframe and contest both the institution and its practices and the bodies in performance as *loci* of political activism. In doing so, we are intertwining perspectives on bodies-in-action, reenactment, politics of representation, and the preservation of this genre, bridging, in the process, understanding conservation, the archive, and the curation of performative actions — those that are yet to disappear.

The first question that emerges from this inquiry is related to the performative possibilities of performance art after the event has taken place. The possible futures of performance art, or the mere possibility of it having a future, is one of the most widely debated topics emerging from Performance Studies over the past few years.[1] The recent trend toward incorporating performance art in museum collections can attest to how the growing interest in performance art preservation has repercussions for the practice itself.[2] Despite the outstanding advances of scholarly work on the possible transmission of performance art pieces for future generations, there is an evident knowledge gap regarding the conservation of highly contextual performance-based artworks, such as politically-driven works created under dictatorships, in revolutionary or (post)colonial contexts.

The Cuban artist Tania Bruguera refers to these artworks as 'political-timing-specific', a term that makes clear their positioning in time and space, and how that time and space are built into the political. In an essay in *Artforum*, Bruguera defines 'political-timing-specific' artworks as part of a genre that 'not only confronts power with its own tools but creates a temporary juncture where those in power do not know how to respond to others' defining what is 'political'.[3] The artist defines this type of art as a form of political resistance that can only occur in the liminal space between a crisis and the adoption of mainstream power moves. She states:

> The window opens and closes very quickly: You have to enter with precision, during a brief moment when political decisions are not yet fixed, implemented, or culturally accepted. Political-timing-specific artworks happen in the space between the imaginary of a new political reality and politicians' existing control of that imaginary. Political-timing-specific art exists within the time it takes for those in power to react.[4]

---

1   See Matthew Reason, *Documentation, Disappearance and the Representation of Live Performance* (Basingstoke: Palgrave Macmillan, 2006).

2   Britta B. Wheeler, 'The Institutionalization of an American Avant-Garde: Performance Art as Democratic Culture, 1970–2000', *Sociological Perspectives*, 46.4 (2003), pp. 491–512 <https://doi.org/10.1525/sop.2003.46.4.491>.

3   Tania Bruguera, 'Notes on Political Timing Specificity', *Artforum*, 57.9 (May 2019), n.p. <https://www.artforum.com/print/201905/notes-on-political-timing-specificity-79513> [accessed 12 February 2020].

4   Ibid.

For the art historian and critic Claire Bishop, the notion of 'political-timing-specificity' seems to resonate particularly in Burguera's early works such as *Homenaje a Ana Mendieta* (Tribute to Ana Mendieta) (1985 to 1996), created after the death of Mendieta,[5] or *Memoria de la postguerra* (Postwar Memory) (I in 1993 and II in 1994), where Bruguera juxtaposed the period of crisis that led many artists and intellectuals to leave the country during *el periodo especial* (1989 to the end of the 1990s) with post-war trauma.[6] Works by other artists also clearly refer to the space between a crisis and the process of assimilation that follows, such as Cildo Meireles's *Insertions into Ideological Circuits — Project Banknote* (1970), in which the artist stamped political messages (i.e., 'Quem matou o Herzog?' [Who killed Herzog?]) onto banknotes only to return them to circulation and, therefore, create an underground network for the proliferation of political statements that would only make sense within their contemporary context.[7] In an interview, Meireles talked about the relation of this work to time, stating that 'the work only exists in the present continuous, when it is circulating', making evident the relationship between art and politics by means of aesthetic operations that are, indeed, timing specific.[8] The artist revisited this work in a 2019 display, questioning the suspicious death of Marielle Franco in 2018.[9] In this case, Meireles created a direct iteration of the question 'Who killed Herzog?' replacing the name with that of Franco. A stamp featuring Franco's picture was also put side-

---

5   According to Bishop, Bruguera also reenacted works by Ana Mendieta years after Mendieta's death, actively inscribing her works in art history. Claire Bishop, 'Rise to the Occasion', *Artforum*, 57.9 (May 2019), n.p. <https://www.artforum.com/print/201905/claire-bishop-on-the-art-of-political-timing-79512> [accessed 12 February 2020].

6   Ibid.

7   In her essay, Bishop identifies 'political-timing-specific' art as being characteristic of Latin American actions created during the recent periods of dictatorship. She provides examples such as Brazilian collective 3Nós3, the Chilean group Colectivo Acciones de Arte, or the Cuban collective Arte Calle. Ibid.

8   See Clara Balbi, 'Em nova exposição, Cildo Meireles questiona morte de Marielle', *GZH*, 29 September 2019 <https://gauchazh.clicrbs.com.br/cultura-e-lazer/noticia/2019/09/em-nova-exposicao-cildo-meireles-questiona-morte-de-marielle-ck0zgmjkd00oh01mtlaq1b9mm.html> [accessed 12 February 2020] (our translation).

9   Marielle Franco was a politician, activist, and outspoken critic of police brutality. She was murdered by two individuals, who shot her and her driver multiple times in the middle of a traffic jam. Ibid.

by-side with a woman's profile symbolizing the republic, juxtaposing ideals of activism, struggle, and democracy itself.[10]

In the Portuguese context, it is also worth mentioning works by Manoel Barbosa — *Identificacion* (1975) — and E. M. de Melo e Castro — *Musica Negativa* (1965) — which created explicit political tensions during the Colonial War (1961 to 1975) and the Portuguese Dictatorship (1928 to 1974), respectively, as well as recent works by a new generation of artists who have been dealing with issues surrounding (de)colonization and social (in)justice. These artists include Vasco Araújo, Ana Borralho and João Galante, and many others.[11]

In this paper, we argue that 'political-timing-specific' works, such as the ones referred to above, demand new methods of adequately preserving their performative practice. Part of preserving them involves accounting for the ways in which the artworks change over time and accept that their materiality needs to convey a moment in time and a situation that keeps challenging any type of normativity. To give an example, Cildo Meireles's banknotes that ask 'Who killed Herzog?' provide a glimpse into a past political action, functioning almost as historical documentation of a practice that no longer exists. The banknotes that ask 'Who killed Marielle Franco?' on the other hand, are sites of political statement and protest, which gain ever-increasing relevance in the current context. In keeping with the form but reframing temporality in the actual object, Meireles brings the artwork to a site of ongoing political action, activating it once more. Bruguera also reflects on this dichotomy in her *Artforum* article. In her own words:

> Form is defined in political-timing-specific art by the political sensibility of the time and place for which it is made.

---

10   For more on this see Daniela Salazar and Hélia Marçal, 'Performance after Performance: On the Material Legacies and their Possibilities for Transmission', to be published in the proceedings of the online conference 'Artist's Legacies: Preservation, Study, Dissemination, Institutionalisation', 20–21 May 2021, organized by FASVS (Fundação Arpad Szenes – Vieira da Silva) in collaboration with the Instituto de História da Arte and others.

11   As an example of Vasco Araújo's work, see *Theme Park* (2016), a video work which contests the existence of a Portuguese theme park full of symbols of the country's colonization, videorecording, 9:48 min, artist website <http://www.vascoaraujo.org/ParqueTematico> [accessed 12 February 2020]. As an example of Borralho and João Galante's work, see the recording of their performance *Art Piss (On Money and Politics)* (2012), online videorecording, 8:00 min, Vimeo, 3 June 2014 <https://vimeo.com/97219167> [accessed 11 March 2021].

> Thus, political consequences become the artwork's meaning and content. Form and content are interdependent, linked to the specificity of a political moment. Any political change requires a reevaluation of the form used to produce political art.[12]

We already see how art institutions sometimes struggle to acknowledge a work that needs to have its materiality revitalized and updated by the means of its production. When these artworks are incorporated in museum collections, with few exceptions, they are usually transformed into fixed and institutionalized entities, which do not always respect the conditions of 'liveness' of the original context of creation.[13] This is the case both when they are incorporated as installations and when performance is presented as documentation.[14] In both instances, decisions are often made *a priori*, without even considering reenactments as means for transmission due to their association with concepts of fakeness or appropriation.[15] Whenever they are indeed acquired and shown as performance, issues relating to where and how the artwork can be activated, and what the consequences of its activism/activation are, become even more significant. These works, as mentioned by Claire Bishop,[16] function differently in different contexts and times, and some of the things that they ought to activate simply do not exist in some parts of the world:

> There is a certain awkwardness to translating political timing specificity to our own milieu. It seems obvious that such interventions will look very different in Cuba, China, and Russia than in so-called liberal democracies, where culture is less micromanaged and dissent has (at least until recently) been viewed as healthy. This difference is manifest in the respective terminologies by which we label opposition: The dissident in authoritarian regimes is referred to here as an activist. Political timing specificity sits between these positions, dissident

---

12   Cf. Bruguera, 'Notes on Political Timing Specificity'.

13   See, for example, Cláudia Madeira, Daniela Salazar, and Hélia Marçal, 'Performance Art Temporalities: Relationships Between Museum, University, and Theatre', *Museum Management and Curatorship*, 33.1 (2018), pp. 79–95 <https://doi.org/10.1080/09647775.2017.1419828>.

14   Ibid.

15   See André Lepecki, *Singularities: Dance in the Age of Performance* (London: Routledge, 2016).

16   Bishop, 'Rise to the Occasion'.

> and activist, yet differs from both, because it seeks to expose contradiction rather than to express indignation or propose solutions.[17]

The question of what to acquire and in which ways then comes to the fore. Is it the province of museums to acquire artworks that are meant to be shown in places where they still work in that liminal space between protest and dissent? Would this mean that the works can only be put on display in contexts where they maintain that practice? What happens to these works when they cease to activate some sort of political action? And who is to decide whether the context is right, and whether the artwork worked or as a political device or didn't? These questions directly affect how the artwork is managed as part of a collection, the conditions for lending the work, and the possibilities for its many futures. Conservation is therefore called to the task of maintaining the artwork and its function and, in this case, implies much more than simply stabilizing a given object or documenting a performance. The museum and its conservators are thus compelled to interrogate the ways in which we can create possibilities for artworks to change as part of their own survival. In trying to reflect on how we can go back in time and still keep these artworks relevant in their political context — allowing them to continue to activate this context and participate in activist forms of artistic practice — we are exploring the notion of reenactment in the context of performance studies.

ON REENACTMENTS

Performance art reenactments consist of informed materializations of a performance artwork after the initial event. Theorists in the field of performance studies, such as Amelia Jones, consider reenactments as 'an activity that preserves heritage through ritualized behavior [sic]', adding fruitful contributions to history as long as they are not based on a premise of 'retrievable original meaning and artistic intentionality'.[18]

---

17   Ibid.

18   Amelia Jones, 'The Now and the Has Been: Paradoxes of Live Art in History', in *Perform, Repeat, Record: Live Art in History*, ed. by Amelia Jones and Adrian Heathfield (Bristol: Intellect Books, 2012), pp. 9–25 (p. 16).

Rebecca Schneider, one of the main authors who developed the concept within the field of Performance Studies, refers to reenactment as a return and, in that sense, as an 'act of survival'.[19] Although the idea of reenactment as a way to pursue the survival of this genre is particularly relevant for the current discussion about performance art conservation, it is essential to understand how it differs from documentation. While documents tend to follow what is considered to be the traditional logic of 'the archive', the inscriptional forms of reenactments are less tangible and, for that reason, often considered more transient and subjective.[20] Like documents, performance art reenactments can be seen as another partial text — having the original event as referent — that needs to be confirmed by an act of reception. Similarly, if documents exist as material remains of the performance artwork, from photos and videos to narratives, technical, or legal documents, reenactments can be considered embodied versions of the work. They can be considered the only way to restore the *practice* of the performance art event, which is only recovered and iterated through what André Lepecki, drawing on Deleuze's terminology, calls *actualization*.[21] Referring to reenactments of Tino Sehgal's 'constructed situations', Sydney Briggs, Associate Registrar at The Museum of Modern Art (MoMA) in New York, explains the importance of embodied knowledge in the preservation or transmission of performance art as follows: if 'a dancer works less, if you cannot actually dance and repeat a choreography, you will forget it'.[22] This way of *actualizing* practice — making it current and consolidating the embodied knowledge that emerges from it — is also something that emerges in the performing arts, such as music and dance. While stopping practice of an instrument makes one less able to play it, the fact that one has been practicing it for years creates embodied memories that cannot be disregarded.

---

19   Rebecca Schneider, *Performing Remains: Art and War in Times of Theatrical Reenactment* (London: Routledge, 2011), p. 7.

20   See in particular the second chapter dedicated to 'Archives' in Reason, *Documentation, Disappearance and the Representation of Live Performance*, pp. 31–40.

21   André Lepecki, 'The Body as Archive: Will to Re-enact and the Afterlives of Dance', *Dance Research Journal*, 42.2 (Winter 2010), pp. 28–48 <https://doi.org/10.1017/S0149767700001029>.

22   Quoted in Vivian van Saaze, 'In the Absence of Documentation: Remembering Tino Sehgal's Constructed Situations', *Revista de História da Arte*, 4 (2015), pp. 55–63 (p. 61) <http://revistaharte.fcsh.unl.pt/rhaw4/RHAw4.pdf> [accessed 13 November 2019].

Performance art is likewise transmitted through practice, as there is no way to communicate a particular gesture, or an aesthetic gaze, in any inscriptional form. In this sense, as documents cannot capture what is not written, not said, or not seen, embodied knowledge is a complement to the archive, which is made of all the inscriptional forms that can be captured and stored. This embodied knowledge has been called 'repertoire'. Diana Taylor, performance studies theorist and founder of The Hemispheric Institute of Performance and Politics, coined the term 'repertoire' in opposition to the notion of the archive — broadly understood as 'stable' inscriptional form of memory:

> The repertoire [...] enacts embodied memory-performances, gestures, orality, movement, dance, singing — in short, all those acts usually thought of as ephemeral, non-reproducible knowledge. The repertoire requires presence: people particip-ate in the production and reproduction of knowledge by 'being there', being a part of the transmission. As opposed to the sup-posedly stable objects in the archive, the actions that are the repertoire do not remain the same. The repertoire both keeps and transforms choreographies of meaning.[23]

If one considers these conceptual demarcations, reenactments can be seen as a way to transmit the unstable and precarious repertoire of performance-based artworks. While documents tend to express the colonial views of the power systems they represent, reenactment also serves as a means to recover alternative and suppressed narratives, which are often concealed by archives more concerned with amplifying their own (official) version of history.

Reenactments thus influence not only the way performance art is preserved or historicized but also demand a sense of perspective re-garding official and neoliberal uses of history. To use Lepecki's words, reenactments work as 'chronopolitical operations', essential in oppos-ing the 'neoliberal impetus to never look back, as if any longing for the past was a mere expression of infantile, regressive, or naïf nostalgia'.[24] In this sense, more than providing a glimpse of the past, reenactments act as sites of critical study of our past interactions in a local and global

---

23   Diana Taylor, *The Archive and the Repertoire: Performing Cultural Memory in the Americas* (Durham, NC: Duke University Press, 2003), p. 20.

24   Lepecki, *Singularities*, p. 21.

perspective, as instruments to resist (or counter-resist) official and normative narratives. Such is the case of the choreographer Vânia Rovisco's rendition of the performance *Identificacíon* (created by Manoel Barbosa in 1975), which was reenacted in the context of her project *Reacting to Time, Portugueses na Performance.*

REACTING TO TIME: PORTUGUESE IN PERFORMANCE

Identificacíon is a performance artwork conceived by the Portuguese artist Manoel Barbosa during the 'Portuguese revolutionary process' (April 1974 to November 1975) and created following his participation in the Portuguese Colonial War (1961 to 1974). Barbosa showed *Identificacíon* in Barcelona in 1975, as a gesture of identification with the Catalan people, still under Franco's rule. The artwork consisted of an action by himself along with two other male and two female performers, aimed at suggesting an atmosphere of oppression and aggression that lingered throughout most of the performance. It ended with a cathartic expression of liberation, enacted through a disruption in time and space, which resonated with the one expressed by the Portuguese dictatorship period and the Colonial War and subsequently the revolutionary process and the liberation wars in Africa. More than forty years after its presentation, the context that led Barbosa to create *Identificacíon* no longer exists in today's Iberia.

When interviewed about the conservation of his work, Barbosa was not opposed to its documentation or its future reenactment. Indeed, he was the first artist to collaborate with Rovisco on *Reacting to Time*, tasked with transmitting Portuguese performance works to the future. According to Rovisco:

> *REACTING TO TIME — the Portuguese in performance art,* wants to update the specific bodily memory of those [Portuguese performance art's, H.M., D.S.] early experiments. Access the source of that information, update it, pass it on by direct experience and present it publicly: these are the goals of this project. It's about building a living archive embodied in the present.[25]

---

25   Vânia Rovisco, 'Reacting to Time: The Portuguese in Performance Art', workshop conducted 19–24 January 2014, online description on the website of the CAAA Centro

Drawing on Lepecki's notion of 'body as archive' to some extent, Rovisco considers that people have an embodied knowledge, and that ignoring such a source, 'which comes from a relation of accumulated reflexive cultural actions [...] is a flaw in the recognition of a heritage that belongs to all of us'.[26] Rovisco recovers artists' memories embedded in their words and in their performative practices (i.e., their bodies) to transmit them through her own body. She argues that she does this by 'transferring' this corporeal knowledge to an undetermined number of week-long workshop participants. The participants, who do not need any previous knowledge or dance practice, engage with this transmission by embodying the score and gestures so that they can present the performance work at a given venue by the end of the week.

This process not only activates and transports memories of the original artwork into a contemporary context through its *actualization*, but, together with the work's presentation, it purports to engage in a conversation between the artist's generation and present and future generations.

Since 2015, *Identificacíon* has been 'transmitted' five times in five different locations, including museums and art centres, and with five different sets of workshop participants. Besides these transmissions, Rovisco, together with her colleagues, has produced a large volume of photographic and video documentation for present and future generations. In this sense, it is possible to consider that the various bodies involved (Rovisco, the participants, and the various audiences) function as repositories of memories.[27]

Rovisco's interpretation of *Identificacíon* can thus be seen as a versioning of the 1975 original event, which at the same time brings about unexpected repercussions. Her participants are not only the vehicles conveying a particular moment of artistic expression but also bring their own perspectives to the work's history and, somehow,

---

para os Assuntos da Arte e Arquitectura, Guimarães <https://www.centroaaa.org/index.php/arquivo-2015-jan-fev-mar/reacting-to-time-workshop-transmissao-ii> [accessed 11 March 2021].

26   Ibid.

27   For more on the process undertaken by Vânia Rovisco, see Hélia Pereira Marçal, 'Conservation in an Era of Participation', *Journal of the Institute of Conservation*, 40.2 (2017), pp. 97–104 <https://doi.org/10.1080/19455224.2017.1319872>.

presentation in the public sphere. However, as the work's creative authority is divided between Barbosa and Rovisco — and arguably the workshop's participants — how can such a fragile work, devoid of substantive materiality, be preserved or transmitted in a museum context? What are the consequences of this practice for museums?

PERFORMANCE ART AND THE MUSEUM IN THE AGE OF REENACTMENT

The museum is arguably where artistic practices are recognized as worthy of being transmitted to future generations. Taking into account the characteristics of the processes involved in the creation of performance art, it is of utmost importance to ask: what place does the museum occupy in the memorialization of performing arts practices, and those in particular that are political timing specific? On the other hand, how can museums account for the memorialization of those practices?

We have seen various efforts emerging from Portuguese institutions in the last few years. 'Projecto P!' (São Luiz Theatre and other places in Lisbon, April/2017) and 'Museum as Performance' (Serralves Museum, Porto, since 2015) are two examples that make visible the relevance and urgency of rethinking the place of the museum in relation to performance and reenactment. 'Projecto P!' was a three-day public, artistic, and cultural programme put on in Lisbon in 2017. Rehearsed as a celebration of the centenary of the 'Futurist Conference' designed and executed by the Portuguese artist Almada Negreiros in 1917, this curatorial programme conjoined artists and scholars in rethinking performance in the public sphere. The 'Futurist Conference' was in itself both an artistic and political manifesto, with Negreiros looking to articulate artistic forms akin to acts of dissent. The political-timing-specific nature of the piece is undeniable, and yet, 'Projecto P!' brought in new perspectives on that specific moment, showing some of the ways performance reenactment can actualize these works both in content and form.

The curator, Ana Pais, created a place for discussing the function and roles of public and artistic institutions in the preservation of memories of performance and the connections between their legacy and contemporary performance practices. Some of the most relevant moments include the artistic projects presented at MNAC — Museu do Chiado, such as the works of Kata Kóvacs and Tom O'Doherty, and, again, the project *Reacting to Time*. Rovisco, in collaboration with Bruno Humberto, presented, in this context, a reenactment of Fernando Aguiar's *Expresiones y Interaccion* (1997).[28] Rovisco's project of transmission once again brought a performance work that lacked historical inscription, both in bodies and documents, into the public sphere. The inclusion of the project into an overarching curatorial programme aiming to discuss the place of performance artworks and their memories in the institutional context additionally rendered a new instantiation of a moment in time that was somewhat forgotten. Still, in the context of 'Projecto P!' it is worth mentioning a new rendition of the 'Futurist Conference', which was reframed by the former artist collective Homeoestéticos as a reinvention of the pivotal event held one hundred years previously (*Zuturismo [or the Penultimatum Zuturista] — Ex-Homeoestéticos Zuturistas — Reinvenções*).[29] In actualizing the performance, to use Lepecki's words, his loose form of reenactment brought the seminal moment of the 'Futurist Conference' back to the present, recontextualizing it and making the theatre a place for memory transmission, political action, and, indeed, chronopolitical operations.[30] As will become clear, the programme 'Museum as Performance' also reestablishes the museum as a place of memory transmission of and in performance.

Presented as a joint curatorial programme by Cristina Grande, Ricardo Nicolau, and Pedro Rocha, curators at the Serralves Foundation/ Museum, 'Museum as Performance' has been taking place over the course of a weekend every year, starting in September 2015. Artists are invited to occupy not only the galleries but also the outdoor space, Parque Serralves. This programme has brought together artistic col-

---

28   *Transmission X, Reacting to Time — Portuguese in Performance*, performance, Vânia Rovisco with Fernando Aguiar in collaboration with Bruno Humberto, MNAC (Museu Nacional de Arte Contemporânea), 12 April 2017. Participants: Mário Afonso, Pedro Castella, Bruno Humberto, Tiago Vieira.

29   Manuel João Vieira, Pedro Portugal, and Pedro Proença, *Reinvenções — 100 anos da Conferência Futurista de Almada Negreiros*, performance, São Luiz Teatro Municipal, 14 April 2017, online videorecording, 16:31 min, Youtube, 27 September 2018 <https://www.youtube.com/watch?v=hz4l8AeoLZQ> [accessed 12 February 2020].

30   See in particular chapter 4, 'The Body as Archive: Will to Re-Enact and the Afterlives of Dances', in Lepecki, *Singularities*, pp. 115–42.

lectives and individual Portuguese and international artists dedicated to the practice of performance. The programme was intended to restore a programmatic, curatorial, and artistic memory related to the institution's founding moments and its historical connection to practice and performance presentation. Therefore, the aim is linked to the continuity of this programmatic cycle, which started in the 1990s. The bodily memory of the institution, which was founded on the possibilities for the museum as a place of performance, is therefore brought together through this programme; more than trying to recover the memories of specific works, 'Museum as Performance' tries to restore the memories of the institution itself.[31]

We cannot ignore the attempts in recent years to engage in international dialogue, with museums such as Tate Modern (London), the Stedelijk Museum (Amsterdam), and the MoMA (New York) developing curatorial and conservation projects particularly dedicated to performance.

Those practices of memorialization indeed express some of the possibilities that emerge from the process of going back and yet always remaining in the present. There are, however, other aspects of museum practice that are not quite so explicit, and that create structures of fixation that hamper the possibilities for these artworks to change. In the Foucaultian and Agambenian perspectives, the museum is both an institutional and confining device, responsible for the selection, control, organization, and hierarchization of history and knowledge through the collection of its memories. In the case of modern and contemporary art museums, colonial practices leading to the legitimization of hegemonic narratives have been progressively questioned. Indeed, the incorporation of installations, video art, or other performance-like artworks attests to a discrepancy between these variable artistic practices and the museum, which is inherently a static and permanent space.

In this sense, museums and reenactments suffer from an inherent anachronistic nature, existing in a liminal space between the past and the future. In both the museum and in reenactment practices,

---

31   This intention was revealed during an interview conducted by Daniela Salazar with the curators of 'Museum as Performance' — Cristina Grande, Ricardo Nicolau, and Pedro Rocha — on 13 November 2015 at Serralves Museum.

the intrinsic liminality contests both the confinement identified by Foucault and the idea of the museum as a repository. The museum is now considered a place of experience, with the concept of performativity being applied in several departments, such as the curatorial department or the department dedicated to public programmes and educational services.[32] For this reason, art historian Dorothea von Hantelmann considers 'the art museum the model of progress [that] is realized performatively'. She adds, 'Within the museum's performative dimension, aimed at the self-formation of the individual (as a politically mature citizen), lies a historical and cultural achievement that not only includes viewer participation but is even exclusively oriented towards it.'[33]

Public participation is, therefore, one of the ways counter-historical narratives endure throughout history in the form of reenactment. Rovisco's participatory practices, rather than centralizing the artwork in the museum structure, or even in the artist's figure, diffract authority in the bodies of all the workshop's participants. Drawing on Lepecki's notion of 'chronopolitics',[34] Rovisco's reenactments advance counter-narratives in the context of the museum. By promoting immediacy and transmission of affects along with the many other interpretations of what has been collected by archives, reenactments function as loci of historical resistance. But how does this affect the preservation of the artistic manifestation? Can Rovisco's process effectively contribute to creating what is usually called 'performance art's afterlives'?

According to the performance studies theorist Louis van den Hengel, the afterlife of performance art can be seen as memory devices that

---

32   If it is true that the practice of reenactment evokes other ways of thinking about museum practices by questioning the museum's temporalities, or its crystallized knowledge and histories, then reenactment is also responsible for reinforcing this tendency of a place of experiences that is growing in the museum institution, not just as a living place, but a place of this new 'experience economy'. This topic falls beyond this essay's scope. For more on this, see Dorothea von Hantelmann, 'The Experiential Turn', in *Living Collections Catalogue*, 4 vols to date (Minneapolis: Walker Art Center, 2014–), I: *On Performativity*, ed. by Elizabeth Carpenter (2014) <http://walkerart.org/collections/publications/performativity/experiential-turn/> [accessed 13 July 2021].

33   Dorothea von Hantelmann, *How to Do Things with Art: What Performativity Means in Art* (Zurich: JRP Ringier; Dijon: Les presses du réel, 2010), p. 99.

34   See Lepecki, Singularities, chapter 4, pp. 115–42.

can be expressed 'through particular bodies and individuals' and yet 'cannot be contained in any single place but rather operates by way of affective interconnections or creative encounters'. In this sense, as Van Den Hengel puts it, memory itself '*works* as a performative practice'.[35]

It is therefore possible to think of reenactment as the potential to develop the 'still non-exhausted creative fields of "impalpable possibilities"' of past performance artworks.[36] In the case of Rovisco's workshop, the 'impalpable possibilities' of reenactment are materialized through the bodies of all participants — both of those who perform and of those who witness the performance. Thus, all agencies appear as instruments to materialize that potentiality of activation. Bodies then become an (an)archive of practices, as changeable as the repertoire itself, since the body is not stable and can neither be contained nor stored. It subsequently becomes a body archive.

The embodied memories of the participants, which constitute the archive in a broad sense, are thus successively constructed, conditioned, and framed, as many times as the archive is either performed or thought.

CONCLUSIONS

This essay has explored the potential of reenactment for recovering counter-narratives of performance art in museums, which are usually seen as contained and static spaces. Political-timing specific artwork is a form of artistic practice that necessarily reframes museum procedures, which are very much programmed to limit the possibilities for change. Artistic projects such as *Reacting to Time, Portugueses na Performance* challenge institutional normativity both because they aim at reenacting political-timing-specific performance artworks in museums, and because they do so through participatory practices that diffract authorial control.

---

35   Louis van den Hengel, 'Archives of Affect: Performance, Reenactment, and the Becoming of Memory', in *Materializing Memory in Art and Popular Culture*, ed. by Laszlo Muntean, Liedeke Plate, and Anneke Smelik (London: Routledge, 2017), pp. 125–42 (p. 127).

36   Lepecki, 'The Body as Archive', p. 31.

Lepecki's notion of performance being constituted by 'impalpable possibilities', along with his idea of the 'body as archive', has ramifications for what constitutes the archive and, more specifically, for the preservation of performance art. Performance art memory then works through reenactment, especially when bodies embody practices and transmit them to future generations. The project *Reacting to Time* has shown how reenactments can indeed bring new contexts of political activism and practice to the museum and activate the space politically in different ways.

Reenactments appear as memory practices, which, rather than repeating (oppressive male- and Western-centric) historical narratives, diffract history in different bodies, perspectives, and memories. In this sense, reenactments are forms of preservation that recall embodied and inscriptional archives, often resulting in interchanging spaces between conservation and curatorial practices. They are forms of contestation in themselves; therefore, they remember both the liminality and insubordinate nature nurtured in the original event and multiply the instances of political dissent, adapting the form of the performance to acknowledge various political circumstances. This is what the original event becomes: a point of origin of multiple instantiations, the start of a life full of expected and unexpected transformations, of turning points that lead to unstable and successive acts of recreation.

ACKNOWLEDGEMENTS

We want to express our gratitude to artists E. M. de Melo e Castro, Manoel Barbosa, and Vânia Rovisco for their abundant generosity. Thank you to Vânia Rovisco and her colleagues for allowing us to observe and experience their process, which was so influential for us. Thank you also to the reviewers and the editors for all the comments that led to the improvement of this paper. A final thank you to Cláudia Madeira, Rita Macedo, and Margarida Alves for all the meaningful and intellectual exchanges, without which this research would not be possible. Finally, this fieldwork research that led to writing this paper and our PhD dissertations was supported by the Fundação para a Ciência e Tecnologia (SFRH/BD/90040/2012, PD/BD/105900/2014). IHC is financed by the Fundação para a Ciência e a Tecnologia, I.P., in the context of the projects UIDB/04209/2020 and UIDP/04209/2020.

'We Are Gathering Experience'
Restaging the History of Art Education
ALETHEA ROCKWELL

> Art is concerned with the how, not the what.
>
> Josef Albers

Draw the negative space between the rungs of a stool. Draw your name backwards. Draw a page of zigzags. Make a rock look like fur. These directives may ring of instruction-based conceptual art, but they predate that movement by thirty years. They are exercises developed by artist and educator Josef Albers to train young artists in what he referred to as the 'how' of art.[1] Albers's emphasis on technical and material experimentation has had a major influence on art education since he began teaching at the Bauhaus in 1923. It is also a touchstone for museum education departments, where there is an interest in shifting audiences' perceptions of works of art as fixed and final objects. Moving away from simply presenting the object (the what), how do museums make present artistic processes (the how)?

This essay considers the restaging of those aspects of artistic practice that fall outside of what is considered a work of art. It specifically

---

1   Frederick A. Horowitz and Brenda Danilowitz, *Josef Albers: To Open Eyes* (London: Phaidon, 2006), p. 82. Cf. Josef Albers, 'The Meaning of Art', paper presented at Berea College, Berea, Kentucky, and Black Mountain College, 12 March 1940.

looks to examples of teaching exercises and therapeutic protocols that modern artists have developed in tandem and dialogue with the body of artistic production that is typically displayed. Actively carrying out these exercises animates the study of how artistic practice is transmitted from one generation of artists to another — whether in formal educational institutions or, as is so often the case, through alternative channels and communities. When presented through participatory programming in a museum context, this strategy of reenacting an artist's specific pedagogical exercises and protocols allows for a richer reading of their material processes and their social and collective ways of working.

The examples given here are drawn from my experience working in the public programming division of the Education department at the Museum of Modern Art (MoMA) in New York. While museums have overarching educational mandates, education staff members are often distinguished from those in curatorial departments through their focus on audiences over objects, or, put differently, their charge to make objects as accessible as possible. The word 'accessible' can take on negative connotations, because it brings to mind the 'watering down' of material. In this paper, however, I echo the scholar Irit Rogoff, who has defined access as 'the ability to formulate one's own questions, as opposed to those that are posed to you in the name of an open and participatory democratic process, for it is clear that those who formulate the questions produce the playing field'.[2] I will return to this idea of access later on, because it can serve as a useful measure for adjudicating the value of reprising pedagogical practices from the past.

Albers's pedagogical theory has a particular resonance for educators at MoMA because of the history of his relationship with the museum. In the early years after its founding in 1929, the museum used the Bauhaus as a model, both in its architecture and its division of departments, which placed equal value on fine arts, architecture, and design. When the Bauhaus was shuttered due to mounting antagonism from the Nazi party, it was Philip Johnson, MoMA's first curator of architecture, who helped secure positions for Albers and his wife and

---

2   Irit Rogoff, 'Turning', *e-flux journal*, 00 (November 2008) <http://www.e-flux.com/journal/00/68470/turning/> [accessed 14 November 2017].

fellow artist Anni Albers at the experimental Black Mountain College in North Carolina. Later, both Josef and Anni Albers would teach through MoMA's education programmes.

Albers's pedagogical innovations began with the Bauhaus *Vorkurs*, or preliminary course, which he took up teaching in 1923. As an introduction to colour and form, it became a central expression of the school's philosophy. It cast off the traditional approach that would have students copy from live models, plaster casts, or the work of the masters, and instead focused on experimental interrogation of the qualities of materials and form. In Albers's words:

> First we seek contact with the material. [...] Instead of pasting it we will put paper together by sewing, buttoning, riveting, typing, and pinning it; in other words we fasten it in a multi-tude of ways. We will test the possibilities of its tensile and compression-resistant strength. In so doing, we do not always create 'works of art', but rather experiments; it is not our ambi-tion to fill museums: we are gathering experience.[3]

After leaving Germany, Albers would further his progressive teach-ing methods at Black Mountain College and, beginning in 1950, Yale University, his students including Eva Hesse, Ruth Asawa, Ray John-son, Cy Twombly, Richard Anuszkiewicz, John Chamberlain, Richard Serra, and Robert Rauschenberg. What makes Albers's educational theory relevant to this discussion is that he had defined methods for students to learn about materials through systematic study. For ex-ample, he would hand out a single sheet of paper and talk about the paper's tendency to lie flat. What can be done with this flat thing to make it more interesting? With a single fold it can stand on edge. With two or three folds, the strength and visual design of the paper becomes more complicated. Albers decried art education that he characterized as 'undisciplined laissez-faire' or 'self-expressionism', just as much as he dismissed the traditional methods that he called 'imitative parroting' or 'discipleship'.[4] For him, moving away from copying the Old Masters did not mean renouncing discipline altogether for a perspective that

---

3   Josef Albers, 'Creative Education' (1928), in Hans Maria Wingler, *The Bauhaus: Wei-mar, Dessau, Berlin, Chicago*, ed. by Joseph Stein, trans. by Wolfgang Jabs and Basil Gilbert (Cambridge, MA: MIT Press, 1969), pp. 142–43 (p. 142).

4   Josef Albers, 'On Education and Art Education', lecture held 28 November1939 at a teacher's meeting in Winnetka, Illinois, published on the website of the Josef

defined everyone as creative, requiring simply the encouragement to express themselves.

That insistence on exercising the eye and the hand through prescribed study means that, while museums cannot reproduce the confluence of individuals that came together in particular intellectual and political climates to make the Bauhaus or Black Mountain College such experimental educational models, they can grant access to this method of thinking through materials. During the 2009 exhibition 'Bauhaus 1919–1939: Workshops for Modernity', the Education department at MoMA ran workshops based on the school's teaching methods. Walter Gropius's daughter, Ati Johansen, who also attended Black Mountain College in the 1940s, taught some of the paper-folding lessons, reprising the curriculum of the original course. Then last year, Fritz Horstman, a scholar from the Josef and Anni Albers Foundation, taught similar exercises according to Albers's methods. Inviting members of the public to test a material in this way, where they can notice the planes and shades created when they crush a sheet of paper, or attempt to construct the tallest freestanding structure using only a single sheet, demonstrates how art is a process and a way of seeing, not simply a set of fixed objects.

Much like performance, pedagogy is ephemeral and contingent, and yet it differs in that it does not establish a fixed spectatorial role. To be understood it must be participated in, for, as Albers said, 'we are gathering experience'.[5] I use Albers as an example because it is clear that his teaching practice informed his artistic production, but it was nonetheless distinct from it. We can take these procedures simply as exercises; they are in no way intended to be works of art. It is freeing that there is no ideal instance or original moment that needs to be carefully reenacted here. These instructions are specific in how they are meant to be carried out, but they are also open, and the way in which a student acts on them will look different each time, particularly because each student is just as much informed by their peers and environment as they are by the directives given to them.

---

and Anni Albers Foundation <https://albersfoundation.org/teaching/josef-albers/lectures/#tab1> [accessed 14 November 2017].

5   Albers, 'Creative Education', p. 142.

Throughout the twentieth century, pedagogical developments aligned with trends in artistic practice toward material experimentation, blurring disciplinary boundaries, and viewer participation. Claire Bishop has established an analogy between post-1968 critical pedagogy's 'insistence on the breakdown of teacher/pupil hierarchy and participation as a route to empowerment' and 'the breakdown of medium-specificity and a heightened attention to the viewer's role and presence in art'.[6] The artist Lygia Clark fits into this analogy as a figure who not only experimented collaboratively with students as a professor at the Sorbonne in the 1970s, but also took up therapeutic practice in the 1970s and 80s, operating outside the typical confines of art. Clients were invited to lie down, and she would use various objects, such as stones, which were placed on different parts of the body, or fabrics, ranging from veils to blankets; she also offered cushions filled with heavier or lighter objects, objects made from stockings containing different materials (i.e., balls, stones, and shells), and plastic bags filled with air, water, or sand.

During the exhibition 'Lygia Clark: The Abandonment of Art, 1948–1988' at MoMA, facilitators in the educational wing of the museum were trained to assist the public in accessing these therapeutic protocols. Two of Clark's disciples, psychologist Gina Ferreira and artist and therapist Lula Wanderley, came to New York to train staff and help them experience first-hand how the artist would have treated her patients. Clark described her sensorial objects as 'gifts' that could shift a user's awareness of their body and the world. She did not create a clear distinction between art and life. This means that, in the museum context, these therapeutic protocols are treated as exercises rather than works of art, which allows visitors to experiment with them. Like Albers's teaching directives, they are specific enough to bring an audience member close to the artist's processes from the past. Yet they are open-ended enough that they can be shared freely with audiences without the anxiety of faithfulness to an original historical object. Granting access in this way allows individual participants to formulate questions that arise from the processes and relationships to materials that structure an artist's practice.

---

6   Claire Bishop, *Artificial Hells: Participatory Art and the Politics of Spectatorship* (London: Verso, 2012), p. 267.

In conclusion, I would like to briefly touch on what critics and art historians, including Irit Rogoff, to whom I referred earlier, have identified as an 'educational turn', emerging around the early 2000s with a rise in artist-led schools or artistic projects that take on educational formats such as discussions, talks, symposia, and workshops. This 'turn' is aligned with the critique of neoliberal pressures on universities and the high costs of education today, but to my mind it also speaks to how sites of education in their ideal form seem to offer the promise of free exchange and emancipatory experiences. One can now think of a school or educational platform as a work of art. Yet in terms of creating access and addressing wider publics within museum practice, I still believe that it is important to position teaching and therapy as existing at the margins of art, which I see as a productively undefined area within which to work. In the historical examples that I have given here, that marginal position allows for reenactment and reprisal without the pressure to make present a fixed, original object from the past. Within museum programming, it sustains the idea that artistic practice need not be passively consumed by viewers, but can enter into the flow of daily life — as it has for artists themselves.

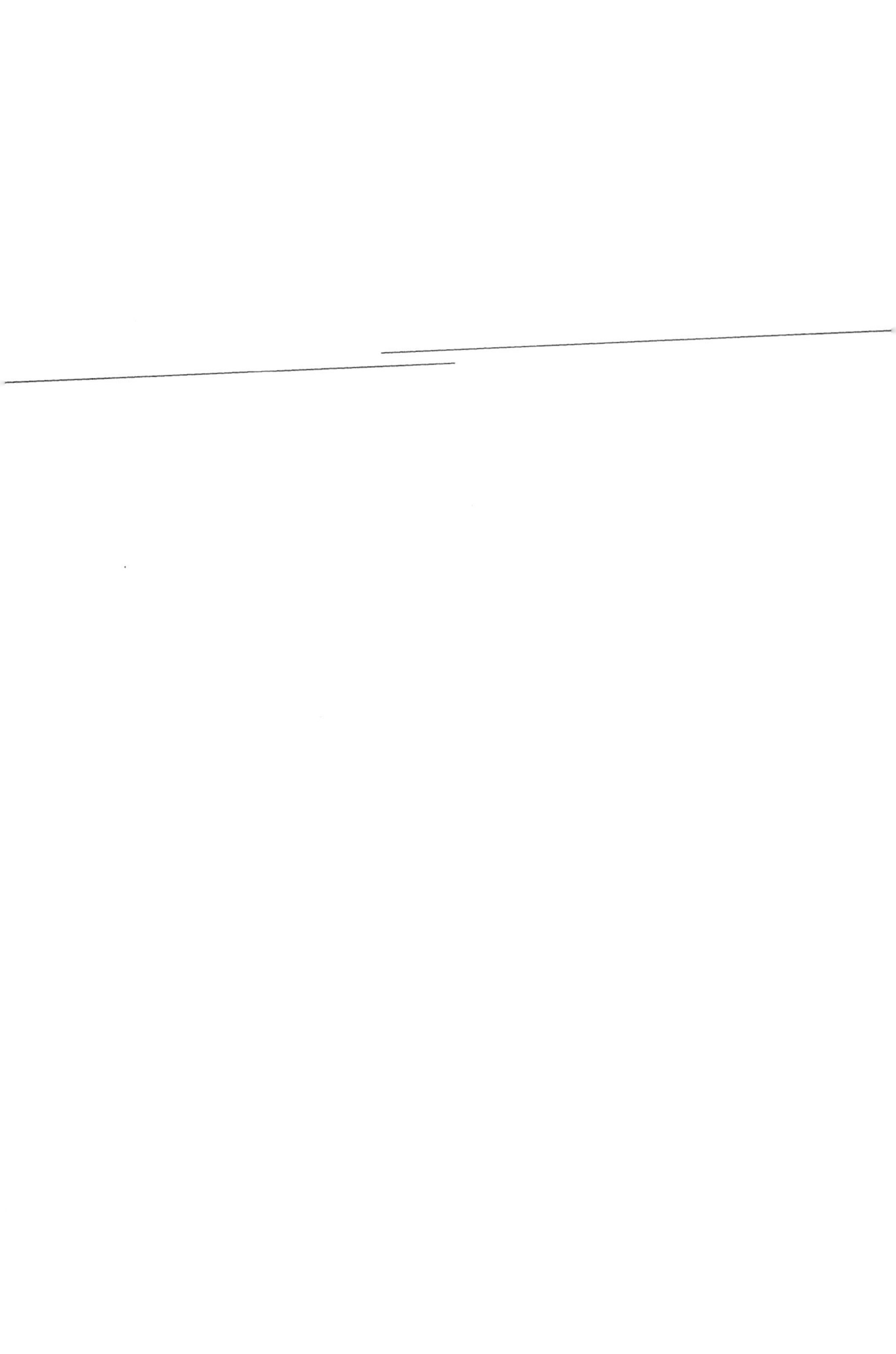

References

BIBLIOGRAPHY

'1975–1987: Rudi Fuchs, Exhibition- and Acquisition Policy', Van Abbemuseum museum website <https://vanabbemuseum.nl/en/about-the-museum/building-and-history/1975-1987-rudi-fuchs/> [accessed 11 December 2019]

Abel, Marco, 'The Cinema of Identification Gets on My Nerves: An Interview with Christian Petzold', *Cineaste*, 33.3 (Summer 2008) <https://www.cineaste.com/summer2008/the-cinema-of-identification-gets-on-my-nerves> [accessed 20 February 2021]

—— *The Counter-Cinema of the Berlin School* (Rochester, NY: Camden House, 2013)

Abramović, Marina, and James Kaplan, *Walk through Walls: A Memoir* (London: Penguin, 2017)

Agamben, Giorgio, 'Difference and Repetition: On Guy Debord's Films', trans. by Brian Holmes, in *Guy Debord and the Situationist International: Texts and Documents*, ed. by Tom McDonough (Cambridge, MA: MIT Press, 2002), pp. 313–19

—— *Homo Sacer: Sovereign Power and Bare Life*, trans. by Daniel Heller-Roazen (Stanford, CA: Stanford University Press, 1998)

—— *Stasis: Civil War as a Political Paradigm*, trans. by Nicholas Heron (Stanford, CA: Stanford University Press, 2015)

Agnew, Vanessa, Jonathan Lamb, and Juliane Tomann, eds, *The Routledge Handbook of Reenactment Studies: Key Terms in the Field* (London: Routledge, 2020) <https://doi.org/10.4324/9780429445637>

Albers, Josef, 'Creative Education' (1928), in Hans Maria Wingler, *The Bauhaus: Weimar, Dessau, Berlin, Chicago*, ed. by Joseph Stein, trans. by Wolfgang Jabs and Basil Gilbert (Cambridge, MA: MIT Press, 1969), pp. 142–43

—— 'The Meaning of Art', paper presented at Berea College, Berea, Kentucky, and Black Mountain College, 12 March 1940

—— 'On Education and Art Education', online publication, website of the Josef and Anni Albers Foundation <https://albersfoundation.org/teaching/josef-albers/lectures/#tab1> [accessed 14 November 2017]

Alonso-Buenaposada, Marta, ed., *Kobro & Strzemiński: Avant-Garde Prototypes* (Madrid–Łódź: Museo Nacional Centro de Arte Reina Sofía–Muzeum Sztuki, 2017) <https://www.museoreinasofia.es/sites/default/files/publicaciones/textos-en-descarga/kobro_ing.pdf> [accessed 18 March 2019]

Anceschi, Giovanni, *Dichiarazione Miriorama 1* (Miriorama 1 Declaration), Preliminary manuscript version, Archivio Giovanni Anceschi, Milano
—— 'How Programmed Art Was Born', in *Arte riprogrammata. Un manifesto aperto. Reprogrammed Art: An Open Manifesto*, ed. by Serena Cangiano, Davide Fornari, and Azalea Seratoni (Milan: Johan and Levi, 2015), pp. 74–79
Antoine, Jean–Philippe, *Farces et Attrapes. Inventer les images* (Genève: MAMCO; Dijon: Les presses du réel, 2017)
Appelbaum, Barbara, *Conservation Treatment Methodology* (Lexington, KY: CreateSpace, 2010)
Arnell, Malin, *Reflect Soft Matte Discourse*, performance, with Clara López Menéndez and Ulrika Gomm, 58 min, part of 'LIKA – a performance evening' at KAMARADE, Stockholm, 24 May 2011
Arns, Inke, and Horn Gabrielle, *History Will Repeat Itself: Strategies of Reenactment in Contemporary (Media) Art and Performance* (Frankfurt a.M.: Revolver, 2007)
Arns, Inke, Igor Chubarov, and Sylvia Sasse, eds, *Nikolai Evreinov & andere: 'Sturm auf den Winterpalast'* (Berlin: Diaphanes, 2017)
Artaud, Antonin, *The Theater and its Double*, trans. by Mary Caroline Richards (New York: Grove, 1958)
The Atlas Group (1989–2004), artist website <https://www. theatlasgroup1989.org/> [accessed 20 January 2021]
Auslander, Philip, 'The Performativity of Performance Documentation', in *Perform, Repeat, Record: Live Art in* History, ed. by Amelia Jones and Adrian Heathfield (London: Intellect, 2012), pp. 47–58
Austin, J. L., *How To Do Things with Words* (Oxford: Clarendon Press, 1962)
'Az információs munka elméleti és módszertani kérdései [The Theoretical and Methodological Questions of Information Work], Állambiztonsági Szolgálatok Történeti Levéltára Budapest [Historical Archive of the State Security Services Budapest], 2 vols. (1977), ɪ:ÁBTL A-3005/30/1
Balbi, Clara, 'Em nova exposição, Cildo Meireles questiona morte de Marielle', *GZH*, 29 September 2019 <https://gauchazh.clicrbs.com.br/cultura-e-lazer/noticia/2019/09/em-nova-exposicao-cildo-meireles-questiona-morte-de-marielle-ck0zgmjkd00oh01mtlaq1b9mm.html> [accessed 12 February 2020]
Baldacci, Cristina, 'For the Future: The Archive as an Artistic Gesture of Resilience', in *Present Archives: Reflections from a Collection of Prints*, ed. by Beatrice Zanelli and Ersilia Rossini (Foligno: Viaindustriae Publishing, 2019), pp. 53–58
—— 'Recirculation: The Wandering of Digital Images in Post-Internet Art', in *Re-: An Errant Glossary*, ed. by Christoph F. E. Holzhey and Arnd Wedemeyer (Berlin: ICI Berlin Press, 2019), pp. 25–33

—— 'Reenactment: Errant Images in Contemporary Art', in *Re-: An Errant Glossary*, ed. by Christoph F. E. Holzhey and Arnd Wedemeyer (Berlin: ICI Berlin Press, 2019), pp. 57–67

Baldacci, Cristina, and Susanne Franco, eds, *On Reenactment: Concepts, Methodologies, Tools* (Turin: Accademia University Press, forthcoming)

Bangma, Anke, Steve Rushton, and Florian Wüst, eds, *Experience, Memory, Re-enactment* (Frankfurt a.M.: Revolver, 2005)

Bann, Stephen, *Romanticism and the Rise of History* (New York: Twayne, 1995)

Bargu, Banu, *Starve and Immolate: The Politics of Human Weapons* (New York: Columbia University Press, 2014) <https://doi.org/10.7312/columbia/9780231163408.001.0001>

Bataille, Georges, *La Notion de dépense* (Paris: Lignes, 2011)

—— *La Part maudite* (Paris: Minuit, 1949)

Baumgartner, Frédérique, 'Reviving the Collective Body: Gina Pane's *Escalade Non Anesthésiée*', Oxford Art Journal, 34.2 (June 2011), pp. 247–63 <https://doi.org/10.1093/oxartj/kcr020>

Becker, Howard, *Art Worlds* (Berkeley: University of California Press, 1984)

Benjamin, Walter, *The Arcades Project*, ed. by Rolf Tiedemann, trans. by Howard Eiland and Kevin McLaughlin (Cambridge, MA: Harvard University Press, 1999)

—— 'Ausgraben und Erinnern', in Benjamin, *Gesammelte Schriften*, ed. by Rolf Tiedemann and Hermann Schweppenhäuser, 7 vols (Frankfurt a.M.: Suhrkamp, 1972–91), IV.1: *Kleine Prosa, Baudelaire-Übertragungen* (1972), pp. 400–01

—— *Gesammelte Schriften*, ed. by Rolf Tiedemann and Hermann Schweppenhäuser, 7 vols (Frankfurt a.M.: Suhrkamp, 1972–91), V: *Das Passagen-Werk* (1982)

—— 'On the Concept of History', trans. by Harry Zohn, in Benjamin, *Selected Writings*, IV: *1938–1940*, ed. by Howard Eiland and Michael W. Jennings (2003), pp. 389–400

—— *Selected Writings*, 4 vols (Cambridge, MA: Harvard University Press, 1996–2003)

—— 'The Task of the Translator', trans. by Harry Zohn, in Benjamin, *Selected Writings*, I: *1913–1926*, ed. by Marcus Bullock and Michael W. Jennings (1996), pp. 253–63

—— 'What Is Epic Theatre? [First version]' and 'What Is Epic Theatre? [Second Version]', in Benjamin, *Understanding Brecht*, trans. by Anna Bostock, intro. by Stanley Mitchell (London: Verso, 1998), pp. 1–22

—— 'The Work of Art in the Age of Mechanical Reproduction', in Benjamin, *Illuminations: Essays and Reflections*, ed. by Hannah Arendt, trans. by Harry Zohn (New York: Schocken, 1968), pp. 217–51

Bester, Rory, 'Trauma and Truth', in *Experiments with Truth: Transitional Justice and the Processes of Truth and Reconciliation: Documenta 11_Plat-*

form 2, ed. by Okwui Enwezor (Ostfildern: Hatje Cantz, 2002), pp. 155–73

Bester, Rory, and Okwui Enwezor, eds, *Rise and Fall of Apartheid: Photography and the Bureaucracy of Everyday Life* (Munich: Prestel, 2013)

Bishop, Claire, *Artificial Hells: Participatory Art and the Politics of Spectatorship* (London: Verso, 2012)

—— 'Delegated Performance: Outsourcing Authenticity', *October*, 140 (Spring 2012), pp. 91–112 <https://doi.org/10.1162/OCTO_a_00091>

—— 'Rise to the Occasion', *Artforum*, 57.9 (May 2019), n.p. <https://www.artforum.com/print/201905/claire-bishop-on-the-art-of-political-timing-79512> [accessed 12 February 2020]

Blanchot, Maurice, *Michel Foucault as I Imagine Him*, transl. by Brian Massumi and Jeffrey Mehlman (New York: Zone Books, 1990)

—— 'Reading Kafka', in Blanchot, *The Work of Fire*, trans. by Charlotte Mandell (Stanford, CA: Stanford University Press, 1995), pp. 1–11

—— *The Space of Literature*, trans. by Ann Smock (Lincoln: University of Nebraska Press, 1989)

Bolter, Jay D., and Richard Grusin, *Remediation: Understanding New Media* (Cambridge, MA: MIT Press, 1999)

Borggreen, Gunhild, and Rune Gade, eds, *Performing the Archive/Archives of Performance* (Copenhagen: Museum Tusculanum Press, 2013)

Bourriaud, Nicolas, *The Radicant*, trans. by James Cussen and Lili Porten (New York: Lukas & Sternberg, 2009)

Brost, Amy, 'From "Certificates of Authenticity" to Authentic Iterations in Variable Media Art' (unpublished master's thesis, New York University, 2016)

Bruguera, Tania, 'Notes on Political Timing Specificity', *Artforum*, 57.9 (May 2019), n.p. <https://www.artforum.com/print/201905/notes-on-political-timing-specificity-79513> [accessed 12 February 2020]

Buchloh, Benjamin H. D., 'Allegorical Procedures: Appropriation and Montage in Contemporary Art', *Artforum*, 21.1 (September 1982), pp. 43–56

Burrows, Jonathan, *A Choreographer's Handbook* (London: Routledge, 2010)

Buskirk, Martha, Amelia Jones, and Caroline A. Jones, 'The Year in "Re-"', *Artforum*, 52.4 (December 2013), pp. 127–30

'Büyük Direniş 2000–2007 Ölüm Orucu' (Great Resistance 2000–2007 Death Fast), *Yürüyüş*, 12 October 2008, p. 10

Caillet, Aline, 'Le Re-enactment: Refaire, rejouer ou répéter l'histoire?', *Marges. Revue d'art contemporain*, 17 (2013), special issue *Remake, reprise, répétition*, pp. 66–73 <https://doi.org/10.4000/marges.153>

Calvino, Italo, *The Castle of Crossed Destinies*, trans. by William Weaver (New York: Harcourt Brace Jovanovich, 1977)

Cangiano, Serena, Davide Fornari, and Azalea Seratoni, eds, *Arte ripro-grammata. Un manifesto aperto. Reprogrammed Art: An Open Manifesto* (Milan: Johan and Levi, 2015)

Carpo, Mario, *The Alphabet and the Algorithm* (Cambridge, MA: MIT Press, 2011)

Castellucci, Romeo, 'Il silenzio dell'eroe', interview by Anna Bandettini, *La Repubblica*, 29 September 2016

Castriota, Brian, 'Meditating Meanings: Conservation of the Staffordshire Hoard', *Postmedieval*, 7.3 (2016), pp. 369–77 <https://doi.org/10.1057/s41280-016-0003-5>

Cavell, Stanley, 'Aversive Thinking: Emersonian Representations in Hei-degger and Nietzsche', in Cavell, *Emerson's Transcendental Etudes*, pp. 141–70

—— 'Being Odd, Getting Even (Descartes, Emerson, Poe)', in Cavell, *In Quest of the Ordinary* (Chicago: University of Chicago Press, 1988), pp. 105–30

—— 'An Emerson Mood', in Cavell, *Emerson's Transcendental Etudes*, pp. 20–32

—— *Emerson's Transcendental Etudes* (Stanford, CA: Stanford University Press, 2003)

—— 'The Philosopher in American Life (Toward Thoreau and Emerson)', in Cavell, *Emerson's Transcendental Etudes*, pp. 33–58

Celant, Germano, ed., *The Small Utopia: Ars Multiplicata* (Milan: Progetto Prada Arte, 2012)

Center for Historical Reenactments and the Johannesburg Workshop for Theory and Criticism, eds, *PASS–AGES, References & Footnotes* (Johan-nesburg: Center for Historical Reenactments, 2010)

Charmatz, Boris, and Isabelle Launay, *Entretenir: A propos d'une danse con-temporaine* (Dijon: Les presses du réel, 2003)

Cixous, Helene, 'The Laugh of the Medusa', trans. by Keith Cohen and Paula Cohen, *Signs: Journal of Women in Culture and Society*, 1.4 (Summer 1976), pp. 875–93 <https://doi.org/10.1086/493306>

Cobbett, Richard, for Daedalic Entertainment, *Long Journey Home* (2017), Microsoft Windows

Collingwood, R. G., *Human Nature and Human History*, Proceedings of the British Academy, 22 (London: British Academy, 1937)

Crimp, Douglas, 'The Photographic Activity of Postmodernism', *October*, 15 (Winter 1980), pp. 91–101 <https://doi.org/10.2307/778455>

—— 'Pictures', *October*, 8 (Spring 1979), pp. 75–88 <https://doi.org/10.2307/778227>

'Dag Hammerskjöld about "Quiet Diplomacy" (1955)', Dag Hammerskjöld Project, Youtube <https://youtu.be/2T4YrDCe5Yc> [accessed 20 November 2020]

Davies, Nick, 'The $10bn Question: What Happened to the Marcos Mil-lions', *Guardian*, 7 May 2016 <https://www.theguardian.com/world/

2016/may/07/10bn-dollar-question-marcos-millions-nick-davies>
[accessed 22 February 2021]

Davila, Thierry, 'Endurance de la répétition, surgissement de l'invention: Le *Remake* et la fabrique de l'histoire', in *Remakes* (Bordeaux: CAPC-Musée d'art contemporain, 2003), pp. 26–46

De Keersmaeker, Anne Teresa, and Bojana Cvejić, *A Choreographer's Score: Fase, Rosas danst Rosas, Elena's Aria, Bartók* (Brussels: Mercatorfonds–Rosas, 2012)

deLahunta, Scott, ed., *Capturing Intention: Documentation, Analysis and Notation Research Based on the Work of Dance Company Emio Greco|PC* (Amsterdam: AHK-Amsterdam University of the Arts, 2007)

Deleuze, Gilles, *Difference and Repetition*, trans. by Paul Patton (New York: Columbia University Press, 1994)

—— *The Logic of Sense*, trans. by Mark Lester and Charles Stivale (New York: Columbia University Press, 1990)

Demand, Thomas, ed., *L'image volée* (Milan: Fondazione Prada, 2016)

Depocas, Alain, Jon Ippolito, and Caitlin Jones, eds, 'Variable Media Glossary', in *The Variable Media Approach: Permanence Through Change* (New York: Guggenheim Museum Publications, 2003), pp. 123–37 <https://www.variablemedia.net/e/preserving/html/var_pub_index.html> [accessed 12 March 2021]

Derrida, Jacques, *Aporias*, trans. by Thomas Dutoit (Stanford, CA: Stanford University Press, 1993)

—— *Archive Fever: A Freudian Impression*, trans. by Eric Prenowitz (Chicago: University of Chicago Press, 1996) <https://doi.org/10.2307/465144>

—— *Demeure: Fiction and Testimony*, trans. by Elizabeth Rottenberg (Stanford, CA: Stanford University Press, 2000)

Deutsche Bank AG, Art, Culture & Sports, Thorsten Strauß, and Franziska Kunz, eds, *Kemang Wa Lehulere, Bird Song* (Berlin: Hatje Cantz, 2017)

Devecchi, Gabriele, *A proposito delle ipotesi Miriorama, Arte programmata e cinetica 1953/1963. L'ultima avanguardia*, ed. by Vergine Lea (Milan: Mazzotta, 1983)

Didi-Huberman, Georges, *Glimpses*, online video recording of a public open lecture for the students of the Division of Philosophy, Art & Critical Thought at the European Graduate School EGS, Saas-Fee, Switzerland, 26 May 2015 <https://egs.edu/lecture/georges-didi-huberman-glimpses-2015/> [accessed 25 February 2018]

—— *The Man Who Walked in Color*, trans. by Drew S. Burk (Minneapolis, MN: Univocal, 2017)

'Directory entry Van Abbemuseum', Art & Education <https://www.artandeducation.net/directory/82357/van-abbemuseum> [accessed 11 March 2021]

Donald, James, ed., *Chamber's Etymological Dictionary of the English Language* (Edinburgh: William Chambers, 1868)

Dophijn, Rick, and Iris van der Tuin, 'Matter Feels, Converses, Suffers, Desires, Yearns and Remembers: Interview with Karen Barad', in Dophijn and van der Tuin, *New Materialism: Interviews & Cartographies* (Ann Arbor, MI: Open Humanities Press, 2012), pp. 48–70 <https://dx.doi.org/10.3998/ohp.11515701.0001.001>

Dray, William H., *History as Re-enactment: R. G. Collingwood's Idea of History* (Oxford: Oxford University Press, 2005)

Duncan, Carol, *Civilizing Rituals: Inside Public Art Museums* (London: Routledge, 1995)

Dunca, Paul, 'Public Collection: An Interview with Alexandra Pirici and Manuel Pelmuş', *Rivista Arte*, 14 December 2014 <https://revistaarta.ro/en/public-collection/> [accessed 23 March 2021]

Eco, Umberto, and Bruno Munari, *Arte programmata. Arte cinetica. Opere moltiplicate. Opera aperta* (Milan: Officina d'Arte Grafica Lucini, 1962)

'Egyptian Foreign Minister Tells U.S. Not to Impose Its Will', PBS NewsHour, February 2011, Youtube <https://youtu.be/TBXVHf_cIEM> [accessed 20 November 2020]

Emerson, Ralph Waldo, *The Collected Works of Ralph Waldo Emerson*, ed. by Alfred R. Ferguson and others, 7 vols to date (Cambridge, MA: Harvard University Press, 1971–)

—— *The Early Lectures of Ralph Waldo Emerson*, ed. by Stephen E. Whicher, Robert E. Spiller, and Wallace Williams, 3 vols (Cambridge, MA: Harvard University Press, 1959–1972)

—— *The Journals and Miscellaneous Notebooks of Ralph Waldo Emerson*, ed. by William H. Gilman and others, 16 vols (Cambridge, MA: Harvard University Press, 1960–1982)

Enstice, Wayne, 'Performance's Art Coming of Age', in *The Art of Performance*, ed. by Gregory Battcock and Robert Nickas (New York: Dutton, 1984), pp. 142–56

'F Tipi Tabutluk Gerçeği' (Truth of the F-Type Coffin), *Ekmek ve Adalet*, 5 June 2002, p. 5

Fanon, Frantz, *Peau noire, masques blancs*, in Fanon, *Œuvres* (Paris: La Découverte, 2011), pp. 45–257 <https://doi.org/10.1522/030294726>

Farocki, Harun, '"Minimale Variation" und "semantische Generalisation"', *film. Eine deutsche Filmzeitschrift*, 7.8 (August 1969), pp. 10–11

Feldman, Allen, *Archives of the Insensible: Of War, Photopolitics, and Dead Memory* (Chicago: University of Chicago Press, 2015) <https://doi.org/10.7208/chicago/9780226277479.001.0001>

—— *Formations of Violence: The Narrative of the Body and Political Terror in Northern Ireland* (Chicago: University of Chicago Press, 1992) <https://doi.org/10.7208/chicago/9780226240800.001.0001>

Feldman, Avi, 'An Interview with Milo Rau', *OnCurating*, 28 (January 2016), pp. 50–53

Fisher, Jaimey, *Christian Petzold* (Urbana: University of Illinois Press, 2013) <https://doi.org/10.5406/illinois/9780252037986.001.0001>

Fisher, Jamey, and Robert Fischer, 'The Cinema is a Warehouse of Memory: A Conversation Among Christian Petzold, Robert Fischer, and Jaimey Fisher', *Senses of Cinema*, 84 (September 2017) <https://www.sensesofcinema.com/2017/christian-petzold-a-dossier/christian-petzold/> [accessed 20 February 2021]

Fiske, Tina, 'White Walls: Installations, Absence, Iteration and Difference,' in *Conservation: Principles, Dilemmas and Uncomfortable Truths*, ed. by Alison Richmond and Alison Bracker (Amsterdam: Elsevier, 2009), pp. 229–40

Flores, Patrick, 'Total Community Response: Performing the Avant-Garde as a Democratic Gesture in Manila', *Southeast of Now: Directions in Contemporary and Modern Art in Asia*, 1.1 (2017), pp. 13–38

Fondazione Prada Team, Journalists, and Friends, 'Why and How: A Conversation with Germano Celant', in *When Attitudes Become Form: Bern 1969/Venice 2013*, ed. by Germano Celant (Milan: Progetto Prada Arte, 2013), pp. 393–421

Forsythe, William, *Improvisation Technology: A Tool for the Analytical Dance Eye* (Ostfildern: Hatje Cantz, 1999)

Foucault, Michel, 'Ariane s'est pendue', in *Dits et écrits*, I: *1954–1975*, text no. 64, pp. 798–99

—— Boîte 53, Foucault Archives, Bibliothèque nationale de France (NAF 28730)

—— *Dits et écrits*, ed. by Daniel Defert, François Ewald, and Jacques Lagrange, 2 vols (Paris: Gallimard, 2001)

—— 'The History of Sexuality', in Foucault, *Power/Knowledge: Selected Interviews and Other Writings*, 1972–1977, ed. by Colin Gordon (New York: Pantheon Books, 1980), pp. 183–94

—— 'Le Langage à l'infini', in *Dits et écrits*, I, text no. 14, pp. 287–88

—— 'Les Ménines de Picasso', in *Michel Foucault*, ed. by Philippe Artières, Jean-François Bert, Frédéric Gros, and Judith Revel, Cahiers de l'Herne, 95 (Paris: L'Herne, 2011), pp. 14–32

—— *The Order of Things: An Archaeology of the Human Sciences*, trans. by Matthew Chrulew and Jeffrey Bussolini (London: Routledge, 2002)

—— 'Les Rapports de pouvoir passent à l'intérieur des corps', interview with Lucette Finas, *La Quinzaine littéraire*, 247 (January 1977), pp. 4–6 (repr. in Foucault, *Dits et écrits*, ed. by Daniel Defert, François Ewald, and Jacques Lagrange, 4 vols (Paris: Gallimard, 1994), III: *1976–1979*, pp. 228–36)

—— 'Theatrum philosophicum', in *Dits et écrits*, I, text no. 80, pp. 885–908, English as 'Theatrum philosophicum', trans. by Donald F. Brouchard and Sherry Simon, in *Essential Works of Foucault, 1954–1984*, ed. by Paul Rabinow, 3 vols (New York: New Press, 1998–2001), II: *Aesthetics, Method, and Epistemology*, ed. by James D. Faubion (1998), pp. 343–68

—— 'What is Enlightenment', in *The Foucault Reader*, ed. by Paul Rabinow (New York: Pantheon Books, 1984), pp. 32–50

Franko, Mark, ed., *The Oxford Handbook of Dance and Reenactment* (Oxford: Oxford University Press, 2017) <https://doi.org/10.1093/oxfordhb/9780199314201.001.0001>

Fraser, Andrea, 'Performance or Enactment', in *Performing the Sentence: Research and Teaching in Performative Fine Arts*, ed. by Carola Dertnig and Felicitas Thun-Hohenstein (Berlin: Sternberg Press, 2014), pp. 122–27

Freud, Sigmund, *Beyond the Pleasure Principle*, trans. by James Strachey (New York: Liveright, 1989)

—— 'Remembering, Repeating and Working-Through', in *The Standard Edition of the Complete Psychological Works of Sigmund Freud*, ed. and trans. by James Strachey, 24 vols (London: Hogarth, 1953–74), XII (1958), pp. 145–57

—— 'Weitere Ratschläge zur Technik der Psychoanalyse: II. Erinnern, Wiederholen und Durcharbeiten', in Freud, *Studienausgabe*, ed. by Alexander Mitscherlich, Angela Richards, James Strachey, and Ilse Gubrich-Simitis, 11 vols (Frankfurt a.M.: Fischer, 1969–75), *Ergänzungsband: Schriften zur Behandlungstechnik* (1975), pp. 205–15

Gallissà, Núria, Maite Muñoz, and Marta Vega, *Folding the Exhibition* (Barcelona: MACBA–Museu d'Art Contemporani de Barcelona, 2014 <https://www.macba.cat/en/learn-explore/publications/folding-exhibition> [accessed 11 March 2021]

'The Game and the Players', exhibition press release, Van Abbemuseum, museum website <https://vanabbemuseum.nl/en/programme/programme/play-van-abbe/> [accessed 11 March 2021]

Geldern, James von, *Bolshevik Festivals, 1917–1920* (Berkeley: University of California Press, 1993)

Giannachi, Gabriella, 'At the Edge of the "Living Present": Re-enactments and Re-interpretations as Strategies for the Preservation of Performance and New Media', in *Histories of Performance Documentation: Museum, Artistic, and Scholarly Practices*, ed. by Gabriella Giannachi and Jonah Westerman (London: Routledge, 2018), pp. 115–31 <https://doi.org/10.4324/9781315645384-13>

Ginzburg, Carlo, 'Morelli, Freud and Sherlock Holmes: Clues and Scientific Method', trans. and intro. by Anna Devin, *History Workshop*, 9 (Spring 1980), pp. 5–36 <https://doi.org/10.1093/hwj/9.1.5>

Giusti, Francesco, 'Passionate Affinities: A Conversation with Rita Felski', *Los Angeles Review of Books*, 25 September 2019 <https://lareviewofbooks.org/article/passionate-affinities-a-conversation-with-rita-felski/> [accessed 25 February 2021]

Glassberg, David, *American Historical Pageantry: The Uses of Tradition in the Early Twentieth Century* (Chapel Hill: University of North Carolina Press, 1990)

Goldberg, RoseLee, 'Performance: The Golden Years', in *The Art of Performance: A Critical Anthology*, ed. by Gregory Battcock and Robert Nickas (New York: Dutton, 1984), pp. 71–94

—— *Performance: Live Art, 1909 to the Present* (London: Thames & Hudson, 1979)

Gombrich, Ernst, *Aby Warburg: An Intellectual Biography* (London: Warburg Institute, 1970)

Goodman, Nelson, *Languages of Art: An Approach to a Theory of Symbols* (Indianapolis, IN: Hackett, 1976)

Graevenitz, Antje von, 'Then and Now: Performance Art in Holland', *Studio International*, 192 (July–August 1976), pp. 49–53

Greenberg, Reesa, '"Remembering Exhibitions": From Point to Line to Web', *Tate Papers*, 12 (Autumn 2009) <https://www.tate.org.uk/research/publications/tate-papers/12/remembering-exhibitions-from-point-to-line-to-web> [accessed 11 December 2019]

Grimm, Herman, *Fünfzehn Essays*, 3rd, rev. and enlarged edn (Berlin: Dümmler, 1884)

—— 'Ralph Waldo Emerson – Ein Nachruf', in *Der Briefwechsel Ralph Waldo Emerson / Herman Grimm und die Bildung von Post-mortem-Gemeinschaften*, ed. by Thomas Meyer, trans. by Helga Paul, Europäer-Schriftenreihe, 14 (Basel: Perseus, 2007), pp. 64–78

Grusin, Richard, 'Premediation', *Criticism*, 46.1 (Winter 2004), pp. 17–39 <https://doi.org/10.1353/crt.2004.0030>

Gule, Khwezi, 'Center for Historical Reenactments: Is the Tale Chasing its Own Tail?', *Afterall: A Journal of Art, Context and Enquiry*, 39 (2015), pp. 88–100

Gura, Philip F., *American Transcendentalism: A History* (New York: Hill and Wang, 2007)

Hamacher, Werner, 'Afformative, Strike', *Cardozo Law Review*, 85 (1991–1992), pp. 1133–57

Hantelmann, Dorothea von, 'The Experiential Turn', in *Living Collections Catalogue*, 4 vols to date (Minneapolis: Walker Art Center, 2014–), I: *On Performativity*, ed. by Elizabeth Carpenter (2014) <http://walkerart.org/collections/publications/performativity/experiential-turn/> [accessed 13 July 2021]

—— *How to Do Things with Art: What Performativity Means in Art* (Zurich: JRP Ringier; Dijon: Les presses du réel, 2010)

Haraway, Donna, *Modest−Witness@Second−Millennium.FemaleMan−Meets−OncoMouse* (London: Routledge, 1997)

Harman, Graham, 'Seventy-Six Theses on Object-Oriented Philosophy', in Harman, *Bells and Whistles: More Speculative Realism* (Winchester: Zero Books, 2013), pp. 60–70

Haugbolle, Sune, *War and Memory in Lebanon* (Cambridge: Cambridge University Press, 2010) <https://doi.org/10.1017/CBO9780511676598>

Hengel, Louis van den, 'Archives of Affect: Performance, Reenactment, and the Becoming of Memory', in *Materializing Memory in Art and Popular Culture*, ed. by Laszlo Muntean, Liedeke Plate, and Anneke Smelik

(London: Routledge, 2017), pp. 125–42 <https://doi.org/10.4324/9781315472171-17>

Hilton, Guy, 'Fifty Is Just the Beginning', *Make*, 73 (December 1996–January 1997), pp. 3–5

Historical Papers (The Library, University of the Witwatersrand) and South African History Archive, *Traces of Truth: Documents Relating to the South African Truth and Reconciliation Commission* <http://truth.wwl.wits.ac.za/about.php> [accessed 6 April 2018]

—— 'Traces of Truth: Select Bibliography of the South African Truth and Reconciliation Commission (TRC)', *Traces of Truth*, 2006 <http://truth.wwl.wits.ac.za/TRCBIB.pdf> [accessed 9 April 2021]

HMKV Exhibition Magazine 2/2019, ed. by Inke Arns, Kata Krasznahorkai, and Sylvia Sasse (Dortmund: Hartware MedienKunstVerein, 2019) <https://www.hmkv.de/files/hmkv/ausstellungen/2019/AGENTS/05_Publikation/HMKV_AGENTS_Magazin_DE-EN.pdf> [accessed 20 February 2020]

Hodkinson, Juliana, 'Creating Headspace: Digital Listening Spaces and Evolving Subjectivities', *Musicology Research*, 3 (Autumn 2017), special issue *Music on Screen: From Cinema Screens to Touchscreens, Part II*, ed. by Sarah Hall and James B. Williams, pp. 163–77 <https://www.musicologyresearch.co.uk/publications/julianahodkinson-creatingheadspace> [accessed 31 March 2018]

—— *Prompt, Immediate, Now / Very Restrained and Cautious* (Copenhagen: Edition Wilhelm Hansen, 2013)

Holert, Tom, 'Exhibiting Investigation: The Place of Knowledge Production in the Visual Arts *Dialogue/Discourse/Research*, 1979', in *Troubling Research: Performing Knowledge in the Arts*, ed. by Carola Dertnig, et al. (Berlin: Sternberg Press, 2014), pp. 28–81

Horowitz, Frederick A., and Brenda Danilowitz, *Josef Albers: To Open Eyes* (London: Phaidon, 2006)

Horwitz, Tony, *Confederates in the Attic: Dispatches from the Unfinished Civil War* (New York: Vintage, 1998)

Huyssen, Andreas, 'The Search for Tradition: Avant-Garde and Postmodernism in the 1970s', *New German Critique*, 22 (Winter 1981), pp. 23–40 <https://doi.org/10.2307/487862>

Hölling, Hanna, 'An Aesthetics of Change: On the Relative Durations of the Impermanent and Critical Thinking in Conservation', paper presented during the symposium 'Authenticity in Transition', Glasgow School of Art/University of Glasgow, 1–2 December 2014, documented online at <https://seminesaa.hypotheses.org/7948> [accessed 16 December 2019]

Iggers, Georg G., 'Historicism: The History and Meaning of the Term', *Journal of the History of Ideas*, 56.1 (January 1995), pp. 129–52 <https://doi.org/10.2307/2710011>

Ippolito, Jon, 'Accommodating the Unpredictable: The Variable Media Questionnaire', in *Permanence Through Change: The Variable Media Approach*, ed. by Alain Depocas, Jon Ippolito, and Caitlin Jones (New York: Guggenheim Museum Publications, 2003), pp. 46–53

—— 'Death by Wall Label', in *New Media in the White Cube and Beyond: Curatorial Models for Digital Art*, ed. by Christiane Paul (Berkeley: University of California Press, 2008), pp. 106–33

Jameson, Fredric, *Postmodernism, or, The Cultural Logic of Late Capitalism* (Durham, NC: Duke University Press, 1991) <https://doi.org/10.1215/9780822378419>

Janicot, Christian, ed., *Anthologie du cinéma invisible. 100 scénarios pour 100 ans de cinéma* (Paris: Jean-Michel Place, 1995)

Jones, Amelia, 'The Artist Is Present: Artistic Re-enactments and the Impossibility of Presence', *TDR: The Drama Review*, 55.1 (2011), pp. 16–45

—— 'The Now and the Has Been: Paradoxes of Live Art in History', in *Perform, Repeat, Record: Live Art in History*, ed. by Amelia Jones and Adrian Heathfield (Bristol: Intellect Books, 2012), pp. 9–25

—— '"Presence" in Absentia: Experiencing Performance as Documentation', *Art Journal*, 56.4 (Winter 1997), pp. 11–18 <https://doi.org/10.1080/00043249.1997.10791844>

Jullien, François, *Près d'elle: présence opaque, présence intime* (Paris: Galilée, 2016)

Kaiser, Céline, 'Auftritt der Toten. Formen des Re-, Pre- und Enactment in der Geschichte der Theatrotherapie', in *Szenotest. Pre-, Re- & Enactment zwischen Theater und Therapie*, ed. by Céline Kaiser (Bielefeld: transcript, 2014), pp. 44–58 <https://doi.org/10.14361/transcript.9783839430163.44>

Kaprow, Allan, *Assemblage, Environments & Happenings* (New York: Abrams, 1966) <https://doi.org/10.2307/1125226>

Kassir, Samir, 'Dix ans après, comment ne pas réconcilier une société divisée?', *Monde Arabe Maghreb Machrek*, 169 (2000), pp. 6–22

Kelmachter, Hélène, 'Interview with Takashi Murakami', in *Takashi Murakami: Kaikai Kiki*, ed. by Hélène Kelmachter (Paris: Fondation Cartier pour l'art contemporain, 2002), pp. 72-105

Kermode, Deborah, and Jonathan Watkins, eds, *Oleg Kulik: Art Animal* (Birmingham: Ikon Gallery, 2001)

Kesting, Marietta, *Affective Images: Post-Apartheid Documentary Perspectives* (New York: State University of New York Press, 2017)

Khoza, Mbali, 'What Difference Does It Make Who Is Speaking?' (unpublished master's thesis in Fine Art, University of the Witwatersrand, Faculty of Humanities, School of Art, 2016)

Kierkegaard, Søren, *Fear and Trembling/Repetition*, ed. and trans. by Howard Hong and Edna Hong (Princeton, NJ: Princeton University Press, 1983)

Kobro, Katarzyna and Władysław Strzemiński, 'Kompozycja przestrzeni: Obliczenia rytmu czasoprzestrzennego', *Sztuka i filozofia*, 13 (1997), pp. 88–99 <https://monoskop.org/images/9/9c/Kobro_Katarzyna_ Strzeminski_Wladyslaw_Kompozycja_przestrzeni_1931_1997_ fragmenty.pdf> [accessed 20 October 2017]

Krasznahorkai, Kata, 'Heightened Alert: The Underground Art Scene in the Sights of the Secret Police — Surveillance Files as a Resource for Research into Artists' Activities in the Underground of the 1960s and 1970s', in *Art Beyond Borders: Artistic Exchange in Communist Europe (1945-1989)*, ed. by Jérôme Bazin, Pascal Dubourg Glatigny, and Piotr Piotrowski (Budapest: Central European University Press, 2015), pp. 125–39

—— 'Surveilling the Public Sphere: The First Hungarian Happening in Secret Agents Reports', in *Performance Art in the Second Public Sphere: Event-based Art in Late Socialist Europe*, ed. by Katalin Cseh-Varga and Adam Czirak, Routledge Advances in Theatre & Performance Studies (London: Routledge, 2018), pp. 127–38 <https://doi.org/10.4324/ 9781315193106-10>

Krasznahorkai, Kata, and Sylvia Sasse, eds, *Artists & Agents. Performancekunst und Geheimdienste* (Leipzig: Spector Books, 2019)

Krauss, Rosalind, 'The Originality of the Avant-Garde: A Postmodernist Repetition', *October*, 18 (Autumn 1981), pp. 47–66 <https://doi.org/ 10.2307/778410>

Kulik, Oleg, 'Return Tickets', in *Live: Art and Performance*, ed. by Adrian Heathfield (London: Tate Publishing, 2004), pp. 50–57

LaBelle, Brandon, *Background Noise: Perspectives on Sound Art* (London: Continuum, 2006)

Ładnowska, Janina, 'Sala Neoplastyczna: z dziejów kolekcji sztuki nowoczesnej w Muzeum Sztuki w Łodzi', in *Muzeum Sztuki w Łodzi: Monografia*, ed. by Aleksandra Jach, Katarzyna Słoboda, Joanna Sokołowska, and Magdalena Ziółkowska, 2 vols (Łódź: Muzeum Sztuki w Łodzi, 2015), I, pp. 326–43

Lambert-Beatty, Carrie, *Being Watched: Yvonne Rainer and the 1960s* (Cambridge, MA: MIT Press, 2008)

Laplanche, Jean, *Essays on Otherness*, ed. by John Fletcher, trans. by Luke Thurston, Leslie Hill, and Philip Slotkin (London: Routledge, 1999)

—— 'Notes on Afterwardsness', in Laplanche, *Essays on Otherness*, pp. 264–69

—— 'The Unfinished Copernican Revolution', in Laplanche, *Essays on Otherness*, pp. 53–86

Laurenson, Pip, 'Authenticity, Change and Loss in the Conservation of Time-Based Media Installations', *Tate Papers*, 6 (Autumn 2006), n.p. <http: //www.tate.org.uk/download/file/fid/7401> [accessed 17 July 2019]

Leeb, Susanne, 'Flucht nach nicht ganz vorn, Geschichte in der Kunst der Gegenwart', *Texte zur Kunst*, 76 (December 2009), pp. 28–45

Le Nemesiache, 'Manifesto per la riappropriazione della nostra creatività' (Manifesto for the Appropriation of our Creativity), trans. by Giulia Damiani (2020), available in the pamphlet from the exhibition *From the Volcano to the Sea: The Feminist Group Le Nemesiache in the 1970s and 1980s Naples,* Rongwrong, Amsterdam (2020)

Lepecki, André, 'The Body as Archive: Will to Re-enact and the Afterlives of Dance', *Dance Research Journal,* 42.2 (Winter 2010), pp. 28–48 <https://doi.org/10.1017/S0149767700001029>

—— *Singularities: Dance in the Age of Performance* (London: Routledge, 2016) <https://doi.org/10.4324/9781315694948>

Leszkowicz, Paweł, 'Gina Pane — Self-Inflicted Pain Is You! Today Photographs Are All That Remain. We Can Only Imagine the Hurt', trans. by Timothy Williams, *Czas Kultury (Time of Culture),* 20.1 (2004), 20.1 (2004), pp. 42–55.

Linder-Gaillard, Inge, 'Stigmata, Icons and Reliquaries', in Gina Pane (Southampton: John Hansard Gallery, 2002) pp. 43–54

Loraux, Nicole, *The Divided City: On Memory and Forgetting in Ancient Athens,* trans. by Corinne Pache and Jeff Fort (New York: Zone Books, 2006)

Lubiak, Jarosław, and Maciej Świerkocki, eds, *Muzeum jako świetlany przedmiot pożądania/Museum as a Luminous Object of Desire* (Łódź : Muzeum Sztuki, 2007)

Lyotard, Jean-François, *The Inhuman: Reflections on Time,* trans. by Rachel Bowlby and Geoffrey Bennington (Cambridge: Polity, 1991)

Lütticken, Sven, 'An Arena in Which to Reenact', in *Life, Once More: Forms of Reenactment in Contemporary Art,* ed. by Sven Lütticken (Rotterdam: Witte de With, 2005), pp. 17–60

—— *History in Motion: Time in the Age of the Moving Image* (Berlin: Sternberg Press, 2013)

—— ed., *Life, Once More: Forms of Reenactment in Contemporary Art* (Rotterdam: Witte de With, 2005)

Madeira, Cláudia, Daniela Salazar, and Hélia Marçal, 'Performance Art Temporalities: Relationships Between Museum, University, and Theatre', *Museum Management and Curatorship,* 33.1 (2018), pp. 79–95 <https://doi.org/10.1080/09647775.2017.1419828>

Mangiacapre, Lina, 'Lava, vulcani e sangue' ('Lava, Volcanos and Blood'), *Il Paese delle donne,* May 2004

Mannheim, Karl, 'The Problem of Generations', in Mannheim, *Essays on the Sociology of Knowledge,* ed. by Paul Kecskemeti (London: Routledge, 1952), pp. 276–322

Manovich, Lev, *The Language of New Media* (Cambridge, MA: MIT Press, 2002)

Marchart, Oliver, *SoDA Lecture 09.07.2014 'The Art of Preenactments',* Hochschulübergreifendes Zentrum Tanz Berlin (HZT Berlin), 9 July 2014, online video recording, Vimeo <https://vimeo.com/114242197> [accessed 10 March 2019]

Marçal, Hélia Pereira, 'Conservation in an Era of Participation', *Journal of the Institute of Conservation*, 40.2 (2017), pp. 97–104 <https://doi.org/10.1080/19455224.2017.1319872>

Mbembe, Achille, *Politiques de l'inimitié* (Paris: La Découverte, 2016)

McEvilley, Thomas, 'Stages of Energy: Performance Art Ground Zero?', in *Marina Abramović: Artist Body: Performances 1969–1998*, ed. by Emanuela Belloni (Milan: Charta, 1998), pp. 14–25

Meillassoux, Quentin, *Après la finitude. Essai sur la nécessité de la contingence* (Paris: Seuil, 2006)

—— 'Potentiality and Virtuality', trans. by Robin Mackay, in *The Speculative Turn: Continental Materialism and Realism*, ed. by Levi Bryant, Nick Srnicek, and Graham Harman (Melbourne: re.press, 2011), pp. 224–36

'MfS-Dictionary: Werbung', *Stasi-Unterlagen-Archiv*, ed. by Der Bundesbeauftragte für die Unterlagen des Staatssicherheitsdienstes der ehemaligen Deutschen Demokratischen Republik <https://www.bstu.de/mfs-lexikon/detail/werbung/> [accessed 17 November 2020]

Miessen, Markus, 'Safe Haven', *Volume Magazine*, 15 (April 2008), n.p.

Mijares, Barbara, 'Militants Reenact Escalante Massacre', *ABS-CBN News*, 20 September 2017 <https://news.abs-cbn.com/news/09/20/17/militants-reenact-escalante-massacre> [accessed 10 March 2019]

Mueller-Vollmer, Kurt, *Transatlantic Crossings and Transformations: German-American Cultural Transfer from the 18th to the End of the 19th Century* (Frankfurt a.M.: Peter Lang, 2015)

Nakass, Kassandra, 'Double Miss: On the Use of Photography in the Atlas Group Archive', in *The Atlas Group (1989–2004): A Project by Walid Raad*, ed. by Kassandra Nakass and Britta Schmitz (Cologne: König, 2006), pp. 49–52

Ngcobo, Gabi, 'Art in Context Africa, Part I: Sabelo Mlangeni's *No Problem*, and a Visit to the Site of Michelle Monareng's *Removal to Radium*', *Art Review*, 66.7 (October 2014) <https://artreview.com/features/october_2014_feature_art_in_context_i_gabi_ngcobo/> [accessed 6 April 2018]

—— 'Does This Window Have a Memory?', *Other Possible Worlds* <http://www.otherpossibleworlds.net/?page_id=453> [accessed 6 April 2018]

—— 'Endnotes. Was It a Question of Power?', in *Condition Report: Symposium on Building Art Institutions in Africa*, ed. by Koyo Kouoh (Ostfildern: Hatje Cantz, 2013), pp. 65–67 <http://historicalreenactments.org/documents/condition%20report/condition.pdf> [accessed 31 March 2019]

—— 'Phantom(pain)', *Glossary of Common Knowledge*, May 2014 <https://www.youtube.com/watch?v=zqgLd_BdNmI> [accessed 6 April 2018]

Ngcobo, Gabi, and Kemang Wa Lehulere, 'Unearthing Skeletons in History's Shallow Graves', in *PASS–AGES, References & Footnotes*, ed. by the Center for Historical Reenactments and the Johannesburg Workshop for

Theory and Criticism (Johannesburg: Center for Historical Reenactments, 2010), p. 10

Nicastro, Clio, 'Undine', *Filmidee*, 24 (October 2020) <https://www.filmidee.it/2020/10/undine/> [accessed 20 February 2021]

Obrist, Hans Ulrich, 'Talking with Marina Abramović, Riding on the Bullet Train to Kitakyushu, Somewhere in Japan', in *Marina Abramović: Artist Body: Performances 1969–1998*, ed. by Emanuela Belloni (Milan: Charta, 1998), pp. 41–51

Ojrzyński, Jacek, 'Historia Muzeum Sztuki w Łodzi', in *Historia Muzeum Sztuki w Łodzi: Historia i wystawy*, ed. by Urszula Czartoryska (Łódź: Oficyna Bibliofilów, Towarzystwo Przyjaciół Muzeum Sztuki w Łodzi, 1998), pp. 6–39 <https://msl.org.pl/media/user/Czytelnia/muzeum-sztuki-w-nnodzi-historia-i-wystawy-1998-1000dpi-pdf.pdf> [accessed 10 December 2019]

Oswald, John, *An Etymological Dictionary of the English Language* (Philadelphia, PA: Key & Biddle, 1836)

'Over and Over and Over Again: Re-Enactment Strategies in Contemporary Arts and Theory', symposium held at the ICI Berlin on 16–17 November, 2017 <https://doi.org/10.25620/e171116>

Oxford University Press (OUP), 'Definition of Simulacrum', in *Lexico.com* <https://www.lexico.com/definition/simulacrum> [accessed 11 July 2021]

O'Dell, Kathy, *Contract with the Skin: Masochism, Performance Art, and the 1970s* (Minneapolis: University of Minnesota Press, 1998) <https://doi.org/10.5749/j.ctttv3g6>

Pane, Gina, *Discours mou et mat*, performance, Brouwersgracht, 28 June to 17 July 1975 <https://deappel.nl/en/events/gina-pane-discours-mou-et-mat> [accessed: 2 February 2020]

—— 'Lettre à un(e) inconnu(e)', in *ArTitudes international*, 15–17 (October–December 1974), pp. 26–35

—— *Lettre à un(e) inconnu(e)*, ed. by Blandine Chavanne, Anne Marchand, and Julia Hountou (Paris: École nationale supérieure des beaux-arts, 2004)

Pasolini, Pier Paolo, 'The Screenplay As a "Structure That Wants to Be Another Structure"', in Pasolini, *Heretical Empiricism*, ed. by Louise K. Barnett, trans. by Ben Lawton and Louise K. Barnett, 2nd edn (Washington, DC: New Academia Publishing, 2005), pp. 187–96

Pastore, Enrico, 'Intervista a Milo Rau', *PASSPARnous Teatro*, 22 (September 2014) <http://www.psychodreamtheater.org/rivista-passparnous-ndeg-22---teatro---intervista-a-milo-rau---a-cura-di-enrico-pastore.html> [accessed 24 November 2017]

Peeters, Jeroen and Meg Stuart, eds, *Are We Here Yet* (Dijon: Les presses du réel, 2010)

Petzold, Christian, 'Interview: Christian Petzold: "Gespenster irren herum"', *Rheinische Post, RP Online*, 12 September 2005 <https://

rp-online.de/kultur/film/christian-petzold-gespenster-irren-herum_
aid-17041845> [accessed 20 February 2021]

Phelan, Peggy, *Unmarked: The Politics of Performance* (London: Routledge,
1995)

Phillips, Joanna, 'Reporting Iterations: A Documentation Model for Time-
Based Media Art', *Revista de História da Arte*, 4 (2015), pp. 168–77

—— 'Shifting Equipment Significance in Time-Based Media Art', *The Electronic Media Review*, 1 (2012), pp. 139–54

Pollock, Griselda, 'The Image in Psychoanalysis and the Archeological Metaphor', in *Psychoanalysis and the Image: Transdisciplinary Perspectives*, ed.
by Griselda Pollock (Oxford: Blackwell, 2006), pp. 1–29 <https://doi.
org/10.1002/9780470691007.ch1>

Quaranta, Domenico, 'RE:akt! Things that Happen Twice', in *RE: akt! Reconstruction, Re-enactment, Re-porting*, ed. by Antonio Caronia, Janez Jansâ,
and Domenico Quaranta (Brescia: LINK Editions, 2014), pp. 43–52

Quarantelli, Ezio, and Gina Pane, 'Travels with St. Francis: A Rare Discussion
with the French Artist Who Is One of the Premiere Practitioners of
Body Art', *Contemporanea*, 1.4 (November–December 1988), pp. 44–
47

Raad, Walid, *Miraculous Beginnings* (London: Whitechapel Gallery, 2010)

Rafael, Vicent, 'Patronage and Pornography: Ideology and Spectatorship in
the Early Marcos Years', *Comparative Studies in Society and History*, 32.3
(1990) <https://doi.org/10.1017/S0010417500016492>

Rancière, Jacques, *The Emancipated Spectator*, trans. by Gregory Elliott (London: Verso, 2009)

Ranke, Leopold von, *Geschichten der romanischen und germanischen Völker von
1494 bis 1535. Erster Band* (Leipzig: Reimer, 1824) <https://doi.org/
10.1515/9783112438268>

Rau, Milo, 'Intervista a Milo Rau', *PASSPARnous, Teatro*, ed. by Enrico
Pastore <http://www.psychodreamtheater.org/rivista-passparnous-
ndeg-22---teatro---intervista-a-milo-rau---a-cura-di-enrico-pastore.
html> [accessed 28 September 2019]

—— *Das Kongo Tribunal*, ed. by Eva Bertschy, Rolf Bossaert, and Mirjam
Knapp (Berlin: Verbrecher Verlag, 2017)

Real, William A., 'Toward Guidelines for Practice in the Preservation and
Documentation of Technology-Based Installation Art', *Journal of the
American Institute for Conservation*, 40.3 (2001), pp. 211–31

Reason, Matthew, *Documentation, Disappearance and the Representation of
Live Performance* (Basingstoke: Palgrave Macmillan, 2006) <https://
doi.org/10.1057/9780230598560>

Rendell, Jane, *Site-Writing: The Architecture of Art Criticism* (London: I. B.
Tauris, 2010) <https://doi.org/10.5040/9780755697533>

Richards, Mary, 'Specular Suffering: (Staging) the Bleeding Body', *PAJ: A
Journal of Performance and Art*, 30.1 (January 2008), pp. 108–19 <https:
//doi.org/10.1162/pajj.2008.30.1.108>

Ricoeur, Paul, *Hermeneutics and the Human Sciences: Essays on Language, Action, Interpretation*, ed. and trans. by John B. Thompson (Cambridge: Cambridge University Press, 2016)

Roelstraete, Dieter, 'Make it Re-: The Eternally Returning Object', in *When Attitudes Become Form: Bern 1969/Venice 2013*, ed. by Germano Celant (Milan: Fondazione Prada, 2013), pp. 423–28

Rogoff, Irit, 'Turning', *e-flux journal*, 00 (November 2008) <http://www.e-flux.com/journal/00/68470/turning/> [accessed 14 November 2017]

Rosenthal, Stephanie, 'Agency for Action', in *Allan Kaprow: Art as Life*, ed. by Eva Meyer-Hermann, Andrew Perchuk, and Stephanie Rosenthal (London: Thames & Hudson, 2008), pp. 56–71

Rovisco, Vânia, 'Reacting to Time: The Portuguese in Performance Art', workshop conducted 19–24 January 2014, online description on the website of the CAAA Centro para os Assuntos da Arte e Arquitectura, Guimarães   <https://www.centroaaa.org/index.php/arquivo-2015-jan-fev-mar/reacting-to-time-workshop-transmissao-ii?lang=en> [accessed 11 March 2021]

Saaze, Vivian van, 'Authenticity in Practice: An Ethnographic Study into the Preservation of *One Candle* by Nam June Paik', in *Art Conservation and Authenticities: Material, Concept, Context*, ed. by Erma Hermens and Tina Fiske (London: Archetype Publications, 2009), pp. 190–98

—— 'From Singularity to Multiplicity? A Study into Versions, Variations, and Editions in Museum Practices', *The Electronic Media Review*, 1 (2012), pp. 87–96 <http://resources.conservation-us.org/emg-review/wp-content/uploads/sites/15/2016/07/Vol-1_Ch-12_VanSaaze.pdf> [accessed 12 February 2020]

—— 'In the Absence of Documentation: Remembering Tino Sehgal's Constructed Situations', *Revista de História da Arte*, 4 (2015), pp. 55–63 <http://revistaharte.fcsh.unl.pt/rhaw4/RHAw4.pdf> [accessed 13 November 2019]

Sacco, Daniela, 'La Jetztzeit del teatro. L'Orestea della Socìetas Raffaello Sanzio/Romeo Castellucci venti anni dopo', *Biblioteca Teatrale*, 119–120.2 (2016), pp. 65–84 <https://doi.org/10.1400/256739>

—— 'Re-enactment e replica a teatro. Riflessioni sullo statuto filosofico della ri-presentazione', *Materiali di Estetica*, 4.1 (2017), pp. 340–51

Sasse, Sylvia, 'KGB: The Art of Performance. Action Art or Actions against Art?', *Artmargins*, 30 December 1999 <http://www.artmargins.com/index.php/2-articles/449-kgb-or-the-art-of-performance-action-art-or-actions-against-art> [accessed 28 February 2019]

—— 'Stasi-Dada. Was KünstlerInnen aus ihren Geheimdienstakten machen', *Geschichte der Gegenwart*, 16 February 2016 <http://geschichtedergegenwart.ch/stasi-dada-gabriele-stoetzer-las-im-cabaret-voltaire-aus-ihren-akten/> [accessed 20 February 2018]

—— *Subversive Affirmation* (Berlin: Diaphanes, 2022)

Schaerf, Eran, 'Scenario Data #39', in *Life, Once More: Forms of Reenactment in Contemporary Art*, ed. by Sven Lütticken (Rotterdam: Witte de With, 2005), pp. 9–16

Schlaffer, Hannelore, and Heinz Schlaffer, *Studien zum ästhetischen Historismus* (Frankfurt a.M.: Suhrkamp, 1975)

Schneider, Rebecca, *Performing Remains: Art and War in Times of Theatrical Reenactment* (London: Routledge, 2011)

—— 'Solo Solo Solo', in *After Criticism: New Responses to Art and Performance*, ed. by Gavin Butt (Oxford: Blackwell, 2004), pp. 23–47 <https://doi.org/10.1002/9780470774243.ch1>

Settis, Salvatore, *Incursioni: Arte contemporanea e tradizione* (Milan: Feltrinelli, 2020)

Settis, Salvatore, Anna Anguissola, and Davide Gasparotto eds, *Serial / Portable Classic: The Greek Canon and its Mutations* (Milan: Fondazione Prada, 2015)

Simondon, Gilbert, *Du mode d'existence des objets techniques*, 3rd edn (Paris: Aubier, 1989)

Skłodowska, Marta, 'Czuła arytmetyka Muzeum Sztuki w Łodzi: Rozmowa z Jarosławem Suchanem', *Obieg* (2009) <http://archiwum-obieg.ujazdowski.pl/rozmowy/9864> [accessed 10 November 2017]

Spielmann, Yvonne, *Video and Computer: The Aesthetics of Steina and Woody Vasulka* (Montreal: The Daniel Langlois Foundation, 2004) <https://www.fondation-langlois.org/html/e/page.php?NumPage=456> [accessed 12 March 2021]

Steyerl, Hito, *Die Farbe der Wahrheit. Dokumentarismen im Kunstfeld* (Vienna: Turia + Kant, 2008)

'Strange and Close: Play Van Abbe', project presentation, Van Abbemuseum, museum website <https://vanabbemuseum.nl/en/programme/programme/strange-and-close-1/> [accessed 16 December 2019]

Taylor, Diana, *The Archive and the Repertoire: Performing Cultural Memory in the Americas* (Durham, NC: Duke University Press, 2003) <https://doi.org/10.2307/j.ctv11smz1k>

Telesko, Werner, 'Der Triumph- und Festzug des Historismus in Europa', in *Der Traum vom Glück. Die Kunst des Historismus in Europa*, ed. by Hermann Fillitz, 2 vols (Vienna: Künstlerhaus Wien, 1991), I, pp. 290–96

Terörle Mücadele Kanunu (Anti-Terrorist Law), Law No. 3713, 12 April 1991 <http://www.mevzuat.gov.tr/MevzuatMetin/1.5.3713.pdf> [accessed 15 November 2017]

Thomas, Kylie, 'Decolonisation Is Now: Photography and Student-Social Movements in South Africa', *Visual Studies*, 33.1 (2018), pp. 98–110 <https://doi.org/10.1080/1472586X.2018.1426251>

—— 'Exhuming Apartheid: Photography, Disappearance and Return', *Cahiers d'études africaines*, 230 (2018), pp. 429–54

Thompson, Jenny, *War Games: Inside the World of Twentieth-Century War Reenactors* (Washington: Smithsonian, 2004)

Truth and Reconciliation Commission, *The TRC Report* <https://www.justice.gov.za/trc/report/index.htm> [accessed 6 April 2018]

—— *Truth and Reconciliation Commission of South Africa Report*, 5 vols (London: Macmillan, 1999)

UMA Pilipinas, '"Cultural Revolution" Pursued in Escalante Massacre Memorial', 20 September 2016 <https://umapilipinas.wordpress.com/2016/09/20/cultural-revolution-pursued-in-escalante-massacre-memorial/> [accessed 10 March 2019]

Warburg, Aby, *Bilderatlas Mnemosyne: The Original*, ed. by Roberto Ohrt and Axel Heil, in cooperation with the Warburg Institute and Haus der Kulturen der Welt (Berlin: Hatje Cantz Verlag, 2020)

Wardrip-Fruin, Noah, *Expressive Processing: Digital Fiction, Computer Games, and Software Studies* (Cambridge, MA: MIT Press, 2011)

Weber, Samuel, *Benjamin's –abilities* (Cambridge, MA: Harvard University Press, 2008)

—— *Theatricality as Medium* (New York: Fordham University Press, 2004) <https://doi.org/10.5422/fso/9780823224159.001.0001>

Weston, Hillary, 'Missed Connections: A Conversation with Christian Petzold', *The Current: An Online Magazine Covering Film Culture Past and Present*, 7 December 2018, hosted by The Criterion Collection <https://www.criterion.com/current/posts/6088-missed-connections-a-conversation-with-christian-petzold> [accessed 20 February 2021]

Wharton, Glenn, and Harvey Molotch, 'The Challenge of Installation Art', in *Conservation: Principles, Dilemmas, and Uncomfortable Truths*, ed. by Alison Bracker and Alison Richmond (Amsterdam: Elsevier, 2009), pp. 210–22

Wheeler, Britta B., 'The Institutionalization of an American Avant-Garde: Performance Art as Democratic Culture, 1970–2000', *Sociological Perspectives*, 46.4 (2003), pp. 491–512 <https://doi.org/10.1525/sop.2003.46.4.491>

Wijers, Gaby, Lara Garcia Diaz and Christian Sancto, eds, *UNFOLD: Mediation by Re-interpretation – Annual Project Review Report, March 2016–March 2017* (Amsterdam: LIMA, 2017) <http://www.li-ma.nl/lima/sites/default/files/Unfold_verslag_excl.pdf> [accessed 12 March 2021]

Wind, Priscilla, 'L'art du reenactment chez Milo Rau', *Intermédialités*, 28–29 (2016) <https://doi.org/10.7202/1041080ar>

Wood, Catherine, 'Re-make, Re-model', *Frieze Masters*, 1 (October 2012) <https://frieze.com/article/re-make-re-model-0> [accessed 27 September 2019]

FILMOGRAPHY

Barbara, dir. by Christian Petzold (Schramm Film Koerner & Weber, 2012)

The Battle of Orgreave, dir. by Mike Figgis (Artangel Media, 2001)

Carnival of Souls, dir. by Herk Harvey (Harcourt Production, 1962)

La carosse d'or (The Golden Coach), dir. by Jean Renoir (Panaria Film, 1952)

Didone non è morta (Dido is not Dead), dir. by Lina Mangiacapre and Le Nemesiache (Le tre ghinee, 1987)

Ghosts (Gespenster), dir. by Christian Petzold (Schramm Film Koerner & Weber, 2005)

How to Sing a Prophecy, dir. by Giulia Damiani (2017)

Nothing Ventured (Nicht ohne Risiko), dir. by Harun Farocki (Harun Farocki Filmproduktion, 2004)

Parallel, dir. by Harun Farocki (2002) <https://www.harunfarocki.de/installations/2010s/2012/parallel.html> [accessed 20 February 2021]

The State I Am In (Die Innere Sicherheit), dir. by Christian Petzold (Schramm Film Koerner & Weber, 2000)

Le Subtil Oiseleur, Foucault de Velázquez à Picasso, dir. by Alain Jaubert (Éditions Montparnasse, 2020)

Transit, dir. by Christian Petzold (Schramm Film Koerner & Weber, 2018)

Vesuvius in Eruption, filmed by British Movietone News (29 July 1929) <https://youtu.be/-7W6BAV0wmw> [accessed 21 November 2020]

Yella, dir. by Christian Petzold (Schramm Film Koerner & Weber, 2007)

Notes on the Contributors

Pio Abad is a Filipino artist living and working in London. He began his art studies at the University of the Philippines before receiving a BA from Glasgow School of Art and an MA from the Royal Academy Schools, London. Recent exhibitions include 'For the Phoenix to Find its Form in Us' (ifa Gallery and Savvy Contemporary, Berlin, 2021); 'Phantom Limb' (Jameel Arts Centre, Dubai, 2019); 'Kiss the Hand You Cannot Bite' (Kadist, San Francisco, 2019); 'Splendour' (Oakville Galleries, Ontario, 2019); 'To Make/Wrong/Right Now' (The 2nd Honolulu Biennial, Hawai'i, 2019). Abad is also a lecturer in fine art at Goldsmiths, University of London.

Roberta Agnese holds a PhD in philosophy and aesthetics. Previously a lecturer in philosophy and cultural mediation at the Université Paris Est-Créteil, she is now in charge of cultural research at the French Ministry of Culture. Her academic work focuses on contemporary visual art and photography, with a particular attention to documentary practices. She published, among others: 'Le Document comme cible et comme instrument. The Atlas Group Archive de Walid Raad', in *Un art documentaire. Enjeux esthétiques, politiques et éthiques*, ed. by Aline Caillet and Frédéric Pouillaude (2017).

Michela Alessandrini, PhD, is a curator at Fondation Cartier pour l'art contemporain, Paris. She is editor of the series on 'curatorial archives' published by Archive Books and of the interview collection *Curatorial Archives in Curatorial Practices* (2018). She is a board member of the École du Magasin Alumni Association and an advisor for private and public curatorial archives and collections. She has been consultant for research at Mathaf: Arab Museum of Modern Art, Doha, Qatar; guest researcher at MACBA, Barcelona, l'Appartement 22, Rabat, and Van Abbemuseum, Eindhoven as well as a curator-in-residence in Switzerland, France, Belgium, and Hungary. www.michelaalessandrini.com

Malin Arnell is a visual and performance artist. She is currently a senior lecturer at Konstfack University of Arts, Crafts and Design (KUNO Stockholm). Over the last twenty years, Malin has been engaged in collaborative practices through 'an embodied and affective *now*'. Through her commitment to a queer feminist, posthumanist, and agential-realist approach she has developed an in-depth practice of knowing-through-doing, based on a strong ecological sensibility. She has developed the 72-hours live PhD thesis in Choreography,

Avhandling / Av_handling (Dissertation / Through_action) (2016), at Stockholm University of the Arts (SKH) and at Lunds University.

Cristina Baldacci is a contemporary art historian and associate professor at Ca' Foscari University of Venice. She was previously a fellow (2016–2018) and an affiliate fellow (2018–2020) at the ICI Berlin. Her research interests focus on the archive as a metaphor and art form; appropriation, montage, and 're-' practices in contemporary art; image theory; sculpture and installation art; art in the Anthropocene. Among her publications are the monograph *Archivi impossibili. Un'ossessione dell'arte contemporanea* (2016/2019) and the recently co-edited volumes *Double Trouble in Exhibiting the Contemporary: Art Fairs and Shows* (with Clarissa Ricci, Angela Vettese, 2020), *On Reenactment: Concepts, Methodologies, Tools* (with Susanne Franco, forthcoming).

Amy Brost is an art conservator at the Museum of Modern Art (MoMA) specializing in time-based media. She works with the Media and Performance collection as well as with the museum's digital repository for art storage. In 2016, she earned an MA in the history of art and archaeology and an MS in conservation of historic and artistic works from the Conservation Center of the Institute of Fine Arts, New York University. She holds bachelor's degrees in studio art and art history from the University of Wisconsin-Madison and a chemistry degree from New York City College of Technology.

Serena Cangiano teaches at the University of Applied Sciences and Arts of Southern Switzerland SUPSI and is a tenured researcher at the University's Laboratory of Visual Culture. Since 2019, she has been the head of SUPSI's Fablab DACD, where she leads applied research projects on digital fabrication, interaction design, and open innovation. Among her publications: *Rebelling with Care: Exploring Open Technologies for Commoning Healthcare*, co-ed. with Zoe Romano, Valeria Graziano, and Maddalena Fragnito (2019).

Giulia Damiani is an art historian, writer, curator, and performance collaborator. She has been the fellow of the 2019–2021 Edition of the Dutch curatorial platform If I Can't Dance, I Don't Want to Be Part of Your Revolution and is currently editing an upcoming book for the organisation. In 2020, she curated the exhibition 'From the Volcano to the Sea: The Feminist Group Le Nemesiache in 1970s and 1980s Naples' for If I Can't Dance at the venue Rongwrong in Amsterdam (October 2020 to May 2021). She's been teaching in the MA programme for curating at Goldsmiths, University of London as well as guest lecturing and tutoring at the Sandberg Instituut, the Dutch Art Institute, the platform SNDO of the Academy of Theatre and Dance at Amsterdam University of the Arts (AHK), and the Gerrit Rietveld Academie.

Davide Fornari is associate professor at ECAL/University of Art and Design Lausanne, where he has led the Applied Research and Development sector since 2016. He has co-edited *Mapping Graphic Design History in Switzerland* (with Robert Lzicar, 2016) and *Bianca e Blu Monica Bolzoni* (with Régis Tosetti, 2019), and co-authored *Carlo Scarpa. Casa Zentner a Zurigo* (with Giacinta Jean and Roberta Martinis, 2020).

Katja Gentric is an artist, art historian, and associate researcher at Laboratoire Interdisciplinaire de Recherche Sociétés, Sensibilités, Soin (LIR3S, Dijon) and at the Institut du Monde Africain (IMAF Paris). She teaches at ESADHaR (École Supérieure d'Art et Design Le Havre-Rouen). Following a post-doctoral project with the title 'Artistic Practices and Use of Language' at the University of the Free State, South Africa, she is currently a fellow at the Günther Uecker Institut in Schwerin with the project 'Günther Uecker — Blickwinkel "South"'. Her research focuses on uses of voice, of language, and of humour in contemporary art practices situated within socio-political frameworks particular to the turn of the twenty-first century, where South Africa holds a key position.

Pablo Gonçalo is assistant professor at the University of Brasília. In 2019, he was a Fulbright Fellow at the University of Chicago and a post-doctoral researcher in partnership with the University of São Paulo. His research centers on the history of unfilmed scripts, focusing on German and Brazilian film history. More recently he has been researching the classic Hollywood era, consulting archives and many original unfilmed scripts of the 1940s, written by Ben Hecht, Francis Marion, Dudley Nichols, and Billy Wilder. He has been published in *Journal of Screenwriting, La Furia Umana*, several edited collections, as well as in Brazilian newspapers and magazines, such as *Folha de São Paulo* and *Revista 451*. Gonçalo also works as film critic and curator.

Juliana Hodkinson is a composer and artistic researcher. Her current work focuses on creating hybrid spatialized electro-acoustic formats for shared performance and experience, often in collaboration with other artists and listeners. She works with objects, instruments, voices, field recordings, archive material, and electronics. She is associate professor of composition at the Grieg Academy in Norway and the Royal Academy of Music in Aarhus, Denmark.

Joanna Kiliszek is a Berlin-based art historian, curator, and cultural manager. She studied at both the University of Warsaw and the University of Cologne. In 2019, she obtained a PhD in the framework of the M. Skłodowska-Curie Innovative Training Network NACCA (New Approaches in the Conservation of Contemporary Art) at the Academy of Fine Arts in Warsaw. From 2008 to 2014, she was the deputy director of the Adam Mickiewicz Institute in Warsaw, from 2001 to 2007, director of the Polish Cultural Institute in Berlin, and, from 1996 to 2001, director of the Polish Cultural Institute in Leipzig. She is a member of the AICA (International Association of Art Critics).

Kata Krasznahorkai, PhD, is a Berlin-based art historian, curator, and writer, currently working as a Gerda Henkel Senior Research Fellow at the University of Zurich. Her research analyses Black Power in Eastern Europe arts and culture. In 2020 she co-curated (with Inke Arns and Sylvia Sasse) 'Artists & Agents: Performance Art and Secret Services' at HMKV Dortmund, which received the German AICA (International Association of Art Critics) award for 'Exhibition of the Year 2020'. With Sylvia Sasse, she is co-editing a comprehensive handbook on art and secret service operations under the same title. Her monograph *Operative Art History or Who is Afraid of Artists?* is forthcoming.

Sven Lütticken, an art historian and critic, teaches art history at the Vrije Universiteit Amsterdam. He publishes regularly in journals and magazines and contributes to exhibition catalogues. His most recent books are *History in Motion: Time in the Age of the Moving Image* (2013), *Cultural Revolution: Aesthetic Practice after Autonomy* (2017), and *Objections: Forms of Abstraction* (forthcoming), as well as the critical reader *Art and Autonomy* (forthcoming). svenlutticken.org

Hélia Marçal is a lecturer in history of art, materials, and technology at University College London and an integrated researcher at the Institute of Contemporary History, NOVA University Lisbon. She was a fellow in contemporary art conservation and research in the Andrew W. Mellon-funded research project 'Reshaping the Collectible: When Artworks Live in the Museum' at Tate (2018–2020). Since 2016, she has been the coordinator of the Working Group 'Theory, History, and Ethics of Conservation' of the International Council of Museums Committee for Conservation.

Vera Sofia Mota is a Portuguese artist based in Berlin since 2011 and in Brussels since 2020. She currently attends the postgraduate program a.pass – advanced performance and scenography studies in Brussels, with a scholarship from the Calouste Gulbenkian Foundation in Lisbon. She studied choreography, performance, philosophy, and yoga in Portugal, the Netherlands, Germany, Belgium, and India, and has been working across these disciplines for the last twenty years. Since 2015, upon the invitation of LIMA Amsterdam, she has been researching the work of visual, performance, and video pioneer artist Nan Hoover. www.verasofiamota.com

Clio Nicastro is a fellow of the VolkswagenStiftung at the ICI Berlin and adjunct faculty member at Bard College Berlin. In 2015 she received a DAAD postdoctoral fellowship to work on the German filmmaker Harun Farocki and from 2016 to 2018 she was a fellow at the ICI Berlin. Her current research focuses on the cinematic representations of eating disorders. Her work on Harun Farocki, Philip Scheffner and Merle Kröger, and Adelina Pintilie has appeared in academic publications as well as in film and art journals. From

2018 onwards, she has been coorganizing 'Spellbound' (with Hannah Proctor and Nadine Hartmann), a series of screenings and reading groups.

Fransien van der Putt is a dramaturge, critic, writer, and radio artist based in Amsterdam. She writes about dance, theatre, and inter- or post-disciplinary performance practices. She has been conducting research into the Nan Hoover archive at LIMA, Amsterdam (with Vera Sofia Mota), and studying cross-disciplinary practices for children and their adult entourage (with Anne-Beth Schuurmans). She is currently writing on artistic and social constellations (with Heike Langsdorf) and working on a radio choreography series (with Netta Weiser) for dance archives in Berlin, Tel Aviv, Cologne, and Vienna. She is the editor-in-chief for De Nieuwe Dansbibliotheek.

Alethea Rockwell is an educator and researcher. She is currently associate educator for studio and artist programmes at the Museum of Modern Art (MoMA). There, she collaborates with artists on experimental projects that expand the museum's public function. She has organized performances, interactive installations, and audio guides with artists Chemi Rosado-Seijo, Amanda Williams, Salome Asega, Michael Rakowitz, and Nina Katchadourian. Rockwell has previously worked on exhibitions and public programmes at the Tate Modern, the Pennsylvania Academy of the Fine Arts, and the Courtauld Gallery. She received an MA in curating with distinction from the Courtauld Institute of Art.

Daniela Sacco is Marie Curie research fellow at the University of Milan and the UQAM, Université du Québec à Montréal. She researches in aesthetics and aesthetics of theatre. She collaborates with the Centro studi classicA of Università Iuav di Venezia. She is the author of a number of books, articles, reviews, and plays, among them: *Pensiero in azione. Bertolt Brecht, Robert Wilson, Peter Sellars: tre protagonisti del teatro contemporaneo* (2012); *Mito e teatro il principio drammaturgico del montaggio* (2013); *Goethe in Italia. Formazione estetica e teoria morfologica* (2016), *Tragico contemporaneo. Forme della tragedia e del mito nel teatro italiano (1995-2015)* (2018).

Daniela Salazar is a researcher, curator, and cultural programmer. She is a researcher at IHA (Art History Institute), NOVA University of Lisbon, and works on both the museological programming of the Cycling Museum (Torres Vedras) and on the management of creative and cultural industries at ArteriaLab (University of Évora). Her PhD research concerned the relation between performance, performativity concepts and practices, museum and curatorial contexts. She was responsible for the Sumol Museum programming between 2013 and 2015.

Pierre Saurisse is a lecturer in contemporary art at Sotheby's Institute in London. His book *La Mécanique de l'imprévisible* (2007) explores the question of chance in art in the 1960s. His recent essay on the image of the artist in films is included in the book *The Mediatization of the Artist*, ed. by Rachel Esner and Sandra Kisters (2018). His forthcoming book *Performance in the Museum* will be published in 2022.

Azalea Seratoni is an art historian. Her curatorial activity complements her critical and research practice. Since 2016, she has been teaching basic design at the Scuola Politecnica di Design, Milan. She is mainly interested in exploring the relationship between art and new media as well as the boundaries of art and design. She is interested in the relationship between the contemporary arts and image theory and visual culture. She is the co-editor of *Arte riprogrammata. Un manifesto aperto. Reprogrammed Art: An Open Manifesto* (with Serena Cangiano and Davide Fornari, 2015).

Özge Serin received her PhD in anthropology from Columbia University, and is currently a visiting assistant professor of politics and anthropology at Whitman College. Her scholarship centres around histories of radical politics, formations of violence, carceral cultures, and corporeal forms of resistance with a particular focus on hunger striking. Her current book manuscript, 'Writing of Death: Ethics and Politics of the Hunger Strike', explores the divide between incompatibly distinct and yet inextricably linked space-times of dying and politics. As a companion to the book, she co-created (with Brian Karl) the video documentary *Death/Fast* (2016), which premiered at Kadist Art Foundation in San Francisco.

Arianna Sforzini is a postdoctoral researcher at the University of Fribourg (2020–2022). She is a member of the Association pour le Centre Michel Foucault, and has been an associated researcher at the Bibliothèque nationale de France (2016–2019), a post-doctoral fellow for the project 'Foucault Fiches de Lecture/Foucault's Reading Notes' (funded by the Agence National de la Recherche (ANR), hosted by both the Centre National de la Recherche Scientifique (CNRS) and the École Normale Supérieure de Lyon, 2018-2020), and a fellow at the ICI Berlin (2016–2017). She is the author of *Les Scènes de la vérité. Michel Foucault et le théâtre* (2017) and *Michel Foucault. Une pensée du corps* (2014).

Ulrike Wagner is a wissenschaftliche Mitarbeiterin at Bard College Berlin and director of its German Studies Program. She received her PhD in German and Comparative Literature from Columbia University and an MA in North American Studies and German Literature from the Freie Universität Berlin. Her current research concerns the relation between religious criticism, education, and culture in the eighteenth- and nineteenth-century history of philology in German Romanticism and American Transcendentalism. Her latest research deals with nineteenth-century Jewish women writers and salonnières in Germany. She is currently completing a book manuscript titled 'Transatlantic Philology: Emerson, Germaine de Staël, Herder, and the Critical Practices of Reordering Religion and Antiquity'.

Gaby Wijers is director of LIMA, Amsterdam, guest lecturer at Amsterdam University, and honourable Research Fellow of the University of Exeter. Previously, she was coordinator of collection and preservation at the Montevideo/NIMk (Netherlands Media Art Institute). She initiated and participated in different international projects dealing with the documentation and preservation of media art and performances.

Index

Abad, Pio 77
Abel, Marco 103 n. 6, n. 7, 104
Aboul Gheit, Ahmed 71, 73
Abramović, Marina 1, 9, 13, 132, 161–166, 169
Acconci, Vito 162, 166, 169
Agamben, Giorgio 50, 51, 94 n. 12, 174, 201
Aguiar, Fernando 250
Albers, Anni 257, 258
Albers, Josef 255–259
Albright, Madeleine 71
Anceschi, Giovanni 141 n. 1, 142, 147 n. 5, 148
Anguissola, Anna 174
Anuszkiewicz, Richard 257
Araújo, Vasco 242
Ardant, Fanny 21 n. 2
Arslan, Thomas 103
Artaud, Antonin 24, 125, 133, 138
Asawa, Ruth 257
Austin, J. L. 15, 114
Baghramian, Nairy 228
Baj, Enrico 145
Balestrini, Nanni 142, 144
Balla, Giacomo 145
Bancroft, George 114
Bann, Stephen 3
Barante, Prosper de 3
Barbosa, Manoel 242, 247, 249
Bargu, Banu 51, 52 n. 13
Bataille, Georges 24, 27, 125
Becker, Howard 189
Benjamin, Walter 3, 4, 66, 67, 91, 92, 136–138, 174, 183 n. 2
Benzien, Jeffrey 59

Berg Holbek, Petra 75, 76
Berio, Luciano 141
Bester, Rory 59, 64 n. 25
Beuys, Joseph 8, 9, 166, 168, 169
Bishop, Claire 9 n. 19, 241, 243, 259
Blanchot, Maurice 24, 26, 47–50, 52 n. 15, 55
Bleeker, Maaike 213
Boccioni, Umberto 145
Boeckh, Friedrich August 114
Bolter, Jay 178
Boriani, Davide 142
Borralho, Ana 242
Borsellino, Paolo 135
Boulez, Pierre 24
Bourriaud, Nicolas 177
Brancusi, Constantin 145
Brecht, Bertolt 137, 138
Brecht, George 8
Briggs, Sydney 245
Bruguera, Tania 166, 240–243
Brzękowski, Jan 220
Burckhardt, Lucius 12
Burden, Chris 1, 163
Buren, Daniel 219, 228, 232 n. 4
Burri, Alberto 144
Burroughs, William 125
Burrows, Jonathan 206
Byrne, Gerard 11
Caesar, Julius 5
Cage, John 8
Caillet, Aline 61 n. 16
Calder, Alexander 145
Calvino, Italo 125, 231, 238
Carpo, Mario 123 n. 2, 128
Castellani, Enrico 142

Castellucci, Romeo 133–135, 139
Cavell, Stanley 113–120
Celant, Germano 174, 176 n. 13, 235
Céline, Louis-Ferdinand 125
Center for Historical Reenactments (CHR) 60–64, 67
Chamberlain, John 257
Chambure, Alain de 20
Chambure, Guy de 20
Charmatz, Boris 12, 206
Cixous, Hélène 158
Clark, Lygia 259
Clinton, Hillary 71
Collingwood, R.G. 5
Colombo, Gianni 142, 148, 149 n. 8
Condorelli, Céline 228
Cook, Sarah 214
Crimp, Douglas 174, 175, 177, 178 n. 17, n. 18
Cummings, E. E. 125
Davies, Stephen 185
Debord, Guy 174
De Keersmaeker, Anne Teresa 206
Deleuze, Gilles ix, 24, 50, 52 n. 14, 54, 55, 133, 173 n. 1, 245
Deller, Jeremy 1, 2, 6
Demand, Thomas 174, 235
Depero, Fortunato 145
Derrida, Jacques ix, 49 n. 5, 52 n. 15, 82, 88, 121–122, 133, 187
Descartes, René 22, 23
Devecchi, Gabriele 142, 146, 148 n. 6, 149 n. 8
de Wette, Wilhelm 114
Diaz, Lara Garcia 196 n. 6, 201 n. 13, 203, 208, 209 n. 4

Dickinson, Rod 1, 2
Didi-Huberman, Georges 84, 87
Doesburg, Theo van 221, 222
Dorner, Alexander 222
Duchamp, Marcel 145
Đukić, Sandro 210, 211, 215
Duncan, Carol 190
Duterte, Rodrigo 6, 42, 44
Eco, Umberto 141–143, 145, 146 n. 4
Eichhorn, Johann Gottfried 114
Eisenstein, Sergei 4
Emerson, Ralph Waldo 113–120
Emio Greco|PC 206
Enstice, Wayne 163
Enwezor, Okwui 59, 64 n. 25
Esche, Charles 233–238
Falcone, Giovanni 135
Fanon, Frantz 65, 67 n. 40
Farocki, Harun 14, 105, 106 n. 10, 109 n. 16
Fast, Omer 1
Feldman, Allen 51
Feldman, Avi 14
Felton, Cornelius Conway 114
Ferreira, Gina 259
Figgis, Mike 2
Fiske, Tina 187, 188 n. 20
Flavin, Dan 11
Flores, Patrick 42
Fluxus 1, 8, 9
Fontana, Lucio 144, 145
Fornari, Davide 141 n. 1, 148, 149 n. 8
Forsythe, William 206
Foucault, Michel ix, xi, 19–27, 92 n. 7, 94, 97 n. 18, 252
Franco, Francisco 20, 247
Franco, Marielle 241, 242
Franssen, Diana 236, 237
Fraser, Andrea 15, 16, 88

Freud, Sigmund 88, 106–108, 139, 178, 226
Fried, Michael 177
Frisch, Max 125
Fuchs, Rudi 232–238
Gabo, Naum 145
Galante, João 242
García Lorca, Federico 125
Gerstner, Karl 142
Giannachi, Gabriella 177 n. 16, 199, 201
Gibbons, Scott 134
Gide, André 125
Gillick, Liam 228
Ginsberg, Allen 125
Ginzburg, Carlo 212
Goldberg, RoseLee 163, 166
Goodman, Nelson 186, 187
Graham, Billy 72
Grande, Cristina 250, 251
Greenberg, Reesa 234, 235
Greene, Graham 125
Grimm, Herman 116, 117
Grimm, Wilhelm 116
Gropius, Walter 258
Gropius Johansen, Ati 258
Grupa Twożywo [Twożywo group] 228
Grusin, Richard 129, 178
Gule, Khwezi 62 n. 18, 64
Hague, William 71, 74
Hammerskjöld, Dag 71, 73
Hantelmann, Dorothea von 252
Haraway, Donna 81, 82 n. 2
Harman, Graham 124 n. 4, 126
Heeren, Ludwig 114, 117
Hegel, Georg Wilhelm Friedrich 3
Heidegger, Martin 114
Heil, Axel 180
Heisenberg, Benjamin 104
Hélion, Jean 221, 222

Hengel, Louis van den 252, 253
Herder, Johann Gottfried 114, 119
Hesse, Eva 257
Hirst, Damien 181
Hitchens, Christopher 71
Hofmannsthal, Hugo von 125
Holert, Tom 12
Holzhey, Christoph 176 n. 12, 178 n. 22
Homeoestéticos 250
Hoover, Nan 199, 205–218
Horstman, Fritz 258
Huszár, Vilmos 221, 222
Ippolito, Jon 184 n. 6, 189 n. 23, 194 n. 1, 201, 202, 209 n. 5
Jabłońska, Elżbieta 226–228
Jaubert, Alain 20, 21 n. 2
Johnson, Philip 256
Johnson, Ray 257
Jones, Amelia 12 n. 22, 44, 140, 169, 187 n. 19, 244
Judd, Donald 11
Jullien, François 140
Kafka, Franz 48, 49 n. 4
Kandinsky, Wassily 145
Kant, Immanuel 25
Kaprow, Allan 8, 9, 162–164
Kashoggi, Adnan 40
Kierkegaard, Søren 187
Kirkegaard, Jacob 71
Klee, Paul 145
Kobro, Katarzyna 220–224, 227
Koolhaas, Rem 235
Koons, Jeff 181
Krauss, Rosalind 174
Krenz, Igor 226, 228
Kruk, Mariusz 226
Kubrick, Stanley 7
Kukama, Donna 59–61, 63 n. 22, 64
Kulik, Oleg 162, 168, 169

Kumalo, Alfred 63, 64, 66
Kurka, Piotr 226
LaBelle, Brandon 70, 71
Lambert-Beatty, Carrie 10, 12 n. 22
Laplanche, Jean 84, 86
Laurenson, Pip 183 n. 1, 184 n. 5, 185, 186, 189 n. 26
Leach, Dawn 210
Lebel, Jean-Jacques 162
Leeb, Susanne 61 n. 16
Lepecki, André 131, 132 n. 1, 243 n. 15, 245–254
Lissitzky, El 222
Loraux, Nicole 94 n. 12
Loti, Pierre 3
Lucier, Alvin 71
Lütticken, Sven xi, 29 n. 2, 32, 175
Lyotard, Jean-François 12, 178
Madeira, Cláudia 243 n. 13
Maderna, Bruno 141
Maeght, Adrien 20
Magritte, Renè 125
Malevich, Kazimir 224
Mallarmé, Stéphane 23
Mandela, Nelson 64, 67
Manet, Édouard 23
Mangiacapre, Lina 82, 83, 87
Mangolte, Babette 10, 11
Mannheim, Karl 162, 165
Manovich, Lev 127, 128
Manzoni, Piero 145
Marcos, Ferdinand 6, 37–46
Marcos, Ferdinand Jr. ("Bongbong") 42
Marcos, Imelda 37–46
Mari, Enzo 142, 145
Marsh, James 114, 115 n. 7
Marx, Karl 13
Mayakovsky, Vladimir 125
Mbembe, Achille 65

Meillassoux, Quentin 123, 124 n. 4
Meireles, Cildo 241, 242
Melo e Castro, Ernesto Manuel Geraldes de 242
Mendieta, Ana 166, 241
Miessen, Markus 232
Milgram, Stanley 2
Minich, Marian 220, 222
Molotch, Harvey 189
Monareng, Michelle 67
Mondrian, Piet 13
Monglond, André 91
Morelli, Giovanni 212
Morris, Robert 10, 11
Moses, Anna Mary Robertson ("Grandma") 37
Mota, Vera Sofia 199
Mroué, Rabih 167
Munari, Bruno 141–146
Murakami, Saburō 167
Murakami, Takashi 162, 167
Nauman, Bruce 166
Negreiros, Almada 249
Nemesiache (Le) 81–89
Ngcobo, Gabi 59, 60, 63–67
Nicolau, Ricardo 250, 251
Niebuhr, Barthold Georg 117, 119
Nietzsche, Friedrich 23, 24, 114
Nixon, Richard 39, 71, 72
Obrist, Hans Ulrich 12, 161
Ohrt, Roberto 180
Ono, Yoko 169
Oppenheimer, Joshua 6
Paik, Nam June 188
Pais, Ana 249
Pane, Gina 151–159, 163, 166
Panofsky, Erwin 10
Pasolini, Pier Paolo 125
Patton, Robert Bridges 114
Pedro, Rocha 250, 251

Pelmuș, Manuel 12, 13
Pérec, Georges 125, 126
Petzold, Christian 101–111
Pevsner, Nikolaus 145
Phelan, Peggy 35 n. 12, 166
Phillips, Joanna 186
Picasso, Pablo 19–25
Picture Generation 175, 178 n. 17, n. 18
Pirici, Alexandra 12, 13
Plato 121
Price, Cedrict 12
Przybos, Julian 220
Putin, Vladimir 14
Putt, Fransien van der 199
Quaranta, Domenico 132 n. 2, 137
Queneau, Raymond 126
Raad, Walid 91–98
Rainer, Yvonne 9, 10
Rancière, Jacques 215
Ranke, Leopold von 3
Rau, Milo 14, 15, 133, 139
Rauschenberg, Robert 257
Reagan, Ronald 39
Real, William A. 185
Rekveld, Joost 198, 199
Rendell, Jane 84, 86 n. 12
Rice, Condoleeza 71
Ricoeur, Paul 178
Ripley, George 114, 115 n. 7
Roelstraete, Dieter 176
Rogoff, Irit 256, 260
Roosevelt, Franklin Delano 72
Rosenberg, Harold 15
Roth, Dieter 142
Rothschild, Edmond de 7
Rovisco, Vânia 247–250, 252, 253
Rumsfeld, Donald 71
Saaze, Vivian van 188, 189 n. 22, 245 n. 22

Saint-Exupéry, Antoine de 125
Schaerf, Eran 6, 7
Schanelec, Angela 103
Schleiermacher, Friedrich 114
Schleime, Cornelia 34
Schneemann, Carolee 169
Schneider, Rebecca 29, 35, 36, 85, 245
Scott, Walter 3, 11
Sehgal, Tino 12, 167, 245
Seratoni, Azalea 141 n. 1, 148, 149 n. 8
Serra, Richard 257
Settis, Salvatore 174, 175, 181
Shannon, Claude 127
Simondon, Gilbert 127
Skog, Susanne 71
Smith, Terry 232
Smith, Tony 11
Sosnowska, Monika 219, 228
Soto, Jesús Rafael 142
Spielberg, Steven 11
Srnicek, Nick 13, 124 n. 4
Stażewski, Henryk 220–222, 228
Stella, Frank 11
Stella, Michael 10
Stjerna, Åsa 70, 71
Stötzer, Gabriele 34
Strand, Liv 71
Strathern, Marilyn 201
Strzemiński, Władysław 219–228
Stuart, Meg 206
Suchan, Jarosław 225, 226, 228
Swaraj, Sushma 71
Szeemann, Harald 235
Sztwiertnia, Grzegorz 226, 228
Taeuber-Arp, Sophie 221
Takiguchi, Shuzo 144
Tatlin, Vladimir 13
Taylor, Diana 246

Thatcher, Margaret 2, 71
Tinguely, Jean 145
Turing, Alan 122, 128
Tutu, Desmond 58
Twombly, Cy 257
Uecker, Günter 226
Ulay 1, 9, 132, 164
Utkin, Boleslaw 222, 224
VALIE EXPORT 166
Vantongerloo, Georges 221
Varisco, Grazia 142
Vasarely, Victor 144
Vasulka, Steina 198
Vasulka, Woody 198, 199
Velázquez, Diego 19–25
Wadsworth Jones, Frances 44
Wa Lehulere, Kemang 59, 60, 64
Wanderley, Lula 259
Warburg, Aby 138, 139, 180,
    181
Warhol, Andy 23 n. 4, 24
Weber, Samuel 133 n. 4, 137
Wedemeyer, Arnd 176 n. 12,
    178 n. 22
Wharton, Glenn 189
Wijers, Gaby 208–211
Williams, Alex 13
Wittgenstein, Ludwig 114
Wittig, Monique 156
Wójcik, Julita 225, 226, 228
Wolf, Friedrich August 117, 119
Wood, Catherine 167
Yozgat, Halit 15
Zweig, Stefan 125

Cultural Inquiry

EDITED BY CHRISTOPH F. E. HOLZHEY
AND MANUELE GRAGNOLATI

VOL. 1   TENSION/SPANNUNG
Edited by Christoph F. E. Holzhey

VOL. 2   METAMORPHOSING DANTE
Appropriations, Manipulations, and Rewritings in the
Twentieth and Twenty-First Centuries
Edited by Manuele Gragnolati, Fabio Camilletti, and Fabian
Lampart

VOL. 3   PHANTASMATA
Techniken des Unheimlichen
Edited by Fabio Camilletti, Martin Doll, and Rupert Gaderer

VOL. 4   Boris Groys / Vittorio Hösle
DIE VERNUNFT AN DIE MACHT
Edited by Luca Di Blasi and Marc Jongen

VOL. 5   SARA FORTUNA
WITTGENSTEINS PHILOSOPHIE DES KIPPBILDS
Aspektwechsel, Ethik, Sprache

VOL. 6   THE SCANDAL OF SELF-CONTRADICTION
Pasolini's Multistable Subjectivities, Geographies, Traditions
Edited by Luca Di Blasi, Manuele Gragnolati, and Christoph F.
E. Holzhey

VOL. 7   SITUIERTES WISSEN UND REGIONALE
EPISTEMOLOGIE
Zur Aktualität Georges Canguilhems und Donna J. Haraways
Edited by Astrid Deuber-Mankowsky and Christoph F. E.
Holzhey

VOL. 8   MULTISTABLE FIGURES
On the Critical Potentials of Ir/Reversible Aspect-Seeing
Edited by Christoph F. E. Holzhey

VOL. 9   Wendy Brown / Rainer Forst
THE POWER OF TOLERANCE
Edited by Luca Di Blasi and Christoph F. E. Holzhey

Vol. 10   DENKWEISEN DES SPIELS
          Medienphilosophische Annäherungen
          Edited by Astrid Deuber-Mankowsky and Reinhold Görling

Vol. 11   DE/CONSTITUTING WHOLES
          Towards Partiality Without Parts
          Edited by Manuele Gragnolati and Christoph F.E. Holzhey

Vol. 12   CONATUS UND LEBENSNOT
          Schlüsselbegriffe der Medienanthropologie
          Edited by Astrid Deuber-Mankowsky and Anna Tuschling

Vol. 13   AURA UND EXPERIMENT
          Naturwissenschaft und Technik bei Walter Benjamin
          Edited by Kyung-Ho Cha

Vol. 14   LUCA DI BLASI
          DEZENTRIERUNGEN
          Beiträge zur Religion der Philosophie im 20. Jahrhundert

Vol. 15   RE-
          An Errant Glossary
          Edited by Christoph F. E. Holzhey and Arnd Wedemeyer

Vol. 16   CLAUDE LEFORT
          DANTE'S MODERNITY
          An Introduction to the Monarchia
          With an Essay by Judith Revel
          Translated from the French by Jennifer Rushworth
          Edited by Christiane Frey, Manuele Gragnolati, Christoph F. E.
          Holzhey, and Arnd Wedemeyer

Vol. 17   WEATHERING
          Ecologies of Exposure
          Edited by Christoph F. E. Holzhey and Arnd Wedemeyer

Vol. 18   MANUELE GRAGNOLATI AND FRANCESCA
          SOUTHERDEN
          POSSIBILITIES OF LYRIC
          Reading Petrarch in Dialogue

Vol. 19   THE WORK OF WORLD LITERATURE
          Edited by Francesco Giusti and Benjamin Lewis Robinson

Vol. 20   MATERIALISM AND POLITICS
          Edited by Bernardo Bianchi, Emilie Filion-Donato, Marlon
          Miguel, and Ayşe Yuva

VOL. 21 OVER AND OVER AND OVER AGAIN
Reenactment Strategies in Contemporary Arts and Theory
Edited by Cristina Baldacci, Clio Nicastro,
and Arianna Sforzini

VOL. 22 QUEERES KINO / QUEERE ÄSTHETIKEN
ALS DOKUMENTATIONEN DES PREKÄREN
Edited by Astrid Deuber-Mankowsky
and Philipp Hanke